W9-BEZ-295

CSALH

1000020728

DISCARDED

HM
136   McClelland, David
.M13   Clarence

        Power

DATE DUE

OCT 13 1978			
SE 22 '78			

POWER
The Inner Experience

David C. McClelland

POWER
THE INNER EXPERIENCE

DISCARDED

IRVINGTON PUBLISHERS, Inc., New York

HALSTED PRESS Division
JOHN WILEY & SONS
NEW YORK   LONDON   SYDNEY   TORONTO

Copyright © 1975 by IRVINGTON PUBLISHERS, INC.

All rights reserved. No part of this book may be reproduced in any manner whatever, including information storage or retrieval, in whole or in part (except for brief quotations in critical articles or reviews), without written permission from the publisher. For information, write to Irvington Publishers, Inc., 551 Fifth Ave., New York City 10017.

Distributed by HALSTED PRESS
A division of JOHN WILEY & SONS, New York

Library of Congress Cataloging in Publication Data

McClelland, David Clarence.
  Power: the inner experience.

  Bibliography: p.
  Includes index.

  1. Power (Social sciences) 2. Control (Psychology) 3. Motivation (Psychology) I. Title.
HM136.M13   301.15′5   75–35603

ISBN 0–470–58169–7

Printed in The United States of America

PREFACE

THIS BOOK has been a long time in the making. I have been thinking about power motivation for most of my professional life; at the least since 1950, when Joseph Veroff made his first attempt to arouse the power motive experimentally. The important further work in defining and measuring the power motive by James Uleman and David Winter in the mid-1960's, culminating as it did in Winter's important book, *The power motive* (1973), gave my thinking along these lines on added stimulus. Unexpectedly our ten-year study of the effects of alcohol on fantasy also shed light on an aspect of the need for Power. But it was not until the early 1970's that it all seemed to come together, at least at the theoretical level. I suddenly thought that I saw a connection between our empirical work on power motivation and the theories of Freud and Erikson. The result is Chapter 1 of the present volume, which provides a theoretical synthesis of these two very different traditions in psychology.

The theory made such good sense to me and to others to whom I showed it, that I immediately used it both to interpret earlier work I had done, and to explain some newer phenomena which were

v

fascinating me. Among the latter was the conversion to Hinduism of my former student and colleague, Dr. Richard Alpert, and his subsequent leading role among a large group of intelligent but alienated young people in America. I spent most of a sabbatical year (1972–1973) in India and Sri Lanka, trying to seek out the roots of these phenomena, particularly in the Eastern view of power. My conviction grew that I was on the right track, and I completed much of the present volume while I was there. My original intention had been to write a more theoretical book; but as the year wore on, my lifelong commitment to empirical validation of psychological theories got the better of me. I wanted to know to what extent my theory could be validated by the empirical and statistical research methods commonly employed in contemporary psychology. Fortunately at this very moment, Abigail Stewart developed a promising measure of Erikson's stages of ego development which made an empirical test of the theory possible. So I decided to postpone publication for a year while I sought for empirical validation of the theory.

The casual reader may not realize what such a decision cost me. For I thought I had developed an exciting new theory which made good sense out of a lot of diverse phenomena and which others felt represented an important breakthrough. Yet I was proposing to jeopardize the whole thing by putting it to the empirical test. What if the results did not confirm the theory? That all too often happens in psychology.

To be honest, it happened at first in the present instance. In a mad scramble to collect data in time to complete this book for the original target publication date a year ago, I decided to obtain the information I wanted from subjects who were serving in an experiment designed for an entirely different purpose. In order to do that, I had to make some compromises that went against my better judgment: the motive measures had to be obtained from the verbal cues used as part of the other experiment. Ever since we reported in *The Achievement Motive* (1953) that verbal cues do not always give the same results as picture cues, I have been dubious about using verbal cues to assess motive variables. Even more important, I had to be satisfied with the other experiment's subject pool, consisting of summer school students at Harvard University. From my point of view they had three distinct drawbacks: they were too young, most of them were unmarried, and nearly all of them were from the educated middle class. Since my research dealt in particular with the characteristics of maturity, it seemed unwise to limit my sample to people in their late teens and early twenties who would not yet have experienced serious adjustments to work and family life. But at any rate I tried it, just to see what would happen.

The result was disastrous. It turned out that the subjects resented having to fill out all the extra forms my research required in addition to what they had to do for the other experiment. And not a trace of what I was looking for appeared in the data. What to do? Was the theory wrong, or should I try again on a better sample? I chose the latter course, with the results reported in Chapters 2 and 8. To my infinite relief, the empirical findings on an adult, more representative sample of people did support in the main my theoretical views as already written into the rest of the book. For those readers who feel that I hunted around amidst all my correlations only to report those that fit the theory, let me reassure them that if the data don't fit the theory, there is no way you can make the results come out right. I tried it in the previous study and failed. It was, therefore, with an even greater feeling of satisfaction that I began to uncover some empirical justification for the theory. I had put the theory in jeopardy, and in the process it had been confirmed and refined.

All this would not have been possible without help from many sources—from Harvard University for a sabbatical leave with half pay; from the National Science Foundation Grant #GS31914X for a study of power and application motives; from my colleagues at McBer and Company for their advice and help in collecting the data reported in Chapter 8; and from my graduate assistants Susan Fiske, Cathy Colman, Robert Watson, and Betsy Harrington, who helped collect, organize, and score the data reported in Chapters 2 and 8. I am grateful to them all. Above all, I owe a special debt to Abigail Stewart and David Winter, who helped formulate many of the ideas in the book. It is no exaggeration to say that without their help the book could not have been written in its present form. Abigail Stewart developed the Social Emotional Maturity scale and the original version of the questionnaire designed to test characteristic expressions of the power motive at different levels of maturity. David Winter helped with these matters and also carried out the final computer analysis of the data. They have been true colleagues and friends throughout. Ram Dass also helped. He read the section on his life, suggested changes more in line with the facts, and helped me understand better the Stage IV orientation towards power.

I also wish to acknowledge with great thanks the fast and efficient help of Martha Adams in preparing the manuscript for publication. She has typed and re-typed various versions and helped check references with a single-minded devotion to meeting the deadline of my departure for Asia, where I hope to find out even more about the role of power in human life.

Alwatte, Sri Lanka

West Cornwall, Connecticut,   David C. McClelland

OVERVIEW
CONTENTS

CONTENTS

PART

A

EXPERIENCING POWER

1

WAYS OF EXPERIENCING
POWER

MAN HAS always been fascinated by power. He has reason to be for, as scholars are fond of reminding him, he belongs to a violent species. Look at his history: a long succession of wars with interludes of peace in localized times and places. His myths and his religion are saturated with concern for power.

The Judaeo-Christian God is almighty. "The voice of the Lord is powerful; the voice of the Lord is full of majesty. The voice of the Lord breaketh the cedars; yea, the Lord breaketh the cedars of Lebanon . . . the Lord will give strength unto His people." "All things were made by Him: without Him wasn't anything made that was made." Jesus said to his followers "He that believeth in Me, the works that I do shall he do also; and greater works than these shall he do . . . ye shall receive power."

In the ancient Chinese Book of Changes, the *I Ching,* there is likewise concern about power —the taming power of the small, the taming power of the great, the power of the light, the power of the

3

dark, the possession in great measure. In the central episode of the Hindu epic, the *Bhagavad Gita,* Arjuna faces a problem of exercising or not exercising power in the war against his kindred. Should he fight or not? The advice given him is that he must fight because it is his duty, but that he should so act as not to be attached to the outcome of his actions; he must feel neither success nor failure, nor joy nor sorrow, whatever the outcome of his actions. It almost seems that religions represent books of changes on the eternal theme of how to deal with man's power relationships. In religion man strives to understand forces greater than himself along with his own urges to attack and destroy or to defend himself against his fellow man.

The need for understanding the psychology of power is even greater today, when man's capacity for destroying himself and the universe has reached a new level of seriousness. The threat of nuclear destruction has not, somewhat surprisingly, evoked an adaptive response, even from thinking and sensitive people. At first it elicited horror and a number of Utopian schemes for controlling man's aggressive urges. Then, as little progress was made toward putting the schemes into effect, people began to adapt to the stress by forgetting it. Even a certain cynicism, mixed with despair, developed; older theories about man's innate agressiveness were revived and gained wide currency. Particularly among the young, groups of people decided, as the Hindus had centuries ago, that to try to eliminate power and power schemes at the social level is hopeless. Rather, an individual should renounce thoughts of power, cultivate his own soul, and live under enlightenment, free from power-based commitments to change the world.

Has the science of psychology anything to contribute to the resolution of these problems? The only power it has is the power to give man added understanding; knowing what underlies his behavior should put man in a better position to control or redirect his destructive tendencies. Yet psychology as an empirical science is a late-comer among those disciplines that have tried to understand the nature of man. Where religion, philosophy, common sense have long dominated the field, to put empirical psychology among them is like putting David among Goliaths. It has its slingshot—that is, a systematic method for measuring and establishing relationships among variables—but to those who are used to the grand sweep of assertion and counterassertion about human nature, it will seem puny indeed, woefully inadequate to a task that has confounded thinking men for centuries. Yet our goal in this volume is no less: it is to report empirical studies of the psychology of power in an effort to arrive at a better understanding of the role of power in human life. More specifically, it focuses on the power motive, that desire for power which plays a major role in the shaping of the human condition. What is its nature? Whence does it come? How does it express itself? Can it be controlled? From what do the pathologies of power derive? Answers to questions like these should give us not only greater understanding but power; for knowledge is also power, the power to alter what we are doing in the light of our better understanding of it.

Measuring the Power Motive

Attempts to isolate and measure the power motive were begun around 1950 and have continued at Harvard University, the University of Michigan, and Wesleyan University. Findings have been reported in a number of scientific papers, and in books such as Veroff's and Feld's *Marriage and work in America* (1970), or *The drinking man* by McClelland and others (1972). Practically all of this work has now been brought together and described in full in an important book by David Winter, entitled simply *The power motive* (1973).

It is worth outlining with some care the approach taken by these studies, because many psychologists, particularly those of a clinical persuasion, have written extensively on the subject basing their conclusions chiefly on case studies of individuals. (See for example *Power and innocence,* by Rollo May, 1972.) The empirical approach to the measurement of power motives started with the simple assumption that a measure of something ought to co-vary demonstrably with the thing it measures. The reason we assume that the column of mercury in a vacuum provides a good measure of heat or temperature is that, as we apply heat to a glass tube containing the mercury, the mercury rises, and as we take the heat away, the mercury falls. The problem in measurement is to arrive at an indicator that will reflect changes in whatever is being measured, and those changes *only*. Thus the purpose of the studies designed to measure the power motive was to implant or arouse power motivation in individuals, and then to search for behavioral indicators sensitive enough to reflect the presence or absence or degree of intensity of the motive that had been implanted.

Many possible behavioral indicators have disadvantages. After arousing the power motive in one way or another, one could in effect ask a person, "How powerful do you feel?" or "How aggressive do you feel?" The disadvantages of such a direct approach are self-evident. For one thing, it is not clear just how to put the question. Since we don't know yet how to define the feelings produced by the power motive, we cannot know whether to ask how aggressive a person feels, or how powerful, or strong, or dominant, or whatever. For another, we know that there are norms governing the expression of such feelings toward others. Though people may indeed feel hostile when their power motives are aroused, they may be unwilling to say so because of fear that it would reflect on their maturity or self-control. Self-reports of motives turn out to be insensitive as a behavioral indicator. Another possibility is to record some action or reaction on the part of a person whose power motive is aroused. The disadvantage of this method is also self-evident. A person may have the impulse to react by hitting something, but there may be nothing appropriate to hit, or he may "control himself" for fear of looking foolish or of inviting retaliation. Actions characteristic of the power motive, indeed, are so apt to be dampened and controlled by social norms that they become very insensitive indicators of the presence of the power motive.

What we need is some direct index of what is going on in a person's head when the power motive is present, and it turns out that the best and simplest way of finding out what is going on in a person's head is to ask him to tell brief imaginative stories to pictures. Under these conditions, he does not know what you are asking—nor do you, for that matter—and thus the stories he tells are unlikely to be influenced by such extraneous variables as the norm of what is socially desirable. In point of fact, fantasy, as reflected in such stories, has shown itself to be the most sensitive indicator of changes in motivational states of all sorts (see McClelland *et al.*, 1953, McClelland, 1958). The further advantage is that such a method does not force the investigator to define in advance exactly what he is looking for, and thus possibly overlook some characteristic effect of the motive aroused. The person is free to write anything at all in his stories, and the investigator to search them for any clues which differentiate the stories produced when the motive is aroused from those when it is not aroused.

The key decision then for the investigator to make is how to arouse the power motive. Here he falls back on common sense; he locates conditions that ought to arouse power motives. But he also has a check on whether he has been right; the fantasy effects of the arousal conditions he has chosen will tell him whether in fact themes reflecting power concerns are more frequent under those conditions. Thus investigators of the power motive relied on four types of arousal: students were asked by Veroff (1957) to write imaginative stories while they were waiting to see if they had been elected to office; by Uleman (1966), after they had served in the powerful role of experimenter, or after they had watched a convincing demonstration of hypnosis; and by Winter (1967) after they had watched a film of the inaugural address of President John F. Kennedy. In the first instance, it was assumed that the concern for power of students who wanted to be elected to office would be particularly heightened just at the point when they might achieve power. In Uleman's experiments, individuals might be supposed to want to be powerful like the hypnotist they had observed, or to continue exercising control over others after having done so for some time as an experimenter. Witnessing the Kennedy inaugural may not seem like a way to arouse power motivation; in fact, Winter originally designed the study to get at the feelings engendered in an audience by a charismatic leader. At the time this film was shown, Kennedy, who had only recently been assassinated, was still a charismatic figure for the students involved. When Winter contrasted the stories written after seeing the inaugural, however, with those produced after watching a neutral film about science demonstration equipment, he discovered that the Kennedy film had in fact greatly increased the frequency with which thoughts of strength, power and confidence appeared in the stories. It was apparent that charismatic leaders are effective because they arouse power motivation in their followers: "The Lord will give strength unto His people."

When Winter sifted through the fantasy effects of all these arousal experiments, he gradually evolved a method of subjectively defining and coding power themes that captured the essence of the fantasy changes in the simplest, most objective and coherent manner. It is impossible to exaggerate the importance of this step in the measurement process. One starts with power-arousing experiences; they produce effects in fantasy which are many and scattered. Out of them all must come a coding definition which makes sense, which covers all the findings observed, and which is so objective that any two scorers can readily agree on the presence or absence of the characteristic being coded. The result is the formal coding definition of the need for Power, generally abbreviated *n* Power in the Murray tradition, to signify its reference to a specific way of measuring the power drive.

What came out of all these studies is a measure of the need for Power, defined as a thought about someone *having impact.* Power imagery is scored if someone in imaginative stories "is concerned about his impact, about establishing, maintaining, or restoring his prestige or power" (Winter, 1973). Concern about having impact may be shown basically in three ways: (1) by strong action, such as assaults and aggression, by giving help, assistance, or advice, by controlling another, by influencing, persuading someone, or trying to impress someone; (2) by action that produces emotions in others. Thus if an act is not in itself strong, but produces emotions in others, it is coded as if it were strong, as in "he leaves, she cries"; (3) by a concern for reputation, for a person concerned about his reputation is concerned about his impact in the most obvious sense. Thoughts of these types increased significantly in stories written following various kinds of power arousal. Thought sequences dealing with such power concerns also contained more references to the prestige of the actors, to instrumental acts they might take to achieve their power goals, to feelings they had about power, or to the effects their actions might have on others, such as a counter attack. All of these additional characteristics became part of the scoring system for *n* Power. They are fully described by Winter (1973), who also provides a method for learning to score them objectively and reliably.

Any given story can obtain a maximum score of 11 points if it contains all of 11 categories scored as part of the *n* Power system. Since usually individuals are asked to write four to six stories, in theory they could obtain scores of 40–60, but in fact most people write only two or three stories which contain any power theme, and each of these contains only three or so characteristics which can be scored. Thus the average score for a group of subjects runs around six to nine. Throughout this book, whenever the term *n* Power is used, it will refer to a score obtained in this way by the Winter system, unless otherwise specified. What needs to be stressed once again is that every aspect of the scoring system was empirically derived from actual experiments. Neither Winter nor any investigator added or subtracted characteristics to be scored on the basis of what they thought should or should not be included as part of the definition of the need for Power. Many groups of men provided these final definitions of need for Power by unconsciously telling different kinds of stories under the influence of various types of power arousal.

The Power Motive in Action

How does a person act who is high in power motivation as measured in this way? It is one thing to develop a sensitive measure of a human characteristic. It is quite another to demonstrate that a reading on the measure will tell anything important about a person — that is, what he will do or think under a variety of circumstances. Much research effort has thus gone into trying to find out how people high in *n* Power behave as contrasted with people low in *n* Power. The results not only validate the power motive measure and demonstrate its importance, but give insight into how the power motive functions in human life; in doing so they define even further just what the power motive is. Winter (1973) has summarized a number of such studies, most of which have dealt with the power-related activities of men in college or in various walks of life in their 30's and 40's. What will concern us here is not the details of these investigations, but rather the main findings.

Whether a motive expresses itself in action will depend upon the opportunity for taking the action and on social norms governing whether the action is appropriate or not. A young man high in power motivation might have the impulse to play competitive sports, but if he is weak or a cripple, or if there are no organized sports in his school, he will have few opportunities for such expression. A number of studies reported in Winter support this assumption. Generally speaking, young men with high *n* Power play and watch competitive team sports both in the United States and Germany; yet in one study of German secondary school students (Kruse, 1971), no correlation was found between *n* Power and sports *participation,* presumably because in German secondary schools there are fewer organized team sports than in a typical American secondary school. To cite another example, Winter provides a table (1973, p. 135) showing that impulsive aggressive acts appear to be an outlet for working-class men with high power motivation. They are more apt to report that they throw things around the room, take towels from a hotel or motel, or fail to show up for a day's work because they just don't feel like it. The correlation between *n* Power score and the frequency of acting in such ways was .36, p < .05. Boyatzis (1973) later confirmed this result (r = .30, N = 144, p < .001) with another large sample of males drawn heavily from blue-collar and lower middle-class backgrounds. But among middle-class males, high power motivation was not associated with such impulsive, aggressive acts; the correlation was only .01. Social norms governing expression of aggression in such ways apparently prevent them from becoming outlets for power motivation among middle-class men. In order to find the most basic types of expression of power motivation, it is necessary to look for those actions least likely to be influenced by opportunity or social norms.

Table 1.1 presents in simplified form the conclusions drawn from studies of the action correlates of the power motive. The activities

Table 1.1—Action correlates of the need for power
(n = 50 males, average age = 33)

Activities	Correlations with:				n Power
	1	2	3	4	5
1. Power-oriented reading[a]	–	– .03	.48**	.43**	.29**
2. Prestige possessions[b]		–	.04	– .05	.25*
3. Competitive sports[c]			–	.61**	.24*
4. Organizational membership[d]					.23*

(From McClelland *et al.*, 1972. *The drinking man*, Bar II sample)
*p < .05, **p < .01 in the expected direction
a. Number of "sporty" magazines listed as read such as *Playboy* and *Sports Illustrated*.
b. Ownership of items like a color TV set, rifle or pistol, convertible car.
c. Number of different non-contact sports played.
d. Number of different organizations in which membership is listed.

listed —e.g., reading "sporty" magazines, collecting prestige possessions, engaging in competitive sports, and belonging to various clubs
or organizations —have been found in a number of different groups to
be characteristic of men with high power motivation (see Winter,
1973, McClellend *et al.*, 1972). All are characteristics originally found
to be associated with *n* Power in Winter's pioneering study of Harvard undergraduates (1967). They apparently represent things that
most men can do that are not restricted in major ways by social norms
or opportunities. The actual correlations given in Table 1.1 are taken
from one particular sample of men, average age 33, of mixed white-
and blue-collar background; see McClelland *et al.* (1972) for a fuller
description of the sample and testing procedure. Since the size of the
correlations is not large, they would be unremarkable except that they
have occurred so frequently in different studies that they invite us to
speculate a little more on the fundamental nature of the power motive
and the ways in which it expresses itself.

First of all, the need for Power leads men to read about sex and
aggression. Those who are high in *n* Power are more likely than
others to read *Playboy* or other "girlie" magazines, and *Sports Illustrated* or other magazines dealing with competitive sports. They also
report watching more violent TV shows. Winter describes them as
satisfying their power motive vicariously through thought and feeling
rather than action. A simpler way to put it might be that they satisfy
their feelings of power by exposing themselves to power-arousing
cues —pictures of nude females, stories of sexual conquest, and victories in competitive sports. They seek ways for the environment to act
on them and make them feel powerful.

An apparently similar way to feel powerful is to drink more

liquor, which regularly increases power fantasies (McClelland, *et al.,* 1972). Drinking heavily, however, also leads to assertive actions; and later research suggests it is more closely associated with such characteristics than with passively arousing power feelings through reading and viewing.

Next, *n* Power also leads men to accumulate prestige possessions. In the group of men referred to in Table 1.1, such possessions included things like a rifle or pistol, a convertible car, or a color TV set. Among college students, Winter found out either through questionnaires or from actual observation of their rooms, the objects they tended to collect—wine glasses, college banners, wall hangings, objets d'art and special items of furniture. The man who is high in *n* Power tends to accumulate whatever signs or symbols give him prestige in the group to which he belongs. This focus on rank was apparent even in the power-arousal studies. One of the pictures used shows a group of men in uniform apparently attending an Army briefing. In the non-aroused group of students, the man giving the briefing was usually described as a captain, but among those whose power motivation had been aroused, he tended to be described as a colonel or general.

In later studies, men were simply asked to put down the number of credit cards they had with them, which serves among older persons as a simpler, more direct index of their orientation towards prestige possessions. Several studies report the number of such credit cards as significantly associated with *n* Power (Winter, 1973; McClelland *et al.,* 1972; Boyatzis, 1973).

Assuming a man to be physically able and opportunities for playing sports to be readily available, the need for Power is also regularly associated with participation in competitive sports. The measure listed for the sample of men included in Table 1.1 is not particularly sensitive, since it deals only with non-contact sports (like baseball, tennis, or basketball). In other studies (1973) Winter has shown that the need for Power in college men is most closely associated with excellence in sports like football, baseball, tennis, or basketball, in which there is a kind of man-to-man competition. In such sports there is a personal power struggle in the sense that each player is trying to outwit or dominate his opponent. The need for Power tends not to be so closely associated with sports like track, swimming, and golf, in which the competition is more with nature or the clock than with a particular opponent. Boyatzis also confirmed in his sample that *n* Power is most likely to display itself by participation in man-to-man sports ($r = .26$, $N = 144$, $p < .01$). The emphasis here is clearly on *assertive actions,* and on other indicators of them, such as the tendency to argue or to behave in an impulsive, aggressive manner which also correlates with *n* Power (Winter 1973; Boyatzis, 1973).

Finally, among older and younger men, both in the United States and Germany the need for Power is associated with belonging to organizations and with holding office in them. Assuming a leadership role is, of course, a direct way of having impact on others, although to compete successfully for such positions, it seems desirable that the person think in terms of exercising power on behalf of others rather than on behalf of himself. Thus, as Chapter 7 makes clear, it is a particular sub-type of power motive which is associated with the tendency to become an officer in organizations. At a simpler level, joining an organization is a good way to feel more powerful through having friends and allies, and an organizational structure and set of norms to guide one: in union there is strength.

What is particularly striking about the results reported in Table 1.1 is that while all of the action outlets correlate moderately with *n* Power, each is quite different from the other. A number of them do not correlate at all with each other, and those that do in this sample do not in other samples. For example, the significant correlations between power-oriented reading and prestige possessions and competitive sports reduce to .03 and .08, and that between competitive sports and organizational memberships to .10 in another similar sample of 108 men (McClelland *et al.,* 1972). What this lack of interrelationship suggests is that the activities listed are alternative manifestations of the power drive. A man with a strong need for Power may express it in one or another of these ways; if he expresses it in one way, he is not any more likely to express it in another. Those who join organizations are not more likely to read sporty magazines, collect prestige possessions, or engage in competitive sports. One must conclude that people get their power kicks in different ways. That, in fact, seems to be a fairly precise way of describing what is happening. Different actions, same effect: a feeling of power. The actions themselves do not have much in common, which is the reason that psychologists have had to suggest a common motive underlying all of them to explain why they belong together in the same table, even though they have little surface similarity.

Can we say anything more than that these are four different ways of experiencing power? Just enumerating outlets of the power drive is basically unsatisfying, since it results in what seems a mere collection of activities with no particular sense in terms of an overall scheme. Can we find a way of classifying these key outlets for the power motive that will tie them in with other things we know about psychology and provide the framework for further investigation of the role of power motivation in human behavior?

A Classification of Power Orientations

A simple method of classification introduces order among the chief expressions of the power motive listed in Table 1.1, and fits them into the well-known scheme for describing stages in ego-development worked out initially by Freud and later by Erikson (1963). The two dimensions of such a classification depend on whether the *source* of power is outside or inside the self, and whether the *object* of power is the self or someone or something outside the self. Such a scheme, as Table 1.2 shows, provides a ready method for classifying the four modalities of experiencing power just described. Power-oriented reading belongs in quadrant I (upper left): the source of power comes from outside the self but its object is strengthening the self. Accumulating prestige possessions fits in quadrant II; the individual acts to expand the self to make it feel stronger. Competitive sports goes into quadrant III because the person tries competitively to win out over others. Organizational membership belongs in quadrant IV because joining makes the person feel part of a higher power which acts through him; he becomes the agent of another source of strength, acting to influence and serve those in the organization. Each of these quadrants also corresponds fairly well to the four stages of ego-development as described by Freud, Erikson, and others. Let us examine each one in more detail.

Stage I. "It" strengthens me. Statge I is the first way that an infant has of feeling strong. If he were able to talk, he might represent his feelings by saying something like, "It strengthens me." It, in this case, is at first a mother or another caretaker who gives emotional and physical support, even milk at the breast, which comes from the outside and which makes the infant feel stronger inside. He incorporates strength from another. In Freudian terminology this is the oral stage, so named because the mouth is initially the chief organ by which the infant takes in his feelings of strength. Later in life, the person continues to draw strength from others —from friends, from a spouse, from an admired leader. He wants to be around such people, to draw strength from them, be inspired by them. Adults in whom this mode of feeling powerful dominates should enter occupations in which they can serve powerful others. Clienthood is their preferred status,

Table 1.2–A classification of power orientations

Object of power:	Source of Power	
	Other	Self
SELF (to feel stronger)		
Definition:	"It" (God, my mother, my leader, food) strengthens me.	I strengthen, control, direct myself. Accumulating prestige possessions.
Action Correlate:	Power-oriented reading	
Developmental Stage:	I. oral: being supported	II. Anal: autonomy, will
Pathology:	Hysteria, drug taking	Obsessive compulsive neurosis
Occupations:	Client, mystic	Psychologists, collectors
Folk tale themes:	Eat, take, leave	I, he, have, go find
OTHERS (to influence)		
Definition:	It (religion, laws, my group) moves me to serve, influence others	I have an impact (influence) on others
Action Correlate:	Organizational membership	Competitive sports, arguing
Developmental Stage:	IV. Genital mutuality, principled assertion, duty	III. Phallic: assertive action
Pathology:	Messianism	Crime
Occupations:	Manager, scientist	Criminal lawyer, politician, journalist, teacher
Folk tale themes:	We, they ascend, fall	Hunt, can

because by being the client of a strong person, they themselves gain strength and feel powerful. They may also become religious mystics, who gain a feeling of power and importance from constant meditation or contact with God, who "strengthens His People." Winter's study shows that this is exactly what happened to the group of young men watching the film of John F. Kennedy's inaugural address; they felt uplifted and strengthened by contact with an admired leader.

Push this modality to an extreme, and the person may develop what are commonly called hysterical symptoms in the sense that forces outside himself govern what he does to such an extent that he no longer feels in control. He may develop an hysterical paralysis or amnesia. In such cases, forces totally beyond his control take over his body and mind, so to speak. Or he may take to drugs, including alcohol, in order to gain the feeling of strength that is no longer being supplied by important people in his life.

People whom this stage characterizes are sometimes described as dependent; and in a sense, they are dependent. They may depend on alcohol, an admired leader, or God. But it is a mistake to think of them as being dependent because they like to feel dependent. Quite the contrary: they are dependent because it makes them feel strong to be near a source of strength. Strictly speaking, there is no such thing as a need for dependency, a need to feel weak and dependent; what is sometimes described as a need for dependency is the act of being dependent or weak, which has as its goal feeling strong.

On the bottom line in quadrant I and the other quadrants are listed folk-tale themes to be discussed in a subsequent section.

Stage II. I strengthen myself. As a child grows older, he soon learns that he can be powerful simply by saying "No." His mother tries to feed him, and he turns his head aside. She urges him to urinate at a particular time and place, and he refuses. Freudians have associated this willfulness, or assertion of self, with the anal stage of development, with learning to control defecation, which provides a major opportunity for learning self-assertiveness and self-control. If the child could summarize his feelings with words, he might say something like, "I can control, that is, strengthen myself. I don't need to depend upon others for strength." The focus of attention may at first be on controlling one's own body and mind. A child learns soon enough that while his mother may make him do something, she cannot control what he thinks; and eventually, by extension, the adult who employs this modality of feeling powerful accumulates possessions which he sees as part of the self. He now seeks to control things like Cadillacs, a color TV set, rifles, credit cards—all of which represent parts of

...self that he can use to make himself feel stronger. For those with a Freudian orientation, it is apparent that we are talking here about the equivalent of what Freud meant when he spoke of feces as the first, most elementary valuable possession, which in time became associated in men's minds with that other most valued possession, money, or filthy lucre.

Or the individual may now engage in body-building exercises, yoga, or dieting in order to feel that he has better control over himself. It is not surprising that Winter has found that students who plan to be and who become psychologists score higher in *n* Power than men in other occupations. Many of them consciously or unconsciously are following a Stage II approach to feeling powerful; by having greater understanding of what makes people tick, they will have better control over themselves. It is not surprising either that psychologists for the most part tend to be self-actualization theorists, if Stage II is their dominant mode of approach to the world. By and large they are against the Stage I modality, condemning it as dependency that a person ought to outgrow, and they are also opposed to the competitiveness of Stage III and the religious orientation of Stage IV. They are apostles for the doctrine of finding sources of strength in the self to develop the self. One of the advantages of the present mode of analysis may be to place the bias of psychological healers in a larger perspective.

The pathology of the Stage II modality is obsessive compulsiveness. A person may end by trying to control his every throught and action. Stolorow (1970) developed an objective method for scoring the extent to which voluntary control was prominent in thought sequences. He found, as predicted, that those in whom a sense of voluntary control was very strong acknowledged practising compulsive rituals, such as not stepping on cracks in the pavement, or following a prescribed sequence for going to bed; whereas those low in a sense of voluntary control reported the hysterical symptom of amnesia more often, as would be expected of a Stage I orientation. He also predicted and found that what we are calling Stage II people (those with a high sense of voluntary control) were more distressed by events involving loss of control over one's destiny, such as failure in school; Stage I people (with a low sense of voluntary control) were more distressed by events involving loss of external support, such as the loss of an important person in their lives. His study confirms the mass of theoretical and clinical evidence supporting the notion that there is a real difference between Stage I (reliance on others) and Stage II (reliance on self). What is slightly different about the present analysis is that we see the stages as leading to different strategies for feeling powerful. In fact, the whole sequence of psycho-sexual or ego development is viewed here as a way of helping us understand the vicissitudes in the development of the power drive.

We are including modalities here that other scholars would not regard as part of the power motive system in quite the same way as we do. Even Winter, at times slips into speaking of the goal of the power motive as "striving to affect the behavior of others," as in his discussion of Dahl (1957), who argues that so far as actual social power is concerned, unless the behavior of another has been affected, you cannot safely infer that power has been involved. It is thus important to stress that, from the psychological point of view, the *goal* of power *motivation* is to *feel powerful,* and that influencing others is only one of many of ways of feeling powerful. The Stage II modality is among the most primitive ways of feeling powerful. You collect prestige possessions or discipline yourself in order to *feel strong.* It may be argued that building up the self in this way represents *potential* power which might be actualized, if needed, to put someone else down. Prestige supplies are sometimes used in just such competitive struggles; a businessman may want his wife to wear more expensive jewels than anyone else's.

But must *all* experiences of power have as their ultimate goal the exercise of power over others? Why is it necessary to make this assumption as Dahl's definition of social power suggests we should? One can, of course, nearly always think of some ulterior motive behind any behavior, but the goal of science is to make as few such assumptions as possible, particularly when they cannot be directly measured. In the case of men with high *n* Power who drink a lot because it induces feelings of strength, why must we assume that they have an ulterior motive to influence others—when, in point of fact, the more they drink the less likely they are to be in a position to influence anybody? Or when a man collects trophies or prestige possessions, why must we assume that he must do so to impress other people? Why not accept the simple fact that sometimes he enjoys being surrounded by his possessions and feeling the power they convey to him, even when others are not around to be impressed? Our definition of the power motive is not oriented as exclusively towards powerful actions or influence as is common in American social science generally. We can conceive of a man high in power motivation who acts in no powerful ways at all, but sits home and reads sex and adventure novels, watches boxing on television and collects rare stamps, which he gloats over in private.

Stage III. I have impact on others. If we return to consideration of the growing child, we find that soon after he learns that he can feel powerful by controlling or building up himself, he also learns that he can feel powerful by controlling others (Stage III). In traditional Freudian terminology, he enters the phallic stage in which he explores the environment in various ways, demonstrating his strength by what he can make happen "out there." As he grows older, simple methods of controlling the environment by physical assertion or aggression gradually give way to more subtle techniques, and he learns to persuade, bargain, and maneuver to control the behavior of others. This is the modality which defines the power goal for many Western scholars, but there is no compelling reason to make it preeminent over the others. Men who fixate on this modality are known as competitors. They try always to outwit, outmaneuver, and defeat other people —in sports, in work, in arguments, and even in ordinary social relationships. Terhune (1968) has shown, for example, that when men with high n Power play a prisoner's dilemma game, they typically try to exploit their *partner*. The game is fixed in such a way that if both players cooperate they can both win, but if each tries to win the most for himself, neither will win. The exploitive mode is to act as if one is going to cooperate, and then defect, because by deception one makes the most money. Those with high n Power act in this way.

There is another type of behavior which belongs in quadrant III, even though it is often thought of as not being power-related at all. It is a type of helping behavior that appears to be the direct opposite of trying to outwit or defeat another. If you help someone, it looks as if you are trying to save him, not put him down, as you would be trying to do if you were competing with him. How can giving and competing be in any sense psychologically equivalent? One way of looking at giving is to perceive that for help to be given, help must be received. And in accepting a gift, or help, the receiver can be perceived as acknowledging that he is weaker, at least in this respect, than the person who is giving him help. Thus, giving and receiving may have a "zero sum" quality analogous to winning and losing. To the extent that one person wins or gives, the other must lose or receive. From this viewpoint, the receiver acknowledges that he is weaker to the extent that he accepts help from the giver. To be sure, most cultures try to minimize the power relationship implicit in giving by arranging for a mutual exchange of gifts, so that neither party need feel dominated, but this very fact underlines the power aspect of giving relationships. Americans have been so taught that helping others is a highly moral thing to do that they have been slow to recognize how such behavior can be used as a form of domination. It was with a start of surprise that white liberals found their efforts to help blacks proudly rejected. Why? The blacks recognized eventually that the more help they accepted, the more they were acknowledging their weakness or their inferior position. The whites could be viewed as satisfying their needs to feel powerful at the expense of blacks.

It is not clear, however, that giving *has to be* perceived in this way, only that it often is, as we will point out in the discussion of Indian values in Chapter 4. There seems also to be a non-manipulative kind of giving that we define as *sharing,* which may be characteristic of Stages I or IV rather than of Stage III, in which nurturance is provided with the implicit or explicit aim of controlling another or establishing superiority over him.

Do we have evidence that people who are high in *n* Power are more likely to help others as well as compete with them? It should be recalled that helping is part of the scoring definition for power, that thoughts about helping increased in those experiments in which power motivation was aroused. At certain stages of development, furthermore, women high in *n* Power are more willing to provide help to others. Winter reports (1973) that men who either are or want to be teachers are regularly higher in *n* Power; and teaching is regarded as a help-giving profession. By definition, it involves sharing information or imparting it to someone who knows less about it than the teacher. What the findings suggest is that men with high power motivation are attracted to the teaching profession because it gives them the opportunity to feel strong by helping others.

While one would also expect criminal lawyers and politicians to be high in *n* Power, it is not so obvious why journalists should be power-oriented, as reported by Winter (1973). But a journalist is someone who is trying to have impact on the largest possible audience. Like the teacher, he may feel that he is providing a service for the public, giving them access to information they would not otherwise have. Once again, helping behavior implicitly involves a power goal, even though those who display it may consciously deny that influencing others in any way motivates them.

The pathology of the Stage III mode of expressing power needs is all too evident: the woman who dominates her son by "smother" love, the man who becomes so fixated on having his way with others that he resorts to crime, to personal violence—to rape, theft, or murder. In legendary form, Don Juan epitomizes these criminal characteristics. In a *tour de force,* Winter (1973) has shown that undergraduates high in *n* Power show many of the behaviors associated with Don Juan; but what is striking about Don Juan is the extremes to which he goes. He brags, lies, deceives, tricks, disguises himself, seduces women and murders rivals. He is the archetype of the man who seeks power satisfaction through the Stage III modality to the exclusion of all other motives and values.

Stage IV. It moves me to do my duty. In Western psychology, it has been widely believed, at least since Freud's day, that all men are innately Don Juans underneath a social veneer. They would seduce, rape, murder, lie, and cheat, if only society did not stop them. Freud's image of man was that of a wolf out to devour or destroy others. From this point of view, all other outlets for the power drive are sublimations of the more primitive urge to dominate others. For this reason, many psychologists have had difficulty taking seriously what we are calling the most advanced stage of expressing the power drive in which the self drops out as a source of power and a person sees himself as an instrument of a higher authority which moves him to try to influence or serve others. To the confirmed cynic about human nature, to whom Stage III is primary, this is sheer hypocrisy. It may even be a clever maneuver to shed personal responsibility for one's power-related acts by claiming that they are dictated by some higher authority —one's religion, the state, the laws, or the norms of the group. But there is simply no compelling evidence that any one power modality is in the service of another. All we know empirically is that some people high in the need for Power get their power satisfaction from joining organizations in which they subordinate personal goals to a higher authority. They say, in effect, "not my will, but thine be done." Great religious and political leaders from Jesus Christ to Abraham Lincoln and Malcolm X have felt that they were instruments of a higher power which is beyond self. Their goal was to act on others on behalf of this higher authority. At a more mundane level, managers of corporations, who are generally high in power motivation, also feel the same way: they regularly act on behalf of the collectivity. They say, "This may not be good for me, or for you as individuals, but it is good for the corporation." Creative scientists also tend to be higher in power motivation (McClelland, 1964) and they, too, are engaged in paying homage to scientific laws that are beyond and above man and govern and control his behavior.

Thus, when the behavioral psychologist B. F. Skinner wrote *Beyond Freedom and Dignity* (1971), he was trying to convince men that they do not have the freedom to choose that they think they have. They should rather concede that their behavior is controlled by forces in the environment outside of the self. What men should do is acknowledge the superior strength and power of the contingencies that control their behavior, as represented in the laws of psychology, and give up their foolish notion that they have free will (a Stage II power strategy) or the power to make things happen on their own (a Stage III power strategy). In short, Skinner recommends a Stage IV power strategy, which oddly enough is psychologically equivalent to the one recommended by all religions. "Yield to higher authority, serve it, and you will feel strong and happy." What is ironic about Skinner's position is that it is psychologically similar to the fundamentalist Christian position he so consciously has rejected all his life.

In Freud, this power modality is typically described as the final resolution of the family struggle for power. When the little boy recognizes eventually that he cannot defeat his father (Stage III modality) in the competition for the mother's love, he ends by identifying with the aggressor. He incorporates the father's image and tries to be like him, gaining his feeling of power from being like him. When the boy grows up, he begins to act out the paternal role that he has incorporated, and begins to act towards others, particularly his wife and children, on behalf of the principle of paternal authority. Bakan (1966) sees this final stage arising when a man and a woman join together and realize that they have a commitment to mutuality which is above and beyond their individual concerns. He calls it communion and argues that it is women who are predisposed to represent this stage, just as men are predisposed to reflect "agency" or the assertiveness characteristic of Stage III. However the stages are conceived, most theorists concede some higher stage of principled assertion that goes beyond the self-assertion of Stages II and III.

The pathology of Stage IV we have labeled simply "Messianism," for the danger is that a person obsessed with this modality will come to think of himself as a direct instrument of God's will. He will no longer be able to distinguish between his personal views and what the higher authority wants—be it God, the nation-state, or even the corporation. He may be driven to extreme acts of violence or persecution in God's name. What he would not dare to do on his own behalf, he will do if he perceives it as his duty to the higher authority. While the pathology of the Stage III modality may result in a few murders, the pathology of the Stage IV modality may lead to holy wars. Power plays based on collective authority carry a far more dangerous potential than power plays based on individual authority. The implications of this fact are dealt with in later chapters.

Legitimating Power

Discussing violence in the name of religion brings the question of legitimacy sharply into focus. Because power-motivated behavior is potentially so disruptive of the social fabric, there is no type of behavior that society regulates more carefully than expresssions of power. The individual learns quickly as he grows up that he may express his power in some ways but not in others. A boy may struggle with another boy to get something, but he must not hit little girls. He may accumulate possessions but not take them from another. He may rely on his mother for strength and support, but if he does so for too long, he will be considered a sissy. How is he to know in a general way what is legitimate and what is illegitimate power behavior?

One clue he learns to heed is that if he acts on behalf of others, his behavior is usually considered to be legitimate, whereas if he acts on behalf of himself, it is often, but not always, illegitimate. Self-defense is an example of egoistic behavior considered legitimate. Nowhere is the vital importance of the distinction between selfish and altruistic power behavior more evident than when the killing of another human being is involved. If a person kills another for selfish reasons, his deed is called murder and society attempts to punish the killer, often in former times by taking his life. If however, he kills on behalf of his country in wartime or for his God, society acknowledges him as a hero and heaps its highest awards upon him. When Arab guerrillas killed Israeli athletes at the Olympic Games, most of the world regarded the act as murder —that is, as totally illegitimate; but in certain Arab nations, the killers were regarded as heroes in a holy war against the Israelis.

In terms of the classifications in Table 1.2, one might assume that power modalities I and IV, based on sources of power outside the self, would on the whole be more legitimate than modalities II and III, where the source of power is the self. Only in the most general sense is this true. It is not just that some personal assertiveness is legitimate, it is that some altruistic behavior, like helping, can sometimes on closer examination appear to be quite illegitimate. And the critical issue in Stage IV power behavior is which higher authority you invoke to legitimize your actions. There are many today who would invoke the higher authority of the survival of the race to label warfare, particularly nuclear warfare, as illegitimate, no matter what lesser authorities like nation-states may do to legitimize it. Thus, while the issue of legitimacy is central in dealing with how the power motive is expressed, the problem is not resolved merely by attaching that label to any of the categories in Table 1.2. The most we can say is that legitimacy is more often associated with acts undertaken for others than with those undertaken for the self.

Maturity

Is there a more mature way to express the power motive? A Stage IV response, since it is learned later in the development of the individual, might seem to be more mature; and in a narrow sense it is, for if a person never gets beyond a Stage I or Stage II strategy for feeling strong, he will be limited in his capacity to deal with many situations. It is proper to speak of immaturity in the sense of a fixation on an early mode of response. A man may, for example, become so dependent upon his mother as a source of strength and support that he never develops the autonomy and self-direction characteristic of Stages II and III. Though he may be able to live satisfactorily as long as his mother is around to support him, he may be unable to take a job that would be suitable for him in another town or even to become free enough from her to marry.

Much of psychotherapy involves helping individuals go from Stage I to Stage II, from external control to internal control. Dependent people often need help in learning to direct their own lives, and to find the strength to exert their own willpower. Other people have difficulty with the transition from Stage II to Stage III; they are unable to be assertive or competitive out of guilt or fear of punishment. (See Chapter 6.) The therapist's job in such cases is to help them become normally assertive. Curiously enough, less attention is given in the psychological literature to the problem of going from Stage III to Stage IV, from self-assertion to selfless service to an ideal. Yet it requires further maturity to be able to subordinate self-interests to some higher good without feeling that one is "losing" himself in the process. Perhaps only Mowrer (1961) among traditional psychologists has spoken eloquently of the importance of learning to feel strong through obedience to higher moral principles.

Do we then conclude that Stage IV is the most evolved state, and that everyone should seek to progress through the other stages and find his feelings of power through a Stage IV modality? In one sense "yes" and in another "no." As we will show, particularly in Chapters 2 and 8, it does appear that men and women who reach a Stage IV expression of *n* Power are more fully actualized. They are more responsible in organizations, less ego-involved, more willing to seek expert help when appropriate, more open with intimates. Yet one also gets the impression that such genuinely mature people have so progressed through all the stages that any modality or expression of power drive is available to them, and that finally they are free to use whichever one is appropriate to the situation. For the fact is, situations play a large part in determining the appropriateness of various modes of expression of the power drive. A young man may appropriately develop Stage II behavior in order to break dependence on home and mother. He may continue to display such autonomy and self-will by marrying, but in the mutuality of the marital relationship it is appropriate for him to feel strong once again, in the Stage I manner, through the support and love of his wife. When he plays tennis on weekends or argues with his friends about politics, he may appropriately show the competitiveness of Stage III; and in trying to be a good Christian, the obedience to higher authority characteristic of Stage IV.

Maturity involves the ability to use whatever mode is appropriate to the situation. Immaturity involves using perhaps only one mode in all situations or using a mode inappropriate to a particular situation. It would be immature to compete for being the most pious Christian, (Stage III behavior) or to be a Christian only to get the immediate emotional and personal support of the minister (Stage I behavior). The developmental model we have in mind is not like the Freudian one in which early learnings are left behind or, if they persist, are viewed as immature abnormal fixations. Rather, the modes of experiencing power are learned in succession, more or less in the order given, each depending on the successful experiencing of the earlier ones. Yet the earlier modes should remain available to provide the opportunity for a richer, more varied life. The scheme is closer to Erikson's notion that earlier Freudian modes should be re-experienced at more mature levels later in life. From this viewpoint it is abnormal to reject any mode of power expression totally or to use one mode at the expense of all others.

The Universality of Power Orientations

We began with four ways of experiencing power repeatedly found among American men. A simple two-dimensional classification scheme by source and object of power both categorized these outlets, and accounted nicely for the four main stages in ego development as described by Freud, Erikson, and others. Thus we gained generality for our classification scheme by tying it to an analysis of the developmental sequence that has wide currency among personality theorists. Yet some nagging questions remain: suppose we had started with four other outlets of the power drive. Why did we have to pick on these four? Aren't there other equally good ways of classifying the action correlates of *n* Power? Hasn't bias entered the scheme by focusing primarily on men, and on American men at that? Although the Freud-Erikson ego-development sequence was worked out from observation on individuals growing up in a number of different countries, starting in central Europe, the people in all of these countries fall basically within the same Western Judaeo-Christian tradition. How do we know the scheme would order power-related activities in other times, places, and cultures?

Supporting evidence for the usefulness of the scheme comes from an unexpected source. In an ambitious attempt to find out what categories of thought were empirically associated with heavy drinking, McClelland *et al.* (1972) collected folk tales from 44 independent cultures located in all the continents of the world—nine from Africa, seven from the insular Pacific, nine from Eurasia, 13 from North America, and six from South America. Using a computerized system of content analysis, the researchers developed some 88 different "tags" for content categories, which consisted of word lists with a common meaning. A computer sifted through the some 400,000 words in the folk-tale collection and counted the frequency with which words under various tags appeared for each of the 44 cultures. Since the purpose of the study was to find which content categories were associated with heavy drinking, we decided to cast a wide net and to include tags covering just about every conceivable type of behavioral activity, from *anger* (words like anger, rage, fury) to *give* (give, let, help) and *want* (want, wish, need). The one important constraint on the development of the tags was that in an empirical analysis they should be related to whether a society drank heavily or not. This constraint was negligible, however, since in the final list of tags only 11 out of 88 turned out to be significantly correlated with the rated amount of drinking in the tribe. What we actually did by focusing on tags associated with drinking was to limit the tags to ones related to power and inhibition; a subsequent factor analysis of the tags showed that the two main dimensions of the factor space—one readily labeled power and the other inhibition—not only accounted for most of the variance but also, taken together, predicted which tribes would drink heavily and which ones very little. If the tribes were high on the power dimension, and low on inhibition, they drank heavily.

In the study of drinking, the tag list was cut down to include only those associated with the male role, since we were primarily interested in investigating male drinking. But the longer list of tags represents a mine of information about the ways in which tribes all over the world think about various behavioral activities, particularly about the ways in which, as it turned out, they think about power and inhibition. Hence we decided to factor analyze the longer list of tags to see if we found any traces of our system for classifying power activities among the widely different groups of people who have not been much influenced by the Western tradition. The list was first pruned from 88 tags to 50 by eliminating second-order tags —combinations of two or more tags —and by cutting out a large number of kinship tags included as an independent means of getting at the social structure of the cultures. The intercorrelations among the tags were factor analyzed and five factors extracted by rotating the principal components according to the Varimax criterion. That is, we decided to keep the factors as independent of each other as possible and to maximize the loadings of tags on each of them so as to make their meaning clear. The analysis was stopped at five factors when it was clear that further factors accounted for little of the variance. Although the loadings on these five factors showed some resemblance to the different types of power modality included in our classification scheme, the tags relating to inhibition were obscuring the picture. The purpose of the analysis was to discover different types of assertiveness, not the interaction of inhibition with different types of assertiveness. So we eliminated all tags which loaded ±.40 or more on the one of these five factors that was clearly the inhibition factor. Furthermore, a few tags like *fear,* which did not load appreciably on any of the factors related to assertiveness, were eliminated. Tags like *child,* however, if they loaded ±.40 on any of the four assertiveness factors, were left in even though they seemed to have nothing to do with assertiveness.

This left 35 tags, the intercorrelations among which were reanalyzed, and four factors extracted according to the Varimax criterion. They loaded highly on content categories which corresponded closely to the way in which we have classified the power modalities. Factor 1 is clearly the equivalent of our Stage I modality. (See Table 1.3 which lists all tags loading ±.50 or more.) Several of the most highly loaded tags have to do with eating, obtaining support and strength by incorporation. The importance of this exchange relationship with an outside source of power is further emphasized by the fact that the only two non-food-related tags to load highly on this factor are *take* (seize, collect), which refers to getting things from the outside world, and *leave,* which taken together with *follow* (.48) suggests the high salience

Table 1.3– Loadings of ×.50 on the four factor solution of the correlation matrix of 35 folk tale tags from 44 cultures

				Source of Power	
		Other		Self	
		Factor 1: Support		Factor 2: Autonomy	
		Eat, take, leave		*I, he, want, have, go, find*	
		Food	.81	Pronoun male	.74
Target		Eat	.77	Singular human terms	.66
	Self	Cook	.69	Have	.59
		Cut, chop	.69	Go, find	.46
		Leave	.63	Want	.46
		Take	.62	Female adjective (pretty)	− .63
of					
		Factor 4: Togetherness, moralized action		Factor 3: Assertion	
		We, they, ascend, fall		*Hunt, can*	
Power		Fall (down)	.79	Capability (can)	.65
		Ascend (up)	.69	Hunt	.57
	Other	We, they	.55	Go, find	− .69
		Domestic	.51	Child	− .64
		Want	− .48		
		Kill	− .60		

of being with or leaving someone. *Give,* which should also be part of this modality, does load highest on this factor (.32) although not at the .50 level which we arbitrarily established as significant. Perhaps the fact that *give* has the meaning of sharing (Stage I) as well as of manipulating or putting down others (Stage III) blurs its profile in the factor space.

Factor 2 loads highest on *pronoun male* (he) and *singular human terms* (I, he, she) and *have.* These tags seem to define directly Stage II autonomy, signifying that the individual is all-important in these cultures and goes about collecting things to make himself strong. It is interesting that the next two highest loadings on this factor are for the words *go* and *find,* and *want* (.46). "I want," or "I have," or "he wants or has," are again ways of defining what we have called the Stage II modality of autonomous will. No explanation comes to mind for the negative loading of words like "pretty" on this factor.

The next two factors are almost equivalent in the variance they account for, which is somewhat less than for the two factors just discussed. One clearly refers to the Stage III modality since the two tags that load highest on the factor are *capability* (can), and *hunt.* The word *can,* to be able to, is in Latin *posse,* from which our word *power* derives. To be able to influence the outside world is often taken to be the defining operation for power. Among these tribes, at least, references to hunting suggest a direct means of expressing power over something that can also exert power; references to competitive sports would have the same meaning in our culture. The negative loadings on *child* and *go* and *find* seem to typify non-competitiveness. The final factor loads highest on the following tags: *fall* (down), *ascend* (up), and *plural human terms* (we, they). The last tags refer unmistakably to the collectivity orientation of the fourth modality: the group is more important than the individual. The clear references to hierarchy in the *ascend* and *fall* tags suggest the obedience to higher authority characteristic of the Stage IV modality. The two negatively loaded tags, *want* and *kill*, reflect an anti-collectivity orientation that would be considered undesirable in Stage IV. The one tag that makes no particular sense is *domestic*, unless one finds in it a reference to togetherness in the family.

What is one to make of these results? There are several reasons for viewing them skeptically. The original tag lists, obtained for another purpose, cannot be guaranteed to represent all the key dimensions of the power experience. Nevertheless they were certainly not collected nor edited with the present classification scheme in mind, since that scheme was developed long afterwards. The factor analytic procedure itself gives cause for uneasiness. A notoriously imprecise tool, it yields different results depending upon which tags are included, how many factors are extracted, and what criteria are used for extraction and rotation. Finally, even after one has discovered which variables load high on a factor, there is a further lack of precision in the way they can be interpreted.

Have we exaggerated the extent to which the particular list of tags loading high on various factors in Table 1.3 actually suggest the four modalities in Table 1.2? The reader will have to judge for himself. In a few cases, such as the loading for female adjectives like "pretty" on factor 2, it is impossible to make sense out of why a tag should load on a particular factor. Nevertheless, we have tried to play fair by including in Table 1.3 every tag that loaded ±.50 on any of the four factors. We have added the next two highest tags in factor 2 only because they further clarified the meaning of the factor.

It is certainly easy to read into the tag list for each of the factors the modalities of power experiences that we have previously identified. Such evidence of the cross-cultural analysis of thought patterns is important in establishing the generality of the classification scheme we have advanced, for it shows that our scheme coincides with the four main ways that people from widely scattered preliterate tribes all over the world think about power experiences. They also think of power as deriving from *support, autonomy, assertion,* and *togetherness.* Knowing this, we use the scheme with greater confidence to analyze varieties of experiencing power among people of various cultures as they go about trying to make sense out of living.

CHAPTER

2

POWER AND MATURITY

THE THEORY outlined in the last chapter is attractive for a number of reasons. It not only begins to put order into the various ways in which the power motive expresses itself, as reported by various investigators like Winter (1973) and McClelland *et al.* (1972), but it does so within the well-known framework of psycho-sexual or psycho-social development originally proposed by Freud and elaborated later by Erikson (1963). If it turned out to be correct, it would go a long way towards explaining the most annoying problem that has plagued research on the correlates in action of the power motive, the fact that findings, even the most significant ones, are not always replicated on different samples of persons.

For a number of years now a questionnaire originally designed by Winter and used in various revised versions by McClelland and others has been routinely administered to various samples of college and adult men and women, in an effort to discover what actions, thoughts, and feelings characterize individuals with high *n* Power. What has proved frustrating in this effort is that a significant correlation obtained on one application of the questionnaire may disappear or even be reversed on a second application of the same questionnaire. McClelland *et al.* (1972), for example, spent years demonstrating that the drinking of liquor is associated with a certain type of power need in older men; but in at least two different samples the same relationship has not been obtained among college men. Or to take another example, college men high in power motivation seem generally *less* willing to lend valuable possessions like a car, a stereo component, etc., whereas college women high in power motivation seem *more* willing to lend such valuable items. In a further study, the results of which will be reported in a moment, it appears that lending things is not at all correlated with *n* Power in men, and only among those women who tend to be oriented towards Stage I in social emotional maturity.

The latter result gives a clue to the understanding of these disparate findings. If, as the theory predicts, the outlets of power motivation differ for different stages of development, then whether or not one finds a correlation between *n* Power and a particular outlet for a given sample depends on the average level of development for individuals in the sample. Thus if the women in a particular sample were primarily oriented towards Stage I, one would expect an overall significant relationship between *n* Power and lending; if they were at a higher stage of development, one would not expect such a correlation. Since it is likely that college women would on the average be at a somewhat lower stage of maturity than adult women, one could expect the former to lend more often than the latter, even though they are also high in *n* Power. To make sense out of seemingly contradictory findings, then it becomes imperative to find out how the power motive expresses itself at different levels of maturity.

Such a study is badly needed also to answer other urgent questions raised by preliminary attempts to define the stages in the new theory and buttress them with action correlates. To begin with, are there important sex differences in the way the power motive expresses itself? Some of the preliminary correlations mentioned above suggest that there are; certainly Erikson's view is that the development of men and women is different. Men are supposed to be more assertive than women, to build more towers; women are more receptive, acting to entrap or enclose.

What about nurturance or child care, then? Is it an expression of the power drive primarily for women, and if so, at what stage? What about aggression? Is it characteristic of the power drive in men but not in women? At what stage are we to classify certain behaviors? By what logic, for example, is the tendency to accumulate credit cards assigned to Stage II, as in Table 1.2? One can argue that credit cards *should* give the individual a greater feeling of power to control things-supposedly characteristic of Stage II —but might one not argue with almost equal logic that credit cards are a kind of assertive display characteristic of Stage III?

The drinking of liquor also illustrates the difficulty of classification by theory alone. In *The drinking man* it is demonstrated that the consumption of liquor increases power thoughts in men. Since drinking is an intake mode, should not liquor consumption be assigned to Stage I? Men seem indeed to be "taking in" a source of power from the outside in order to make themselves feel stronger, exactly according to the definition of Stage I. Yet it is also true that most men who consume appreciable amounts of liquor behave aggressively or assertively, in a manner characteristic of Stage III. So on the basis of theory alone, therefore, it is difficult to be certain whether liquor consumption is a Stage I or a Stage III expression of the power drive.

While the theory seems promising, even persuasive, it is in fact badly in need of a rigorous empirical test. The same objection has been raised to Erikson's theory of psycho-social development; it seems reasonable enough, but how can we be sure that individuals do develop in that way or that the stages he describes actually exist? In a sense the theory is almost too persuasive, for it is couched in such general terms that almost anything a person does may be interpreted as belonging to any stage. If a man is said to be fixated at the oral stage, then his drinking will be interpreted as "oral intake." If he is supposed to be at Stage III, the same activity will be interpreted as "phallic display." Although leeway must of course be allowed for clinical judgment, such flexibility does not promote precision in the understanding of the stages of development. Measurement, on the other hand, can contribute directly to that end.

A Measure of Social Emotional Maturity

What is needed is a measure of ego development or the level of social emotional maturity. A measure of the need for Power already exists, and a questionnaire can readily be constructed to get at activities, feelings, and attitudes that characterize various stages of maturity; but in order to test the general theory it is necessary to have a direct measure of the level of maturity that can serve as a moderator variable —that is, as an indicator of which outlet n Power will seek. Conceptually, maturity level may be thought of as a kind of switching mechanism to channel the need for Power into one activity or another. What is lacking is some way of estimating the condition of that switching mechanism for a given individual.

Such a measure became available midway in the preparation of the chapters in this book. Most of them were written, indeed, before it was designed and tested, and have been only slightly revised since, in the light of the new findings. The more theoretical and clinical analyses presented in some of the later chapters brought home to me the urgent need for such a measure. They contributed in addition all sorts of items for the questionnaire prepared to tap outlets for the power drive at various levels of maturity. Some readers of a theoretical bent may in consequence want to skim over this chapter, which describes in detail how a measure of maturity level was derived and used to test the theory empirically according to all the usual statistical methods. Others, on the contrary, may not want to read the later chapters until they have some firm evidence that the theory has a basis in empirical fact.

The measure of social emotional maturity was developed by Abigail Stewart (1973). Her approach was empirical rather than exclusively theoretical, as had been the case in previous attempts to measure Erikson's stages. One obvious way to go about the problem of designing a measure is to read Erikson's descriptions of the stages and then to write questionnaire items that presumably tap the feelings, attitudes, and activities called by Erikson characteristic of each stage. This approach, while seeming to be simple, actually involves a triple translation of what is happening in behavioral or phenomenological terms. First there is Erikson, observing the thought processes or behavior of an individual in a given stage and trying to find words that communicate to others what he is perceiving. Next there is the questionnaire designer, who takes Erikson's descriptions and translates them into items supposedly capable of tapping the actions or feelings Erikson described. Finally, there is the reader of the questionnaire items, who attempts to decide whether they describe his thoughts and behaviors or not. In the repeated translations, error or misunderstanding is undoubtedly introduced, whereas what the investigator really wants to know is whether the present subject is showing the same thoughts, feelings, or activities as the person whom Erikson originally identified, let us say, as belonging in Stage I. Looked at in this way, it is not surprising that attempts to measure Erikson's stages through questionnaires have not proven successful.

Stewart approached the problem more directly by identifying individuals who, according to objective criteria, seemed definitely to belong in Stages I, II, III, or IV of Erikson's or our scheme. She then attempted to isolate carefully the different ways in which they thought about various matters. In this respect she followed the procedure successfully used to develop a measure of human motives: the first step is to get two groups of individuals who clearly differ with respect to a motive, and the second step is to search their thought processes for characteristics that differentiate them.

Her subjects were Harvard freshmen, their average age about 18, of the class of 1964. Their thought processes were sampled through a version of the Thematic Apperception Test in which they wrote short, five-minute stories about ambiguous pictures at the opening of college in the fall of 1960. The subjects were chosen because large amounts of information were subsequently collected about them as part of the Harvard student study conducted by King (1973). Stewart chose fantasy as the place to look for codes of differentiation, rather than some of the other measures obtained in the same study, because fantasy has regularly proven to produce more subtle measures of human characteristics than questionnaires and check lists. She assigned her subjects to stages by picking the six cases out of eighty-five young men in the sample whose reports were highest in each of the following areas and low in the other three:

Stage I. Oral. Eating breakfast regularly, having a substantial snack after dinner, smoking at least half an hour a day.

Stage II. Anal. Have a regular time of getting up and going to bed, and listing many bedtime rituals such as: taking a shower, emptying the pockets of one's clothing, brushing one's teeth, urinating, opening the window, etc.

Stage III. Phallic. Having dated a lot in high school with different girls, and citing "reputation enhancement" and "sex" as the most important motives for dating.

Stage IV. Genital. Having a steady girlfriend to whom one is faithful, and reporting that on dates one studies and talks and makes love, as compared to doing other things. The criteria here are Freud's "love and work."

Several points are immediately obvious about such a method of classifying individuals into stages. The criteria are physical rather than psychological or social. There are two advantages: whatever measure is developed is tied directly to bodily functions or psycho-sexual stages, just as in Freud and Erikson: and it is easier for the subject to report the relevant data accurately and for the observer to believe the report. More subtle types of behavior, such as attitudes, beliefs, or preferences, are subject to bias in reporting. Another point is that by choosing the most extreme cases on each dimension, Stewart seemed certain to get individuals who would be relatively "pure" in representing a particular stage. Even if the individuals classified as in Stage III were exaggerating their claims of sexual conquest their concern for sexual exploitation would be an equally diagnostic sign of a Stage III orientation.

A final point to be noted is that these particular criteria are obviously bound to the particular time and sample of individuals tested; there is no reason to think that they would be the same for samples drawn from different populations. Sexual habits, for example, have so changed among undergraduates in the 1970's that sleeping with the same girl on a regular basis could not be taken as the same sure indicator of psycho-sexual maturity that it presumably was for an eighteen-year-old in 1960. Among older men living under different circumstances, or among women, almost certainly other criteria would have to be used. But from the point of view of *deriving* the system for coding thoughts, all that matters is that these criteria have theoretical validity for assigning this particular group of young males to the various stages.

After reading and comparing stories written by these twenty-four students, Stewart developed a coding scheme (1973) that significantly differentiates among the four criterion groups and that cross-validates on a larger sample of subjects. The code is objective and reliable in the sense that, after training, two observers coding the same material achieve high inter-rater agreement. It is described in full elsewhere (Stewart, 1973) along with supporting data on its reliability and validity. Table 2.1 summarizes the general outline of its contents and is to be read is as follows.

Take first the theme of *relation to authority.* In the stories written by students classified in Stage I, Stewart found that authority appears significantly more often as benevolent, whereas in the stories written by those in Stage II, it appears as critical. Stage III students wrote stories about rebelling against authority. Characters in the stories of Stage IV students did not seem to be subject to any kind of personal authority, but when authority did appear, it took an institutional or abstract form. What is remarkable about the coding system —developed as it was from differences obtained in the stories written by these four groups of subjects —is the extent to which it reflects what one would expect from the clinically based theories of Freud and Erikson. That is, descriptions written by individuals in the oral stage reveal that for them authority is the benevolent provider of what a person needs to survive, that loss of such support leads to feelings of despair and

Table 2.1—A brief outline of the Stewart coding system for social-emotional maturity

Criterion group:	High oral intake	Excessive bedtime rituals
Thematic elements	Stage I (Intake)	Stage II (Autonomy)
A. Relation to authority	Authority is benevolent	Authority is critical
B. Relation to people/objects	Gets what he wants	Doesn't get what he wants
C. Feelings	Loss, despair	Incompetence (unable)
D. Action	Passive	Clears disorder
Criterion group:	Mutuality in making love	Sexual exploitation
	Stage IV (Generativity)	Stage III (Assertion)
A. Relation to authority	Removed from personal authorities	Rebels against authority
B. Relation to people/objects	Differentiates among them	Escapes
C. Feelings	Complex mixtures of joy and sorrow	Hostility, anger
D. Action	Schedules what is to be done as appropriate	Leads to failure

melancholy, and that the predominant mode of action is in fact passive —waiting to be fed, so to speak. In Stage II, the individual breaks away from the dependency of Stage I, and develops autonomy or will-power as he attempts to control his own life. He sees authority as critical; he often feels unable to keep things in order; he worries about his incompetence in this regard. Then in Stage III his orientation turns outward, away from the self, toward others. Rebelling against authority, he begins to escape the network of family relationships and to explore the world outside. Although often aggressive in his new-found assertiveness, he is plagued by a fear that he may fail to make it entirely on his own. In Stage IV, which Erikson calls the stage of mutuality or generativity, he begins to think in more complex terms of a newfound togetherness as part of some larger "institution" like marriage or a love relationship. His actions and feelings, less dominated by particular modes, are more appropriate to time and circumstances.

The fit between the code empirically derived and the code theoretically expected is so close as to support the Eriksonian view of a close linkage between psycho-sexual and psycho-social development. What is remarkable about the themes in the maturity code is that they do not reflect in any direct way the bodily functions used to assign the students to the four stages. It appeared, after the fact, that Stewart had chosen well in using the criteria she did for selecting individuals to represent pure cases of various stages. Yet all of the categories summarized in Table 2.1, while they make good theoretical sense, were included only if they differentiated among the four groups. Nothing was added to the code because it made theoretical sense if it also failed to discriminate empirically. The code is thus based on fact rather than on theoretical or clinical logic.

The scheme yields a score for each stage for each individual. For example, a person may receive scores of 1, 3, 4, and 0 for stages I, II, III, and IV, respectively, and his modal stage would be phallic (III). The modal stage score is sometimes used to classify individuals. Since this individual also has strong elements of Stage II, however, Stewart computes an overall Maturity score representing his average standing on a scale of 1–4. The first application of such a scoring system to the eighty-five college freshmen in the sample showed that the most frequent modal score was for Stage II; on the assumption that college freshmen are just breaking away from home and taking charge of their own lives, the score makes theoretical sense. Other applications suggest that by the senior year the modal stage has shifted upwards, and that if one applies the system to adult married men, the modal stage is IV. Such preliminary findings are promising in that the scores seem to be yielding results that make developmental sense for groups of people, but they still need checking, for the pictures used to elicit stories from these samples were different. The whole matter of validity of the scoring system will be treated in a separate publication. Here we merely assume that the measure is sufficiently promising to be used as a way of testing the general theory outlined in Chapter 1.

The crucial question is: if this scheme is used to measure the stage of individuals, will the need for Power lead to actions, thoughts, and feelings theoretically characteristic of a given stage? To answer the question with this measure involves trying to lift ourselves by our bootstraps. Since we know neither whether the measure is good, nor whether the theory is right, how can we use one to test the other? Indeed, if we do not obtain an expected result, it is impossible to know where the difficulty lies; the measure could be inadequate, or the theory could be wrong. Positive results, however, are meaningful. If an expected result is obtained, then one gains confidence both in the measure and in the theory. If enough positive results are obtained, one may gain so much confidence in the measure of maturity level, that failure to obtain a theoretically predicted result could lead to questioning or refining the theory; it would be impossible to reject the measure without rejecting all the positive results already obtained. Hence we decided to use the Stewart measure of social-emotional maturity in a major study to locate outlets of *n* Power for men and for women at different levels of maturity.

Power Motivation among Adults

Samples of men and women aged 25–50 were recruited in the metropolitan Boston area through a newspaper advertisement in which potential subjects were asked to come to Harvard University to take some tests for which they would be paid eight dollars for about three hours of testing. We decided to limit the study to adults because previous work had suggested that habits and patterns, particularly in areas like drinking, had not settled down enough among students of college age to give stable results. It would be particularly desirable to have subjects settled in an occupation and marriage and family life, since these are the major experiences that might modify habits, attitudes, and feelings in all sorts of areas. Only married women were recruited because of the requirements of another study in which we asked some of them to participate. Such a restriction has the advantage that it includes only women who have been exposed to the opportunities and limitations of family life, but it of course restricts the generalizability of the findings so far as women who do not marry are concerned. Although recruiting through advertising introduces an unknown bias, we thought that the amount of money offered was enough to attract a broad range of people with varying interests in psychological research. The procedure does have the advantage that it attracts people from both the working and middle classes.

The people who volunteered were given the option of coming at several different times for testing, in the evenings and on Saturdays, to make it possible for working people to come. From fifteen to twenty-five arrived at a particular time, and they were given all the measuring instruments in a group setting. They first wrote brief imaginative stories to the following pictures: a ship captain talking to someone, two women working in a laboratory, a couple in a bar, and a man and a woman in a trapeze act. See Appendix I B. The pictures were chosen primarily to elicit stories dealing with power, but secondarily to present situations that would be appropriate for either men or women. Next the subjects answered a long questionnaire (a copy of which is included in the Appendix I A), based on questions originally designed by Winter (1967) to get at various outlets for the power drive, later expanded in *The drinking man* (1972), and still further expanded for this study to include the thoughts, feelings, or actions characteristic of the various stages described in Erikson's writings. So far as possible the items referred to operant actions, since they have been found to be most characteristic expressions of motives and most easily reported. Thus a person quizzed on specific actions —how often he drinks coffee, gets into arguments, or slams a door—can identify easily what he is being asked about. In addition, they are operant; he can perform them spontaneously. Anyone can argue, slam doors, or drink coffee, whatever his or her life circumstances, which means they are more apt to be a pure reflection of motives. Although we included a few attitude items to get at matters not easily tapped through reports of actions, for the most part we avoided them as likely to be influenced by response bias factors such as social desirability.

General Effects of Power Motivation

Eighty-five men and one hundred and fifteen women showed up for the testing. They averaged around thirty-five years of age; two-thirds of the men were married, and nearly all of the women. They were on the whole a rather highly educated group, the men having completed on the average nearly four years beyond high school and the women nearly three. About a third of them came from working-class backgrounds. Nearly one third of the men and one half of the women reported that their mothers had worked (see Appendix Table 2.1). The best that can be said for the sample is that it is miscellaneous, although it is in no sense a random sample of the general population. It is more urban, better educated, drawn more heavily from the middle-class than would be typical for the country as a whole. But certainly there is a wide enough range of backgrounds within the sample to give the results fairly general applicability.

A question of prime importance is whether the Stewart maturity score yields results for women comparable to those for men. Since it was derived on a sample of young males, one might legitimately question whether it could be indiscriminately applied to women, although the themes it covers, as outlined in Table 2.1, do not appear to be sex-linked. It was reassuring to discover that the mean score for each of the four stages differed little for the two sexes (see Appendix Table 2.2); the means differed significantly only for Stage I, the women scoring higher on the average ($t = 2.65$, $p < .01$). Whether this difference reflects some measurement artifact or a real tendency for women to show a stronger Stage I orientation is impossible to say. The latter possibility would be consistent with traditional views of the woman's role as requiring a more dependent or "intake" orientation. So far as the present analysis is concerned, this small difference does not matter, because we are concerned with variations in scores for a given stage rather than with absolute levels; mean scores for the two sexes for the four stages seem comparable enough not to cause major distortions in the range of such variations.

The modal stage scores show a somewhat more disturbing difference between the two sexes. We arbitrarily decided that a stage score would be considered the mode if it was at least two points and if it was higher than the scores for the other three stages. Ties were resolved in favor of the lower of the stage scores. On this basis there is a significant difference in the distribution of modal scores between the two sexes, more of the women showing modes in Stages I and II and more of the men in Stages III and particularly IV. The proportion of men with a mode in Stage IV is significantly higher than the proportion of women (X^2 = 7.6, p < .01). See Appendix Table 2.2. Yet it seems unreasonable on theoretical grounds to assume that a miscellaneous sample of adult men is "more mature" than a similar sample of married women. Thus it may well be that there is some bias in the theory, the scoring system, or more probably in the particular set of pictures used: that is the picture cues might elicit more Stage IV type responses in men than in women. Although the mean difference is small, it is sufficient to contribute to a higher mode at Stage IV for men than for women.

For this reason we decided not to use the modal stage score in the following analyses. One logical approach to testing a theory is to assign each individual to a stage and then to see how his or her n Power correlates with various "outlets." If the correlated actions differ significantly for individuals at various levels of development, then the theory might be tested. Assigning people to stages on the basis of the modal score, however, seems for a number of reasons a highly dubious procedure. It would be contaminated by the sex bias just noted. It would be highly unreliable, since a score of just two points can assign a person to a stage. It would greatly reduce the number of cases on which correlations have to be based —to as few as eleven in the case of men classified at Stage I. And it would treat as similar two individuals whose stage scores might be as different as 2, 2, 2, and 3 and 0, 0, 0, 2 for Stages I–IV respectively. We thought it preferable to deal with the actual stage scores for each individual rather than to assign him to a stage according to his modal score.

How these stage scores correlate with each other and with n Power is also of interest. See Appendix Table 2.3. The stage scores themselves are unrelated with each other except that in both sexes the Stage I score ("intake") has a significant negative correlation with the Stage III score ("assertion")—not surprising in view of the fact that the two modes are directly opposite. The other major finding for both sexes is that the n Power score is strongly and significantly associated with the Stage III score, as well as somewhat positively correlated for both sexes with the Stage II score.

Both sets of correlations argue that the n Power scoring system itself may be biased towards the expressive modality in which the self, rather than some outside force, is the source of a person's feelings of power. On the surface it looks as if the scoring system for n Power might be influenced by the Western bias towards self-reliance or toward an acceptance of the individual as the ultimate source of powerful acts, a bias which we discussed in Chapter I. The distortion is not likely to have come from the methods of arousing the power motive. Winter's method of presenting the film of an inspiring leader seems typical of Stage I, as Uleman's method of encouraging people to be manipulative experimenters is of Stage III; and Veroff's method of tapping fantasies while candidates were waiting to see if they were elected to office seems to be representative of Stage IV. Only the Stage II modality is not represented, in which, for example, a person might be encouraged to show marked independence of or control over a potentially disorderly situation. The bias appears likely to have entered into the scoring system as American psychologists pored over the stories looking for characteristics differentiating the aroused and unaroused subjects. As psychologists they were probably sensitive to the individually assertive acts characteristic of Stages II and III, and they also probably chose pictures more likely to elicit such themes.

The bias also appears in Appendix Table 2.2, which presents the mean n Power scores of individuals assigned to various stages by their modal scores. For both men and women assigned to Stages II and III the average n Power scores are much higher than they are for those assigned to Stages I or IV, in which the individual theoretically gets power from the outside rather than displays it in his own actions. Here is still another reason why the analysis cannot be made in terms of variation in n Power within stages. The mean n Power score for men in Stage III, for example, is over nine, whereas it is only about four for men assigned to Stage I. Thus a variation upwards from these two very different means might have quite different significance, and in that case the range of n Power scores to be correlated with various outlets would not be comparable across stages.

Finally, the mean n Power score for men is significantly higher than it is for women, a fact which may once more reflect the assertiveness bias built into the scoring system, or at least into the particular picture cues used in this study. Fortunately the probable bias in the *n* Power measure, while troublesome, does not totally undermine our ability to use the data to test the theory. All it can do is make some of the relationships less obvious or significant, particularly in the Stage I and Stage IV areas. What it suggests is that, since the *n* Power scores for men and women with these two orientations may be underestimated, we may not obtain some of the relationships which we otherwise would. But once again our primary concern is the variations of the *n* Power score in connection with the stage scores. Even though that variation may not be as large or as valid as it might be without the bias in the *n* Power scoring system, enough of it should remain to enable us to test the theory.

Our overall objective was to combine the *n* Power and stage scores in such a way as to correlate the resultant score with various actions, feelings, and attitudes supposedly representative of the various stages. In the end we decided simply to add the *n* Power and stage scores, having first made their means and variances comparable by converting them to standard scores. They could have been multiplied, but both the empirical results and theory (see Couch, 1960) demonstrate that a product yields less variation in a resultant score over its components than a sum does. We were interested in maximizing the differences, say, resulting from combining *n* Power with the Stage I score over what either *n* Power or Stage I score alone would yield.

One other major methodological problem had to be solved: previous theory and research have shown that motives characteristically express themselves in alternative ways. An example from *The drinking man* (McClelland *et al.*, 1972) will illustrate the point. Heavy drinking, an accumulation of prestige supplies, frequent gambling and many aggressive impulses were all correlated at a low positive level with the measure of personal power orientation (called p Power). Yet none of these variables showed any correlation with the others; a person who gambled a lot did not necessarily drink a lot nor did the man who reported many aggressive impulses necessarily drink heavily or gamble a lot. The assumption seemed reasonable, therefore, that these were *alternative* outlets for the personl power drive. If the person could gratify his p Power by gambling heavily, he had no need to engage in any of the other activities. Accordingly each of these measures was standard scored and the maximum standard score for each individual chosen from among the four. This maximum score, which represented the most that anyone displayed of any of these personal power outlets, correlated more highly with the measure of p Power than either any of the outlets alone or their sum. A high motive score, in other words, indicates only that a person will show some extreme form of power activity, not which particular form. Thus the correlation of the power motive score with any particular outlet may be low, because those who are high in power motivation but using some other outlet will show up as contributing zeros to the correlation with the first outlet.

Since the logic is involved, we have presented a numerical example in Appendix Table 2.4 for the reader who wants to follow it more closely. Two measures from the present study are chosen by way of illustration: the tendency to report either that one has frequently committed impulsive aggressive acts like yelling at someone in traffic or deliberately slamming a door hard, or that one "hasn't but would like to." These can easily be understood as alternative outlets for the power drive. A person may tend either to act aggressively or to think about such behavior without actually indulging in it. If his need for Power is strong, he will probably develop a consistent mode of responding, but will be unlikely to report *both* controlling *and* expressing his anger. In such a case one can readily see how the correlation of power motivation with either one of these alternatives taken alone might be low whereas it would be much higher with the maximum expression of either.

We can apply precisely the same logic to the expression of the power motive at different levels of maturity. If an individual is at Stage I, his power drive may find one outlet, if he is at Stage II another, and so on. But if a sample of individuals consists of people at all levels of maturity, then the first order correlation between the power drive and any one of these outlets may be small or insignificant. The analytical problem is to find the set of alternatives to include in the cluster, the maximum expression of any of which is to be correlated with n Power. The most rigorous course would be to find some statistical technique, akin to multiple regression, in which one could maximize the correlation with n Power through testing various sets of alternatives until one found the particular set that yielded the best results using the maximum score within a set. So far I have been unable to discover such a technique. Simply taking factorial combinations of two hundred possible alternatives two at a time, three at a time, and so forth —a kind of "main strength" method—is impracticable, even by computer.

In choosing alternatives to include in a set, therefore, we have of necessity been guided largely by theoretical considerations as well as by suggestive although not definitive empirical findings. The first step is to try to find for each stage one outlet for *n* Power that best typifies that stage. If we are successful in picking these outlets, and they are genuine alternatives preferred by people with different stage orientations, then the need for Power should correlate significantly with the maximum expression of any one of the four. If a person were high in *n* Power and also in Stage I score, for example, he should choose the first alternative; if he were high in *n* Power and high in Stage II score, he should choose the second alternative, and so on.

Three criteria were used in choosing the alternatives. First, an alternative must exhibit the characteristics of that stage, according to the theory outlined in Chapter 1. Second, the correlation of the alternative in question must be higher with *n* Power plus that stage score than with *n* Power plus the other stage scores, for *both sexes*. Third, the outlet must be measured in terms of more than a dichotomy in order not to place artificial restraints on the maximizing procedure applied to a cluster. In some parts of the questionnaire, for instance, the individual simply checked an item or not, such as whether he tended to interrupt others in coversation. When a presence/absence measure like this is introduced into a cluster, it restricts the range of scores for that item, and this fact places an artificial restraint on the maximizing procedure. In a few cases, however, this requirement was abandoned where it was difficult to find alternatives that satisfied the first two criteria.

Table 2.2 shows how the operation was carried out. The subjects were asked to list the magazines they read regularly, and the number that could be classified as power oriented was simply recorded. They consisted mainly of magazines dealing with sex, like *Playboy,* or with competitive sports, like *Sports Illustrated.* The measure satisfies the theoretical criterion because it is an "intake" variable characteristic of Stage I; indeed it is the same variable used to illustrate Stage I in Chapter 1. It satisfies the second criterion because for women it correlates positively, and for men it correlates significantly with *n* Power plus Stage I score, and in both cases the correlations are higher for this than for any other stage.

For Stage II we could have used credit cards possessed, the variable discussed in connection with Table 1.2; it meets the second criterion also, significantly for women and less so for men. We had three reasons for not using it. (1) In these samples men had only half as many credit cards with them as women, suggesting some sex bias in the variable. (2) Credit cards seem a less clear illustration of Stage II than admitting to many aggressive impulses that one controls. (3) The

Table 2.2–Correlations among 85 men and 115 married women between n Power and actions characteristic of four stages of maturity

	Correlations with			
	n Power		n Power plus same stage score	
Characteristic associated with	Men	Women	Men	Women
Stage I. Power oriented reading	.13	.11	.27*	.12
Stage II. Controlled anger	.15	.12	.22*	.17†
Stage III. Expressed anger to people	.07	.04	.10	.17†
Stage IV. Organizational memberships	−.01	.23*	.12	.30**
Correlations with maximum expression of any of the four alternatives				
Whole sample	.32*	.21*		
Random half of sample	.31*	.33*		
Other half of sample	.35*	.14		
Correlations with average expression of the four alternatives	.19	.27**		

†p < .10, *p < .05, **p < .01.

control of aggression versus its expression—the Stage III outlet chosen here—seem more genuinely alternatives as required by the model than the possession of credit cards versus the expression of aggression.

The Stage III outlet chosen—the frequency with which people admit to having carried out impulsive aggressive actions against people—has the merit of representing the assertive mode characteristic of Stage III, although its correlation with *n* Power plus Stage III score is not high for either sex. Competitive sports, the alternative mentioned in Chapter I, could not be used here; using precoded alternatives such as bridge and bowling, in an effort to make the item suitable for women, destroyed the usually obtained correlations of *n* Power with this variable.

Finally, organizational memberships was the defining variable used for the characteristic Stage IV inclusion in a supra-individual unit. For Erikson such a unit meant marriage and parenthood; from our point of view any institution was meaningful.

What is particularly striking about Table 2.2 is that the first-order correlation between *n* Power and any of these variables is insignificant in seven out of eight instances. If we were simply looking for correlates of *n* Power, without the theory of different outlets for different stages, we would have to conclude that none of these variables is significantly correlated with *n* Power. Furthermore, they are uncorrelated with each other, at least for men, as a correlation matrix from a previous study shows (Bar II sample in *The drinking man*, 1972). As expected, the tendencies to act on one's aggressive impulses or to control them are correlated exactly .00, n = 108. In fact, only the tendencies to engage in power-oriented reading and to commit aggressive acts are significantly correlated, and these only at the level of .20. All four of these variables, in short, seem unrelated to each other and to *n* Power. There would be no particular empirical justification for combining them —as, for instance, to get an overall measure of the tendency of *n* Power to express itself in these ways.

Hence it is amazing to discover from the correlations at the bottom of the table that in fact they do represent alternative expressions of the power drive just as the theory predicts they would. The correlations of *n* Power with the maximum expression of any of the four alternatives are significant for the whole sample of men and of women, and for random halves of the sample for men. For women the correlation holds up for the first random half but drops considerably for the other half, for reasons that are not clear. Also, as predicted by the theory, the correlation of *n* Power with the *average* expression of the four outlets is insignificant, and considerably lower, at least for the men, than it is with the maximum expression of any of the four. For the women the two correlations are about the same, although it should be remembered that, since the measure based on scores for single alternatives is less reliable, its "true" correlation with the criterion (*n* Power) may well be greater.

The results are encouraging. Positive findings, as we said, tend to confirm the whole chain of logic used in obtaining them. On the basis of these results one has somewhat more confidence in the Stewart measure of levels of maturity as well as in the general theoretical model that *n* Power will express itself in alternate ways at different stages of social emotional development. Without the theory, indeed, it is doubtful that we would have found the outlets of the power drive characteristic of men. One could never have predicted from the first-order correlations of various characteristics with *n* Power that the correlations of the maximum expression of any of them would be higher and more stable for men than for women. The finding illustrates the major difficulty in relying exclusively on empirical first-order correlations in deciding which set of alternatives to put in a cluster. First-order correlations may be used as a guide; but if they had been the sole criteria here, they certainly would have led us to exclude organizational memberships for men. Lacking a clear empirical method of picking the alternatives, I have relied most heavily on theory for deciding on the outlets for a particular cluster of alternatives.

Sex Differences

To test the theory in its most general form was the first objective, which required finding the four most characteristic outlets for *n* Power at each stage, both for men and for women. The next logical question seemed to center on whether power motivation expresses itself differently for men and women regardless of stage. The answer involves going through the list of correlations of each variable in the questionnaire with *n* Power separately by sex, and picking out those that correlate significantly with *n* Power and with *n* Power in combination with every stage score. As an example, consider the first variable in Table 2.3. The subjects were asked "recall and describe two of your dreams that were unusual or that you have often." A number of people were unable to recall any dream whatsoever, or at the most one, a fact not true of men high in *n* Power. They were not only more likely to recall their dreams, but more likely regardless of their stage scores, the correlations being .35 for *n* Power in combination with Stage I score, .24 in combination with Stage II score, .33 in combination with Stage III score, and .28 in combination with Stage IV score. For what suggestive significance it may have, the highest correlation for the combination *n* Power plus stage score is listed in Table 2.3 together with the stage number involved. It can be seen by glancing down the righthand column in Table 2.3 that the characteristics selected in this way do seem representative of the whole range of stages, except for Stage IV among men.

The procedure yielded seven non-stage-specific characteristics that correlated significantly with *n* Power for men and seven for women, six of which were included in the cluster of alternatives. Interpreting these results seems hazardous without some kind of cross-validation inasmuch as they have been selected out of two hundred or more such correlations and could be significant by chance alone. How do we know that we are not interpreting chance results?

We made two checks. First, the samples of men and women were randomly split in half and all of the correlations run in each half separately to see if the relationship found in one sample cross-vali-

Table 2.3–General, non-stage specific characteristics of men and women high in n Power

Associated characteristics	Correlations with n Power	Maximum r with n Power plus Stage score	Stage
Men			
m More dreams recalled	.32**	.35***	I
m Get into arguments more often	.26*	.26*	II
m Share information about sex life	.21†	.20	I
m Reason not so crucial	.32**	.38***	I
m Non power-oriented alternative jobs	.27*	.32**	III
m Don't check on home security	.24*	.24*	III
m Have trouble sleeping	.28*	.31*	III
Correlations with maximum expression of m alternatives, whole sample (N = 85)	.48***		
Random half of sample (N = 43)	.45**		
Other half of sample (N = 42)	.57***		
Correlations with average expression of m alternatives N = 85)	.59***		
Women			
m Discipline body (e.g., diet) more often	.31***	.34***	I
m More credit cards	.24**	.26**	II
m More unpleasant dreams	.20*	.19*	II
Play tennis more often	.25*	.29*	III
m Concerned about appearance of clothes	.21*	.19*	IV
m Willing to donate body parts after death	.13	.15†	I, III, IV
m High fluid intake per day	.27**	.21*	II, III, IV
Correlations with maximum expression of m alternatives, whole sample (N = 115)	.36***		
Random half of sample (N = 58)	..24†		
Other half of sample (N = 57)	.44***		
Correlation with average expression of m alternatives N = 115)	.49***		

†p < .10, *p < .05, **p < .01, ***p < .001

dated at approximately the same level in another. For the variables in Table 2.3 this was mainly the case. In one half of the sample of men, for example, the correlations between dreams recalled and *n* Power was .33, and in the other half it was also .33. Since we ourselves have argued above that first-order correlations like this may vary depending on the particular distribution of stage scores in a sample, we decided to cross-validate the whole pattern rather than the individual items that make it up. Consequently, the variables correlated with *n* Power for each sex were grouped as alternatives in a cluster and the maximum expression of any of them correlated with *n* Power both for the whole sample and for random halves of the sample. The results were impressive, expecially for men. The correlations (r = .45 and .47) are not only higher than are usually obtained in motivational research of this sort, but high enough to provide a challenge to those who like Mischel (1971) believe there is not enough consistency within personality to account for any significant proportion of the variance in human behavior. The *n* Power score for these men accounts for 20–25% of the variance in their tendency to show some extreme form of an element within a power-related syndrome of thoughts and acts.

Also listed in Table 2.3 and in similar tables to follow are the correlations of *n* Power with the *average* expression of the alternatives in a cluster. If anything, they tend to run higher than the correlations with the maximum expression of any of the alternatives, a finding that means one of two things: either outlets *within* a stage tend to be more positively correlated than *across* stages, as in the previous table, so that the average score works better than the maximum alternative score; or the greater reliability of a measure made up of many items (as in the case of the average score) provides a better estimate of the true correlation with *n* Power. Thus if we were to estimate the true validity of a measure based on a single alternative vs. one based on the combination of alternatives, it might well be that the former approach would give a higher correlation. The data are simply not adequate for deciding whether outlets for *n* Power within a stage are genuine alternatives or simply summate. Since the theoretical model of motivation tends to favor looking on them as alternatives, and since it is surprising to observe them serving so effectively this way, the emphasis throughout the chapter will be on viewing them as alternatives.

Leaving the statistical and methodological arguments aside, suppose we take the results at their face value. What do they show? So far as non-stage specific characteristics are concerned, they suggest that men high in *n* Power tend to be *assertive* in one way or another and *emotional*. They tend to get into arguments; they share information about their sex life with friends and family —probably with a view to boasting about it. They are not bothered about going back to check on things they might have left undone in their living quarters, such as locking the door or turning off the lights. They report that they have trouble getting to sleep or staying asleep. One gets the impression of energetic men who charge ahead at a high level of tension, an impression supported by the fact that on several items in the questionnaire they tend to downgrade reason and understanding. They feel that good will is more important than reason, that action is more important than a knowledge of the truth, and that it is not necessary to understand everything. This kind of emotional assertiveness apparently also reflects itself in their tendency to dream a lot or to be able to recall their dreams.

The only puzzle in the cluster of alternatives is the one derived from asking them to list the three occupations "you have been in, would like to be in, or would strongly consider" —including the one they are currently working in, which was to be listed first. All the jobs were coded as being power-oriented or not, according to the empirical findings presented by Winter (1973); teaching, journalism, and management were considered power-oriented jobs. Although the men higher in n Power listed fewer career possibilities that were power oriented, they tended more often to be already in a job that was power oriented. This means in effect that they were particularly unlikely to list jobs other than the one they were in that would be power oriented. The result may be due to chance, since the correlation was only .07 in one half of the sample and .40, $p < .01$ in the other half. Pressed for an interpretation one might speculate that they are in power-oriented jobs now because they have rejected non-power alternatives that they consider only in fantasy. Yet the overall picture is reasonably clear: the man with high n Power seems to have an emotionally assertive style regardless of his stage of ego development or maturity.

The picture for women is less clear, although what emerges is somewhat more novel and surprising than the expected assertiveness found in men. We were generally less successful in finding outlets for n Power in women, perhaps because we had had less experience over the years in preparing items for questionnaires that would tap women's life styles. The item dealing with tennis was not included in the cluster analysis because it was such a low-frequency item that when it was combined with other competitive games, the correlation dropped to insignificance. The item dealing with willingness to donate parts of the body to others after death was included because of its theoretical importance and because for three out of the four stages it correlated at a near 10% level of significance with *n* Power, even though the overall correlation was somewhat lower. The correlation with the maximum expression of the six alternatives included in the cluster with *n* Power was a substantial .36 and held up fairly well for random halves of the sample. The correlation of the average expression of the six alternatives was even higher (.49, p < .001).

What comes through clearly in this set of correlations is the concern women with high *n* Power show for their bodies. Such a woman disciplines her body more often, through yoga or exercise or particularly by dieting. She fills it with more fluids every day; she is concerned with the appearance of the clothes she wears, as reflected in the number of adjectives used to describe them. The women were asked to list as many clothes that they wore the day before yesterday as they could remember; the number of adjectives used in describing the clothes was then counted as an index of how concerned they were about their appearance. Women were also more likely to say they wanted to and might already have made arrangements to donate parts of the body like an eye or a kidney to others after they were dead. Even credit cards can be considered as a kind of extension of the self, as if women wanted to be big and capable. It is as if they see their bodies as a resource, just as the males see themselves and their bodies as something to use for instrumental purposes. The results thus fit into traditional psychological notions of male and female roles. The male is pictured by sociologists as the aggressive, assertive protector of the family, the female as the resource, the person who produces children, food, and emotional support for the other members of the family. What these findings suggest is that individuals high in power motivation tend to play out these roles more definitively. Even the tendency of women of high power motivation to have unpleasant dreams fits the picture because most of their unpleasant dreams have to do with being threatened or attacked by monsters or other vague figures. Seeing themselves as the object of attack, they once again underline the preciousness of their selves, just as when they fill themselves with liquids, and diet to make sure they look attractive.

At the most general level, then, the picture that emerges appears almost reciprocal. The male high in *n* Power has an emotionally assertive approach to life, whereas the female high in *n* Power focuses on building up the self which may be the object of that assertiveness. He finds strength in action, she in being a strong resource. This is an over-simplified picture, dealing largely with stylistic approaches transcending the levels of maturity. We must now turn to sex differences as they appear at various stages of social emotional development.

Power Orientation: Stage I

Table 2.4 assembles separately for each sex those variables that correlated optimally with *n* Power combined with a Stage I score but not when combined with the other stage scores; it presents, in short, the stage-specific characteristics of the power drive when combined with a Stage I orientation. For the sake of comparison, the correlations of each variable with *n* Power alone are also given. The variables at the top of each list, labeled m, were selected for inclusion in the cluster of alternatives, the maximum or average expression of which was correlated with *n* Power plus Stage I scores. Once again, statistically speaking, it appears that we were successful in picking ways in which individuals with a Stage I power orientation expressed themselves. The correlations of the maximum (and average) expressions of the alternatives within the clusters are moderately high with *n* Power plus Stage I scores, highly significant for each sex, and fairly stable from one sample to the next. Note particularly that these correlations are much higher than with *n* Power alone, or with *n* Power plus other Stage scores, indicating that Stage I maturity diverts *n* Power particularly into these channels. Of greater interest is the picture these correlations give of the power-motivated adult still oriented toward the first stage in development.

The power-motivated man with a Stage I orientation reads magazines focused on sex and aggression, just as one would predict for an "intake" stage. He also shares information about himself of a kind that many people regard as confidential. Part of the questionnaire consisted of items taken from Jourard's Self-Disclosure Scale (Jourard, 1963) in which a person is asked to indicate the extent to which he has talked about a number of items with his father, his mother, his male friend other than husband, female friend other than wife, or spouse. He records a zero if he has told the other person nothing about that aspect of himself, a 1 if he has talked in general terms about it, a 2 if he has talked in full and complete detail about it or an X if he has lied or misrepresented himself to the other person. The items covered:

> the worst pressures and strains in my work;
> the kinds of things that make me especially proud of myself, elated, or full of self-respect;
> whether or not I now have any health problems —e.g., trouble with sleep, digestion, female complaints, heart condition, allergies, piles, etc.;
> all of my present sources of income —wages, fees, allowances, dividends, etc;

Table 2.4–Correlations of n Power with characteristics at Stage I ("Intake") level of maturity

Associated characteristics	n Power	Correlations with n Power plus scores for			
		Stage I	Stage II	Stage III	Stage IV
Men (N = 85)					
m Power-oriented reading	.13	.23*	.12	.03	−.02
m Share more secrets	.20†	.31**	.18†	.15	.19†
m More intraceptive (psychic minded)	.11	.17	.10	.10	.09
m More unpleasant dreams reported	.17	.35**	.12	.13	.18†
Pre-Oedipal identification (N = 35)	.27	.35*	.20	.26	.27
Interruptive talker	.00	.23*	.12	.03	−.02
Check car carefully	.06	.27*	.15	.05	−.07
Fewer car accidents	.12	.27*	.08	.09	.09
Correlation of maximum expression of m alternative for whole sample	.13	.33**	.09	.10	.14
Random half of sample (N = 43)		.36*			
Other half of sample (N = 42)		.30†			
Correlation of average expression of m alternatives (N = 85)	.23*	.42***	.06	.13	.07
Women					
m Male inspiration stronger than female	.13	.22*	.07	.05	.10
m List more precious possessions	.00	.11	.00	−.04	−.02
m If given $10,000 would invest it	.16†	.24*	.10	.11	.13
m Loaned more things	.08	.12	.05	−.00	.01
m More frequent physical symptoms	.09	.19*	.11	.08	.06
Oedipal identification (N = 51)	.23	.29*	.13	.08	.36**
Correlation of maximum expression of m alternatives for whole sample	.17†	.29**	.04	.08	.26**
Random half of sample (N = 58)		.36**			
Other half of sample (N = 57)		.21			
Correlation with average expression of m alternatives (N = 115)	.21*	.37***	.12	.17	.16

†p < .10, *p < .05, **p < .01, ***p < .001.

the facts of my present sex life—including knowledge of how I get
sexual gratification; any problems that I have; with whom (if anybody)
I have relations;

what feelings, if any, I have trouble expressing or controlling;

whether or not I now make special efforts to keep fit, healthy, attractive,
(e.g. calisthenics, diet, etc.)

The summary score for all seven of the items is particularly
associated among men with a strong Stage I power orientation. Summary scores for disclosure to father, mother, male and female friends
and spouse all showed high correlations for this group of men. They
were people who opened themselves out, as it were, to family and
friends. As the lower correlations with other stage orientations suggests, such high self-disclosure is not characteristic of men in other
stages of development. In a sample of college men, there was if
anything a tendency for those with high n Power to disclose less about
their private lives.

The next variable helps explain further what men high in
n Power with a Stage I orientation are like, for they report themselves
as more intraceptive or psychically minded in a number of questionnaire items which were combined to make a single score—items like
"My fantasies are a most important part of my life," "It is very important
for me to understand the underlying motives of other people," "I often
think about and try to understand my own dreams and fantasies,"
"Sometimes I think of natural objects as possessing human qualities,"
"The rich internal world of ideals, or sensitive feelings, reverie, of self-
knowledge is a man's true home." The items make up a scale drawn
from Murray's Measure of Intraceptiveness (1938) and used by Sharaf
(1950) to assess what he called psychological mindedness. By sub-
scribing to such sentiments these men reinforce the impression that
they live in a world of fantasy and feeling, in a manner uncannily
similar to traditional Freudian descriptions of the way the omnipotence of thought dominates the oral character. Such individuals read
more about sex and aggression and share their innermost thoughts and
feelings with others; even natural objects have psychic qualities for
them.

In view of this similarity to the classic picture of the oral character, it is also interesting to note that those who were classified as
having an identification with the pre-Oedipal mother tended to score
high in the Stage I power orientation. The identification was measured
as follows (following a procedure used by Slavin, 1972): they were
asked whom they resembled most, their mother or father, and how

they resembled him or her. The second part of the question was used to check whether they had answered the first part correctly. If they were unable to cite any reasonable basis for resemblance, their answer on the first part was discarded. Then in another part of the questionnaire they were asked to read over a number of images or metaphors that a poet might use to symbolize the idea of death, and to rank the images from most to least effective. The alternatives consisted of several "castration" images (a satanic wrestler, a grinning butcher, a hangman with bloody hands, a crumbling tower) and several non-castration images (an infinite ocean, silent birds, a compassionate mother).

The ranks assigned metaphors were standard scored within the individual to control for variation in the ability of the subjects to rank properly, and the average standard score for the castration death metaphors computed. They were, as might be expected, somewhat less preferred on the average than the other metaphors. Then we determined whether an individual's average standard score for the castration metaphors was above or below the population mean. If it was above the mean, he was classified as preferring the castration metaphors somewhat more than the average person. If he stated that he resembled his father and preferred castration metaphors more than average, he was classified as Oedipal in orientation. If on the other hand he claimed to resemble his mother and preferred castration metaphors less than average, he was classified as pre-Oedipally identified with the mother. Other cases were classified as mixed. As Table 2.4 shows, only thirty-five men could be classified as either Oedipally or pre-Oedipally identified. Of those who could be so classified, however, those who were pre-Oedipally identified (approximately half) were much more apt to be high in a Stage I power orientation. The finding fits also with Sharaf's discovery that college men high in "psychological mindedness" (the same sentiments on which these men scored high) tended to be identified with their mothers.

Once again the link with Freudian theory is unmistakable. It is as if such a man has "etherealized" his mother, so that all of the universe—the earth, nature—become imbued with psychic qualities. The growing boy with a Stage I orientation wants to fuse with her or be united with her by sharing in the psychic world that has assumed so much importance for him. (We will return to this world view in more detail in Chapter 4 when we consider how it has been institutionalized in the religious and cultural life of India.) Thus a strong empirical link has been established among characteristics previously associated only through clinical evidence and theorizing. It is also worth recalling that in a previous paper (1964) I showed that creative physical scientists are at least moderately high in *n* Power and tend to view nature as having psychic qualities, although an attempt to link them to a pre-Oedipal identification via preference for female metaphors for nature failed. In view of the present findings, it may be that this approach was too direct. One would now predict that scientists should be power-oriented in a Stage I fashion and that this circumstance would explain their preference for endowing nature with human qualities.

The men with a Stage I power orientation also reported more unpleasant dreams, mainly of a kind that could be classified as indicating insecurity. They felt strange, they were being chased or attacked, someone had died, and particularly they would feel they were falling or the world was somehow shifting around them. Such a finding is consistent with their focus on being "at one with the maternal ground of being"; their greatest anxiety would be separation from the source of strength and security.

In typical conversations with friends they often find themselves interrupting to say something—another detail in which the data confirm a classical clinical syndrome; explosive talk is generally supposed to be one of the key characteristics of the oral character. But what are we to make of their report that they often go back to their parked car to make sure that they have turned off the lights and the radio and locked the doors? We might be inclined to dismiss the finding as a correlation significant by chance, except that it remains significant in random halves of the sample and that it is confirmed by their report of having fewer accidents, again nearly significantly in both halves of the sample. Since they did not report that they go back to check on things in their living quarters after leaving, we cannot attribute the behavior to a general carefulness syndrome. We have to ask, therefore, what is peculiar about a car for them?

One interpretation that comes to mind is that the car is for many men a projection of the self; automobile advertisements stress this fact. A car is a symbol of masculine pride and assertiveness. In a sense, then, they are concerned about making themselves secure. They drive more carefully and have fewer accidents. One is tempted to speculate that they see driving as penetrating nature, which we have already shown has psychic qualities for them—perhaps symbolizing the mother. Thus they have a special reason to be careful.

What about the women with a Stage I power orientation? Although they too tend to take in more power fantasies through reading (see Table 2.2), more important is the fact that they are inspired by men. All subjects were asked to jot down the initials and sex of people in their lives who had been a real inspiration to them, and to rate the strength of their influence on a scale of 1 for "not very strong" to 3 for "very strong, they made a big difference in my life." The number of males minus the number of females listed was computed, and the average difference in strength of influence of the two sexes was also obtained. These women reported a greater inspiration from men than from women, and also showed up with a more frequent Oedipal identification (father resemblance plus relative preference for castration metaphors).

Beyond this, a major theme in the correlations appears to concern growing big in order to have more to share, although the picture is fainter in particulars than it might be. When the women were asked to list their most precious possessions, they named more than the men. The circle of their selves was larger; they "owned" more precious things. When asked three things they would do with a hypothetical gift of ten thousand dollars, they were more likely than the men to list investing it as one of the alternatives. They seemed to want what they had to grow bigger. They complained too of physical symptoms—getting to sleep, loss of appetite, difficulty in getting up in the morning, and feeling "you just couldn't get going." The common idea behind this listing of symptoms seems to be: "there's often something wrong with me; I just don't have what it takes, the resources that life requires to meet its demands." Again to have the health and strength to face life is the key issue.

Furthermore they are a little more likely to report that they have lent something important—their car, household equipment, or clothes—or that they lend such things readily. It is worth recalling from Table 2.3 that power-oriented women with this stage orientation are also a little more willing than men to donate parts of their bodies after death. Of particular interest in this set of correlations is that it gives a picture of power as a physical resource, a concept also present in the non-stage-specific characteristics of women high in n Power; women seem to want to have more so that they have more to give. This concept becomes explicit in the themes discussed in the culture of India in Chapter 4.

Specifically suggested here is the source of the concept in the growing child. In line with clinical findings, it is easy to speculate that the little girl looks to her father for "inspiration" which in turn makes her grow big (big with child?) In these data the idea, though sublimated or generalized, retains its main outline: men are seen as inspirational; women, if they are power-oriented at Stage I, see themselves as wanting to be big and strong so as to have more to give.

In other chapters we will be concerned with general characteristics of this stage not specific to either sex. What are they? Two seem to stand out. Individuals with a Stage I power orientation are as they should be according to theory, oriented towards "intake," towards obtaining a sense of power and strength from outside. How they get those outside resources —whether through reading or talking or being with admired figures —may differ by sex but the orientation towards intake is clearly present. The other major characteristic is a concern for health or suffering. Although it is obvious in women, who complain more about physical symptoms, it is also present in men, as in the items dealing with self-disclosure to family and friends. Those with a Stage I power orientation are particularly likely to talk about their health problems with others. The correlation with n Power plus high Stage I scores is .19, p < .10, higher than for the other stages. The concern is revealed a little differently in the two sexes. The men talk about their health problems, the women report that they have more health problems; the concern with relief from suffering is definitely present in both sexes —a point of great theoretical importance, as we shall see later in dealing with the psychological sources of Indian religions like Buddhism.

Power Orientation: Stage II

Table 2.5 assembles the variables particularly correlated in each sex with n Power plus the score for Stage II. Once again the correlations of the maximum or average expression of selected alternatives with the Stage II power score are moderately high, significant for both sexes, and reasonably stable for random halves of the samples.

Among men, two themes characterize the outlets for this stage orientation. The first appears to be an emphasis on control, autonomy, or will power. The men report many aggressive impulses that they have controlled or not acted upon. They have been able to control their smoking. And they drink more coffee. Although the latter relationship is small and almost non-existent in one half of the sample, one could speculate that drinking coffee is undertaken to build up will power to get things done. The other theme, a modification of the first, is that these individuals reject institutionalized authority and any responsibility to it. They were asked to rate how likely they were to get personal help from such sources as a minister, a psychiatrist, parents, or friends. They reported being less apt to get personal help from their parents, whom they seem to be rejecting as authoritative sources of advice.

Table 2.5—Correlation of n Power with characteristics at Stage II ("Autonomy") level of maturity

Associated characteristics	n Power	Correlations with n Power plus score for			
		Stage I	Stage II	Stage III	Stage IV
Men (N = 85)					
m Controlled anger	.15	.01	.22*	.13	.06
m Don't seek personal help from parents	.10	.08	.18†	.11	.06
m Rejects institutional responsibility	.18	.06	.22*	.21	.02
m Drinks more coffee	−.02	−.04	.11	−.01	−.08
Like children as responsible adults relatively less	.07	.11	.16	−.05	.08
Less apt to smoke	.07	.08	.19†	.11	.08
Work considered boring and tedious	.16	.05	.20†	.14	.05
Time spent with opposite sex at party	.03	.06	.29**	.03	−.03
Correlation of maximum expression of m alternatives for whole sample	.26*	.15	.33*	.20	.15
Random half of sample (N = 43)			.43**		
Other half of sample (N = 42)			.23		
Correlation of average expression of m alternatives (N = 85)	.22*	.16	.38*	.17	.00
Women (N = 115)					
m Controlled anger	.12	.10	.17†	.01	.13
m More distress from loss of voluntary control	.06	.05	.14	−.10	.07
m Freedom from restrictions on love	.11	.07	.20*	.11	.07
m Religion promotes clean living	.15	.04	.20*	.08	.03
Total help seeking lower	.08	.06	.15†	.08	.02
Lie to family and friends	.06	−.01	.13	−.01	.07
Low sharing with mother	.07	.09	.16†	.11	−.02
Correlation of maximum expression of m alternatives for whole sample	.17†	.04	.27**	.09	.06
Random half of sample (N = 58)			.24†		
Other half of sample (N = 57)			.26†		
Correlation of average expression of m alternatives (N = 115)	.20*	.14	.33***	.11	.14

†p < .10, *p < .05, **p < .01.

Another section of the questionnaire contained items dealing with institutional authority. They were asked: whether they enjoyed feeling part of an organization like a church because it made them feel more useful; whether higher authority is really essential for guiding a person; whether people regarded them as responsible individuals who volunteered for jobs that needed doing. In all cases they rejected such ideas, and their overall score on this variable tended to be low.

In another item they were asked how they liked children at four different ages, each representing a different stage: as babies, helpless and nice to hold (Stage I); as school-agers, looking after their own things (Stage II); as teenagers, energetic, exploring their skills (Stage III); and as young adults, just married and learning to be responsible (Stage IV). The men with the Stage II power orientation particularly disliked the last alternative. Again the word *responsible* appears to be the key reason for their dislike.

Asked how they felt about their present work, they were likely to describe it as boring and tedious. Work would also seem to imply obligation or responsibility, and once again these individuals dislike it. Finally, even their report that they are more apt to spend time talking to the opposite sex at a party can be interpreted as fitting under this heading. Clearly they are not talking to the opposite sex for romantic reasons; in an item dealing more directly with their interest in the opposite sex, they show no special interest in a variety of heterosexual relationships. One is therefore left to speculate that they avoid talking to people of the same sex because they represent responsibility, perhaps particularly responsibility to work, since friends of the same sex are often associated with one's work. So they talk to the opposite sex to avoid talking about what bores them and involves responsibility. Although these men want the autonomy that is theoretically characteristic of Stage II, a strong element in their desire for autonomy seems to be the rejection of institutional authority, beginning with parents. Quite simply, they want neither to be told what to do nor to feel that they have to do what is expected of them.

The women with a Stage II power orientation are also interested in control and autonomy. They too report aggressive impulses that they have not expressed. When asked to describe briefly three incidents distressing to them personally, they are likely to list incidents involving a failure in voluntary control. The scoring system used here was developed by Stolorow (1970), who, as noted previously, found that loss of voluntary control is particularly distressing to obsessive compulsives (Stage II according to the present scheme). Typical events would include some kind of personal failure such as flunking a course, embarrassing a friend, running a car into a tree, etc. The fact that women with a Stage II power orientation reported more such distressing incidents indicates the importance voluntary control has for them.

They were also asked whether, with members of the same sex, it was most enjoyable to (1) have a single relationship, (2) have one main relationship, with freedom for others, or (3) have several relationships. If they were presently married, they were asked to answer as they would have before being married. They were given a "non-monogamy" score of 1–3 for checking the alternatives in the order listed; this score is the one reported in Table 2.5. In this instance, however, the score reflects primarily a choice of the second alternative rather than the third; these women prefer to have one main relationship with freedom for others. "Freedom for others" is the important condition to them rather than "playing the field" (having several relationships), which we will see in a moment is characteristic of Stage III males.

Another item dealt with the appeal of religion as characterized in the four different stages. These women tended to rank higher the Stage II alternative: religion appeals because of "the way it helps people to lead good, clean, ethical lives, rather than messy or selfish lives." It may seem odd in this connection that they also show a slight tendency to report that they lie more to family and friends, but lying is one way to maintain control over one's life. While the men with a Stage II orientation report getting less personal help from their parents, the women report less willingness to seek help from any source, and they also share less personal information with their mothers.

The contrast between the men and women at this stage is interesting. Though they are both interested in autonomy, in controlling their lives, the men seem concerned with *freedom from* established authority and the women with *freedom for* controlling their lives. Developmentally this contrast makes sense. The boy is breaking away in this stage from the dependency on his mother characteristic of Stage I. What he must establish above all is his independence, his freedom from the strong attachment to an external source of strength that characterized him earlier. The little girl's problem in growing up is different. She previously saw herself as a more or less passive recipient of male inspiration. Now her problem is to change from being passive to being actively in control of her own life and not waiting around to be inspired. She now needs to show in every way possible that she is *in charge,* free from help of all kinds, free to control her own life.

The picture is clear and the empirical data strongly support the theoretical analysis of this stage in development. Yet one important element is missing. One of the main characteristics of individuals with the Stage II power orientation, as we shall see, is a desire to have knowledge, particularly foreknowledge of what is to come —presumably so that one can plan how to control things when they do happen. We attempted to tap this dimension by framing a number of attitude questions dealing with the importance of knowledge or reason; but, as Table 2.3 has already demonstrated, individuals with high *n* Power — particularly men, but also women —tend to deny that knowledge is of such central importance. Thus the expected correlation between *n* Power plus Stage II score and desire for knowledge did not occur. With the benefit of hindsight, it seems clear that the items were wrongly formulated, especially if what is important is not merely reason or knowledge for its own sake, but foreknowledge. The items did not reach the issue of knowing in order to control. A more direct way of getting at such an interest would have been to ask whether the subjects had ever visited fortune tellers or psychics who could forecast the future. Only one item touched on the point tangentially. Among the alternative sources for personal help was listed "a spiritual or holy person (guru, monk, mystic, etc.)". The women with Stage II power orientation did report that they were more willing to seek help from such a source (r = .16, p < .10) than were power-oriented women with other stage orientations, and it is reasonably clear that they were not seeking such a person for religious reasons since they did not report that they were more likely to go to a minister, priest, or rabbi. Among the men in the same category there is the same greater willingness to seek help from a mystic than a minister, but the correlation is only a very insignificant .05, and we can only regret that the question was not asked properly. Although it seems reasonable to assume that the women might have interpreted the term "mystic" in the sense of a spiritualist or psychic, and that therefore the correlation is more meaningful for them, nevertheless the empirical support for the theoretical view that foreknowledge is very important for the Stage II power-oriented person is slim indeed.

One other problem exists with the data. What happened to prestige possessions? In Chapter I we pointed to ownership of them as most characteristic of Stage II power-oriented people, yet there is no evidence for such a trend in Table 2.5. The number of credit cards possessed was larger for individuals in this category, although it was larger for all women with high *n* Power regardless of stage; and the correlation was positive, but insignificant, for men. Particularly disappointing was the fact that the more general measure of prestige possessions owned did not correlate with *n* Power for either men or women at any stage of development. At first glance, the result is surprising because in at least three previous studies the number of such possessions has shown a significant positive correlation with *n* Power in men (McClelland *et al.*, 1972; Boyatzis, 1974). Apparently we destroyed the relationship in changing the measure to accommodate it to both men and women. In previous studies when the men had been asked whether they owned particular prestige items such as a color television set, a tailor-made suit, a Playboy Club key, and the like, we had always worried as to whether the "prestige" of these items might not differ appreciably for men of different social background, or even for men of the same background at different times. In making out the present questionnaire, we felt handicapped by the lack of experience as to what would be considered a prestige item by women. Hence we simply asked the subjects to list whatever they considered to be their most precious possessions. Although that solved the problem of what the person considered valuable, apparently it also significantly altered the nature of the responses, perhaps by introducing the social desirability factor. A man might own a Playboy Club key, for example, which would be symptomatic of his high *n* Power, but he might not feel it appropriate to list it as a "precious possession." So the theoretical contention that owning prestigious or power-oriented objects is characteristic of Stage II power orientation has to remain a likely possibility, not confirmed by these data.

Power Orientation: Stage III

The chief variables associated with the Stage III or assertive power orientation are listed in Table 2.6 for men and women separately. For the entire sample of men, the correlation of the maximum expression of the selected alternatives with Stage III power orientation is the highest obtained for any of the stages, but at the same time it is unstable from one half of the sample to the other. Part of the explanation undoubtedly lies in the fact that one variable involves lying to family and friends. In talking about one's private life admission to lying was extremely rare, only about one in five men owning up to even one lie. Thus when the sample was split in half, it was easy to get most of those who admitted to lying in one half of the sample, leaving very few for the other half, so that the correlation was highly significant in one half and even slightly negative in the other. It would have been possible to gain higher stability by including a less infrequent

Table 2.6—Correlations of n Power with characteristics at Stage III ("Assertion") level of maturity

Associated characteristics	n Power	Correlations with n Power plus score for			
		Stage I	Stage II	Stage III	Stage IV
Men (N = 85)					
m Freedom to love several women	.17	.05	.13	.25*	.20†
m Lie to family and friends	.00	−.09	.06	.22*	.01
m Collect valuable objects	.14	.17	.10	.22*	.07
m Heavier alcohol consumption	.17	.15	.10	.19	.10
Reasons for drinking problematic	.19†	.13	.12	.27*	−.02
More frequent physical symptoms	.15	.13	.12	.20†	.15
Dislike child care more	.25*	.17	.12	.25*	.21†
"Compassionate mother" metaphor disliked	.18†	.00	.08	.20†	.17
Correlation of maximum expression of m alternatives for whole sample	.22*	.07	.18	.41***	.13
Random half of sample (N = 43)				.67***	
Other half of sample (N = 42)				.12	
Correlation of average expression of m alternatives (N = 85)	.21	.17	.24*	.38***	.02
Women (N = 115)					
m Expressed anger to people	.04	.01	.01	.17†	.02
m Like to travel	.05	.06	.05	.19*	.05
m Like to try new foods	.18†	.13	.12	.25**	.18†
m Keep sex life secret	.19†	.10	.08	.20*	.05
m More intraceptive (psychic minded)	.12	.11	.02	.20*	.04
Feeling of "oceanic oneness" with world	.21*	.14	.18†	.24*	.14
Low n Affiliation	.32***	.07	.18†	.40***	.23*
Parents taught few sociocentric values	.22*	.14	.17†	.23*	.09
Relative preference for action therapy	.13	.11	.00	.16†	−.03
Correlation of maximum expression of m alternatives for whole sample	.11	.08	.01	.30**	−.02
Random half of sample (N = 58)				.36**	
Other half of sample (N = 57)				.28**	
Correlation of average expression of m alternatives (N = 115)	.24**	.09	.04	.43***	.19†

†$p < .10$, *$p < .05$, **$p < .01$, ***$p < .001$.

item in the cluster of alternatives; but this one has such theoretical importance, it was chosen over the others. Because of its low frequency, one can have somewhat more faith in the correlation for the whole sample than in the smaller half samples.

The correlation of the average expression of the alternatives in the cluster is also substantial for the men and for the women. The correlation of the maximum expression of any of the alternatives and Stage III power orientation for women is somewhat lower but remains relatively unchanged from one half of the sample to the other.

It is interesting that the defining characteristics of the phallic stage come out near the top of the list of significant correlations for men with a Stage III power orientation. They definitely prefer a "non-monogamous" style in relation to members of the opposite sex, but unlike the Stage II power-oriented women, they check the alternative of having several relationships significantly more often ($r = .28$, $p < .01$). They prefer to "play the field" sexually. Furthermore, they admit to lying more often to family and friends, as one would expect if they are carrying on relationships with several women at once.

When asked if they had ever collected such objects as shells, stamps, rare books, china, neckties, etc., they listed more kinds of things collected. This was another way of trying to get at the ownership of prestige possessions, and it gave somewhat different results from asking people to list their most precious possessions or the number of credit cards owned. These collections of rare objects appeared to signify a desire for display characteristic of the assertiveness of Stage III rather than a desire for collecting resources to support one's independent strength and autonomy the way credit cards do.

The men with a Stage III power orientation also drink more heavily. The measure here is a little different from the one employed in *The drinking man* (1972). There the emphasis was on quantity and frequency of hard liquor consumed. Here it was decided to record for each person the *maximum* consumption of either beer, wine, or liquor. In other words, we judged it unimportant in what form the person consumed large amounts of alcohol. Rather the issue was how much he consumed, how often. Since each man reported the average quantity and frequency with which he drank each type of beverage, it was a simple matter to record for him the maximum product of quantity times frequency of any type of beverage. This was the measure on which men with a Stage III power orientation scored higher. They were also asked to score various reasons for drinking from +2 for "very important" to 0 for "not at all important." Half of the reasons might be considered normal (e.g., I drink to be sociable) and half have been found by other studies to be associated with problem drinking (e.g., "I drink when I want to forget everything"). The Stage III power-oriented men tended to rate the problematic reasons for drinking as more important to them. Furthermore, they reported more physical symptoms in general, such as inability to sleep, loss of appetite, difficulty in getting up in the morning, etc. These symptoms may of course result from drinking heavily, but they also may indicate a kind of narcissistic concern with the body such as we thought the same characteristics implied for Stage I women.

Of particular significance is the fact that this cluster of attributes so closely matches the characteristics of the Don Juan image both in legend and among contemporary American undergraduates, as summarized by Winter (1973). The Don Juan type of male attempts and practices serial seduction. He "abandons women as soon as he has seduced them, and he takes greater delight in the 'sport' of tricking and cheating women than he does in the act of sex itself" (Winter, 1973, p. 170). He lies to obtain his ends, just as our subjects with high Stage III power orientation do. He boasts about his importance or his prestige. He drinks. He is narcissistic and self-centered. He even kills the father of one of the women he has seduced when it becomes necessary for him to escape. Aggressiveness, however, appears to be an incidental rather than a chief characteristic; in the present sample the correlation between Stage III power orientation and aggressive acts to people is only .10. In short, the Don Juan image, used by Winter as an archetype of the power motive, describes very well the male with high n Power who also has a Stage III level of maturity. It also fits the description of the man oriented towards personal power (p Power) in *The drinking man* (McClelland *et al.*, 1972). Although the p Power variable was not scored in the present study, an indirect measure of it was obtained in the following way.

The p Power scoring system was derived from subjects high in power need and low in a measure of restraint called Activity Inhibition, which consists in the number of times the word "not" appears in imaginative stories also scored for motives. Thus an estimate of p Power orientatation can be obtained by calculating the relative strength of n Power among subjects low in Activity Inhibition. In the present instance we did so by subtracting the standard score fo n Power from the standard score for n Affiliation among subjects low in Activity Inhibition. This score correlated significantly both with the maximum quantity of alcohol consumer ($r = .30$, $p < .05$) and with Stage III power orientation ($r = +.60$, $p < .001$). In each case it is the estimate of p Power which uniquely correlates with the variable in question.

The *n* Power minus *n* Affiliation score does not correlate with maximum alcohol consumption if Activity Inhibition is high, and the p Power estimate correlates significantly higher with drinking than *n* Power combined with other stage scores. It seems clear, in other words, that the Stage III power orientation, which indicates phallic assertiveness, nicely captures the spirit of what Winter has called the Don Juan archetype and what in other publications we have called the personalized power drive.

Winter also ties this type of power orientation to a fixation on the pre-Oedipal mother. "Don Juan seeks fusion with his mother through seducing a series of women; yet he fears this very fusion because . . . (it carries) the threat of his own destruction" through being incorporated or swallowed up. He is attracted to and fears women at the same time. Is there any evidence from our study to support this notion? As Table 2.4 makes clear, the men with a pre-Oedipal identification by our measure tend generally to be higher in *n* Power at all stages of maturity, although they are highest in Stage I orientation, not Stage III. If one accepts the argument that the Don Juan style is chiefly characteristic of a Stage III power orientation, therefore, there is no special evidence that it arises from a fatal attraction to the mother. On the other hand, it is at least interesting to note that Winter ends his discussion of the Don Juan image as follows: "Don Juan lives out the secret ideal of many men, and has a career of glorious conquests — until his courage and energy drive him to destruction . . . yet in the end power is a fleeting illusion, because in death it inexorably ends with the swallowing up of even the most powerful man. Power is everything; yet it is nothing, for man can never escape 'the encircling arms'" (Winter, p. 200). The men in our sample with the Stage III power orientation dislike most the metaphor describing death as "a compassionate mother" ($r = .20$, $p < .10$). Is this because they are especially ambivalent about connecting death with the mother figure? Do they dislike the thought because that is precisely what they fear the most?

In view of Don Juan's tendency to "love 'em and leave 'em," it is not surprising to discover that our men with Stage III power orientation particularly dislike child care. We asked how often they volunteered to look after children, not because they had to but because they wanted to, on a scale of very often to never. These men rarely volunteered their services. Being tied down to family responsibilities is something Don Juan always avoids.

The image of the assertive Stage III woman, as outlined in Table 2.6 is less familiar either in legend or in psychological literature. She comes through, above all, as active and assertive. She expresses her anger openly, swearing or screaming at those who get on her nerves, or at other drivers in traffic. She says that she enjoys travelling alone in new places, and she likes to try eating foods she has never eaten before. She does not disclose the secrets of her sex life to others, and for personal help she prefers an action type of therapy rather than going to a minister, a psychiatrist, to friends or her family. Perhaps as the obverse of this same syndrome, when asked to list the three most important things her parents tried to teach her, she lists fewer socio-centric virtues like kindness to others, tolerance, and social poise. She also lists more ego-centric virtues like being intelligent and energetic, but so do all women with higher need for Power. She tends to be significantly lower in the need for Affiliation than women with low need for Power and low Stage III orientation. Her assertiveness as a woman, in other words, seems to imply a lessening of concern for others, typical of the traditional sex role for women.

Somewhat surprising is the inclusion in this cluster of two variables that suggest an intraceptive orientation. Women with a Stage III power orientation state on the questionnaire that they are psychically minded, that is, that they believe fantasies and dreams are important; they are interested in the motives and emotions of others; and they even think natural objects are sometimes alive. Sometimes they have even had a feeling of being one with the external world as a whole, which "someone has described as an oceanic sensation of eternity." In the case of the men who reported these feelings we showed that they had more often been able to associate them with a pre-Oedipal identification with the mother. Among these women, however, the correlation with the pre-Oedipal variable is only an insignificant .08. The correlation with mother resemblance alone is even reversed, −.15. It makes good developmental sense, however, to argue that, having broken in Stage II the dependence on male inspiration of Stage I, the girl should now go on to identify clearly with a kind of "female principle in the universe," even though that may not be properly represented in the women she has known, such as her mother. She does not report being more inspired by women than by men, perhaps because in point of fact the women do not reflect this basic principle in its pure form, but are themselves more apt to be Stage I oriented women. If we search in legend for a figure to sum up the Stage III power-oriented woman, it would have to be the Greek Artemis, or Diana the Huntress, as she is more commonly known in her Roman form. She liked to travel, was active, energetic, and kept her sex life secret. She hunted deer with bows and arrows and spent her time largely with other women. As the patron of homosexuality in women, she would be in active pursuit of her own interests, not tied down by traditional affiliative bonds to men and children.

Power Orientation: Stage IV

Our questionnaire was least successful in discovering the outlets for the power drive at the highest stage of maturity. As Table 2.7 shows, the four items selected for analysis among men, did not correlate very highly with n Power plus the score for Stage IV. Moreover, the correlation of the maximum expression of any one of them with Stage IV power orientation was low and insignificant, even though the average expression of all of them was higher. It may be that there is some incompatibility between n Power and a Stage IV orientation, at least as n Power is scored with its bias towards Stage II and Stage III characteristics. Individuals whose modal score was in Stage IV, it will be recalled, scored lower in n Power both in the male and female samples. Some further support for this notion comes from the fact that the Stage IV score alone, leaving out n Power, correlates at a significant level ($r = .23$, $p < .05$) with the maximum expression of any of these alternatives.

According to theory, we should have found that these men respected institutional authority, and showed responsibility for passing on power from a normative source as members of an institution. Yet the attitude items in the questionnaire, though designed to get at this view, did not correlate with this stage orientation as expected. They proved useful only in showing how men with a Stage II power orientation rejected institutional responsibility. To a certain degree the variables listed in Table 2.7 do reflect the expected orientation. Men with a Stage IV power orientation belong to more organizations, as would be expected. They are somewhat more willing to seek help of all kinds, particularly from an authoritative source like a psychiatrist. At a party they say they try to meet new people—a responsible thing to do. And they report that religion appeals to them less because it teaches charity and helping those less fortunate than themselves. Oddly enough, though this item was designed to test a Stage IV orientation, with the benefit of hindsight we can understand that an emphasis on personal charity would be less appealing to people with a strong institutional orientation.

Aside from the greater institutional orientation, we expected that a Stage IV power orientation might show itself in greater mutuality

Table 2.7—Correlations of n Power with characteristics of Stage IV ("Generative") level of maturity

Associated characteristics	n Power	Correlations with: n Power plus score for			
		Stage I	Stage II	Stage III	Stage IV
Men (N = 85)					
m Organizational memberships	−.01	.07	.06	−.02	.12
m More willing to seek help	.11	.06	−.01	.01	.14
m Seek out new people at party	.08	.07	.02	.05	.16
m Few possessions	.01	−.06	−.07	−.02	.19†
Religion appeals least for					
helping poor	.21†	.17	.06	.09	.20†
Sharing with wives	.21†	.26†	.12	.15	.20†
Shorter	.12	.01	.07	.18†	.22*
Correlation of maximum					
expression of m alternatives for					
whole sample	−.01	.06	−.08	−.05	.14
Random half of sample					
(N = 43)					.16
Other half of sample (N = 42)					.10
of m alternatives for female					
cluster IV (below)	.19†	.17	.23*	.24*	.23*
Random half of sample					
(N = 43)					.24
Other half of sample (N = 42)					.21
Correlation of average					
expression of m alternatives					
for male cluster (N = 85)	.08	.22*	.04	.17	.30**

and fewer hangups or ego-centric attachments. There is some slight evidence in support of this hypothesis. These men, if they were married, reported sharing more private information with their wives. They also shared more information with both their fathers and mothers (r = .20, p < .10, and r = .12 respectively), as if they had no particular hangups in talking to their parents. In all cases, however, this sharing was less than for men with a Stage I power orientation. Finally, they reported having fewer possessions, as if in fact they were less attached to such things, as they are supposed to be. Apparently they are also helped towards mutuality or equality by being shorter than the average male, or more nearly equal in height to the average female.

Yet these are only hints of what we had expected. A better set of alternatives for the prediction of the male Stage IV power orientation includes the four that successfully predicted the corresponding female Stage IV power orientation; but these same alternatives predict power

Associated characteristics	n Power	Correlations with: n Power plus score for			
		Stage I	Stage II	Stage III	Stage IV
Women (N = 115)					
m Organizational memberships	.23*	.15†	.24*	.14	.30**
m Knowledge less important (than acting)	.14	.11	.10	.18†	.26**
m Sharing with husbands	.10	.11	.07	.08	.20*
m Prefer psychiatrist for personal help	.05	.04	−.07	.01	.22*
Share things that make me proud	.11	−.05	.03	.11	.23*
Working in power oriented job (e.g., teaching)	.07	.08	.01	.01	.15†
No betting	.13	.11	.09	.12	.22*
Oedipal identification (N = 51)	.23	.29*	.13	.08	.36**
Prefers castration death metaphors	.15†	.18†	.08	.02	.22*
Mother's education	.11	.14	−.00	.13	.18†
Correlation of maximum expression of m alternatives for whole sample	.28*	.26**	.24**	.20*	.39***
Random half of sample (N = 58)					.39**
Other half of sample (N = 57)					.38**
Correlation of average expression of m alternatives (N = 115)	.22*	.13	.13	.15†	.41***

†p < .10, *p < .05, **p < .01, ***p < .001.

orientation at other stages also, both for men and women. In other words, we did not succeed, either for men or women, in finding alternatives uniquely associated with a Stage IV power orientation. The most that can be said for the women's correlations at the bottom of Table 2.7 is that they are lower for Stage I, II, and III power orientations than they are for the Stage IV power orientation; and they continue to point to the kind of institutional authority orientation we would expect on theoretical grounds. Women with a Stage IV power orientation belong to more clubs; they prefer an authoritative or expert source for personal help (e.g., a psychiatrist); they are more active. They tend to be working in a power-oriented job, like teaching. They talk more with family and friends about things that make them "especially proud, elated, full of self-esteem or self-respect." Perhaps they are less apt to bet because it doesn't fit in with such a self image, although the betting item may be of chance significance since it doesn't cross-validate in the second half of the sample. They are able to share more of their private lives with their husbands. It may look as if they have an Oedipal identification, but actually this correlation is caused almost entirely by their preference for castration death metaphors rather than direct father identification for which the correlation is only .12. To see death as castration derives almost certainly from their action orientation, since death can seem as the ultimate frustration of pride in one's accomplishments.

These appear, indeed, to be more liberated women—a view supported by the fact that in general their mothers have had more education. They are likely apt to be working in a power-oriented job in which they take pride. They both participate in more organizations and share more as equals with their husbands. It is clear in the case of a woman how, having broken away from her Stage I attachment to males and gone through a phallic assertiveness stage, she can emerge more as a person in her own right who can share on an equal basis with her husband and join in an organization or in her role as a family member without losing her sense of identity. How the men behave as they emerge into the stage of mutuality and generativity is less clear, although what clues there are point to a diminished importance of power motivation for attaining the highest level of maturity.

Perhaps this is the place to ask the more general question of what additional information has been obtained by combining the *n* Power and stage scores over what we would have learned from considering either one alone. We began our analysis to discover what outlets *n* Power has at different stages of psycho-social development. The patterns of outlets discovered for the four main stages fit fairly closely the major orientation of those stages as described by Freud and Erikson. The question naturally arises: what role does power motivation play in contributing to each of these patterns?

Neither Freud nor Erikson spoke directly about power motivation. They thought in terms of a universal sequence of development to be undergone by every individual, whether his power motivation was high or low. To clarify the problem we might ask whether the same pattern of outlets for each stage would have been obtained, if the *n* Power score had been omitted and only the stage scores used. A complete answer would require analysis of all the correlations of each of the stage scores alone, which would go beyond the limits of our present concern; but a partial answer emerges from examining the correlations between the stage scores alone and the clusters of outlets selected for each of the stages, presented in Tables 2.4 to 2.7.

If we consider first the correlation of each stage score with the maximum expression of the selected alternatives for that stage, we find that they are all highly significant, being .31, .25, .48, .23, for the men, and .24, .28, .41 and .24 for the women for Stages I to IV, respectively. For the *average* expressions of the alternatives for each stage, the same correlations are also highly significant, being .34, .36, .44, and .38 for men and .32, .34, .49 and .33 for women for Stages I–IV, respectively. Even if we leave out the *n* Power score altogether from the calculations, therefore, the stage scores alone will predict that people will behave in ways we have considered theoretically characteristic of those stages. Missing from the data is information on alternative outlets correlated with each stage score, alternatives that were not selected because the combination of stage plus *n* Power score did not point to them.

So far as maximum expression of alternatives is concerned, if we compare each of the above correlations with its opposite number obtained for each stage score with *n* Power included, we observe that half the correlations decreased, and half increased. So far as the men are concerned, the same is true of the correlations for individual items listed in Tables 2.4 to 2.7. Approximately half of the correlations increase when *n* Power is added to the appropriate stage score, and half decrease. For the women, adding *n* Power to the stage score more often increases the correlation for individual items; twenty-one increase, ten decrease, and one stays the same. An examination of the possible reason for this difference will help shed light on how *n* Power interacts with stage scores.

The difference is most marked for Stage IV. Adding *n* Power for the men *decreases* the correlation with the cluster of alternative outlets from .23 (p < .05) to an insignificant .14. Adding *n* Power for women *increases* the same correlation from .24 to a highly significant .39. Now if Stage IV represents moving towards mutuality and equality, as the theory maintains, then it is easy to see that a high *n* Power, tending to accentuate the assertive male role, would make it more difficult for men to show behavior characteristic of Stage IV. Just the opposite is true of women: if they are to move towards mutuality, they must behave in a *more assertive* way than is characteristic of traditional women. Thus a high need for Power among women makes it more likely that they will behave in ways characteristic of the mutuality of Stage IV.

Such an analysis also underlines the fact that the interaction of power motivation with stages will require a detailed analysis beyond the scope of our present concern. Since our focus here is on expressions of the need for Power, not on stages of development, we must be content for the moment to observe, as shown in Tables 2.4 to 2.7, that knowing the person's level of maturity in addition to his *n* Power score will increase our ability to predict what he will think, feel, and do. The *n* Power score alone, in short, does not predict the clusters of behaviors in these tables nearly as well as the *n* Power score *and* the stage score, or the level of maturity of the person involved.

Thus we have found a way to explain why correlations of *n* Power with a given outlet may vary from one sample to another; the average maturity level differs. Note, for example, in Table 2.7 that a sample of men may report having *fewer* possessions if they are primarily stage IV oriented (as in our adult sample) but *more* possessions if they are primarily Stage II oriented (as in Winter's college samples). Fortunately the Stewart maturity scale provides future researchers with a measuring instrument geared to help account for such inconsistencies.

It is worth recapitulating what our findings show about how power-oriented men and women develop socially and emotionally. Of course our study is cross-sectional rather than longitudinal; we are dealing with adult males or females who have remained relatively oriented more towards one stage of development or another. From these orientations we can make sensible inferences as to the orientations all males may have experienced as they went through various stages of development. Our argument is that some adults simply stay oriented more towards one stage than another, and that from their current activities, feelings, and beliefs we can get a general picture of what characterized a particular stage in an earlier part of the life cycle. To judge by the way power-oriented males with a strong Stage I orientation respond, boys start out normally by identifying strongly with their mothers. They tend to see the whole universe as psychic. They want to share their innermost thoughts and feelings with others. They are caught up in the world of thought, fantasy, and dreaming, as if they want to remain united in this way with a kind of mother principle, the source of all life. If they advance, they find it necessary to break with all organized responsibility and to show signs of self-control and self-direction, to be strong on their own. This trend is accentuated at Stage III, when they become typically more assertive, identify with the "male principle," and begin to act like miniature Don Juans. They start showing off, drinking, chasing women, and generally behaving in an assertive "sporty" manner. Finally, if all goes well, they give up their ego-centric assertiveness, submit to institutional authority, and join in a mutually rewarding relationship with their wives.

The female life trajectory is a little different. Women start out by seeing themselves as the objects of male inspiration. As such, their goal is to have strong and resourceful bodies, which presumably enable them to produce more children and generally share what they have to give with others. If they go beyond this stage, they do not feel the same need to reject the kind of overwhelming nurturant support, as the boys do; but they want very much to be in charge of their own lives and to show that they need no help from others. In the third stage this tendency towards taking charge develops into a full-blown assertiveness. They become active and assertive, trying all kinds of new things and, oddly enough, identifying for the first time with the fundamental female principle in the universe, as reflected in their increase in intraceptiveness, and their oceanic identification with the external world. Thus in both sexes it is only at Stage III that the boy or the girl identifies with his or her own sex, properly speaking. At the start both are oriented mainly towards the opposite sex; they break this tie in Stage II, and begin to come into their own as men or women in Stage III. This stage, of course, often creates many more social problems than the earlier stages, and it is often difficult for adults to perceive that it represents an advance in development over earlier stages; only if the individual becomes a fully identified man or woman, however, can he go on to the final stage of mutuality. In Stage IV our data show that women are ready for genuine communion, in Bakan's sense (1966), having first themselves gone through a stage of agency. They are now able, in short, to share with men, having developed a sense of self-respect and an ability to act on their own. Although communion with men is quite possible for women who remain at the Stage I orientation, theirs is a much more dependent and passive role.

Throughout these stages of development certain male and female styles of expressing the power motive are apparent. The men with a strong *n* Power appear to be more tense and argumentative, more emotional than reasonable. They dream more, or remember their dreams better. It is as if they were leaning forward tensely into the wind, projecting ahead what impact they are going to have upon the world. The women with a strong power drive are focused more on themselves, particularly on their bodies, thinking in terms of having resources to share. Though strongest in Stage I, this orientation persists throughout all stages. Women are more concerned about having and sharing; men more about pushing ahead.

On the whole the findings of this study are encouraging. They support the notion that the Stewart measure of social emotional maturity does measure what it is supposed to measure; on its own or when combined with the *n* Power score, it gives results that would be expected according to the theory outlined in Chapter 1. The theory itself gains support from use of the measure, because we were able to demonstrate that *n* Power does express itself in different but expected ways at different stages of maturity.

Not everything, of course, came out as we wanted it to. We found little evidence of fascination with a knowledge for predicting the future that we still think is characteristic of Stage II power orientation. The defining characteristics of Stage IV maturity in men were not outlined well, and further research will be needed to define them further. The issue of whether nurturance in women is a form of active assertiveness like aggression in men was likewise not clarified. But psychological research seldoms answers all important questions in a single study. What was discovered seems more than enough to encourage us to use this theory in interpreting other phenomena in the chapters that follow.

On the plus side also, in the course of testing the theory we validated what appears to be a very important notion for personality theory and research —the idea that a set of actions may be alternative manifestations of a given motive and that if one wants properly to test the impact of a motive on action, one must correlate it with the maximum expression of any of the alternative outlets. In this way correlations are found that indicate a higher consistency within personality study than is typically found in single variable correlations.

Finally, the empirical correlations have added substance and precision to the general theory of psychosocial development as outlined by Freud and Erikson on the basis of clinical evidence. We believe that the correlations reported in Tables 2.4 through 2.7 will point future theorists to a more precise idea of the actions, thoughts, and feelings correlated with these stages of development. In particular, they show how the female course of development, while it follows the main outlines of male development, differs in important ways that have not been so clearly defined in the predominantly male-oriented, clinical literature.

B

ACCUMULATING POWER

THE NEED for Power has been here defined as the need primarily to *feel strong,* and secondarily to act powerfully. Influencing others is just one of several ways of satisfying the need to feel strong. The difficulty, as we have pointed out, is that Americans are so action oriented; they tend to slight Stages I and II in the developing power need and to assume that even being near a strong person (Stage I) or controlling oneself (Stage II) are potential means of acting powerfully at some later date.

To get outside this set and appreciate the early stages of the power drive, we have to study groups for whom these stages are of central significance. We must go beyond the Western tradition, which has glorified the powerful act, and consider Eastern tradition, which has maintained that it is more important to be strong than to be powerful (in the sense of acting powerfully). Anderson (in Holt, 1972) contrasts the Western conception of power with the Javanese conception. He writes "the central problem raised by this (the Javanese) conception of power, by contrast with the Western tradition of political theory, is not the exercise of power but its accumulation. Accordingly, a very considerable portion of the traditional literature deals with the problems of concentrating and preserving Power rather than with its proper usage" (1972, p. 8). Or again, "the most obvious sign of a man of Power is, quite consistently, his ability to concentrate: to focus his own personal Power, to absorb Power from the outside, and to concentrate within himself apparently antagonistic opposites ... One typical image, which links this type of absorption with the concentration of opposites, is a battle between the hero and the powerful adversary, in which the defeated adversary in death enters the hero's body, adding to his conqueror's strength" (1972).

The striking contrast to Western thought comes in the fact that defeating someone in battle, which would be the ultimate aim of power in Western thinking, in Javanese thought becomes the *means* to the primary goal of accumulating or having power. The sequence is the exact reverse of what scholars in the West assume it to be. In Javanese thought, the ultimate public sign of power is not influencing the behavior of another, but a kind of radiance (*wahju* or *tedja*) "which was thought to emanate softly from the face or person of the man of Power." President Sukarno even spoke of Hitler's "tedja," which alarmed Western observers because they could not think of someone having power without judging the morality of its use. In terms of the scheme outlined in Table 1.2, the Javanese emphasize Stage I and Stage II aspects of the power motive, both of which have as their aim accumulating power in the self, or feeling powerful, rather than trying to influence others.

In Chapter 2 we found some evidence of this concern for building up strength and sharing it, particularly among women high in *n* Power. In the next chapter, we will see that in the West it is almost as if the modes of expressing power have been sex-typed—women traditionally showing more interest in *being* strong (having resources and sharing them) and men in *acting* powerfully. We will also observe that women high in power motivation appear to focus on building up their resources so that they have more to give. With a Western orientation it is difficult to conceive of giving without seeing the gift as a means to some end. When women are asked why they lend things, they sometimes say it is so that they will be appreciated more, or because it invites reciprocity, or for some other such reason. Yet these answers seem in theoretical terms to be secondary rationalizations of a Stage III sort, in which the person is trying to justify her act in terms of how it influences others. They do not express true Being orientation of the ideal Stage I modality, where a person accumulates resources and shares them in the same way that a brighter light sheds more radiance.

Sara Winter (1966) found evidence for the phenomenon in a direct way in her analysis of the fantasies of mothers while they were nursing their babies. If power is influence, one might expect the fantasies would be about feeding the child in order to make it grow strong and healthy. The mere word *nurturance* implies a means-ends relationship that appears to be a Stage III mode: "I am strong to be doing this for you to influence you (make you stronger)." Indeed, when women are asked why they nurse their babies, they usually give such answers. But Winter found no evidence of such instrumental fantasies in nursing mothers; instrumental thinking of all types was even significantly less during such a time. The mothers were very Being, present-time, pleasure-oriented. It was as if they were "radiating" strength, which they felt but did not think of as sharing "in order to" accomplish something.

In the next two chapters we will explore Stage I and Stage II vicissitudes of the need for Power by studying first the traditional feminine life style and then the value orientations of traditional Hindu culture. In both instances we will be able to see more clearly how giving has come to be particularly valued as showing strength. We start with this mode because it is less appreciated and understood in the West and because according to our scheme it develops earlier in life, but is not on that account in any sense more primitive. It might rather be considered more basic to all forms of expression of the power need.

CHAPTER 3

POWER AND THE
FEMININE ROLE[1]

IT IS clear from the results reported in Chapter 2 that women with a high power need behave differently from men with a high power need. Sex role is a key variable in determining how the power drive is expressed. It deflects the power drive into different channels. To understand just how and why, we must examine more thoroughly the nature of the "moderator variable." In what ways does sex role shape behavior? How are women expected to behave differently from men, and do these expectations affect their actions in major ways? Sex role turns out to be one of the most important determinants of human behavior; psychologists have found sex differences in their studies from the moment they started doing empirical research. The difficulty in drawing conclusions from this mass of data is that they have tended to regard male behavior as the "norm" and female behavior as some kind of deviation from that norm.

81

Psychological Sex Differences

Most such studies have shown that woman is still perceived by both men and women as Adam's rib—despite all the efforts of feminists from Lucy Stone to Simone de Beauvoir and Germaine Greer. She is defined not in terms of her self, but in terms of her relation to men: Adam's rib, Adam's temptress, Adam's helpmate, Adam's wife and the mother of his children.

To sharpen the point, let us consider the findings of just one psychological study in which men and women in many countries were asked to rate adjective pairs, like large vs. small, according to how well they described man, woman, male, female, husband, wife, father, mother (Osgood, 1964). Around the world, the male image is generally characterized by both sexes as strong—as large, strong, hard, and heavy. Where does this leave the women? The female image is characterized as small, weak, soft, and light. In the United States and many other countries it is also dull, peaceful, relaxed, cold, rounded, passive, and slow. Two conclusions immediately follow.

First, women are regarded as the opposite of men. Possibly this is the psychologist's fault, for a respondent who seeks to describe a woman as "not strong" must place a check mark closer to its polar opposite, weak. Yet a woman may obviously be "not strong" without being weak; in fact, the strong-weak dimension may not apply to her at all. Since it is useful in describing male behavior, she is commonly dragged in and placed somewhere on it, not only by the psychologists, but by the man in the street. Again, Adam's rib. Woman is perceived in terms of where she stands on a male characteristic.

Secondly, most of the terms describing the female image have a negative tone. Who wants to be small, weak, light (a light-weight?), dull? By such a definition women must be pretty feeble creatures, pale reflections of men. No wonder they have been dissatisfied with the image and have reacted either with open resentment or secret doubts as to their own real worth. The obvious reaction is simply to deny the charge. The early feminists argued that women could be just as loud, rough, strong, ferocious, sharp, and fast as men, as several proved by their own behavior. If females were not often like this, they contended, it was either because they were kept in subjection by men or because they were lazy and without the will to amount to anything. Some women have always wondered if this line of argument is really satisfactory. Do they, or should they, want to be so rough and tough — so masculine? Or does accepting the issue as joined in this way concede too much to the male image? Is it possible to fashion a female image that is not identical with the male image, consisting of a set of quite different characteristics altogether? Then the answer to the question of how assertive a woman can be rated would be: "The category doesn't apply. You simply can't stuff women into that pigeonhole."

If we cannot, then, use male categories to describe accurately women's characteristics, what ones can we use? As we shall see in a moment, women generally do not like pigeonholes of any kind as well as men do; so we are playing a male game, but one that may be justified on the ground that it could help some women entertain a higher opinion of themselves and their role in life. Fortunately, our search will not suffer for lack of facts on which to base conclusions. In psychology's short history, literally thousands of studies have been reported that show significant sex differences. Men and women, boys and girls, differ in dozens of ways —in abilities, in interests, in their reactions to various types of treatment, in the way they are "put together" psychologically. The problem is not lack of information, but making sense out of a surfeit of facts, the mere listing of which is enough to bore and confuse most people. What follows is an attempt to bring some order out of this chaos, an attempt to find dimensions that characterize the way women actually function. Although there is no guarantee that we shall find the ideal in the real, that we shall discover how women should behave from the way they do behave, the facts should be helpful, particularly if they can be ordered in a meaningful way that is not the mirror opposite of the male image.

To begin with an obvious male trait, men are more assertive than women. Many studies show that boys are stronger, more active, more aggressive or "pushing" practically from birth on (see Terman and Tyler and Pratt, in Carmichael, 1946). The characteristic appears to have some physiological basis in the dominance of the male sex hormone, but nearly all cultures (roughly 85 per cent) strengthen it by training boys more than girls in self-reliance and achievement (Barry, Bacon, and Child, 1957). Males get into more trouble in school (Williams, 1933), in college (compare bills for furniture repair in men's and women's dormitories), and in later life (male crime rates are higher; see Tyler, 1956). In the words of Kagan and Moss, "Traditional sex-typed values regard some forms of aggression as critical attributes of masculinity. Thus boys who are striving to identify with a masculine ideal will be prompted to push a peer, to grab a toy, to jeer at a teacher. These behaviors may not necessarily reflect hostile needs but may be the child's way of announcing to the social environment, 'I am a boy, I am capable of executing those behaviors that help to define my role.' Thus a boy may employ a shove or verbal taunt as a way of greeting a peer —a 'hello' if you wish. This use of aggression in a girl is unlikely" (1962, p. 274).

These authors report the results of a long-term study in which the same people were followed from infancy to adulthood. Two characteristics more stable or consistent over the years for boys than for girls were aggressiveness and active interest in the opposite sex. This they interpret to mean that neither of these assertive traits was likely to be interfered with in boys, because they are considered to be normal and proper masculine characteristics. The authors also found that men were quicker than women at detecting aggressive scenes flashed briefly on a screen. Others have shown that even three-, four-, and five-year-old boys play more violently with dolls than girls do (P. S. Sears, 1951).

Boys prefer rough games, physically strenuous, adventuresome activities (and stories about them), selling activities, showers over baths, driving racing cars, hunting.[2] They report more often than girls that they feel "entirely self-confident" or like picking a fist-fight with someone. They much more often enter occupations expressive of their assertive interests, like selling, soldiering, engineering (adventurous activities), and law (which allows considerable play for aggressive interests). In the United States it is interesting to note that entrants into the last two occupations have remained over 95 per cent male despite the freedom of at least a couple of generations of women to enter them (Davis and Bradburn, 1961). Of course the "freedom" is only relative: The strong prejudice still remaining against women lawyers and engineers has doubtless kept many women from venturing into these fields. But what we are concerned with here is traditional role expectations, not whether they are justified or not.

Women have shared much less in these assertive interests and activities; yet to say they are not assertive in this way is to say very little. It is to fall into the traditional trap of explaining women as "not men." If they are not so vigorously acting on the world about them, what are they doing? All the evidence suggests that they pay more attention to what goes on around them and modify their behavior accordingly. They care more about relationships. They are interdependent. The characteristic shows up at the motor level just as assertiveness does for boys. Girls excel at tasks involving rapid, fine motor adjustments, as in tests of finger dexterity and clerical aptitude (Tyler, 1956, p. 254). Their organism seems more finely tuned to making adjustments to stimulus changes. Their interaction or interdependence with the environment is greater than for boys, who are likely to barge ahead assertively, no matter what is happening around them.

The female concern for interdependence is most striking in the social field where interrelationships with people are concerned. Women recognize more readily than men scenes of interdependence flashed quickly on the screen —of a child clinging to an adult's knee (Kagan and Moss, 1962). Findings like this are sometimes interpreted as indicating dependence in women, but interdependence is a better word, and for an obvious reason: it is not clear whether the female observer identifies with the dependent child or the nurturant parent. Overwhelmingly; the evidence points to the conclusion that women are more concerned than men with both sides of an interdependent relationship. They are more highly trained in nurturance (child care, looking after people) in 82 per cent of the cultures on which data are available (Barry, Bacon, and Child, 1957); and they are also more dependent on others in the sense of being more easily persuaded by others to change their minds (Janis and Field, 1959). In one study, where couples were working together on a problem in which the success of one might mean the failure of another, a confederate at one point asked his partner to "please slow down." The girls responded to this plea by slowing down; the boys did not (Walker and Heyns, 1962). Child care obviously involves this kind of give-and-take or interdependence, where one's actions are continually dependent on reactions of others.

It is not surprising, then, to find that women disclose more of their secrets to others (Jourard, 1963), feel less dislike for all sorts of odd people (infidels, people with gold teeth, spendthrifts, etc.), and are most attracted to fiction and movies dealing with interpersonal relationships, sentimental stories, romances, social problems, etc. Many tests like the Allport-Vernon-Lindzey *Study of Values* show women as more concerned for the welfare of others and as more moralistic (women are more likely to report, "I become quite irritated when I see someone spit on the sidewalk."). In both instances, concern and morals, they are simply expressing a social awareness which covers all sorts of interrelationships of people from child care to proper social behavior, including proper dress, makeup, etc. (Tyler, 1956).

It follows that they enter occupations like nursing (78 per cent female), social work (68 per cent female), or teaching (59 per cent female) (Davis and Bradburn, 1961). Researchers report, indeed, that female occupational interests show only one major pattern (as contrasted with several for males) which covers whatever it is that housewives, office workers, stenographers, nurses, and teachers have in common. The men who did the study with the usual male bias called the factor "Interest in Male Association." Leona Tyler (1956), noting that this label does not cover teaching very well, noncommittally calls it "Typical Feminine Interests," whereas actually all these occupations fit in the interdependence category we have been using to describe one of the main dimensions of female interest and actions.

To summarize, women are quicker to recognize their own interdependence; they are more interested in situations where interdependence is important; they enter jobs where this characteristic is salient, from child care to teaching or office work. One can even explain in these terms their general tendency to score higher on tests of neuroticism (Tyler, 1956; Gurin *et al.,* 1960). They are willing to admit to concern about interpersonal problems of which men are simply less aware. Consider the following test item: "I get very tense and anxious when I think other people are disapproving of me." Women, far more likely to report "True" to such a statement than men are, are correspondingly likely to get a higher score for "worries" or "neurotic problems." Since interpersonal relationships are more important for women, therefore it is more worrying, more necessary to make an adjustment, when someone disapproves. The men may not notice or not care. To be fair, one should point out that men are just not on the interdependence dimension: they are often deaf, dumb and blind to what is going on around them because they are so busy assertively concentrating on a task. In work groups, women make comments that relate to social and emotional relationships in the group; men make comments that relate to the task itself (Exline, 1962; Strodtbeck and Mann, 1956). Perhaps it is women's concern for interdependence that explains why so few of them, as compared with men, have isolated themselves for long periods of time voluntarily as hermits or solitary sadhus.

To move on to a different but related characteristic difference between men and women, men are interested in *things,* women in *people.* Such a contrast, though scarcely surprising, is remarkably prominent throughout life. In nursery school little boys are apt to draw pictures with physical objects in them (toys, buildings, etc.), girls with people (Goodenough, 1957). The interest continues throughout the school years. Twelve-year-old boys, asked to "construct an exciting movie scene," often chose blocks and vehicles (Erikson, 1951). They like mechanical and scientific activities, from reading *Popular Science* or radio magazines to "repairing a door latch" or working with a chemistry set. They are much better than girls at those activities in school, scoring higher on "mechanical-aptitude measures, such as mazes, puzzle boxes and tests calling for the assembly of small objects" (Tyler, 1956, p. 253). "In Bennett's Mechanical Comprehension Test there is not a single item for which women average higher scores than men" (Tyler, 1956, p. 252). The superiority reduces basically to a greater interest in and ability at manipulating spatial relationships or "things in space."

Later in life, men enter far more often than women occupations like engineering and physical science, where these interests and abilities are all-important. The girls, in the meantime, continue to show their interest in people by preferring dolls to cars, by liking dramatics, stories about love relationships, charades, or just "being with one another." They are also better than boys at tests of verbal fluency; they talk earlier, think of words more quickly, and usually see or write more in a given period of time. One can argue that this is because language is *par excellence* the means of interacting with people, of communicating with people and responding to them. Since girls care about people more, they learn the means of interacting with them better. That the interest is not in language *per se* is shown by the fact that girls are not better at tests of verbal meanings.

Ian Fleming was not a professional psychologist, but he was making use of a scientifically established fact when he had his famous detective, James Bond, remark that women tend not to be good drivers because they more often take their eyes off the road to look at whoever is with them. In carefully controlled studies, it has been found that in small groups women typically look more often and longer at each other's faces than men do (Exline, 1962). College girls are more likely to fill their imaginative stories with living creatures — animals and people — than boys are.[3] These interests, like the corresponding male interest, tend to draw women to occupations like nursing, teaching, and office work where they will be satisfied. They apparently even influence the choice of the scientific field that attracts the largest proportion of women — namely, biology, and particularly biochemistry (44 per cent female entrants), the science that is concerned with the ultimate source of life itself.

Running through these differences is another theme which contrasts the way men and women go about dealing with the world — their respective *styles*. Again, the male style is easier to describe; it is, very simply, *analytic and manipulative*. If boys start early assertively moving things about in the environment (trucks, toys, stones, etc.), it is scarcely surprising that they end up better able to abstract common elements out of changing situations. They are better, as we have seen, at tests involving restructuring of spatial relations, taking puzzles apart, or noticing what is wrong with a picture. Numbers are abstractions *par excellence,* and males generally are better at tests involving the use of numbers in new combinations—so-called mathematical reasoning tests (Tyler, 1956, p. 252). Consequently, among college males roughly two-thirds of the College Board Quantitative Test Scores are higher than their Verbal Test Scores, while the reverse is true for women.

Nowhere is this male ability more clearly demonstrated than in certain perceptual tasks, such as finding a simple figure hidden in a complex design (Witkin *et al.,* 1954) or trying to see apparent motion between two visual displays flashed on and off successively (Gardner *et al.,* 1959). The men take longer to see the apparent motion than women do, maintaining a more "analytic" attitude. For the same reason men are quicker to notice that something has changed when small increases are introduced in the size of squares that are briefly presented one at a time (Gardner *et al.,* 1959). They also make fewer errors in adjusting a rod to the vertical position when they are sitting in a tilted chair or a tilted room (Witkin *et al.,* 1954). In short, men spend more time actively inspecting the environment, pulling things apart, taking things out of context and putting them back together in a new way. Constantly manipulating, analyzing and restructuring as they are, they do better at tasks that require these abilities.

Since women are more influenced by the tilt of the room in adjusting the rod to the upright, they have typically been described as "field dependent" or "passive acceptant." Again, these terms have a clear, if unintentional, negative connotation based on the bias that the male mode of reacting is the right one. In this case, it happens to be more appropriate to the task requirement, but it would not be difficult to set up a situation in which compromising among conflicting cues would be the task requirement. Then women should do better because their style is *contextual* rather than analytic; they have a more complex interdependent relationship with the world than men do. They are more "open" to influence, where men are "closed." It is amusing to note that such an interpretive statement is literally reflected in figure preferences shown by a test developed for cross-cultural use by John Whiting (unpublished). He and McClelland and Watt (1968) have found that women generally prefer figures like those on the left, men those on the right.

Note how much easier it is to describe the male style: it shows a preference for the simple, the closed, the direct. In contrast, women are more interested in the complex, the open, the less defined. They

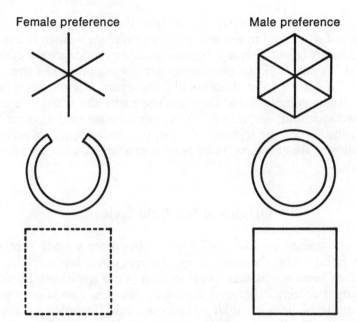

Female preference   Male preference

are quicker to see similarities or "equivalences" among objects and to observe apparent motion (Gardner *et al.,* 1959). Hence they are much more interested in art and generally score higher on Art Appreciation Tests (Tyler, 1956, p. 261). They also like the subtleties of poetry, which is not simple and direct enough for the average male. It may be that this characteristic accounts also for their superior memory, particularly for details (Tyler, 1956, p. 254). Since women pay more attention to context, the *whole* picture, while men are abstracting something out of it, women should be better able to recite from memory, for example, a story which has just been read aloud —and this is indeed the case (Tyler, 1956, p. 254). Male bias unfortunately shows up in labeling this female superiority as "rote memory," or "memory for details," terms which make women seem to be robots recording unimportant details (to men, that is). The contextuality label seems preferable. Women are concerned with the context; men are forever trying to ignore it for the sake of something they can abstract from it.

In trying to make this point clear to students, I have several times asked them to read Virginia Woolf's famous feminist essay, "A Room of One's Own." Her chief argument is that women have not become famous like men chiefly because they had little privacy and less support —either financial or emotional—for independent effort. In terms of our present analysis, she is right, though the lack of privacy may be self-generated in the sense that the average woman is less able than a man to *ignore what is going on around her,* to forget the context. Virginia Woolf's style in presenting her argument makes the point beautifully. Most of the students like the essay, but the boys in the class typically complain that they don't see why she is so circumstantial, so roundabout, so "literary." Why can't she get to the point? Why doesn't she lay out her argument in one, two, three order? Most of the girls (but not all, of course!) like her circumstantial, complex, contextual style.

Origins of Sex Role Styles

Must women be like this? Or are they simply underprivileged human beings who, because of male oppression, are forced into a shape they need not assume? Few women in our age like to think that "anatomy is destiny," that they cannot become truly great or anything they want to be because of an accident of birth. If women are the way they are largely because of social rules and expectations, why not change the rules? As in most things human, a good case can be made for the effect of both biological and social factors in producing sex differences. That the genes play a role is suggested by such facts as: (1) that sex hormones differ and are known to affect characteristics like assertiveness in other animals; (2) that sex differences in motility and sensitivity show up in neonates before culture could have had much effect (Hendry and Kessen, 1964); (3) that some of the differences, such as the ease with which apparent motion is seen, appear to be unrelated to any of the usual types of sex role expectations or training; (4) that practically all cultures train their boys in one way—for assertiveness—and their girls for another—interdependence. If there were no biological bias in these directions, would it not be more likely that the differences in training would be randomly distributed between the two sexes?

On the other hand, it is easy to demonstrate the crucial importance of training. After all, a few cultures can and do reverse the uusual sex-typing, as Margaret Mead demonstrated long ago in describing the Tchambuli women, who are assertive, and the men, who are timid, artistic, and dependent. At the individual level moreover, there is such an overlap in traits that, while there are average differences between the sexes, fully 40% of the women may be more assertive than the average male, and 40% of the men more interdependent than the average female. French and Lesser (1964) and more recently Stewart

(1971) have shown that career orientation among women is itself a powerful moderator variable that affects the way they behave. Career oriented women, who are more self-defining, behave like men in many ways. They project their own achievement motivation into stories involving females rather than males. They are likely to hold office in college, to have taken the initiative to telephone a man, to major in natural or social science rather than the humanities, and to have indulged in loud arguments (Stewart and Winter, 1974). Women who see their careers in traditional terms as housewives and mothers are more apt to behave in the interdependent fashion we have described; they tend to mention friends and their approval as the main pleasure in life rather than achievement or an active hobby (Stewart and Winter, 1974). Since it hardly seems likely that these two groups of women differ in any biological way, we have evidence of the importance of sexually determined expectations in shaping female behavior.

Furthermore, Horner has demonstrated in a series of studies (1972, 1974) that white American women tend to "fear success." Given the opportunity to complete a sentence like, "when Mary found she was at the head of her class in medical school, she . . .," a high proportion of women conclude with negative endings such as, "she discovered it was a mistake the registrar had made in computing her average," or "she lost her boyfriend who didn't want to marry someone who was smarter than he was" or "she went into research and gradually went out of her mind from studying so much with no social life." When the word "John" was substituted for "Mary" in this sentence, the women wrote that he went on to fame and success; but for a woman to be so conspicuously successful evoked associations of disaster. It is as if women have learned that if they stand out, or are assertive, they are very likely somehow to get hurt. Society not only does not expect them to be assertive, it punishes them if they are: men avoid them; they are told they go crazy if they have no social life; ways are found to justify not promoting them or paying them the same as a man, etc. Small wonder that on the average they learn to avoid being assertive! Interestingly enough, black American women do not show the same fear of success; in their sub-culture they have been taught that the woman is rewarded for being assertive and looking out for herself and her children more than the black man, who has been ruthlessly suppressed by white society at the first sign of rebellious assertiveness (Hamilton, 1974).

Does all this evidence suggest that society's expectations about woman's role are completely arbitrary, and not based *at all* on biological facts? To accept the importance of expectation in shaping women's behavior and the ease of changing them, is not necessarily to deny that biology may play some role in building sex role expectations. Some sociologists have long argued, for instance, that in the family functional roles exist and are likely to be assigned to different family members. If the family is to survive as a unit, the argument goes, someone must be assigned the role of bringing outside supplies into the unit and protecting it against attack. Because the male is usually stronger, he is in most societies assigned this assertive role. On the other hand, relationships within the unit must be the responsibility of someone, or fights will break out, supplies will not be properly divided, the weak will not be cared for, etc. (Zelditch, 1955). Women are normally assigned this role because they are not strong enough to play the male role. The needs of a functioning society, plus one biological factor (greater male strength), the sociologists argue, are sufficient to account for the existing bias in sex-typing. According to such a theory, as the need for male strength decreases in a technologically modern society, the basis for sex-typing disappears—particularly since no biological basis for the female superiority in interdependent relationships is assumed. Some would even argue that the family itself may be outmoded, a fact which would mean it could hardly be used any longer as a basis for sex-role typing.

Yet it is difficult to reject altogether the role of biology in shaping behavior patterns. Anatomy may not be destiny, but it is one of the facts of existence that shapes the learning of boys and girls. Every boy experiences the phallic tumescence-detumescence cycle literally thousands of times from birth onward. The association between rise-pleasure-assertion should be firmly fixed by this recurrent experience. Girls, on the other hand, learn early that they are penetrated in the sexual act, that the often painful experiences of menstrual flow and childbirth are difficulties that lead to pleasure and happiness, that to bear a child—one purpose for which their bodies are obviously constructed—they must relate to another, who will support them during childbirth and their somewhat dependent state thereafter, etc. So there may be common learning experiences based on anatomical facts that help create some of the psychological reactions observed more often among women—their interest in interdependence, their idea that they must give up one thing to get another, etc.

Nothing, to be sure, is absolutely foreordained about these learnings. Women can and do learn the male patterns; men can fail to learn them. All anatomy does is to make some associative patterns *more likely* in one sex than the other if nature takes her course, and if nothing is done to change what would normally be learned. Society builds its expectations on these "natural" learnings, which unfortunately tend to be far stronger and more restrictive than anything a biological bias could conceivably justify. They can arbitrarily dictate to a woman that she *must* be interdependent or socially defined, that she *cannot* be assertive. If she tries to go against this rigid stereotype, she is made to suffer by the scorn heaped upon her or by the many realistic deprivations and punishments that society can invoke against those who break the "cake of custom." Unfortunately, women who break the mould often do suffer and lead such unhappy lives as a result that the biological determinists can turn their example into evidence that women should accept their traditional role. One hopes that the days of women's enslavement to traditional sex typing are passing.

Why then talk at all about sex differences? Their mere existence might provide support for a too rigid view of explicit feminine behavior. There is some risk of that, of course; but I have taken the risk, over the violent protest of some contemporary feminists, of exploring more fully and trying to build greater acceptance for a life style that traditionally has been more characteristic of women because of the biologically based "normal learnings" I have referred to. It should be emphasized, however, that there is absolutely no reason why a woman has to or should adopt this life style or why a man for that matter should not adopt it. My own belief is that the traditional male's single-minded, specialized assertive life style is far too dominant and too much valued in so-called advanced societies. Both women and men are drawn to it—to full-time specialized careers, for instance—because that is the only way to be fully respected in contemporary Western society. The traditional male life style has won out and exerts an even subtler form of oppression on women who feel increasingly worthless if they pursue the traditional feminine social emotional role rather than the male instrumental role. I devote the rest of this chapter then, without further apology, to an exploration of the traditional feminine role, its strengths and weaknesses as a life style, in full recognition that, though the study has to be based on women, I see no reason why more men could not or should not adopt such a role also.

Power Motivation and the Traditional Feminine Life Style

Knowing how women typically behave as contrasted with men has put the findings reported in the previous chapter in a broader perspective; for women's behavior is shaped by role expectations rooted in history and in society, and power motivation expresses itself in terms of how women are expected to behave. Because their role has traditionally been to manage social and emotional resources in the family, women are interdependent and especially interested in people and the life process. Their contextual style is adapted to dealing with the many demands that are made on them at once. They have not been instrumental specialists like men but generalists who have learned to pay close attention to all sorts of information, particularly of an interpersonal sort, and to give of their time and resources to manage interpersonal relationships more successfully.

What then if they are high in power motivation?

The answer lies in the information in Table 3.1 assembled from the study of adult men and women reported in the last chapter. At the top are listed a number of responses reflecting female sex-role behavior as we have described it on the basis of considerable empirical evidence. The women generally are more interdependent: they are more strongly inspired by others, belong to more organizations, have been taught sociocentric virtues, and *like* looking after children. They also give more of their resources, being willing to lend important possessions and share a gift with charities.

By and large, increased power motivation does not strongly accentuate these traditional role behaviors. There is a slight tendency for it to increase the giving-loaning expressive modality, particularly at the Stage I level of maturity, but its general effect is on *building up one's resources*. Five of the six main items listed in Table 2.3 as more characteristic of women high in *n* Power, regardless of their stage score, are also significantly more characteristic of women in general than of men. (See the bottom half of Table 3.1) Thus women in general diet more often than men, accumulate more credit cards, etc., but women high in *n* Power do so even more. We interpreted these responses in Chapter 2 as efforts to build one's resources up, particularly one's physical-material resources, so as to have more to share. One item even reflects this sharing concern directly —the willingness to donate parts of one's body after death. Women's social role as defined in the items at the top of Table 3.1 already insures that women will be more interdependent and share more of their resources; what power motivation does is focus them on having more resources to share.

This whole trend is modified by the level of the woman's maturity, as can be illustrated by various items. Although women in general are significantly less likely than men to report that they like to travel

Table 3.1—Women's behaviors which are and are not accentuated by power
motivation

Behaviors more common in women than men	Women	Men	Women-Men	
		Mean scores		
A. Not accentuated by power motivation regardless of maturity level	(N = 115)	(N = 85)	diff.	p value
Strength of inspiration by others[a]	4.80	4.14	.66	<.01
Number of organizations belonged to	2.17	1.35	.82	<.01
Number of sociocentric virtues taught by parents (out of 3)	2.12	1.87	.25	<.05
Things loaned lately	2.36	1.67	.69	<.001
Share $10,000 gift with charity (out of 3)	.23	.08	.15	<.01
Volunteer to look after children because you like to (scale 1–5)	3.63	2.96	.67	<.01
Like babies especially scale 1–6)	5.35	4.40	.95	<.01
Disclose private feelings	3.55	3.28	.27	~.21
B. Accentuated by power motivation regardless of maturity level				
Discipline body (diet) frequency 1–4	2.24	2.07	.17	<.10
Number of credit cards	4.00	1.94	2.06	<.01
Number of unpleasant dreams (out of 2)	.78	.54	.24	<.05
Average daily fluid intake (juice, coffee, etc.)[b]	2.95	2.55	.40	<.01
Willingness to donate parts of body after death (scale 1–4)	2.55	2.28	.27	<.05

a. Number of admired figures of either sex plus strength of influence of each one on a scale of 1–3.
b. Average frequency of drinking various fluids outside meals (scale 1–5).

alone in new places, women high in power motivation who are also at the Stage III level of development are more likely to do just that (Table 2.6). Joining organizations is more common among all women, but power motivation increases the tendency to join primarily at Stages II and IV—the two stages where control is more important. Recall too our conclusion in Chapter 2, that power motivation apparently helps women develop into higher stages of maturity, just as it hinders men.

All this adds up to the need for caution in talking of "general trends" for women. Obviously it depends on what kind of women we are talking about, at what stage of maturity. But if we remember this all-important qualification, it is still appropriate to try to understand the traditional feminine style better, as it is accentuated by power motivation.

The Demeter-Persephone Life Style

Female role behavior deserves a more positive, simple designation. It is more than just not being assertive like a man. It invokes interdependence, building up resources, and giving. Since psychologists have turned to ancient Greek mythology to describe the traditional male role in terms of the Oedipus story, let us turn there again for female role models. They are not hard to find, for the Greeks had a way of representing profound insights into human psychology in mythological terms that remain as appropriate today as when they were conceived. The female life style is dramatically illustrated by the stories of Demeter and her daughter Persephone or Jason and his wife Medea. In both, the woman submits, is taken advantage of, and triumphs.

Medea helps Jason find the Golden Fleece at considerable sacrifice to her own people, only to find that he in the end deserts her for another. Although she retaliates by killing their children, she returns to a successful life at home while Jason loses out. Her self-sacrifice is crucial to the story: the fact that he fails to recognize it is his undoing. In the end she wins anyway.

The story of Persephone, as told in the Homeric *Hymn to Demeter*, is not only more revealing, but is particularly appropriate for our purposes because the *Hymn* was associated with the Eleusinian Mysteries, celebrated in ancient Greece for over 2,000 years. Although it is fashionable to conclude that no one knows what went on in the Mysteries (Myonas, 1961), it is known that they are probably the most important religious ceremonies, even partly on the historical record, which were organized by and for women, especially at the onset before men by means of the cult of Dionysos began to take them over (see Harrison, 1903). Thus the *Hymn to Demeter* may be regarded as a special presentation of feminine psychology.

The plot of the hymn focuses on the psychology of a mother (Demeter) and her daughter (Persephone). Persephone is out playing in the meadows with her girl friends when she sees a beautiful narcissus, which she runs to pick. As she does so, the earth opens, and Hades in his horse-drawn chariot comes to take her back with him to his kingdom in the underworld. Demeter so mourns her lost daughter that she refuses to let anything grow. She is the all powerful Earth Mother on whose resources everyone depends for life. Crops are ruined, men and animals suffer and die, until Zeus takes pity on man's suffering and persuades his brother Hades to send Persephone back to her mother. Persephone returns but only after she has eaten some pomegranate seed, which means that she must spend part of the year with Hades in the underworld. Demeter is overjoyed to have her daughter back, and while they are together, the crops grow, the trees flower, the animals give birth to their young. Earth's creativity is enhanced in every way by the return of her long-lost daughter. During the months of the year when her daughter is back in the underworld, however, Demeter sorrows again and refuses to let anything grow. The story is used to explain the seasons—Spring and Summer, when Persephone returns to her mother, and Fall and Winter, when she is away underground.

The psychological themes of the story are clear: *women are the source of life* and *going without brings increase.* Going down under (Persephone's submission) or going without (Demeter's loss of her daughter) is followed by a return which produces fertility and joy. The message is clothed in the age-old image of sowing and harvesting. "Except a corn of wheat fall into the ground and die, it abideth alone; but if it die, it bringeth forth much fruit" (John 12:24). Almost certainly the Mysteries had to do with "first fruits" and the harvest. Demeter is pictured as overjoyed when Persephone returns after her forced absence; in her delight she causes the earth to yield far more than normal, just as the grass, the plants, and the trees grow so much faster and greener in the spring after the long deprivation of winter.

The theme of going without to enhance the value of something was played out in other ways in the Mysteries at Eleusis. To begin with, the rites were probably the most secret ever enacted in the ancient world. Although thousands of people were initiated over the centuries, none gave away what happened, so dreaded were the penalties for revealing the secrets. Once Alcibiades started to explain what went on at a drunken party and as a consequence lost all his possessions and nearly his life, although he was a national hero at the time. Towards the end of their celebration the early Christian fathers, like Clement of Alexandria, made some horrid guesses as to the rituals enacted, but scholars have seriously doubted whether they really knew. The secrets were extraordinarily well kept, and, psychologically, what is the purpose of secrecy? It is precisely to enhance the value of what goes on in secret. So the secrecy of the rites is explicit testimony to their enactment of the theme of doing without in order to make something more valuable. Jourard (1963) has shown that women particularly value letting people in on secrets—a fact confirmed for feelings only at a moderate level of significance in Table 3.1. Women more often than men tell others about aspects of their private lives, particularly their feelings. The Eleusinian Mysteries suggest they do so because they are acting out a fundamental theme in traditional feminine psychology, which is to enhance the value of one's resources by restricting information about oneself and then letting others selectively in on the secrets.

Furthermore, the part of the ritual that was carried on in public involved purification. Before the march to the temple at Eleusis, for example, each of the Athenian celebrants drove a little pig to the sea and washed it and themselves in the ocean. The celebrants had to go without certain foods and abstain from sexual intercourse. The psychological purpose of purification is also to wash away or take something away in order to enhance the value of what is left. The person becomes better, purer, by going without or doing without. During the ceremonies at Eleusis, at least two events occurred that underline the same theme. It is fairly certain that, as in other women's rituals, something like pig's flesh was let down into caves under the temple and allowed to rot and later hauled up to spread on the fields as fertilizer to increase the yield of crops (Harrison, 1903). The association between death, decay, going down, and increased life and fertility is clear. It is known too that part of the ceremonies were carried out in the dark and under ground and that at a certain critical moment the celebrants came up into a scene brilliantly illuminated. Again, going without in order to get is emphasized by going down in order to come up, and by darkness followed by bright light. Other less certain speculations about what went on fit the same theme: ritual marriage, birth of a child, first fruits. What all of these rituals are saying to the celebrant is: "You must give in order to get, go down in order to come up, yield in order to win." Every participant surely had the story of Demeter and Persephone in mind, the central part of which deals with the same theme. Persephone submits to a man by force, is *taken* by a power greater than herself, goes down under—and the result is greatly enhanced fertility and joy when she comes up out of the experience.

The story captures so eloquently the essence of traditional feminine psychology as we have uncovered it in various empirical studies that it seems appropriate to refer to the traditional feminine role as the Demeter-Persephone life style.

To remind ourselves once again that it need not be exclusively associated with women, we have only to recall that Jesus Christ was a perfect example of this life style. He died on the Cross to win—to save—mankind. "He who loses his life for my sake, shall find it." It is perhaps because Christianity absorbed some of the feminine-oriented imagery of Greek mystical cults like the Eleusinian Mysteries that it had such a wide appeal for women as well as for men.

A whole culture can come to value this life style highly, or to see it is essential to the life process itself. Christianity, as we shall see in Chapter 9, made only a half-hearted move in this direction. But traditional Indian culture, as we see in Chapter 4, valued giving or going without above all other modalities, and in this sense made the Demeter-Persephone life style paramount. In such a society it is the traditional male mode—straightforward assertiveness—which is a variant pattern, and the traditional female role is normative. It is worth remembering this in the United States where the male mode is so valued by both men and women that the Demeter-Persephone style is considered deviant, passive, and a sign of immaturity.

Measuring the Demeter-Persephone Life Style

Evidence for the Demeter-Persephone life style is so far indirect. It consists of our attempt to make sense out of some sex differences in behavior, particularly as they are exhibited by men and women high in the need for Power. To find myths which express the main themes in these differences, and give them a Greek label, is not very convincing proof that the themes actually exist. Robert May (1966) tackled the problem more directly. If the supposed differences in sex-role styles really exist, he argued, they ought to show up in their own right in the imaginative thinking of men and women. With the Demeter-Persephone myth in mind, he had male and female college students about 18 years old write stories based on the picture of a man and woman doing a trapeze act in mid-air against the dark background of a circus tent. Stories evoked by such a picture could readily focus on falling and rising, helping, letting go, rising to peaks of glory, etc. He found some striking differences, later confirmed with other pictures, in the themes of the stories told by men and women. The following is a typical male story:

> This picture suggests a dynamic, intimate relation between the man and woman —hence the light is around their bodies and the rest is dark. This picture is a climax to a period in which they have come to understand each other. Both are completely lost in the thought of their union. They are totally occupied. From such heights they can only go down.

Note that the acrobats have reached a climax from which they "can only go down." Sixty-one per cent of the male stories, vs. 30 per cent of the female stories were of this type, in which the acrobats worked themselves up to a peak and then a letdown, often a fall, occurred. Professor Murray (1955) has dubbed this psychological theme in its more extreme form the Icarus Complex; Icarus flew high on his wings toward the sun, but the wax melted and he fell into the sea. This is the male image of achievement. The straight line projecting upward to a peak of glory until, with the failure of assertiveness — perhaps just with old age —he falls.

The women's stories were more complex. Here are portions of four typical female stories about the same picture:

> Mary is learning to do a change between trapezes. She is about to swing to the next and her teacher, old Mr. Picken, is going to become instantly ill, and she is going to catch him from falling by a lucky chance. He will then train her to circus stardom.

> A lovely circus act, great daring and beauty. Fortunately the man is upside down, or you'd see he's not so young; actually he's her father, and not as bright as she . . .

> What do you think, Best Beloved? Daddy is going to slip, Mamma screams from the ringside seat reserved for her, Tony (her boyfriend) drops his cigar, Petronella saves Daddy.

> She is terribly afraid. She *knows* deep down that he will catch her, but that moment of freedom in the air, far above the ground is frightening. Suddenly as he takes her hands, she feels tremendously released from tension.

Note that in these stories there is a crisis which provides the opportunity for great release or pleasure. Dependence —threatened falls—become the occasion for great joy. May found that in 70% of the female stories, as contrasted with only 32% of the male stories, the same theme occurred. In more general terms problems occur, in which the girl or her partner is in danger, and she or he acts to save the situation. The sequence is pain-pleasure, the reverse of the male pleasure-pain sequence. It is as if women have learned to think of going through suffering, anxiety, or problems to pleasure on the other side, much as Demeter and Persephone suffered to create an occasion for great joy.

May's scoring scheme was in terms of Deprivation (D) — Enhancement (E): he measured whether more D units or more E units occurred before or after a story's pivotal incident. Women's stories in general showed more D—E sequences in which deprivation units preceded enhancement units. For each person May could get a score that reflected the extent to which she (or he) showed a Persephone-like thematic style. He came to feel, however, that "the categories of 'deprivation' and 'enhancement' seem to have been defined with the typical male mode of functioning in mind . . . the labels are loaded in the direction of male values tending to equate 'giving' with 'giving up' . . . Giving up or suffering has overtones of finality for men, whereas for women it can be a means to an end, almost an opportunity" (Robert May, 1966).

The significance of May's work is that he ended with a measure of individual differences in sex-role orientation so that it was no longer necessary to categorize people merely in terms of their biological sex. Many women show the E-D Icarian sequence, and many men the D-E Demeter-Persephone sequence. In a later study McClelland and Watt (1968) were to report that while housewives showed the Persephone pattern predominantly, working women did not. Sixty-seven percent of the former told two out of three stories with a feminine or D-E score, as contrasted with only 25% of the latter—about the same percentage as a composite group of working men. The woman's assertiveness style, in short, matched her life situation, either because she adjusted it to the situation or because she chose to work or be primarily a housewife because of her assertiveness style. Women who were housewives thought in terms of the interdependent world in which they live. A woman who must respond to all the demands put upon her by her children, her housecleaning, the cooking, her neighbors, the school, and her husband, cannot do one thing at a time, as a working person can. She must often postpone what she is doing to respond to an immediate need, give over and over again as she nurtures one person after another in her life situation. A working woman can and does learn to respond like a man —to think in terms of a straightforward, attack on the problem.

Abigail Stewart approached a similar measurement problem in the following way: she wondered how the fantasies of career-oriented college women would differ from those of girls who were not definitely planning a career but who were thinking in terms of a traditional woman's role, as wife and mother. In the imaginative stories they wrote she obtained differences (1971) corresponding in general terms to those found by May. The girls oriented towards the traditional woman's role told fewer stories characterized by causality or purposeful plans of action (the Icarian sequence), and more in which higher powers *acted upon* characters in the story (the "deprivation" part of the D-E sequence). She did not find signs of "enhancement" following yielding or adjusting, perhaps because her orientation in choosing pictures etc. was towards the self-defining woman. But her measure has some of the same correlates as May's: non-self-defining women are less apt to have a mother who works; they major in the humanities or arts; they do not assert themselves in college; they take major pleasures in their friends rather than in work; and they describe their fathers not in terms of his objective qualities but in terms of his relationship to them ("he loves me"; "I hate him". (Stewart and Winter, 1974). So there are at present at least two measures of individual differences in traditionally feminine vs. more assertive role styles.

Feminine Masochism

The willingness of women to give of themselves for others has usually been referred to, especially in psychoanalytic literature, as feminine masochism (Deutsch 1944). Supposedly the growing girl renounces her aggressive urges for the sake of being loved. Since the aggressive impulses are not totally exhausted by the act of renunciation, they are turned against the self, and the girl enjoys suffering in the act of being loved. May summarizes some of Deutsch's examples of this type of masochism in women (1966): "Subjecting oneself to a man's will, being attracted by suffering, a painful longing and wish to suffer for the lover, renunciation in favor of others, a feeling that suffering is compensated by love, rape fantasies, and the willingness to serve a cause or a human being with love and abnegation." Although all of these instances are examples of the Demeter-Persephone life style, we have avoided using the term masochism because it suggests pathology and because the Freudian derivation erroneously regards male aggressiveness as the normal outlet for aggression and regards traditional feminine giving as a deviation from the norm.

A Demeter-Persephone complex can become the basis for pathology, however, and when it does, then it is proper to speak of feminine masochism. In an earlier paper I traced a special variant of the Persephone theme which focuses on the "demon lover"—on Hades who comes to take Persephone away to the underworld. Since in later forms of this myth in the Western world, he came to be called Harlequin, I call this variant of the Persephone theme the Harlequin complex. Greenberger (1965) felt that if it was true that women took a masochistic pleasure in suffering, or associated joy with pain, then a critical test of the hypothesis might be a study of the fantasies of women dying of terminal cancer. According to her theory, approaching death might be mythically associated with Hades or Harlequin, the demon lover, who would take them down under but still give them joy. Thus college women, more than college men, might judge that referring to death as "a gay seducer" would be an appropriate poetic metaphor, a finding first reported in McClelland (1964) and confirmed later by Stewart, though at a lower level of significance. Greenberger found that lower-class women dying of cancer in a public hospital had more frequent fantasies of punishment (deprivation) and illicit love affairs (enhancement) than a matched control group of women hospitalized elsewhere for minor illnesses. Imminent death evoked two opposite fantasies—one fearful, involving punishment, and the other vaguely pleasurable, involving sexual seduction. Women faced by a powerful threat from without (death) reacted as predicted: they showed signs of the Harlequin complex in fantasy.

In elaborating on the implications of all this for feminine psychology, I was led to suggest (1964) that severe difficulties in sex-role styles might be related to pathology, such as schizophrenia; I cited one of French's cases in which a woman had crippling delusions of being dead, delusions clearly associated with her sexual experiences and impulses. Could schizophrenic women be suffering from an extreme form of the Persephone or Harlequin complex—totally victimized by forces beyond their control, and therefore in a sense dead, unable to move on their own? Or might they for some reason have such anxiety over playing the traditional yielding female role that they had lost totally a sense of sexual, and subsequently, personal identity? To check these possibilities we gave both male and female schizophrenics and comparable normals a series of tests of sex-role identification (McClelland and Watt, 1968). Schizophrenics of both sexes showed some alienation from normal sex role styles, particularly the males, who were non-assertive and tended in a number of ways to behave like women. But the schizophrenic women showed less rather than more of the masochistic, D-E pattern, using May's measure. In this respect they were like working women. Were they anxious about the Persephone style or were they just more masculine and assertive than typical women?

It took a more sensitive measure to shed light on the question. Robert May (1968) measured the inhibition or anxiety that normal and schizophrenic subjects of both sexes showed in response to pictures showing individuals in normal and reversed sex-role relationships. The schizophrenic men, thus confronted, again showed a tendency toward sex-role reversal; they showed less anxiety than normal men to pictures such as a man feeding a woman or a woman with a knife. On the other hand, they showed more anxiety to normal sex-role relationships —to a woman feeding a man or a picture of a man in anger. For the schizophrenic women the situation was reversed: they showed more anxiety than normal women to reverse-role pictures — to the woman with a knife or the man feeding a woman —and less anxiety to "normal" sex-role pictures. Normal women, in short, had more difficulty with pictures like one of a woman feeding a man or of a man beating a woman —which might be considered part of "traditional" sex-role expectations. Schizophrenic women, on the contrary, had less anxiety over the pictures: in a sense they could accept the idea of a man beating a woman more masochistically than normal women, who resisted the idea.

Watt *et al.* (1970) found supportive data from the school reports of children who later turned out to be schizophrenic. Such reports are especially valuable because they are not biased by the knowledge that the child is going to be schizophrenic. The boys, it seemed, were clearly recognized as "queer"; they did not behave in normal assertive ways, being either withdrawn or impulsively annoying. Girls who were future schizophrenics, on the other hand, were "supernormal": they tended to be rated favorably by their teachers because they were especially conscientious and "good." They showed to an extreme the traditional Persephone, yielding, compliant role. It seems likely that they were forcing themselves into yielding, when the very essence of the ideal D-E role involves being able to give willingly, to feel oneself an instrument of a larger power than the self.

Giving as Fulfillment

Defining the traditional feminine life style by its pathology is unsatisfactory. It distorts the picture by emphasizing the negative aspects of the role. Words like "masochism" and "yielding" inevitably conjure up the image of a person helplessly victimized by forces beyond her control. Psychologists from Freud on have far too often attempted to perceive the normal dimly through the anxieties of individuals who come to them only because they are unhappy and need help. Even Persephone and her mother are depicted as harrassed women who found joy and creative sharing only after suffering.

The alternative approach, as Maslow convincingly argued, is to define the normal through the supernormal, by finding and describing lives of actual people. Thus at least one could correct the impression that most women lead lives of quiet desperation, trapped in a life style that frustrates their creativity or drives them insane. See Chessler (1972). So I should like to close this chapter with the case study of a woman who regards her life as having been tremendously exciting and fulfilling, even though her name will not go down in the history books. One of the difficulties in finding people who represent the giving life style, as I said earlier, is that they indulge so little in a self-forwarding activity to focus attention on themselves, that they seldom get into the history books. They live in and through other people. They seldom concentrate enough on their own actions to produce a great book, run a military campaign, make a scientific discovery, or pursue high public office. History glorifies the specialists, even though there would be no history books if there were only specialists. Even those we recognize as epitomizing the giving role—like Christ, or the Buddha—tend to be men, because they specialized in the role in a dramatic enough way to call attention to themselves. All the more reason to present as a model here someone who is not famous, yet whose life could be an example for many—both women, and men.

Before I describe her, a word is in order about how I happened to choose her. One of the games psychologists play, particularly male psychologists, is to keep secret the sources of their scientific generalizations. They like to believe that their abstractions are objective and based solely on the evidence. The facts, of course, are often quite otherwise. Many times their generalizations are based on vivid personal experiences of which they may not be aware or which they even deny, fearing that if the truth were known, the public would distrust the objectivity of their reasoning. As Bakan (1958) has pointed out, although many of Freud's methods and generalizations derive from his own personal experiences with the Hassidic Jewish tradition, he and his followers concealed the fact lest it undermine the acceptability and objectivity of psychoanalysis. Freud even presented and analyzed his dreams as if they were those of another person. There may on occasion be legitimate reasons for the anonymity and "objectivity" that psychologists love, but, as Jourard has pointed out (1963), it is men who generally fail to share information about themselves, not women. Thus when I asked the subject of the present case study if she wanted to be anonymous, she said please to call her by name. So following her example, I have decided to introduce the case by being open about my background experiences with her and with women, even though I am well aware that as a man, such a procedure makes me particularly vulnerable to attack. My experiences with women have been unusual.

My father was president of a women's college in Jacksonville, Illinois, and I spent some of the formative years of my life in a women's dormitory where the President and his family lived. The climate was one strongly supportive of careers for women, and women's rights generally. The college, then called Illinois Woman's College (IWC), had been founded by Methodists in 1846, and it was for over a century (until 1956) one of the few colleges west of the Alleghenies devoted exclusively to the education of women. To survive, it had to convince the farmers in the surrounding communities to spend hard-earned money to give their daughters a kind of education not available at the less expensive coeducational state university in Urbana. I early accepted the notion—which I have never entirely lost—that if women are to compete successfully in the male world, they must have special preparation in colleges of their own. Coeducation did not mean to me and others at IWC so much equal rights for women as attendance at a college whose goals, curriculum, and extra-curricular arrangements were defined by men for men.

My mother was typical of the small group who in the early twentieth century had fought for higher education for women, for the vote, and against "demon rum." She herself had graduated from Goucher College in 1910, at a time when few women went to college. She was active in the church and in the temperance movement, and as the wife of the president played an important administrative role at the college. She assumed, as did others at the college, that intelligent women like my sisters should go to college and if possible have careers. Outstanding women were regularly given honorary degrees at commencement as examples of the accomplishments to which the young graduates could and should aspire.

Behind all this pressure for career development, there was always some unease, some conflict, because obviously most of the girls did not have careers, but shortly married and "settled down." Since my father was also a minister, he often officiated at the ceremony that effectively put an end to the expectation that this girl would have a career in which she could make obvious use of her higher education.

He used to like to recall that when one of the seniors came to him at graduation and asked, "Doctor Mac, will you marry me?" he answered, "This is so sudden!" As in most good stories, his answer had more than one meaning. There was an undertone of disappointment, well-concealed by humor. Although there was ample justification for turning out educated wives and mothers, there was an inevitable disappointment that more of them did not go on to make use of the great talents they had shown in class. The conflict between career and marriage was felt to some extent by all the girls, and by the college. It created unhappiness, a conviction that choosing either one would bring a certain lack of fulfillment. The pressure was particularly hard on my sisters.

There was, on the other hand, one group of women who seemed to me to be truly fulfilled. They were the unmarried teachers at the college. I had known many of them, of course, as I was growing up, but two in particular influenced me greatly; the only coed in a girl's college, I studied languages with them in the year after I graduated from high school and before I went away to college. They were impressive people—vivid, vigorous, tremendously knowledgeable, humorous, excellent teachers who cared what each individual student learned. I include them among the four or five great teachers that I have had. As far as I could see, they were not "frustrated old maids." In fact I was astonished later to discover how many men felt that "old maids" had to be "frustrated" or somehow unhappy. That was far from my experience. It is certainly not necessary for women to be wives and mothers to be completely fulfilled.

Yet to be completely honest, I had an experience while I was planning this chapter, that shed a new light for me on exactly how they led such fulfilled lives. I revisited one of those teachers, Dr. Frieda Gamper, who had taught me German forty years earlier. She was in her mid-eighties, bent over with age, but still as vigorous as ever mentally. She lived alone with her books, unable to go out much, visited occasionally by former students. What surprised me was that she was running something she called a kind of "animal hospital." She wasn't quite sure how many cats she had, but thought there might be seventeen, including five baby kittens that she fetched to show us with pride and joy. She said she suspected that people left sick animals with her because they knew she would look after them. The previous winter she had even looked after a sick cow! The message came through to me clearly: even though she had seemed to me to be the model of the assertive, proactive self-determined career woman, uninvolved with husband or children, her teaching all along had been an example of the sharing life style. When the students had gone out of her life, she had found another way of expressing her needs in sharing with animals.

From this female-oriented environment, I went east to an all-male college where the view of women was totally different from the one I had known. Talk at the fraternity house table centered on sex and aggression. Women were discussed as objects for sexual exploitation who were brought to campus three times a year for house parties; such gatherings provided the opportunities for making as much headway sexually as one could hint at having achieved. My critical view of this male chauvinism has been tempered somewhat by the realization that these "rap" sessions were functional; they prepared men for the assertive role society insists they play (Stage III assertiveness). Unfortunately there are men who never outgrow their adolescent assertiveness and who continue to think of women this way throughout their lives —justified in their own eyes for continuing to exploit women in all sorts of ways.

In the summer after my junior year, I went to a work camp in Tennessee, where I met, fell in love with, and a year later married a Quaker girl from Germantown, Pennsylvania. When I was introduced to her family, I was astonished to discover that they were part of the Quaker community which had been settled in that area since William Penn had started his Holy Experiment in Philadelphia two hundred and fifty-odd years earlier. When I took her away from Philadelphia, in fact, I discovered that she was the first member of her very large family on any side who had left the area for nine generations! It was a closely knit, strongly religious community, in which everyone seemed to be related to everyone else by blood or marriage. Knowing them was a totally new experience for me, since like most Americans I was third generation; my grandfathers on both sides had immigrated to America and their families had spread out all over the country.

What struck me particularly about the Quaker society was that the women seemed to be so much more self-assured and important in the community than even the career-oriented feminists I had known at Illinois Woman's College. They were vigorous, self-confident, and obviously influential. They were wives and mothers, for the most part, and not career women, but many had strong intellectual and artistic interests, even though few of them had gone to college. I realized that my feminist upbringing had led me to take it for granted that the "housewife" role would be weak or passive, a second best that many women had to choose. But here were women who gloried in their role, regarding it in no way as a hindrance; yet I could not dismiss them as simple homebodies. As I wondered how this could be, I realized that Quakerism as a religion gives strong support to the sharing rather than the assertive life style. Since Quakers in this traditional community did not have what they called "paid ministers," there was no male hierarchy of authority typical of most Christian churches. Everyone is equal before God, and in the silence of the Quaker meeting God may speak through anyone, male or female. Indeed, some of the best known Quaker ministers —those who spoke in meeting—were then and had always been women. For every male in the Quaker pantheon like John Woolman, who worked persuasively against slavery in mid-eighteenth century America, there was a woman like Elizabeth Fry who led prison reform in England or like Mary Dyer who was hanged for her beliefs on Boston Common. Each person served in the organization of the Society of Friends according to his or her abilities rather than according to his or her sex.

Quaker faith and practice, moreover, center on mystical communion with God, which promotes sharing power rather than that assertive power more typical of males. Thus the religion in its essence supports the life style traditionally adopted by women; and it strongly discourages the assertive, competitive Stage III expression of the power drive more characteristic of men, because Quakerism has from its beginning been pacifist. Young boys learn that they must not be aggressive and competitive; they learn, as girls do, that the ideal life style is to collaborate and share.

I found the emphasis on career muted among both men and women. When my future mother-in-law saw that I was worried about marrying so young, before my plans for the future were settled, she wrote me: "Why should it be necessary for thee to decide definitely about thy career just now? Why not plan to get married, then you will be so much more settled and adjusted that things may open out easily for thee." The life goal was to develop a certain character and to live in a simple, harmonious way rather than to achieve a career of great significance. It is the only society I have ever entered in America in which the first question asked of a man is not "what do you do?" but "who are you?" In fact I discovered that many of the women seemed to have only a very vague idea of what their men did. Though they realized of course that it was necessary to have an occupation and to earn money, that was not the most salient or valued feature of a person's life, as it is nearly everywhere else in contemporary America.

The religious culture, then, was "being"-oriented rather than "doing"-oriented, an attitude that directly favored a sharing life style. That so many women found they could live happy, fulfilled, vigorous and important roles in such a society was therefore not surprising. I came to know many such women, but best of all, my mother-in-law, Grace Waring. (Quakers do not traditionally use titles like Mrs. or Mr. because everyone is equal before God.) So I should like to present her story.

Why choose her? Perhaps I am moved a little to protest the traditional view in America that mothers- and sons-in-law never get along, because our relationship was a peculiarly productive one. Then too, she was typical of the strong women I had observed in the Quaker community. Most of all, however, I have chosen her because I have known her for thirty-seven years and still have in my possession letters from her spanning that entire time. This last is particularly important, because it enables me to present her life as she sees it, rather than as I would interpret it. One of the difficulties in writing about someone close to one, particularly a man writing about a woman, is that he may project his own needs and feelings and thoughts into his description. Hence in this account, I will try to use her own words as far as possible—her words as they have come to us in letters or in my interviews with her about this project. This is her life as she sees it, with occasional interpretations by me to explain how what she is saying fits into the overall scheme I am using in this book to sort out observations about power behavior. She herself has read it all over and agrees that I have managed to highlight some of the most important aspects of her life style.

Looked at for the moment in the framework of the power motivation syndrome, her influence has been great. As a grandmother in her seventies and eighties, she was Nana to her seven children and their spouses and to her twenty-three grandchildren and *their* spouses, Gracie to everyone else—to all the dozens of people who have come to her for counsel and support. I first felt the impact of her support and strength when I proposed marrying her daughter thirty-seven years ago at a time when I was barely twenty-one, had just graduated from college, and had what the world regarded as very uncertain prospects for supporting a wife. My family indeed thought it was unwise to undertake family responsibilities when I was just starting graduate school. One of the best-known marriage counselors of the time, whom I consulted, simply reported to me the statistics showing that the proportion of marriages contracted at my age which ended in divorce was very high. Yet my future mother-in-law decided that she had faith in me and in the marriage, whereupon she went to work very effectively, in a long and persuasive letter which I still have, to remove my own doubts about the wisdom of such a course.

I was not, after all, hard to convince, but the letter is an impressive document just the same. It recognized that the marriage involved risk, but "if we are to live at all, we must all take risks. Why not seize life and all its glory and not be afraid of it?" Pointing to the emotional dangers of a long engagement, she reasoned that once we were happily married and adjusted, I would be in a better position to face whatever uncertainty the future brought with greater strength and confidence. "The risks and sufferings and sacrifices and work and disappointments and joy and fulfillment are all worth it, *as long as you are together.*" What was most important about the letter was not the particular arguments, but the feeling of confidence and hope it created in me at a time when, though much in love, I was quite uncertain whether I could successfully manage a marriage and a career. I felt that I had miraculously found a powerful ally —a feeling that has never left me in the years since. Not only was her support spiritual and emotional; it was also practical and financial. She saw to it that both her family and mine contributed enough to our support to enable us to live during my years of graduate study.

Never was there any doubt in her mind or in mine as to where these resources came from that she shared so prodigally with me. She received that strength directly from God. "I had an unusually quiet day on Saturday and spent the whole day praying that David would make the *right* decision and that it might come clear to you both. I had no feeling for or against anything, just for the *right.* By Sunday I felt all was settled and at peace" (1951). Or a year later, "I have promoted you on my prayer list. I am not leaving you to last and going to sleep over you just because I have so much faith in you. There are too many important crises in your life and you need all the help you can get and all the light." Her words and her life express a relation to power that had begun at Stage I and progressed to Stage IV, in terms of the scheme presented in Chapter I. "It (God) strengthens me" (Stage I) "and this strength I share with others" (Stage IV), to serve and strengthen them.

Such a giving life style expresses itself in various ways. In its simplest form, it is reflected in the joy of being alive, of feeling a kind of communion or oneness with nature and the life process. "Last evening we were invited to a clambake on the lighthouse beach. There are so many lovely beaches here with rocks and some with tall, high sand dunes. It was a lovely soft evening with a cool sea breeze, dark clouds to the west, edging off into opal, and lavender, and gentle pink. There were lots of young people . . . then the stars came out and the meteors began, after we got back to our own garden" (1937). But this communion was best expressed for her always as a relationship to God, who represented a real power in the universe.

"I really deeply believe that Nana [her mother] despite all the bad psychological mistakes she made (with me, especially) had what she called 'power in prayer,' and through this power carried her children and grandchildren through many deep rivers. I know she prayed for us every day. Kids are really mystic, I believe, and feel so many things we have become too toughened to be sensitive to. I fail so much in all these kinds of faith, but now and then get hold. It is a sort of surrender to the will of God and letting power flow through. (But gosh, I know you can't help getting impatient and cross and do everything wrong— but I guess God understands and forgives just as the kids do)" (1950).

Although she often said that the two most over-used words in the English language were love and God, there was no doubt in her mind that God's love was reflected most directly and joyfully in the love of one's family and friends. She was one of five sisters, all of whom married happily and had children. Her oldest sister died in late middle age leaving a widower who was still vigorous but lonely. When after some time he decided to marry again, the whole family gathered joyfully to welcome their new sister-in-law. "We had the most beauti- ful. and blessed weekend—love and laughter ruled. Our fun began early in the morning at breakfast in bathrobes in the kitchen. I really don't see how any family could love and enjoy each other so much" (1947). Twenty-four years later she was writing, "It is that deep and tender yet questioning *sharing* of each other's lives that keeps vibrat- ing long after a visit is ended." All her family and hundreds of friends felt the warmth and joy and love and concern that she radiated wherever she was.

Put that way, her warmth sounds like a natural gift, something she was born with and spontaneously expressed. But such an impression would be misleading. She was not at all Pollyannish in her views of people; she was, on the contrary, a realist in her awareness of their faults. Some of her most pungent remarks had to do with the need to love imperfect people. "I am not afraid to love sinners, but I don't enjoy selfish ones." Or, "We have to love people but God doesn't say we have to enjoy them all." Or, "I can't help loving her, but that doesn't mean I trust her." Yet she loved sinners and never gave up believing that they could change for the better, that God might work in their lives. "Willingness to be open often involves *change,* meaning to me the possibility of *revelation.*" As part of her Quaker faith she accepted that there was something of God in every man. That idea she translated practically into the conviction that different people had different gifts, and that these gifts could be made to develop through faith and prayer —and a knowledge of scientific psychology. (That was where I came in!) She genuinely believed that every individual had in him a divine spark —represented by actual human qualities that could be developed into something of value. People who came near her sensed that she believed there was something really good in them, felt warmed by her confidence, and often tried to live up to her expectations. In other words, she regularly produced in others what Robert Rosenthal (1966, 1968) later called "the experimenter bias" effect. He found that teachers who expected their children to be intelligent indeed encouraged those children to behave in more intelligent ways (1968). In her terms she thought that belief in people's potential helped to bring them out. In my own case, she always expected great accomplishments, which I found both exciting and a little embarrassing. "Within thee, thy mind, thy soul, are all the great possibilities that must have time for full development."

Thus love, for her, meant belief in the other person's potential, a belief that people who love each other have, and that helps each bring the other out. When I scolded her sometimes for worrying excessively about accidents that might have happened to us if we were late, she would always say I was exactly right, that she did worry too much and that I was helping her by pointing it out. Not at all defensive she looked even on criticism positively. She was married twice and believed that both of her husbands helped bring her out. "They both felt I had something to express." Her first husband helped her develop socially, made her feel at ease with others. "He also thought I had psychic insight and would believe anything I would tell him along those lines." Her second husband firmly backed her in managing a large and complex family and the social concerns she developed later in life. "He had never failed me through all these years —financially, spiritually, or sympathetically. We have seen the family through some rough going too" (1949). Love for her meant mutual support and mutually positive expectations for the possibilities in each other.

As to negative things in people, she considered that it was extremely important to know about them. She was always afraid that people would not tell her things to spare her, and felt strongly that only if you knew things, even the worst, could you deal properly with them. Knowing the worst, however, was not the same as dwelling on it or expecting it to continue. When she learned something negative about a person, she would often throw it in what she called her "forgettery." She wanted to be realistic but positive. "I took care of poor little X yesterday. She is not very attractive and has a general determination and set against things. But she has character and personality and will grow better looking." She didn't believe in overemphasizing the negative. "I remember being a hateful child, screaming, sucking my thumb, biting my nails and resorting to twiddling —but I have had a *good* life notwithstanding. I don't think my mother ever nagged over these minor things."

Her general dislike for trying to correct faults in others is perhaps best expressed in this passage from an early letter, "It is only the very unusual case where the thwarted emotional life blossoms into a beautiful fruition . . . as we heard in meeting on Sunday, the pruning and cutting of the vine is not the main cause of its development, but the sunshine and good soil."

She quite literally says, and means it, that she can never give up loving anyone. When her daughter was divorced, she insisted on keeping on good terms with her ex-son-in-law and his new wife. Again, when one of her beloved grandsons was divorced, she kept close to his ex-wife and her new husband. It was not that the separations were not painful to her: they were. Yet she *could not* stop loving and caring for someone with whom she had once shared her life. Small wonder that people in trouble, particularly young people, beat a path to her door for advice and help. They sensed that they could not shock her into abandoning them no matter what they had done, and that she would go on believing in them and strengthening them to make the *right* decision.

Initially her counseling was done chiefly in her large family, but later when her children grew up, she began to take a more formal part in marriage counseling, and in helping people with troubles. When she helped set up a marriage committee in the Friends meeting, many young couples came to her for advice. She always included very down-to-earth sexual advice and information about contraception along with spiritual and emotional help. Love for her was always physical as well as spiritual. She always said she believed that "love children," those conceived at a moment of great passion, were physically more beautiful. Even in the late 1960's, when young people were supposed to be alienated from the older generation, the teenagers kept coming to her in her eighties to tell her their problems and to get her sympathy and help. "They just keep calling me up and telling me they want to come over and talk." So, at a time of life when most old ladies are minding their knitting and their canaries, she is deeply involved in discussions with young people about sex and drugs and protests against the evils of a corrupt society.

Thus she continues to live in and for others. Let her sum it up in her own words. When she was sixty-four she wrote, "I think your children are *wonderful,* wonderfully energetic! Wonderfully intelligent! Wonderfully imaginative! Wonderfully honest! Of course I may be a bit prejudiced, so don't show that to anyone. I feel that I am the luckiest of women with such a husband, such children, and what an exciting batch of grandchildren! Not to mention sisters! and friends. So the world seems full of golden light right here at the moment. Of course I know it won't last (I might even get bored if it did). The world at large is bad enough to make up." Twenty-odd years later, she writes "It is interesting to me that the longer I live and the more varied my personal experiences and sharing, the *less* I become involved with my own ego. It almost seems as if I am going slowly and peacefully down the drain and leaving beautiful and vicarious living behind." In her own mind she thus emphatically represents feminine fulfillment in the traditional sense: she shared what resources and power she had.

How did it come about? It sounds as if she must have had a happy childhood, full of love and happiness. But she didn't—at least not in her own eyes. A closer look at her early development will help us trace how what we have been calling the power need evolved in her life to the form it finally took. "I hated my mother and aunt when I heard them say that it was too bad that Grace turned out to be a girl and homely . . . I was very sensitive about it and reacted by making an imaginary life of my *very own* . . . I never wanted to be a boy. I never thought of a career, but my teachers wanted me to go to college. I wanted to but Father couldn't afford it and besides, he thought a college education would make us *unmarriageable.* I never got on well with my father. He thought I was queer and awkward and had colds in my head. But my parents did feel that I had beautiful hands, teeth, and skin." As good Quaker parents, they tried to find something nice to say about her, but in her own mind she was the Cinderella in the family in comparison with her beautiful sisters. "They thought I was so healthy I could stay home with the servants while all the family went to Atlantic City for a vacation. The day of my older sister's wedding, I got up at 5 a.m., scrubbed the floor, went and taught kindergarten before the ceremony. She was so beautiful." "I got the notion it was a good idea to be unselfish, though I later realized that it could be selfish to hog all the unselfish jobs in order to be holy. I was a little martyrish about it."

Her first marriage brought her great release and happiness. She was deeply in love with her husband, they had three children, and then not long afterwards they discovered that he had incurable tuberculosis. She suffered through many months of his last illness at a sanatorium while she simultaneously tried to look after three young children. Though she was left penniless and emotionally exhausted, the family rallied around and each contributed a little money to support her until she was able to earn a living at least partially by going back to teaching kindergarten.

Despite the fact that it had been the dying wish of her first husband that she not marry again, some years later she married a widower who also had four children and together they built a happy family. It was not easy. The children were different in temperament and were used to doing things in different ways. Competition, jealousy, dislike might easily have developed, but they did not. In the end the children became more devoted to each other than natural brothers and sisters often are. "The family worked mostly on account of Pa's firm devotion to sharing all the material and spiritual values and my warmth, love, flexibility and thinking it was really *fun* with all its problems." But disaster was never out of her life for very long. One son-in-law was killed in an airplane crash, leaving two fatherless children to care for. Then she went through the emotional trauma of her daughter's divorce —a particularly difficult experience for her, not only because it was the first divorce ever in the family, but also because she loved her son-in-law deeply.

Not long afterwards, she discovered that her second husband had a cancer, "too far gone to be operated on. He could hardly bear to tell me, but made a clean breast of it when he did. It was an awful burden for me to bear alone —so I guess I led his daughters to be suspicious. I must keep myself from entanglements so that I can give all my time to him when he needs me . . . I do not want to fail him and wish to be at his side when he goes down into the dark valley." He was to live nine more years and they were to have many happy times together, but since he was many years older than she and developed heart complications also, she had to curtail her natural desire to live life fully and remain at his side looking after him. A few years after he died, she had a severe stroke while she was out walking by herself. She fell to the ground, lost consciousness, and was partially paralyzed on one side of her body for nearly a year afterwards.

Then she discovered that her own beloved oldest son also had cancer, and once again she had to live through a period of years hoping he might survive as each new treatment was tried, but slowly watching him succumb, in the end very painfully, to the disease. After that, one of her husband's daughters developed cancer, and she watched and sympathized with her and her family as she wasted away and died. There were many other emotional and psychological problems to master, and no one should get the idea that her joy in living and thankfulness for God's gifts grew out of a life unmarked by sorrow. She had more than her share of suffering. But her view of sufferings characteristically was that they "should be assets in helping and understanding and sympathizing with other people."

To all her misfortunes she reacted with vigor and an attempt at imaginative reconstruction of the event, just as she had reacted to the initial trauma of feeling rejected by her parents. It is worth dwelling on this adaptive reaction for a moment, because it provides the key to understanding how her power motivation developed and matured. She thoroughly accepted the feeling, characteristic of Stage I, that there was a power beyond herself —God —who could strengthen her and others. As she says, in spite of all the bad psychological mistakes her mother made, she nevertheless had a power in prayer that carried her children across many deep rivers. On the other hand, since Gracie felt rejected as a child, particularly by the father who is the first object of inspiration at Stage I, there was no danger that she would stay fixated at that stage. She could not rely wholly on outside forces to be beneficent; she had to take action herself. Hence as a child and growing girl she withdrew into herself, actively creating a world full of fantasies of her very own where she could be in control. She created imaginary playmates and lived in a world of books. She was, so to speak, catapulted into Stage II where she felt: "I can have power by controlling things myself."

Although this push out of Stage I was good in the sense that it helped her mature and escape the dangers of self-love and dependency, it had negative consequences also, because it was forced. Her Stage II behaviors, being compulsive, were often an annoyance to herself and others. She was obsessed with cleanliness and getting rid of dirt and disorder. She wanted to have voluntary control of everything. She was always ahead of time and hated waiting for other people. Only in this area was she ever "martyrish," as she put it, or masochistic. "I really had dreams about all your messes. Your life sounds full of dirt and confusion . . . everything seems very peaceful and tidy around here. I am getting old maidish again and enjoying it." "I am having my usual *hellish* visit from the X children . . . they fight with each other . . . I feel as if in the last day I had aged ten years and become a completely useless, brainless, and hateful old woman . . . but I'm *not qualified* for little *children anymore!*" In fact she never was good with babies and little children because of the noise, confusion, disorder, and dirt they created. She preferred children in their teens when she could talk to them about psychological and emotional and spiritual problems, and material considerations were not part of her responsibility. She kept house compulsively well, but never in a relaxed, joyful way. She never enjoyed cooking. Her pleasure came only at the moment when all the disorder and dirt were banished.

So Stage II was not a comfortable resting place for her either. The fact that she had been forced into it in an attempt to prove herself to her parents showed up in the compulsiveness with which she carried out its activities. The fact that she was exposed to so many traumas also reinforced her rather anxious method of coping with disasters.

To her discomfort in Stage II behavior she developed two adaptive reactions. One was her strong feeling, developed very early, that more psychological *knowledge* was the way to straighten out human problems. She read Freud when his books first became popular, and "I knew I had all sorts of unconscious things in me —fascinating!" Psychology was going to straighten things out. When there was talk of developing a new Institute of Human Relations in Philadelphia in the early 1950's she wrote, "It seems to be just a combination of remote visions I had, along educational lines, when I first read Freud over thirty years ago and *sort of* realized that religion had to be tied up with some new and far-reaching science. Now I can supply the old-time religion with prayer and faith in God, and D and G can supply the science and organization." Twenty years later she was writing, "I feel far from happy about the world. I still feel that psychology is the only answer, if it can keep pure and straight. I guess not in our lifetime." The desire for knowledge is a Stage II expression of the power drive if it involves trying to create more order in the world; but psychological-mindedness represents a move into Stage III behavior for the power-oriented woman (Table 2.6).

Her other adaptive reaction to the discomforts of Stage II was to move forward to Stage III in expressing her power motivation. From the time of her first marriage, she had realized that the best way to leave the world of private, controlled fantasies was to act on the world, to move outside herself and her martryish concern with dirt and disorder to do things with and for other people. Curiously enough, when she was studying to be a kindergarten teacher, she had become absorbed in writing a paper on "self-cause." She remembers it as a very important intellectual discovery. She concluded in her paper that there is "an invisible third" (self-cause) which is beyond God (Stage I) and conscience (her Stage II martyrish tendencies). In a reaction against the simple Christian fundamentalism in which she had been brought up, she concluded that people were somehow responsible for their own lives. Thus she felt that she was not wholly determined by

God's will or by her conscience, but was free to take initiative herself in acting on the world. The tendency to take the initiative grew to be one of her strongest characteristics.

In 1937 she wrote, "But (if we are to live at all) we must all take risks. Why not seize life in all its glory and not be afraid of it?" In 1951, "One thing I have noticed is that seeking security and safety seldom brings it—certainly not spiritual security." "I feel we must go on our way, erect, not crouching, and take what comes." Shortly after her stroke she wrote, "I am happy about dying—I *think* it will be just at the *right* time. I don't think yet awhile and I don't particularly care when. I don't want my family ever to have any regrets if I should kick off after an ecstatic time. It would always be worth it." In fact, her cerebral hemorrhage had happened when she had insisted on participating in an exciting but exhausting race relations meeting in the south, at a time when she was worn out from having nursed her husband through his final illness and resettled her whole life afterwards. But her attitude always was that that would have been an ideal way to die, living life at its fullest.

Earlier, when her son-in-law had been killed in an airplane crash, she wrote, "D feels the way I do about death and tragedy. It is like meeting a heavy surf—if you turn away and try to evade the great waves, they may destroy you. Only by rising to them and diving into them and being carried by them does one find oneself safe beyond the breakers." The image is an apt one for her because she has always been a great swimmer. She enjoyed swimming hundreds of yards out to sea while the lifeguards ran frantically up and down the beach blowing their whistles at her. As she nears her eighty-seventh birthday, she still swims far out, even though in walking she is wobbly and has a hard time getting to the lakeshore and into the water. Once the S.S. Grace is launched, as she puts it, she is in her element. Swimming in the surf almost perfectly expresses her attitude towards life: she knows that she, like everyone else, will be buffeted about by the waves of life, and she has a healthy respect for powers beyond her control, but she feels that the only way to live is to meet them head-on and "be carried by them," in a kind of exhilaration of the spirit. This is a more positive way of feeling about the Demeter-Persephone theme of "giving to win": it is more like diving in to win.

She showed other characteristics of the Stage III power-oriented woman. She loved to travel. Even at eighty, when she was not physically strong, she delighted in taking the opportunity to fly to Ethiopia to visit us. An undeveloped country, far from civilization as she knew it, primitive living conditions, strange foods, long exhausting

flights—they all presented a challenge in which she gloried. Once we
were met by a Land Rover at a tiny airfield in the central mountains
near the rock churches of Lalibella to which there was no access by
road. The car proceeded to bump and tilt along the mountain track to
our destination. Although she was certain it was going to tip over—
not an unreasonable notion at all—she consoled herself with the
thought that this would be as good a place to die as any and furthermore that her soft body might cushion our fall and thus help us out!
One of her favorite quotations is from Christopher Fry's *Sleep of
Prisoners:*

> "Thank God our time is now when wrong
> Comes up to face us everywhere
> Never to leave us till we take
> The longest stride of soul man ever took
> Affairs are now soul size."

But her Stage III vigor, initiative, and assertiveness had no
quality of competitiveness or p Power in it. From the very beginning it
had been socialized into a Stage IV desire to help others. "I don't
think such a thought as to *career* ever entered my mind but I wanted to
do something special *for* people." She even considered being a missionary for a time. Then she taught kindergarten before her marriage
and after her first husband's death. As her children grew up, her
organized social concerns (Stage IV) took many forms. She was active
in the formation of the Marriage Council in Philadelphia, as we have
noted, and herself counseled many young couples and people in
trouble.

Her other great cause was race relations. Her grandfather had
travelled widely setting up schools for the freed slaves in the south
after the Civil War. She was the only one of her sisters who developed
a passionate interest in helping the underprivileged—possibly because
she felt she was underprivileged in her family. At the practical level
most of her energies were directed toward bettering the lot of the
Negro. She was active in the formation of Fellowship House, one of
the early and most successful attempts to improve understanding
between the races in Philadelphia and to get whites to accept blacks as
equals under God. Strongly pacifist by conviction as well as by Quaker
tradition, she opposed all wars from World War I on, and even served
with her husband as co-director of a Civilian Public Service Camp for
conscientious objectors in California during World War II. In 1951
she wrote, "What is really upsetting me greatly (I can hardly stand

reading any news anymore though I know I must) is that, as a nation, we are losing *everything* we *say* we are fighting for and the U.N. knows it, and all intelligent people know it, and yet we go right on down the road to destruction of our civil liberties, freedom and conscience and intellect and all the liberal thinking that should be the heritage of our children and grandchildren." In 1968, "The world of course is teetering, politics are awful, McCarthy (Senator Eugene) having a rough time. Conservatism in the saddle? Black power and integration at loggerheads and all mixed up. Philadelphia a mess. Poor people's march a failure. Steve C. and some other young Quakers in jail." So hers was by no means a private life limited to her family and friends. Her power concerns expressed themselves in attempts to do something about the state of the world to the limits of her ability.

Gracie thus represents one type of feminine fulfillment—a type seldom glorified in the history books and even rejected at this moment in American history by some leaders of the feminine movement who see her as locked into a traditional role, a victim of oppression. Always a firm advocate of woman's rights, she herself laughs at the notion that she is the "victim" of anything and worries that some leaders in the woman's movement reject fundamental femininity, which she values greatly. Though she glories in being a woman, notice that her power motive matured to the stage where she was anything but passively dependent on male or anyone else's initiative. It is true that little girls, perhaps even more than little boys, may become fixated at Stage I because they are pretty and loved and cared for to the point where they believe it is unnecessary to take initiative because the world will look after them. They may become so thoroughly enslaved in a kind of narcissistic dependence on others that it may prove necessary to stress the importance of women being proactive and self-actualizing to break those dependency ties. Yet it does not follow that the only way for a woman (or for a man) to become fully mature is to have a specialized career of the type that men so often have, just because such careers more often bring public recognition. Gracie's life proves otherwise. Her power motive matured in the sense that she progressed through all the stages without stopping at a particular level, and in the sense that she is able to express the behavior characteristic of each stage comfortably, except for Stage II. Though she would deny no woman a career, she feels that her own life has been fulfilled and that she has been one of the luckiest women ever born. She has had enormous impact on those around her. She has strengthened them and helped them sort out their tangled lives, and she has repeatedly created joy and love, even amidst suffering. All this she has done by taking initiative to share those resources with others that God has given her in her daily attempts to understand and do His will.

Notes

1. A revised and expanded version of a paper which appeared previously under the title of: "Wanted: a new self-image for women" in Lifton, R. J. *The Woman in America*. Boston, Mass., Houghton Mifflin, 1965.

2. Whenever preferences of this sort are described in the text, they are drawn from standard test instruments developed to measure "Masculinity-Feminity" of such interests. That is, the items have been selected from a large pool of such items according to the extent to which they show distinctive preferences by men or women (largely in the U.S.). An early study in this field was carried out by L. M. Terman and C. C. Miles and reported in their book *Sex and Personality: Studies in Masculinity and Feminity* (New York: McGraw, 1936). Items are drawn from their study and also from Strong's *Vocational Interest Test* and the Masculinity-Femininity Scale of the *California Personality Inventory*.

3. I am indebted to one of my students, Mrs. Ruthanne Cowan, for this finding based on coding the imaginative stories of a representative sample of Harvard and Radcliffe freshmen.

THE POWER OF GIVING: TRADITIONAL INDIA[1]

THIS CHAPTER analyzes some of the major themes in traditional Indian culture. In the process I hope to pursue two other objectives as well: (1) to show explicitly how I believe a psychological study of national character can and should be carried out, since I will be using that approach in other chapters as well; and (2) to describe in detail how a culture functions that has elevated giving—the traditional feminine life style —to a position of central importance as an expression of the power drive.

To attempt to make any generalization about India is immensely difficult and, for a foreigner, somewhat presumptuous. Not only is it a huge country with a long and complex history, but it is a tremendously varied one. Is it proper to speak of "a culture" embracing all of India? As Narain in his book *Hindu Character* observes: "The Hindus are an old and complex people. It is by no means an easy task to understand and explain them" (1957, p.34).

123

Yet many have tried, perhaps because, despite the obvious variety, certain Hindu characteristics such as the stress on non-violence or the caste system have appeared so striking, even to the casual observer. Furthermore, one suspects that the core values of Hinduism must have represented a strong unifying force in that they have managed to resist and transform several major attempts to take over the country politically by foreign invaders from the Greeks under Alexander the Great, to the Moghul emperors, or more recently to the British Empire builders. Even though such attempts were buttressed by other major religious traditions, like Christianity and Islam, one gains the impression that in some sense Hindu character overwhelmed and transformed them all. Thus there must be a hard-core unity in all this diversity, and many have sought to discover what it is —including Indian scholars like President Radhakrishnan (1948, 1957) or Nirad Chaudhuri (1966) and Westerners like W. S. Taylor (1948) or Morris Carstairs (1957). Such contributions have been ably reviewed by Narain (1957), who has also added much himself to our knowledge of Hindu character.

By what right do I try to join such a distinguished company of observers? If Narain feels handicapped by his inability to read Sanskrit or any of the South Indian languages, how much more handicapped am I —I who cannot read *any* Indian language? I have not even lived in India for any extended period of time. In fact I have made only a number of short visits there, touching base in such key spots as a North Indian village, Delhi, Bombay, Varanasi (Benares), Hyderabad and two smaller cities in South-central India —Kakinada and Vellore, while missing many important parts of the sub-continent. Perhaps my one claim to first-hand knowledge in depth is based on our intensive work over a period of years with businessmen in Kakinada and Vellore; they joined us in an effort based on modern psychology to develop the spirit of enterprise in their cities. This project has been fully written up in a book elsewhere (McClelland & Winter, 1969); paradoxically, my experience with it left me with the predominant feeling that Indian businessmen are pretty much like businessmen I have worked with everywhere else —in the United States, in Spain, in Tunisia, and in Mexico. Perhaps there is an advantage in studying a culture at a distance. The closer one gets to it, the more one becomes aware of our common humanity.

Narain has also pointed to this possibility: "to study the culture in which one is born is a double-edged affair—he can see things from within, but he cannot look at them from without" (1957, p. 186). To look at them from without, and from a distance, may give one more perspective but is also in its way extremely dangerous. If one cannot see very well or very clearly, one tends to imagine what is there. As modern psychology has demonstrated again and again, people tend to project into an ambiguous stimulus what they themselves wish and believe. Westerners have for a long time tended to create an image of the "mysterious East" which fulfills their own desires to escape from the hectic demands of an achievement-oriented civilization. From Thomas Mann and Hermann Hesse to young Americans in the 1970's extolling the virtues of the Yogic experience, the Westerner has all too often created an image of a peace-loving East in which people live out a kind of other-wordly existence unaffected by the materialistic demands that confound the West. So, while the Indian may feel too close to his culture to see it clearly, the Westerner has his special problem of coping with his need to see things that aren't necessarily there.

As if these problems were not enough, the dominant view among behavioral scientists today is that national character studies should not be attempted without national sample surveys. Inkeles and Levinson (1954) argue that the only scientific meaning national character can have is in reference to modal personality traits—that is, beliefs, attitudes or acts factually shown to characterize the mode for a random sample of the human beings living in a given nation state. Clearly no data of this kind exist for the Indian sub-continent nor are they likely to exist in the near future. From what factual base, then, are we to infer the themes that characterize Indian culture? Why attempt something that can have no scientific basis in national sample statistics?

The answer lies in my different conception of the nature of the task involved in delineating national character or finding themes in a given culture. National sample statistics are clearly helpful in such an effort, but they are not essential. To me culture is a shared cognitive system. Members of the culture learn to operate in terms of this system often quite unconsciously, in much the same way as they learn to speak a language. Though they learn to speak the language correctly—that is, according to the implicit rules of the linguistic system—they may be quite unable to formulate those rules and describe them to an outsider. It is the job of the behavioral science observer—the anthropologist, sociologist or psychologist—to try to discover those rules and formulate them as simply and parsimoniously as possible.

For this purpose it may be more efficient to go directly to the rule books rather than to infer what the rules are from the actions of modal classes of people in a culture. By "rule books" I mean those documents which lay out more or less explicitly in words the cognitive systems which the members of a culture are supposed to share. In the case of India they would certainly include such popular epics as the *Bhagavad Gita* and the *Ramayana*, as well as such other forms of popular culture as the films and proverbs analyzed by Narain (1957). I personally have found children's stories particularly useful for this purpose because they often express the general rules of conduct quite simply and directly. If they are explained simply enough for children to learn, perhaps even behavioral scientists can understand them!

The genesis of this paper lies in an analysis I made of 21 such stories sampled at random from third-grade readers used all over India around 1950 (see McClelland, 1961). I had undertaken the task because I thought the results might be helpful to the Indian business-men when they were considering the virtues of a greater achievement orientation in the light of certain traditional Indian values. We had planned to discuss the themes I had observed in the stories, reading them more or less as a clinical psychologist would, in terms of whether they promoted or inhibited the changes in the activities that these men were considering. The discussions never took place, partly because I could not be present personally to conduct them, and partly because the Indian staff responsible for the courses wondered how these "psychological insights by an American" would be received. It proved better to deal indirectly with possible value conflicts between tradition and new ways of behaving under discussion in our achievement motivation courses for businessmen.

So while I found the culture of India fascinating and its children's stories even more so, I have hesitated to publish these notes for fear of being presumptuous. I would not have done so now had it not been for the urging of A. R. Desai and D. Narain of the University of Bombay. Even with their kind invitation I hesitate to expose these thoughts to the public. The ideas are certainly less authoritative than I would like them to be, based as they are on an inadequate knowledge of Indian languages, history, religion, and culture. Perhaps the only excuse for publishing them is that they represent an approach which in more knowledgeable hands may be pushed to a more authoritative conclusion. The reader should realize that what follows is, at best, only a rough sketch of a few of the main features of the cognitive map in terms of which Indians appear to operate.

How to Analyze National Character

Let me begin by stating the nature of the task as I understand it. The goal is to explain or understand the characteristics of Indian culture —its customs, beliefs, institutions, the typical actions of members of the culture, much as I have done for American and German culture elsewhere (1958). To accomplish this purpose two steps are necessary. First, we must make a list of the facts to be accounted for; second, we must discover the fewest possible themes or propositions that seem to account for them. Possibly the themes themselves can be organized into a coherent whole on the assumption that the culture "makes sense" psychologically in the same way that a language does. The different rules should "hang together" in some way, or at least not contradict each other. This is not to say that there will be no conflicts among the various themes; but if there are, there at least should be culturally defined ways of coping with them.

What facts need to be accounted for? Obviously the universe is very large. Table 4.1 presents a sampling of such facts, some of which have figured in previous interpretations of Hindu character, and some of which have not. The list illustrates a number of points about an analysis of this kind.

To begin with, we must deal with a *sample* of facts. We could not possibly either list them all or account for them all. Furthermore, though we are sampling facts, not people, as in a national sample survey, in deciding how to do so we may follow the same principles used in sampling people. Just as a sample of people must be representative of all the different classes of people in India, a sample of facts must be representative of all the different classes of facts. If it is truly representative, the sample need not be large. There is as yet unfortunately no commonly accepted system for classifying facts, though a few simple categorizations suggest themselves. First, we ought to sample facts from different areas of cultural life —from child-rearing, from political behavior, from religion, from art and so on —from all the major categories in an anthropological handbook like *Notes and Queries*. Secondly, we should sample not only the ideal but the real. Thus we note that Indians stress the ideal of non-violence, yet we must also account for the fact that in reality they are among the most disputatious people in the world (see below). We must account not only for their highly abstract philosophy of religion but also for the fact that the common people worship tree spirits. Thus Table 4.1 includes facts of apparently very different levels of importance. There is the doctrine of Karma, which everyone would doubtless agree is of central importance, along with such apparently trivial facts as the tendency of gods and goddesses to have four hands or of people to shake their heads in a sidewise motion in conversation. According to the theory being presented here, any analysis of Indian character must account for the trivial as well as the sublime, for folk culture as well as for consciously idealized culture. To test the generality of interpreta-

Table 4.1—Some miscellaneous observations of Hindu cultural characteristics

1. Crowded occupancy of space.
2. Wide variations in personal life style (in everything from dress to religion).
3. Non-violent ideal (vegetarianism).
4. High rate of litigation and disputation.
5. High dominance and succorance (asking for help) rates in children, compared to other cultures.
6. Sacredness of the cow.
7. Why are gods and goddesses represented as having four arms and hands?
8. Caste system, dharma (duty in "calling").
9. The law of Karma (action and reaction, permanent record of merit).
10. Moksha—the goal of enlightenment, withdrawal from the world.
11. Stress on ritual purity, non-contamination (touch taboos).
12. Feeding and food offerings as signs of devotion and respect.
13. Not eating (fasts) as a means of constraining the behavior of others, showing anger, curing disease.
14. Two types of leaders—wealthy men, men of no wealth (Sadhus).
15. Yoga as self-purification.
16. Traditional restriction of freedom of movement of women.
17. Women mythologically considered dangerous, active.
18. Women have higher positions of political power in modern India than any other nation.
19. Excessive concern over privileges in bureaucracy (size of office, rug, desk, number of peons, etc.)
20. Insistence that even important men must be always available to callers in their offices, even though they are already in conference.
21. Fights between mothers-in-law and daughters-in-law.
22. Dangers of open praise for another's performance (or beauty and good health of a child). Emphasis on criticism.
23. Side-wise head shaking.
24. Love of discussion of abstract moral issues.
25. Importance of sexual imagery in worship (the *lingam* in the *yoni,* etc.).
26. Frequent ritual worship (asking for help and protection) from a variety of power figures (as gods, performing "pooja," or in real life, the "bapu" syndrome).

tions, it is desirable to include a random sampling of facts, both trivial and sublime, from all areas of cultural life.

The careful behavioral scientist will want to know when a fact is a fact. While he must agree that many Indians are vegetarians, if he is at all knowledgable, he will be quick to point out that many millions of Indians eat meat and have always eaten meat. In what sense, then, can we say that vegetarianism is a characteristic of the culture of India? Why not say that non-vegetarianism is a characteristic of the culture of India? Is the matter to be decided by majority vote? Obviously not, according to the mode of analysis adopted here. Vegetarianism is a fact characteristic of the culture of India in the sense that practically every Indian knows that vegetarianism is an ideal practiced by many Indians. It is part of his culture in exactly the same sense as a word might be part of his vocabulary which he could understand if it was spoken, even though he might never use it himself.

But vegetarianism is more important even than that to our understanding of Hindu character. If it were practiced only by a minority and the majority knew nothing about it, it could be helpful in our analysis because it is relatively unique cross-culturally. Unique, uncommon, or strange facts are particularly useful in permitting inferences about national character because of the logic of inverse probability.

In making an analysis of this kind we are trying to infer an explanation A, from a manifestation of it B. Unfortunately under normal conditions we cannot infer A from the existence of B. There are many other antecedent conditions, X, Y, and Z, that may have been responsible for B. There is only one condition under which we can safely infer the antecedent A from the consequence B: that is when A and *only* A can product B. If B is a common event like eating meat, we would be lost trying to infer reasons for it, since most peoples eat meat and there presumably are all sorts of reasons for doing so. If B is a rare or unique event, however, such as not eating meat, we have a much more restricted universe of antecedent events A from which to pick an explanation. We are then more likely to be in a position to say that A and *only* A could produce B. The reader with a more technical interest in this problem should refer to discussions of the laws of inverse probability (cf. Bakan, 1967).

But our skeptical methodologist may still not be wholly satisfied. Though he might be willing to accept the fact even without a national sample survey that the cow is considered sacred in India, he is certain to question our assertion that there is "excessive concern" over privileges among bureaucrats in India. What do we mean by "excessive"? Is it truly greater than in any other bureaucracy? What proportion of Indian bureaucrats are "excessively" concerned about privileges? It would be better if we had some statistics to answer these questions because the way the "fact" is stated implies a comparison of some kind. Thus we feel more comfortable about fact 5 in Table 4.1 because we know that careful comparative studies made by the Whitings and Longabaugh (1974)[2] have demonstrated that seeking dominance is highest and seeking help is second highest for Khalapur Rajput children in samples of children from six cultures where observations were made under identical conditions. Still, in the absence of such comparative data, we are not quite willing to abandon the statement about "concern over privileges" altogether because Indians themselves so often talk about how prevalent it is. Whether on an international basis Indian bureaucrats are more concerned than others with privileges or not, it is a fact that Indian commentators find the concern objectionable; in this sense at least the issue of privileges needs to be accounted for in any complete picture of Indian national character.

One other characteristic of the "facts" listed in Table 4.1 is that, so far as possible, they represent "observables" rather than interpretations. I have tried not to list traits such as "femininity" or "otherworldliness," sometimes attributed to Indians; femininity, which seems more of an interpretation than a fact, belongs as such in the second part of the analysis. In the first part we list the stress on nonviolence, but if we want to interpret that as meaning femininity, we have a great deal of work ahead of us yet. We would have to show that women are less violent than men cross-culturally, that Indian men are in fact non-violent, and so forth. We would also have to define other behavior characteristics of women and see if Indian men display them more than men in other cultures do.

In making an analysis of the sort proposed here, it is methodologically essential to list the facts in advance of their interpretation. Otherwise we fall into an unsystematic, anecdotal procedure of making a few informal interpretations and then looking around for illustrations to bear them out. Science is devoted to the notion of being more careful than that, of setting the facts up in such a way that they could jeopardize interpretations offered. The listing in Table 4.1 is by no means definitive. It is indeed something of a random jumble, but since it has the merit of having been made in advance of the interpretation, we cannot be accused of selecting the facts to fit the theories. If anyone does not like the interpretations about to be offered, moreover, he has an opportunity of developing his own alternative hypotheses; or he can insist that certain key facts have been overlooked and must be included in the list. When we have finished, we can look back and see whether we have accounted for all of these facts reasonably well and whether any of them are left over. Only by systematically checking our interpretations in such ways can we lay claim to being engaged in a scientific enterprise.

Given the facts, then, how do we go about finding interpretations for them? To attempt psychological explanations based on Western experience is dangerous. Suicide and suicide threats, for example, are commonly associated in the West with low self-esteem, often following desertion by a loved one. To interpret suicide threats in India in these terms, would be a mistake. Instead we must turn to the explanations Indians themselves give for what they do. There are three main sources of information on such matters. First in importance are the formal rule books—the sacred texts containing religious and philosophical explanations understood by every knowledgeable adult. Thus it is not hard to find out why cows are considered sacred in India. "The Vedic writers held cows in high regard, used them as their standard of exchange, and identified them with earth, nourishment, and motherhood" (Minturn & Hitchcock, 1963, p.268).

Great popular epics like the *Ramayana* and the *Mahabharata,* which includes the *Bhagavad Gita,* are examples of such religiophilosophical texts. Narain quotes President Radhakrishnan as saying that the *Gita* "is the most popular religious poem of Sanskrit literature . . . It is a book conveying lessons of philosophy, religion and ethics." Narain continues, "The Hindu turns to it when he is serene as well as when he is ruffled. It may be a daily ritual with him or it may be his only hope when crisis threatens. The occasions on which the *Gita* is read and its teaching are taken to heart are as numerous as they are varied. From a minor emotional disturbance to the most intense spiritual distress, the *Gita* is looked up to as the last word and the unfailing source of help. It has exerted on the Hindu mind an immeasurable influence. Its teachings have percolated down in some form or other to the common people" (1957, p.78). Narain then devotes an entire chapter to analyzing the psychology and philosophy of the *Gita.*

The *Ramayana* is scarcely less important. Told and retold down through the ages, nowadays it forms the basis for a series of films that are immensely popular in India. The student of Indian national character is fortunate to have at hand such a well-defined set of popular religious texts to provide explanations for the kinds of facts listed in Table 4.1.

Formal explanations, however, have limitations. They deal more with the ideal than with the real. So it is often necessary to interview ordinary people to find out just how they understand formal religious and psychological doctrines. Minturn and Hitchcock (1963), for example, report that Rajput adult men understand very well the principle of non-violence which they accept as a traditional Hindu ideal. When asked by anthropologists about quarrels and stick fights, therefore, they at first deny any knowledge of them. On further questioning by an Indian adult male like themselves, however, they admit that fights occur frequently and that in fact they encourage their boys to learn how to defend themselves in stick fights. Here the formal rule about not fighting was being supplemented by an informal norm that encouraged fighting in self-defense.

To take another example, many abstract philosophical explanations can be found for the law of Karma, some of which sound like scientific determinism; but the way it is understood by an ordinary man should also be taken into account. Minturn and Hitchcock report, for instance, that "a Rajput man explained this concept by saying that God keeps something which resembles a court file. During the course of a man's life his meritorious deeds are entered on this file, together with his sins. The file is first consulted when the man dies. At this time the balance between his good deeds and his bad deeds determines the length of his soul's stay in a 'small heaven' . . . The file is consulted a second time when the soul is to be reborn. This time the balance between good deeds and bad determines the status into which the soul is to be reborn" (1963, p.276). Whatever the merit of this explanation in abstract philosophical terms, it is important for trying to define the themes characteristic of Indian culture.

Finally, there is popular literature —the films and proverbs that Narain has analyzed or the children's stories that form the basis of our analysis. Popular literature often provides clues for psychological interpretations unobtainable in formal texts. Suppose we wanted to know why Hindu gods and goddesses sometimes have four hands. The *Ramayana* makes clear that as a symbol of their power demons have a hundred hands. But why are hands a symbol of power at all, and why are extra hands also attributed to gods? One of the children's stories suggests the psychological meaning. A tailor is given one wish by a tree spirit he has disturbed. He dreams of becoming a king, but his wife insists that he ask for two more hands. "With four hands you could make more cloth, sell it and make more profit." In other words, hands are for making and getting things, for increasing the exchange one has with the world. Giving and receiving are central attributes of existence, a fact the gods symbolize by having extra hands. One might have guessed this in advance, but finding it in a text diminishes the likelihood that the interpreter is putting his own thoughts into the explanation.

To take another example, we also find in the stories an instance of a suicide threat. A crocodile has befriended a monkey, but unfortunately the crocodile's wife conceives a desire to eat the monkey's heart, and insists that her husband get it for her.

Immediately the he-crocodile told his wife, 'How can you make such a request! How can I ever kill my friend? If you want, I will get you some more fruits.' The she-crocodile threatened her husband and said, 'If you don't get me the monkey's heart, I will go to the land and commit suicide.' Now what could the he-crocodile do? With tears in his eyes he went near the monkey.

The suicide threat has nothing to do with grief or mourning over a lost love object, as such an act would be interpreted in the West; instead, it is a power play explicitly designed to force somebody to do something. Although one might obtain such an explanation from an Indian informant, since such threats seem common (see Chaudhuri, 1966 and Minturn and Hitchcock, 1963), the stories provide a quick and convenient way of finding interpretations for otherwise puzzling acts. The fact that the explanation occurs in a popular text of this sort, moreover, gives it greater credibility than if it were given by one or two informants. Since the stories are read by millions of children, one can assume that they represent the shared cognitive systems of members of the culture. Here, for example, is what the translator has to say about the Hindi stories included in our sample:

> "This Reader has been compiled and published in the stage of Uttar Pradesh (Northern India) in Hindi—the language which is officially becoming the national language of the country. It is prescribed as a textbook for children aged 9 and 10 in the public schools throughout the state which has a total population of 60 million . . . The stories in this Reader are steeped in the culture of the country. They are drawn from Hindi mythology, from the great epics, from Indian history and from social customs and scenes . . . Three of the stories are from the ancient Hindu epics—the Ramayana and the Mahabharata. Every Indian, young and old, is familiar with these and can aptly quote from them. Sentries on duty and children on playgrounds shout happily from them and scenes from them are performed annually by communities throughout the country."

Indians read and speak in many different languages. Which stories were chosen for analysis? In an attempt to obtain a sample representative of the whole of Indian culture with stories from different cultural-linguistic areas, we chose 21 stories completely at random—six from Hindi readers, seven from Telugu readers, and eight from Tamil readers. Although the sample is short on stories from North India and the Hindi-related languages, this fact compensates somewhat for the North Indian bias that appears in our other sources of information, in particular the detailed anthropological account of the Rajputs of Khalapur. Furthermore, a comparison of the themes found in the three sub-sets of stories suggests that they do not differ in major ways. Rather they support the impression that, despite linguistic-cultural differences, there are common themes that run through the popular culture of India.

The themes were arrived at inductively beginning with an analysis of the children's stories. The various ideas in the stories were gradually sorted out and classified under major headings, which were then used in an attempt to explain such facts as those listed in Table 4.1. Since it would be tedious to take the reader through this laborious process, we shall reverse the procedure and present the themes that were arrived at as the end result of the analysis.

Giving and Receiving

If I were to sum up the core theme in Indian culture in one word, I should choose the word *giving.* No one word is adequate for so awesome a responsibility, but if it is understood in its fullest sense, *giving* does the job fairly well. Giving implies a giver, a gift, and a receiver. It also implies an *exchange,* an event that takes place in time with a beginning, a middle, and an end, and that can occur over and over again, and is not going anywhere in time —as for example in a means-ends progression like building a road across a country. One might almost refer to India as the recycled society. Let us try to put all this into a sentence.

1. GIVING AS A KIND OF REPEATED EXCHANGE IS AT THE CENTER OF THE NATURAL AND MORAL UNIVERSE

This basic idea is formulated at many different levels of abstraction in Hindu culture. In the *Upanishads,* theological texts written in the 6th century B.C., "the Absolute is described as a Being not only transcendent but also immanent. All created beings are only His partial manifestations" (Sarma, 1961, p. 23). Each man's soul, the Atman, represents a portion made manifest of the world soul, the Ultimate Reality, Brahman. "The souls of animals, plants, and even inanimate objects are merely separate manifestations of this world soul" (Minturn & Hitchcock, 1963, p. 269). These material manifestations of course keep changing. Men, as well as plants and animals, are born, live for a while, and die. Thus a gift, so to speak, of the world soul is made manifest for a time in a man's life; but when he dies, he is reabsorbed into the infinite. Man's ultimate goal, indeed, is to return to and become one with the world soul, so that Atman and Brahman become one. The idea of an exchange between the spiritual and the material world, of a going back and forth between the divine and its manifestations, is explicit in this doctrine. As we discovered in Chapter 1, belief that reality is fundamentally psychic is characteristic of a Stage I power orientation in males.

At a more concrete level the Hindu conception of Trimurti or the three-fold form of God also expresses the same idea. God is to be worshipped in his creative aspect (Brahman), his protecting or preserving aspect (Vishnu), or his dissolving or destroying aspect (Shiva). Once again this image seems to symbolize the "gift of life" or a concrete manifestation which comes into being, lasts for a while, and then dissolves into the original source of creation. If this idea of exchange, or recycling, is central, we are not so puzzled to find that the gods are often pictured as having four hands—not only those concerned with wealth like Ganesh and Lakshmi, but the three main aspects of God himself—Brahman, Vishnu and Shiva. The extra hands symbolize, as we have already noted, exchange, giving and getting power, which is of the very nature of God. The world is made up of an endless series of exchanges between the spiritual and the material world, and it is the nature of the gods as personifications of this process to be involved in, or to facilitate, those exchanges.

The idea of exchange was worked into a moral code for man in the law of Karma. A man is supposed to build up merit in one manifestation as a living person so that he can be reborn at a higher level in his next incarnation, until finally he is able to escape material manifestations altogether and become one with the divine world soul. The notion of giving and getting now becomes considerably more concrete, with strong moralistic overtones. One of the children's stories explains in down-to-earth ethical terms what is involved in this birth-death-rebirth cycle of all men. It begins:

> "The world is an illusion. Wife, children, horses and cows are all just ties of fate. They are ephemeral. Each after fulfilling his part in life disappears . . . As long as we live, it is wise not to have any attachments and just think of God . . . Don't get entangled in the meshes of family life. Just to learn that wife and children are ties of fate, listen to this story."

The story then goes on to tell about a man who took his child as soon as it was born out to the graveyard and asked, "Who are you? Why are you born to me?" The child replied that in his previous life he had sold the man a load of wood but was not paid for it. "I am born to you so that I can get it." So the man gives him what he owes him, and the child dies. After this happens a few more times the wife begins to suspect that her husband is burying live children. Finally, however, a child is born to him who actually owes him money from a previous existence. Hence the child will stay alive so long as the parents never collect this debt by taking anything from him. Unfortunately one day after he has grown up, his mother accidentally picks up some money that belongs to him, and immediately he dies because he has paid his debt to them.

What are we to make of this strange story? The idea of exchange has now been given a distinctly moral tone. It involves concrete obligations of one individual to another. A child is born to collect a debt or to pay a debt. Life represents so to speak an incomplete exchange. As soon as the exchange is correctly completed, the person dies. Ideally it would be better to escape the whole business —a theme to which we return below. For now it is enough to note that giving and getting are central, and that they are part of a prescribed code governing interpersonal obligations.

The central idea of giving or exchange can be broken down into several subsidiary themes which may be more explicitly stated. Implicit in what has already been said is the notion that the world soul, the source of life, of everything given, is clearly superior to any of its material manifestations; and it thus deserves to be worshipped either in its personifications as various gods or as an abstract principle. The reverence for the creative life force is often coupled with an explicit or implicit rejection of its opposite, the world of matter; but since the rejection of the material world has other deeper motivational roots, we will postpone a discussion of it.

The second theme may be summarized then as follows:

2. WORSHIP EVERY LIVING THING AS A GIFT OR MANIFESTATION OF THE DIVINE

The respect Indians show for living things —even including plants and animals —is too well known to need elaboration. Some of its obvious forms include: representations of animals as major gods and heros (Ganesh, the elephant god; Hanuman, the monkey god); vegetarianism (arising from dislike for killing animals); non-violence (because aggression is likely to cause injury to life); and respect for the cow, which has become particularly symbolic of the nurturant, life-giving force in the universe since it yields so many valuable products —calves, milk, curd, butter, urine and dung —all of which are sacred even among farmers today (Minturn & Hitchcock, 1963, p.269). Water is also actively worshipped, especially in the holy river Ganges, as a representation of the divine life force which heals, purifies, and strengthens, just as it produces crops in the dry plains of North India. The prominence of sexual imagery in various aspects of Hindu religion can also be derived from this theme, for the sexual act symbolizes particularly well the workings of the creative principle in the universe. It involves exchange which is symbolized by the lingam or phallic-shaped stone (male principle) resting in the yoni or saucer-shaped stone (female principle) in thousands of temples throughout India. Certain priests to Vishnu use a similar sign painted on their foreheads, a straight line penetrating a semi-circle, representing coitus. Sexual Union (Maithusra) creates life, and a child is particularly valued as a representation of the divine life force. Thus, fertility in women is highly prized. Not only is pregnancy celebrated by a special ceremony, but a prominent abdomen is an object of pride and display among traditional Indian women, not something to be hidden as long as possible, as in some Western cultures.

Worship for life is illustrated in one of the children's stories called the "Child Monster." It gives an "ant's eye" view of what a "monster-child" is like whose height is "like a small hillock" and who "killed hundreds of people (ants) with his hands and feet and for the sake of play." The moral is clearly drawn: "We should not give trouble to insects like ants and flies . . . Those who do not sympathize with living beings are like monsters." Worship for life, however, does not automatically imply sympathy for the individual living being. Indians can be cruel to animals, leaving them diseased and starving, twisting bullocks' tails until they are broken, etc. Such acts are not seen as inconsistent with respect for the divine spark so long as they do not put it out. Pain and suffering too are to be honored as part of divine creation.

If one worships a kind of life-giving force, it is a logical moral step to infer that if one wants to be a good person, he should imitate that divine principle by giving also.

3. ATTAIN MERIT BY GIVING

In its simplest and earliest forms giving took the form of sacrifice or *Yajna*. "Rita was originally the order of natural events such as the succession of seasons or the harvest of crops. But soon it came to mean not only the cosmic order but also the moral order . . . The order of the universe was supposed to be maintained by sacrifices. In fact, according to the famous *Purusha-Sukta,* the universe itself is the result of a sacrifice performed by the gods. Thus Yajna or sacrifice became the means, and *Rita* the end" (Sarma, 1961, p. 5). These gifts or sacrifices were a way of imitating the divine creative force and a way of initiating an exchange with the gods. Animal sacrifices were early abandoned as violating respect for life. They were replaced by gifts of food, specially prepared, as they are for nearly all Hindu ceremonies to this day. Such gifts of food among the village people are interpreted as exchanges with the gods —either in the form of *do ut des* ("I give in order that you give") or *do ut abeas* ("I give in order that you stay away") with particular reference to the disease goddesses. It is still common in Benares, as you start off on an ordinary journey in a car, to make a gift to Durga, one of the manifestations of death, that she may stay away. Ceremonious giving of food to divinities and upper castes is common in Indian village life (Minturn & Hitchcock, 1963, p. 275). Brahmans, for example, representing as they do the most spiritual class, are fed by the lower classes and provide spiritual guidance in return.

Self-sacrifice is the most meritorious form of giving. One of the children's stories is about a king (Emperor Shiva) who agreed to give protection to a dove pursued by a hawk. The hawk was indignant, arguing: "I am dying of hunger. How can you take away my food? This dove is my food. If I die of hunger you will commit the sin of killing an animal." Note that the hawk is well aware of theme 2 above (worship of life, in this case, his own). So the king in order not to harm either the hawk or the dove finally cuts off his own flesh and says, "Eat me." The story ends with the statement that the gods were pleased and sent him to heaven. The moral of the story is that the most meritorious form of giving is literally of one's own resources —of one's own flesh if other food is unavailable.

The Rajput mothers have difficulty controlling their children because they cannot conceive of punishing them by withholding rewards. "What we have, we give," they say over and over again (Minturn & Hitchcock, 1963, p. 29). At a practical level self-sacrifice often takes the form of fasting, as when wives go without food to help their husbands recover from an illness. The reason self-denial is so meritorious apparently lies in the fact that it represents an attempt to reject the material world and to become one with the divine spirit of the universe (Themes 1 and 2 above). Self-sacrifice is an attempt to become holy.

Here is also another reason why aggression is considered so bad. It not only can result in the sin of wiping out a life; it is also the direct opposite of the most meritorious act, which is to sacrifice oneself in the act of giving and becoming one with God.

It also is clear that one must: 3a) *accumulate in order to give.* This is exactly the formula we found in Chapter 2 to be characteristic of power-oriented women.

We now begin to run into some of the conflicts within the Indian value formulas. At first sight it seems paradoxical to ask a person to get (which is the opposite of giving) in order to give. Yet how can a person give if he has nothing? The paradox is reflected in the respect Indians give not only to poor wandering Sadhus with no worldly possessions but also to men of wealth and power. In the Rajput village the leaders are clearly those with the most possessions in land and worldly goods. The Indian businessmen repeatedly wrote stories about men who were successful and became wealthy *so that they could be of service* to the people.

The contradiction is more apparent than real, though it can at times lead to interpersonal difficulties. The norm is explained in a children's story about some birds that deserted a banyan tree after they had eaten all its fruit. The tree complains: "Til now the birds were living happily with me. Now I have neither leaves nor fruit. Therefore . . . they leave me. Only if we possess something will people go after us." The moral seems to be that respect comes from having material things like fruit to give to others. But the author of the story draws a somewhat different moral. "Boys! The words of the tree are true. Therefore you must read well. Only if you read well you can live well. Then all people will be searching after you." Apparently knowledge, such as the knowledge obtained from reading, is like material possessions; it too can be accumulated and given. It is for this reason that the Sadhus and wandering holy men must be respected. Though they have no material possessions, they have accumulated wisdom and spiritual merit which they can share with or transfer to others.

There is also the notion implicit here that: 3b) *giving exhausts the giver* (the tree has no more fruit). In a sense then all giving is self-sacrifice, because it involves giving away one's resources, and one must constantly store up resources if one is to go on giving. As a curious example of this point, Carstairs (1957) has noted that loss of male semen is considered debilitating, so much so that one drop of semen is equivalent to the loss of forty drops of blood.[3] Summed up in this idea are several of the themes already mentioned: semen as representing the life force is valuable; it is given in an exchange which starts life; but the gift weakens the giver; it is in a sense a sacrifice of the self which is the most meritorious form of giving.

4. GIVING EXPRESSES POWER NEEDS

At the empirical level we have reported in Chapter 2 that giving can be a means of expressing the power need, especially in women in the United States. We have also examined what we called the Demeter-Persephone life style in which the individual, often but not always a woman, finds ultimate satisfaction in giving. What is fascinating about traditional Indian culture is that it has institutionalized giving as the central value in life. Hence we have an opportunity to examine in detail some of the personal and social consequences of making a "feminine" life style the normal way of expressing the need for Power. In the United States and Western Europe, sharing is a secondary or alternative mode of expression, while the "masculine" direct assertive or aggressive mode is primary. The reverse is true in India, where men are trained to respect most what the West reserves as a life style suitable for women.

If this contention is correct, women should have a position of greater strength in India than in the West, since they at the very least have a superior natural claim to resources in a giving-oriented culture. Indeed the ultimate creative force in the Universe, Shakti, is feminine. Like the sacred cow, women produce children and provide milk to nurse them, in ways biologically denied to men. Here a "rule of nature" should help establish feminine merit. The mother-son nurturing relationship is in fact particularly important in India, as we shall see. At a more practical level, legal ownership of property like a house is normally vested in the wife, not in the husband as in the West, because she is the one who controls resources. In folk tales and mythology, women are depicted as wielding considerable power. The female consorts of the gods Shiva and Vishnu are more active than the rather passive males. The goddess Kali is enormously aggressive, maiming and chewing up human sacrifices.

In the children's stories, the crocodile's wife forces her compliant husband to go after his monkey friend's heart, and the tailor's wife forces him to ask for another pair of hands even though he wants something else. In modern films, Indian wives often play very forceful roles, even to shooting lovers (see Narain, 1957). But usually they are seen as bad—powerful but dangerous. It is almost as if the men realized that women have a superior natural claim to merit in the Indian value system and that therefore they must be checked and confined. In traditional households women could not even leave the courtyard after marriage. As these "old-fashioned" checks on women's power are eased in the modern sector, Indian women have risen to positions of greater political leadership than in most other cultures. Both they and the men know that in a value system which stresses power from accumulation of resources, they have a special claim to strength. The current Prime Minister of India, Mrs. Gandhi, is not just an isolated example. The prime minister of Sri Lanka is also a woman, as are several chief ministers of Indian states. Women may also be chosen because, as we shall see, men get into difficulties trying to seek leadership by sacrificial giving. Thus, a woman becomes a natural choice both because she avoids intense competition among men for leadership positions and because she has a natural claim to superior strength in the Indian value system.

Such analyses make the study of national character valuable for studying the behavior of nations. One might well be curious as to why women are political leaders in India and not, say, in Mexico. Political theorists or historians tend to fall back on *ad hoc* explanations in terms of particular individuals or events. But armed with a knowledge of power-related themes in the two cultures, they would have no difficulty in understanding why women would be likely to be political leaders in India, and very unlikely to be in Mexico.

Even where there is no superior natural claim to merit by virtue of one's sex, power struggles are apt to develop in ways that are clearly outlined in Indian stories. Everyone there is out to win a competition for superior moral merit, which is a power goal—that is, to be a bigger, more worthy, or more respected person, who will ideally be reborn in a higher status. Such a competition for merit through giving inevitably involves people in certain difficulties, the reasons for which are not always explicit. Four such reasons can be discerned.

4A. GIVING IMPLIES A SUPERIOR-SUBORDINATE RELATIONSHIP

I can give only what others will receive. If I give and you receive, I by definition have more resources and more power than you have. This can make for trouble. You may think you are my equal and not like the idea of the inferiority implied in taking something from me. Not many years ago there was a famous international incident when Mrs. Gandhi, the Prime Minister of India, said in public that the United States got more out of all the billions of dollars of aid it had given India than India had. Whatever economic gains she may have had in mind, she was certainly speaking correctly within the framework of Indian values. The act of giving itself is meritorious, and India in accepting gifts from the United States was acknowledging its superiority—which India was not happy about. President Nixon, responding within a very different value framework, did not understand what she was saying. He immediately recalled the United States Ambassador, and a few days later a new program of aid for Pakistan was announced. The U.S. was saying in effect, "If you don't appreciate our help, we'll give it to someone else." But this attitude implies that giving is a means to self-gratification or to gaining one's ends, which is not at all meritorious in the Indian value system. All in all, it is difficult for an Indian to know where he stands in the giving game. He should be generous to inferiors and they should acknowledge his superiority with respect, but he had better be careful to even things out with equals, and himself to give respect and gratitude to superiors who have given to him.

Above all, he owes respect to his parents since they have given so much to him from the time of his birth. In one very well-known story, Ganesh (the elephant god) won a competition to see which god would be worshipped first by showing the greatest respect for his parents. The Creator had decreed that the god who was first able to circumnavigate the universe would be worshipped first. While bigger and stronger gods hastened off on their journeys, Ganesh rode a mouse around and around his parents, and won because he had defined them as the "universe." Note the implicit message of this story: everyone is in a competition for merit, the object of which is to see who will be worshipped first (be the biggest god). But superiors, especially mothers, have a way of finding out that they can control other people's behavior in a system like this by giving more, and thus demanding more in return. This situation can lead to real power games.

In response to Professor Maslow's published request for more information on the lives of normal people to balance the abundance of information on pathological cases, an Indian banker whom we will call AB kept a revealingly honest diary of all his thoughts and activities over a period of nine days. Many of AB's thoughts had to do with his mother, who lived with his family.

"I then called my mother to the pooja (worship) room and prostrated before her. I wept. She wept. In the process, my forehead struck the floor with some force. It did not hurt me, however. Just a small bump for some time. What a feeling of relaxation and an understanding of mother and son, I thought! I remember her telling me some time back that I did not like her. Such remarks she passes often, without meaning too much by them perhaps, but they still are irritating. After all, I am her only living child and she prays for me nearly 16 hours a day! She has to be tolerated."

Not only that. He had to do what she wanted. He had a little dog that he loved very much, but the dog startled his mother, and made her unhappy. So he had to give the dog away. After all, she prayed for him sixteen hours a day, etc. The mother's sacrificial giving was a powerful tool in controlling his behavior, and he was obviously ambivalent about the power bind that he found himself in with her. He felt manipulated by her and inferior in power, because she has the superiority of having given so much to him.

Chaudhuri (1966) is particularly eloquent as to how a wife can use her sacrifices in fights with her husband. He sees the Hindu wife as exhibiting "the split personality most typically. In one of her personalities she does not seem to remember any grievance, and goes about quietly doing her work, and even shows affection to the husband. But once a quarrel has begun, it does not remain limited to the occasion; every quarrel since the day of the wedding is recalled; all the grievances become connected; in retrospect the sorrows gain accumulative fury, and the anger is poured out in red hot streams of lava. Listening to the words, one would naturally imagine that a resumption of married life could not take place, and as long as the fit lasts both the husband and wife think so. But in actual fact no such calamity comes about . . . So one might say that for most Hindu husbands the wife is a beautiful bath of gleaming porcelain with both cold and hot water taps, with this difference, however, that the taps are not under control but flow as they list, and by turns the husband is bathed in the cool spray of love or scalded in the geyser of anger" (1962, p. 277). Chaudhuri has described with wit and vividness how the moral code of being a self-sacrificing wife can result in a tremendous reserve of hostility if the husband does not appreciate sufficiently what she is doing. As the story of the crocodile's wife makes clear, suicide threats on the part of a wife are also bald power plays aimed at forcing the husband to do something she wants. In short, self-sacrifice may seem highly moral, but it can also be an ill-disguised power play. The superior moral position of having given to another can be used to dominate the other person directly—and Indians know it.

That renunciation, yielding, and self-sacrifice often serve only to mask a strong urge to power, is clearly recognized in the children's stories. A bird and a rabbit had a dispute over property rights and went to search for someone to settle it. They finally "found a cat sitting by the side of a small pond. He had a string of beads on his head. He had had his bath in the pond, applied sacred ashes to his forehead and started contemplating. The bird and the rabbit thought he was a saint." So they decided to ask him for help in settling the dispute, but the cat claimed he was hard of hearing and insisted that they come closer. They were a little afraid, but he reassured them as follows: "Don't you see what I am now? I have committed many sins in my life. I am waiting for my death. What more hatred have I got? I am just thinking of God and spending my life. So don't be afraid." So they came closer, got lost in their argument until "the cruel cat caught them within his paws all of a sudden and killed them."

In another story a tiger got so old that it could no longer search for its food. It sat "with a golden bangle by the side of a lake with eyes partly closed like one who performs penance." A traveler saw him and started to run but the tiger called out: "Brother, why are you running? I don't kill lives. If you come to me, I shall give you the golden bangle." The hapless traveler drew near to get the bangle, got stuck in the lake, and was killed by the tiger. The message of such stories seems clear: a superior moral humility all too often is a means of getting power over others.

4B. THERE IS A DANGER THAT GIVING WILL NOT BE NOTICED

Indian children are taught that they must not be assertive, and that the best way to win recognition is by being modest and self-sacrificing. In one story the teacher decides to hold a "beauty contest" and to award a prize of a book and play material to the child who appears most beautiful. The girls in the class are very much excited, put on "their best dress and ornaments and beautify themselves." Note that the competition is over a resource—an asset like beauty—not over an achievement like who can spell the best or solve the most math problems. Sakuntula was the prettiest and her parents thought she would win the prize, but Rupavathi wore the costliest ornaments with great pride; Sakuntula became jealous and refused to speak to her. But the poorest girl, Valliyammal, won the prize although her face was black and she had given away her only ornament. She won because she was not proud, but was cheerful, and self-sacrificing. The nature of the goal of the contest—who has the most merit in terms of assets—is clearly stated and also the means of winning it—by being humble and self-sacrificing, and by not trying to win.

The insistence that one must not *seek* resources is so strong that it seems counter-phobic, as if everyone recognized that the pressure to do so is very great in a system that requires people to accumulate resources to attain merit. Indian mothers, for example, report that they almost never use praise as a technique of teaching children because "praising children 'to their faces' will spoil them and make them disobedient" (Minturn & Hitchcock, 1963, p. 325). In hundreds of observations these authors found only one or two instances of a parent praising a child (p. 326, p. 359). Instead, the children were constantly criticized and scolded; the work they did around the house was belittled to others, etc. Why? It is almost as if praise would bring to the surface in an unbearable way the wish for recognition or need for Power that is being stimulated all the time. If a child were praised, that might encourage him to be proud and to seek merit directly by aggressive action rather than by renunciation and humility as practiced by the girl who won the beauty contest.

But what if nobody notices that you are being humble and giving things away to others? In theory of course it shouldn't matter, because you will gain merit in the next rebirth; but in practice, as such stories make clear, one should get recognition in this life as well. The banker tells what happened in a case of this sort that happened to him. After getting out at a station stop he returned to his compartment in the train, to discover that a man and his wife and daughter had taken his and his companion's seats despite the fact that they had left their belongings there. He spoke to the station master about it and discovered that the man was a doctor who worked for the railroad. He refused an offer of help from the station master. "I told him that the so-called doctor had no concern for others. He volunteered to help me and enquired whether I felt any inconvenience by the doctor's occupying the compartment. I assured him I didn't feel any and would make myself comfortable . . . The train started. I never went inside my compartment . . . The conductor asked me to take the seat meant for him in the corridor. I said I was comfortable. I thought I must convey to the doctor my feelings, that I wished him to have some concern for others, not only for himself and his family. I went inside and took my book . . . (he paid no attention) . . . I inquired if he was comfortable. He said 'yes' and made no other response to my inquiry."

AB was getting more and more disturbed that the doctor took no notice of what was happening. Finally he persuaded his companion to sit on the same small conductor's seat with him in the corridor and got the conductor to go in and ask the doctor if he wouldn't step outside. "I was sitting with my hand on the shoulder of my friend, in a very comfortable posture and told the doctor that we were very comfortable. He appeared disinterested—a selfish fellow, I thought."

At that point AB exploded. Having tried in every way he could think of to get the doctor to acknowledge the merit of his sacrifice, and failed, he finally "told him point blank that he did not have the least concern for others. He did not have the ordinary courtesy even to ask whether we would like to sit inside, when I inquired as to his comfort." This incident shows how self-sacrifice can on occasion misfire: people are supposed to notice and respect it. Although AB kept insisting he was comfortable, which was meritorious giving, unfortunately the doctor didn't notice the sacrifice, even when it was stuck under his nose. He simply accepted the sacrifice. Nothing could be more frustrating in such a system, for there is always the danger that trying to get something by not trying to get it can simply fail —if others don't notice and reward you for not trying. Hence the importance to AB of educating the doctor to show a concern for others.

4C. MORALIZING POWER NEEDS ACCENTUATES CONFLICT

AB was not allowed by the Indian value system to get his seat back simply by asking for it. Though that seems quite proper, say, to an Englishman or an American, it would have seemed to him selfish. I recently observed an English couple face a similar situation on a Ceylonese train, where someone was sitting in one of their seats. The man simply and directly, but authoritatively, asked the man to move, in a tone of complete assurance that brooked no questioning. An American might have tried to soften the blow by apologizing or making a joke of it so as to avoid conflict, but he would almost certainly have asked for his seat back. Both would regard such assertiveness as normatively quite permissable, in fact desirable; but not the Indian. The necessity to disguise one's assertive desires in the form of doing good to or for others can lead to some extraordinary tangles and more than ordinary conflicts among people; one side feels unjustly treated, as AB did, and the other manipulated in the name of morality for a personal end, as the doctor did.

The result is that the Indian stress on non-assertiveness seems to lead to *more* conflict than if direct assertiveness were allowed. Minturn and Hitchcock (1963) found the average man in Khalapur had been engaged in an unusual number of legal fights. The Whitings also reported (1974) in their observation of children from six cultures that in India both boys and girls turn out to *dominate others* more often than children from any of the other cultures; whether older or younger, they spend more of their time telling each other what to do than children in any of the other five cultures. In the light of the constant advice to be humble and non-dominating, this finding seems paradoxical. Yet it can be understood in terms of the need to express one's power through reminding others to be good. Its seeming paradox lies in the natural tendency for pro-social dominance, to use the

Whitings' terms, to short-circuit into ego dominance. For a child to say to another, "Stop eating that, it will make you sick" is perfectly all right in the value system: it is pro-social dominance or giving good advice to another, like AB's advice to the doctor to show concern for others. The admonition often shortens, however, simply to, "Stop eating that," with no reason given for the command other than that "I (an important person, commanding much knowledge, having prestige, etc.) tell you to do it." Thus what in the formal value system is a good (pro-social dominance) readily turns into something which the same system regards as bad (ego-dominance). Small wonder that Indians often see themselves as two-faced because in the effort to become holier than the next person they end by being at times extraordinarily unholy to each other.

4D. CONFLICTS ARISE FROM COMPETING FOR RESOURCES

Though people are encouraged to accumulate resources so that they will have something to give, the effort often appears selfish to another who might have wanted the same resource so that *he* could be generous with it. In this context one can understand most easily the extent to which Indian bureaucrats become emotionally involved over the privileges they are entitled to. Why should they care whether they are assigned a larger office, a larger number of *peons,* or a car with a driver? In many cases these items are not demonstrably related to doing a more efficient job of work. But they are tremendously important if one is seeking to be in a position to be of service to other people. One must accumulate resources in order to give, and privilege represents resources.

I know of an instance in which the head of a Government of India's Institute was upset because it seemed to him his car was being driven too rapidly through a crowded section of the city. Yet he could not bring himself to speak directly to the driver to ask him to slow down. Instead he had to ask someone who was in the car with him please to ask the driver to go more slowly. Why could he not speak directly to his driver? It is certainly only a half-truth to claim that he was mimicking his former colonial masters, the British.

No, the explanation lies in the Indian value system. One must accumulate resources in order to be useful. Privileges represent accumulated resources and the meritorious leader is one who can help others precisely *because* he has privileges which symbolize control over resources and put him in a position to help others and be worthy of respect. Not speaking to someone does not signify disrespect as it would in many cultures, but ideally it means: "I am maintaining a position in which I can be of service. Maintaining my distance from people is one of the ways in which I can show that I have power and only if I have power can I be useful."

Needless to say, the person not spoken to does not always see it this way, unless he is clearly of lower status. Endless squabbles and even fierce fights may break out if two people of undetermined or nearly equal status are each trying to get into the position of having more resources, power, and privileges than the other. Yet it is obvious to Indians that these unseemly struggles for power are directly opposed to the part of their value system that stresses humility and self-sacrifice. Thus the Indian who told me the story about the Institute head and his driver was very critical of him for behaving in this overbearing manner.

Newspapers in India are more critical of men in power than perhaps any other newspapers in the world. Chaudhuri in *The Continent of Circe* excoriates practically every person or group in Hindu society that might have any pretence to power. He seems, indeed, to like only the aboriginals or tribal peoples—presumably because they have no claims to any power or resources whatsoever. But in doing so he is operating solidly within the value system we are attempting to describe. The irony of it all is that no one seems to realize that the system has a built-in inconsistency. It demands that people accumulate resources in order to be able to give, but then punishes them severely for attempting to do so because they violate the ideal of being humble.

Nowhere is the competition for resources more poignantly revealed than in the conflicts, proverbial in Indian culture, between mothers-in-law and daughters-in-law. Narain (1957) is a little puzzled by the intensity of this particular conflict. Why, he asks, shouldn't there be similar conflicts between, say, sister-in-law and daughter-in-law, if it is just a matter of being forced to live together? Yet the conflict is understandable if we realize that mother and wife are competing with each other to gain merit (power) by giving to the same person. The mother has expressed her power need by giving all her life to her son. Now a daughter-in-law enters the picture to threaten the mother's position of power. Though the mother usually wins out at first because of prior and stronger claims to sacrifice, the daughter-in-law begins to move in because she too is under a compulsion to attain merit by giving to her husband.

The trouble is that the husband has a limit on what he can receive. If he accepts attentions from his wife, he cannot then accept them from his mother, who becomes jealous of her daughter-in-law. On the other hand, if he accepts them from his mother, he makes his wife jealous, because she is being put down in the system of merit by her mother-in-law who is managing to do more for her son. The situation is made worse by the fact that the fierce inter-personal competition is disguised and moralized in terms of self-sacrifice or giving. The husband/son understands well enough that there is some kind of struggle going on, but there is little he can do to mitigate its intensity. So for the most part he tries to withdraw, and in time the young wife learns to turn her attentions to her son rather than to her husband.

Competition over resources is a major theme in the children's stories. Often a key problem is sibling rivalry—which child will get the father's affection by sitting in his lap (King Uttanpad and Duruv) or which one will succeed to the throne (the Ramayana). In another story, while a bird was away, a rabbit moved into his nest in the bank of a river. When the bird returned, he said: "This is my house. Get out." The rabbit replied, "How can you say it was yours? When I came here it was empty. So I occupied it." The story of AB in the railroad train all over again!

In similar fashion land disputes and arguments over prestige and preference are endemic in Indian villages (see Minturn & Hitchcock, 1963). In interviews with 38 men between the ages of 25 and 65 in Khalapur, Minturn & Hitchcock found that they had been involved in a total of 59 separate court cases, eliminating duplications and not counting the disputes that never got to court. Nearly all the cases involved control of resources—disputes over land ownership, allocation of income from land, water rights, alleged thefts, etc. In many cases the material value involved was trivial, but material gain was not the point of the dispute: the real struggle was for the respect and merit derived from control of resources. In India, as in many cultures, it is common to think that resources are by their nature limited, so that what one person gains another person inevitably loses. By definition, therefore, people are always trying to accumulate the *same* resources.

Precisely on this ground Sinha (1967) has been critical of our attempts to develop achievement motivation in Indian businessmen. Since India is a country of limited resources, motivating businessmen will only make them compete with each other more strenuously for scarce resources, and the net effect on the community as a whole will be that they will get in each other's way. Part of the belief in limited resources derives from a conviction that India is a poor country. It is a commonplace to pick up almost any Government of India publication and find sentences like, "The Indian farmer is poor and backward." He may in fact be neither of those things. It would be just as possible to write, "The Indian farmer has rich soil which is amply watered, and given the conditions under which he works he does a remarkable job of farming the land." But, as we have seen, it is against Indian values to praise or point with pride. If one is to be morally superior, one must always be critical and humble. The idea of the "limited good" thus derives in part from the Indian's tendency to belittle everything. He is convinced "there isn't enough to go around" and what there is, everyone is trying to accumulate so that he can attain merit by giving it.

How to Avoid Power Struggles

We are now in a position to understand one of the most famous passages in Hindu epic literature, that in which Lord Krishna advised Arjuna in the *Gita* to give up his attachments to the world. Arjuna is pictured as unnerved, in doubt as to whether to go into battle because it may involve killing his relatives. Krishna advises him that he must fight because it is his duty, but that he should fight without any concern for the outcome. "To action alone hast thou a right and never at all to its fruits; let not the fruits of action be thy motive; neither let there be in thee any attachment to inaction." He develops the doctrine of detachment from the world even further by arguing that sensory attachments, pleasure and pain, love and hate, all these are temporary; the wise man fit for immortality is he who remains steadfast, ignoring all of these earthly feelings and attachments.

This doctrine, extremely influential in Hindu thought, is also puzzling. As Narain points out, "Krishna's psychotic concept of mind can only lead to wholesale banning of emotions" (1957, p. 95). He goes on to say, "Krishna has outlined a chain of reactions which originates in attachments to sense objects and ends in the destruction of the individual" (p. 97). This chain may be summed as follows:

Sensations → attachment to material objects → desire → anger → bewilderment → loss of memory → destruction of intelligence → death.

The only way to escape this chain of disaster is to give up attachment to sense objects and desires altogether. But Narain asks quite sensibly, why should desire automatically lead to anger? If desires are fulfilled, they lead to pleasure and satisfaction. Krishna seems to have left out an important link in the chain of connected events; desire leads to anger only if it is disappointed. Narain points out that in terms of modern psychology this doctrine is self-defeating; it never permits a person to learn to cope with his disappointments, and to use anger in socialized ways. Frustrations, sorrow, and pain can, after all, be *constructive* forces in the development of character if properly handed.

While I agree with this analysis, it is still an interesting psychological question to ask why the author of the *Gita* overlooked this obvious psychological fact. Why did he think that desire would automatically lead to anger? Surely it is not reasonable to infer that the author of the *Gita* did not understand that desire does not always lead to anger. I would credit him on the contrary, with giving a profound expression to the central conflict in the Indian value system. Desire for material objects *will* lead to anger in a system where giving resources is a virtue of great importance, precisely because giving in India often involves a power game which results in intense interpersonal competition. In other words, giving produces the disappointments and feelings of inferiority that for all the reasons just reviewed evoke aggression. It implies inferiority in the receiver. It forces one to seek merit by not seeking it. It exaggerates conflicts by moralizing non-assertiveness. Above all, it defines merit as having resources, often completely material in nature, to share. So a person is involved in competition with others who may want the same resources. He realizes he must not compete for these resources, that he who is most humble is certain to win —and winning is important! He is almost certain to become angry at those who try to prevent him from being meritorious, at himself for being pushy (assertive) and at others for not noticing how humble and worthy he is. Both within himself and with others he is locked into power struggles that are extremely painful and self-defeating. It is not surprising that the Visuddhimagga, the definitive Buddhist commentary, states that "Lovingkindness has greed as its near enemy."

Small wonder that Krishna counsels withdrawal from such a world! He tells Arjuna that one should play the prescribed game (do one's duty), but without having any of those dangerous feelings of love, hate, attachment, pleasure, and pain that inevitably arouse hostility in such a game. The hope is, as we shall see in Chapter 6, that the person can eliminate the power drive from such conflicts by renouncing the ego's interest in the outcome, shifting from Stages II and III to IV. It would be good advice if ordinary people could follow it with any regular hope of success. And it is just one among several of the devices developed by Hinduism to cope with the psychological conflict induced by making giving the central value in the culture. It is time we turned to these devices.

5. POWER ASPECTS OF SHARING RESOURCES MAY BE MANAGED BY RENUNCIATION, RULES, REQUESTS, AND REASONING

It seems paradoxical that the simple act of giving, conceived by most cultures as meritorious, should create so much conflict in India. One cannot argue that it *must* create these conflicts, or that since giving often expresses power needs, one must therefore avoid giving. Rather the shoe is on the other foot: the conflicts arise because giving in India is so power-oriented, not because giving in itself produces them. Giving, as religious Indians note, ought to lessen the strength of the power drive. What we have tried to show, however, is how easily giving *can* produce trouble when it is in the service of a strong power drive.

We may in fact go further and speculate that giving is more apt to create these conflicts when it becomes the dominant mode for men. Cross-culturally, the image of giving is not associated with competition for scarce resources; it more often goes with an image like the miracle of the loaves and fishes or the miraculous pot of honey that is never used up. Folk tales often tell about wonderful resources that never give out or are used up, but supply all needs. The natural biological basis for such an image is the mother's breast: the more the baby sucks, the more milk the mother has to give.

If our arguments in Chapter 2 are sound, it is doubtful too that normal women perceive giving as "using up" something. The notion of scarcity of resources and of external material supplies that are exhausted in giving, seems more likely to be a male concept. Again the biological image supports this view: giving semen is like losing blood; the act of sharing weakens rather than strengthens the giver, unlike the process of nursing a baby. What we appear to have in India is a male "perversion," if one may use so strong a term, of a traditional female mode of expressing strength. If the female concept were genuinely accepted, it is doubtful that power conflicts would develop in the same way or in the same intensity, for the very simple reason that in the feminine mode sharing creates rather than uses up resources.

Men seem best able to get a feeling for this mode through meditation, mysticism, or becoming one with the Divine source, as we shall see in Chapter 6. For now we must return to how Indians regulate the conflicts inherent in the way they use giving to implement their power needs.

5A. RENUNCIATION OR NON-ATTACHMENT TO THE MATERIAL WORLD

As Indian sages like Buddha or the author of the *Gita* have stressed over and over again, one effective way to handle power struggles is to become non-attached, to *reject all impulses or desires for anything,* so that a person does not get entangled in the desires that lead to conflict. He must renounce his *attachment* to the world. Note that the notion of attachment to material objects is similar to the notion of high n Power Stage III males that a possession is something you collect (Table 2.6). So *renouncing* attachments to "possessions" has meaning to such people (Stage IV. Table 2.7).

Though a man cannot avoid acting and participating in power struggles, such as Arjuna's war with his family, he can give up all feeling or caring about the outcome of his actions. He should go through life impervious to the "slings and arrows of outrageous fortune," concentrating wholly upon God, unattached to the world of the senses and material objects. As President Radakrishnan put it, Hindus regard themselves naturally "as strangers and pilgrims on earth, fit for heaven but of no earthly use" in the sense that they seek for union with the supreme, universal spirit and regard earthly attachments as standing in the way of that goal.

The average Indian of course does not reach such a level of detachment. Yet he may manage to avoid involvement or commitment to a degree that some Westerners find extraordinary. The sidewise headshaking, for instance, so characteristic of Indian encounters is at first baffling to the Westerner. Is the man saying yes or no? The answer is that he is doing neither. He is avoiding commitment for the moment, but is attempting to facilitate the interpersonal exchange by saying in effect: "Go ahead; I read you loud and clear." My wife is an artist who has drawn people in public places all over the world—in Ethiopia, Tunisia, Italy, Mexico, Hong Kong, Thailand, Sri Lanka. The problem everywhere is that the people she draws get curious to see what she is doing. They become self-conscious and compulsively interact with her by asking her questions and interrupting what she is doing. But not in India. She found it easier to draw ordinary people in India than in any other country. They seemed unbothered by her attention, quite remote from her, as if they were indeed strangers and pilgrims on earth.

Practically speaking, this means that very young infants and old people who are about to leave the world are considered holier because they are less involved in material attachments. The death of an infant is not traditionally considered a major tragedy in a village family, since a child is a recent spark from the divine returning home unsullied by the world. In middle life Hindus recognize that they have to get involved in the material world, but ideally in old age "a man and his wife should retire to a forest and live there as celibate hermits, devoting themselves to a life of religious contemplation" (Minturn & Hitchcock, 1963, p. 274). Though few practice the ideal, it shapes their view of the materialistic world as unworthy. The hierarchy of the caste system is essentially built on renunciation of contact with the world: the most revered castes are the most spiritual and have the least contact with material things which can pollute them; the untouchables as the lowest caste must handle the most "materialistic," sense-arousing objects —like slop and feces. Rajput women cannot handle blood or fluid-stained clothes after childbirth and must wait for a lower-caste midwife to come and clean up. Anything material that arouses the senses and the passions is potentially polluting by making a person more attached to the worldly, and less spiritual.

5B. RULES FOR AVOIDING POWER STRUGGLES

Another technique for handling conflicts is to work out a set of *rules* for who does what for whom under what conditions and gets what in return. The Hindu view of the life cycle helps soften the full force of the doctrine of detachment from the material world by putting off withdrawal to the end of life. The purpose of life is fourfold, "namely, *dharma* (duty), *artha* (wealth), *kama* (desire) and *moksha* (liberation). The first three of these constitute the path of *pravritti* (active life) and have to be gained in domestic life. That is, a man has to be a member of society and discharge his duties as a householder and citizen. He has to acquire wealth, gratify his legitimate desires, and at the same time practice virtue. The final stages of life for which his whole career has been a preparation is one of *nivritti* or complete surrender and hence *moksha* or liberation" (Sarma, 1961, p. 21).

The caste system is of course the most elaborate set of rules for determining who has the resources (superior merit) to give to others. To base a claim to merit on things that have happened in previous incarnations is a useful way to avoid conflict, since the merit is not open to dispute at this time. If a man can prove by genealogy that he is a Brahman or Ksatriya (of the warrior-ruler caste), he is by definition superior to an untouchable, who must show him respect. Emphasis is placed on maintaining clan or family status by elaborating rules governing who can marry, touch, or eat with whom, or by developing genealogies claiming high status through connection with a famous ancestor (Minturn & Hitchcock, 1963, p. 216). It has always seemed paradoxical to observers that Indians who stress the virtue of humility have traditionally spent so much of their time demonstrating their status as members of a superior caste. Yet their activity is functional in that it eases power conflicts that would be inevitable if all people had equal claims to merit and had to fight out their rank with everybody else.

Bureaucracy, as we have found, can substitute for the caste system; a person may have a superior claim to merit by having a position with all the external signs of superiority—more servants, a larger office, etc. While envy still arises, at least establishing a "pecking order" by a set of bureaucratic standards helps resolve direct power confrontations. Sex too serves to regulate who gives to whom. Although at the unconscious level women are considered to be powerful because they have more to share, fear of them is correspondingly great. So they have been kept in their place until modern egalitarianism has released them and allowed them to rise to positions of exceptional political leadership—at least in comparison with cultures governed by the patriarchal myth (see Chapter 8).

Age, sex, caste, bureaucratic position have all been used to define one's power and establish rules for who gives what to whom under what conditions, thus easing power conflicts.

5C. REQUESTING HELP AS A WAY OF ESTABLISHING A MERIT HIERARCHY

A simple way to avoid competition for power in a giving-oriented society is to *request help*. The person who asks for help automatically assumes an inferior position and admits from the outset: "You are stronger and more powerful than I am. Therefore give to me." To ask for help is in itself a sign of respect, since the asker tacitly acknowledges the superiority of the person asked. A person would not ask help of someone he clearly perceived as his inferior, unless it were a service expected of someone in a clearly subordinate role. In such a system, training for self-reliance in children obviously has no merit; instead children learn to ask or demand from their parents, who clearly have superior status and are in a position to give. Indian children, indeed, show more demanding behavior than the children from four of the five other cultures studied under comparable conditions (Whiting & Longabaugh, 1974).

"The extent to which the children were capable of insistently demanding was brought home to us almost daily . . . Throughout our stay we were rarely out of earshot of the whining cry 'give me my photo' . . . Nor did the mothers reprimand their children for this persistent begging. Many mothers were, in fact, only slightly less demanding in this regard than their offspring" (Minturn & Hitchcock, 1963, p. 336). This has sometimes been called the "Bapu" or dependency syndrome in which Indians seem to be endlessly asking for protection, advice, and assistance of all kinds from superiors. Arjuna shows it in the *Gita* when he gives up in effect and says to Krishna, "With my mind bewildered about my duty, I ask thee, Tell me, for certain, which is better, I am thy pupil; teach me, who are seeking refuge in thee." The same attitude is reflected in the daily acts of "pooja" (worship) of many Indians like AB, in which they give an offering and respect to a deity while asking for protection in return.

Westerners or even Indians who are bothered by these insistent demands might be more tolerant if they understood that the suppliant is doing the man a favor by acknowledging him openly as a superior who has a greater control over resources. Competition for power can be avoided simply by one person acknowledging at the outset that the other has more to give. The person asked is supposed to share his greater resources by giving darshan (spiritual support) or even by giving materially if he can—but privately. If he were to give publicly, the suppliant would seem even more inferior and would be enraged. Anyone interested in the niceties of these moral points need only read Chaudhuri's description (1966) of his anger when someone announced publicly that he had given him a typewriter.

5D. REASONING AS A MEANS OF ESTABLISHING A MERIT HIERARCHY

Another technique for coping with power struggles is to rationalize them in such a way as to prove someone's moral superiority. Thus *reasoning* and discussion are highly valued in Indian culture. One of the most striking characteristics of Hindu religious thought is its extraordinary variety and subtlety. Its philosophers have been famous for millenia, and new sects or religious movements have constantly appeared based on subtle theological differences. The Rajput villagers spend hours on the men's platform talking and arguing. They must be able to reason cleverly in the many lawsuits they are involved in.

Indians appear to enjoy discussion the way some people enjoy action. By contrast one need only remember how New England farmers used to spend hours together sitting around a stove in winter, scarcely exchanging a word.

The solution of power struggles is not the only virtue of reasoning; it has many virtues in the Indian value system. It involves exchange among people, the giving and receiving which is so basic a part of the Indian world view. It avoids the dangers of commitment to action, which may entangle a man in its consequences. It is part of the whole push toward dematerializing or intellectualizing the universe, for it attempts to replace the world of the senses and emotions with talk. But above all it is a necessary part of the maneuvering that goes on, in court and out, to gain control of resources, since direct instrumental activity is in theory forbidden.

There is a children's story about four businessmen who bought a cat to keep the rats from getting into the bales of cotton they kept in a warehouse. Each man owned a leg of the cat. One day the cat injured a leg; the owner of that leg tied an oily rag to it which caught fire when the cat went near the fireplace, and so the whole warehouse was burned to the ground. With so serious a loss of resources, something had to be done. The three businessmen brought suit against the man who tied the oily rag to the cat's leg on the ground that he was responsible for their misfortune and should pay damages. The magistrate after considerable argument delivered the following judgment: "The leg on which the defendant tied the oily rag was an injured one. Therefore if was unfit for walking. It was only because of the other three legs owned by you three that the cat ran. The great loss occurred only because the cat ran. Therefore you three have to pay for the loss of the defendant."

Thus, the humble man who renders a service wins, as he always should in an Indian morality tale; but the reasoning by which this outcome is reached is typically Indian in its subtlety and in the cleverness with which the tables are turned on the one who thought he had a superior moral position at the outset.

These analyses of the power aspects of giving in Indian culture can be pushed a step further to include their relationship to the stages of expression of the power need outlined in the first chapter. Indian culture is in these terms heavily invested in Stage I and Stage II expressions of the power drive. It stresses feeding, sharing, ultimate reabsorption into the Divine Matrix (Stage I), and control of many aggressive impulses (Stage II). Stage III "masculine," direct assertiveness creates anxiety and is forbidden; yet self-sacrifice can be such a manipulative way of controlling the behavior of others that it can be considered an alternative Stage III mode of expression of the power need, modeled somewhat inaccurately on the female mode of expressing power by sharing. Later, in Chapters 6 and 8, we speculate on why a culture or an individual should develop anxiety over expressing assertiveness directly, in a Stage II expression of the power drive. All we can say here is that the most generally acceptable explanation appears to lie in an intense mother-son relationship, which leads the son to value the traditional female mode of attaining power by giving (Stage I fixation, Cf. Table 2.4) and to feel guilty about being directly assertive. Of course this does not explain which came first—the psychological complex or the historical family situation that forced a close mother-son tie.

Relating these findings to the theory of the power motive we also note that Indians do not typically advance to Stage IV in which the individual exercises his aggressiveness on behalf of a higher moral authority. Rather they ideally turn away from society to personal salvation (Stage I). This in turn explains why Indians have difficulty in maintaining public order, or forcing others to do things on behalf of the general good, a theme to which we will turn in a moment.

The Meaning of Work

So far, we have stressed how the Indian copes with gaining power through the moral superiority of giving. Little of what has been said seems to bear directly on such immediate problems as getting a job done or managing other people to achieve some collective goal. How does the average Indian look at work? To judge by a number of critical comments, he is not sharply focused on the problem of getting work done. The following episode reported by an American Peace Corps volunteer is fairly typical of what often happens:

"Storm ripped an opening in the Block's poultry house. 'We've got to get this fixed,' I told the Block development officer. 'Yes, yes,' he agreed. Nothing happened, however. When I asked him about this several weeks later, he said the engineer was preparing a detailed estimate of cost involved.

"Six weeks passed. In the meantime, a mongoose got into the poultry house through the hole made by the storm. Half of the birds were slaughtered by the mongoose or crushed in their frenzied efforts to escape.

"The day after this happened I asked the engineer if the cost estimates had been prepared. The engineer turned to the Block Development Officer and said something in Hindi. They didn't think my Hindi was good enough to understand—but I understood. The BDO hadn't told the engineer to prepare the estimate."

(BRADFORD, 1968)

Observations like these are not limited to Westerners. In his story, "Man how the Government of Indian run!" (published in *A Bride for the Sahib and Other Stories,* 1967), Khushwant Singh, one of India's most distinguished men of letters, has provided us with a witty and perceptive account of how little Government of India clerks manage to accomplish in a day.

Can it be that the BDO cared nothing about the chickens, that he and the clerks of the Government of India are just plain lazy and disinclined to work? There is another possibility:

6. WORK IS VIEWED AS A FORM OF GIVING, AS PROVIDING SERVICE TO OTHERS

Lord Krishna, supported by many Hindu sages, had advised all Indians: "Work alone art thou entitled to, and not to its fruit. So never work for rewards nor yet desist from work. Work with an even mind, oh Arjuna, having giving up all attachment." One must not focus on the outcome of work, on getting something accomplished that will give satisfaction. Of what value then is work?

It can be made to fit into the major theme of giving or providing services to others. A Block Development Officer, a clerk, or a joint secretary is in a sense doing a favor to people by working; he is providing services, out of his resources, for others. But of course he must *have* some resources —e.g., privileges, prestige, respect. So his major focus of interest is not the outcome of a job but whether or not he has the resources to do the work. Viewed from this perspective, the Peace Corps volunteer who advised the BDO to fix the poultry house effectively *prevented* him from doing anything. The person who gives advice, in the Indian value system, has more power than the one receiving it. By acting on it the BDO would have been admitting his inferiority, and to admit inferiority is to say that you do not have the resources to do your job properly. A person wise in the ways of getting things done in India knows that suggestions for action of this sort must be made indirectly and if possible in such a way as to make the superior think it was his own idea. Only then will he feel that he has not been undercut in his capacity to do his job.

Similarly the clerks may feel it is more important to show how fatiguing their jobs are (after all, giving exhausts the giver) than actually to do the job. From this point of view, it is not unreasonable to spend a lot of time in tea breaks, since they emphasize how tiring the work is and how important it is for the workers to build up their resources to cope with it. Thus, the clerk is more involved in the question of his *capacity* to do the work, his power to provide the service, than in actually doing it. This is exactly how a person with high *n* Power looks at work.

It also follows that high value would be placed in India on working *for others* rather than working for oneself. One can avoid the dangers of taking the initiative by admitting humbly, as Arjuna did, that he needs to be told what to do by a superior. Working for another person can be perceived also as a form of giving. The ideal situation is one in which the person is working for a superior master (e.g., the Government of India) who tells him what to do, yet at the same time can establish his importance as a public servant by working for others rather than himself. Once again the key issue is not the work he accomplishes, but his moral position of power, as an important person who, from his accumulated resources, can provide services for the people.

In all of this there also seems to be some actual fear of too much involvement with work. In the children's story, the tailor who received four hands as a gift from the tree spirit was stoned to death as a freak by the other villagers when they saw him. Giving and getting too much, or working too hard, can apparently lead to one's downfall. People are afraid to praise others for their work, as we have said, because praise might lead to pride. So Indians are also taught to fear success, because it means standing out, being proud rather than humble. They resort almost entirely to criticism as a means of attempting to control the behavior of others. Psychology has shown, however, that punishment is a less effective way of encouraging learning than reward; it tends above all to instill a fear of failure in work, a fear that what one does will be criticized. So intense is the fear in Indian school boys that in studies of achievement motivation made by Mehta (1967), certain story characteristics—like descriptions of personal failings or difficulties in the world—were not mentioned at all in India, in contrast to stories written by similar children in other countries in the world. These boys were so counterphobic about difficulties that they failed even to mention them as possibilities. At least part of the reason seems to be in the conception of work as an interpersonal service; failure is thus perceived as a failure of personal resources rather than simply as a failure caused by the difficulty of the task.

Disinterest in Controlling Others

As for public order, there is little in the value system of India to promote its maintenance. Rather the idea seems something like:

7. NO ONE SHOULD BE PREVENTED FROM REPRESENTING GOD IN HIS OWN WAY

A major characteristic of Hinduism is its tolerance of other religions. At the village level, the Rajput farmers adopted a Moslem saint. In modern Hindu temples leaders of all great religions are represented and worshipped —Christ, Mohammed, Buddha, etc. "No true Hindu ever tries to uproot another man's faith nor revile his God nor boast of the superiority of his own religion. For you may accept any creed, follow any prophet and belong to any organization, provided you are able by these means to reach your goal of realization of God" (Sarma, 1961, p. 235). The extent to which the ideal of toleration is practiced in everyday life in India is at first startling to the Western observer, for it appears that there are no norms of dress or behavior and that no one ever interferes with another in the name of public order. The range of permitted behavior is greater than in almost any culture. Men can wear dhotis, "pajamas," or Western clothes, refuse to cut a hair on their heads like the Sikhs, or wear no clothes at all for fear of crushing tiny insects, like a few very religious Jains. No one objects or tries to foist his convictions on another.

Streets, even in major cities, are often in indescribable confusion. Every living being, including especially cows, have a right to go anywhere, in any direction. No one really likes to make streets one way, to prohibit them to animals, or even to push cows out of shops. Chickens, cows, or goats are seldom fenced in, not because farmers are too poor —in many places all they would have to do is pile stones into a wall —but because it is not right to interfere with other living beings. Above all, one must not sacrifice one life for the welfare of another. To the average Indian it is inconceivable that he might drown three kittens in a litter of five so that the remaining two would have enough to eat to live well. Everyone has a right to life, no matter how miserable. It has proven extremely difficult, even in major cities, to get ordinances enforced for killing off packs of diseased, starving dogs.

The result of such tolerance has been a great deal of public disorder. Few have been willing to put the common good above the welfare of individuals. Hinduism is interested primarily in *individual* not group salvation. Thus conservation is difficult to teach because it often means weeding out the unfit for the sake of the rest. Public health measures arouse no interest because they often require a family to stop doing something (like fouling a water supply) that is bad for the general public. Public cleanliness suffers the same fate. Indians are intensely interested in being personally clean (uncontaminated by the material world), but they see nothing especially valuable in clean *public areas* —sidewalks, streets, bathrooms —since maintaining public cleanliness may interfere with the personal habit of keeping clean by throwing refuse into the public domain.

In politics factions develop as people maneuver to accumulate their resource base from which to exercise power; but the factions are tolerated, even respected. Husbands and wives or brothers and sisters may head different political parties which struggle fiercely against each other, but no one would think of invoking family solidarity in an attempt to silence his opponent (see Erikson on Gandhi, 1969). Though one may maneuver to form a stronger faction, one should not invoke party discipline to keep a splinter group in line. Even the fairly mild party discipline of Western democracies is alien to the traditional Indian spirit. The severe discipline of the Communist party is even more so.

Tolerance inevitably promotes disorder, though Indians have not always seen the two phenomena as intimately connected. If one carries respect for individual differences to the extreme, it produces confusion.

There must always, however, be some system for promoting the public interest, for at least on some occasions sacrificing the freedom of the individual to the welfare of the group. All societies maintain some kind of balance between individual freedom and public order. India for centuries achieved a semblance of such order by an hereditary caste system which constructed a fixed model of social organization within which all individuals and groups had a place. At times she also achieved order by rule imposed from without, as during the Moghul or British periods. It has often been noted too how much more successful Indians seem to be outside their own country, in communities scattered from East Africa to Southeast Asia. One reason may well be that they can function better in a society where *someone else* imposes the public order which they are reluctant to impose on themselves.

In terms of power, we would say that Indians have difficulty in sacrificing to the good of the whole because their power drive has not followed the normal course of proceeding through Stage III (personal assertiveness) to a socialized power drive (Stage IV) in which a person can be aggressive towards or control another on behalf of higher authority.

How the Themes Account for Indian Traits

Let these seven themes complete the analysis. Obviously many more could be added, but one of the goals of this type of effort is to keep the analytic structure as parsimonious as possible, lest it become in the end as complicated as the facts it is trying to interpret. What I have tried to do is show that many facts about Indian culture, some apparently paradoxical, can be interpreted in terms of a few relatively simple variations on the central theme of giving or exchange. Though I feel that I have not managed yet to state the themes exactly right, my hope is that these ideas may be helpful to some Indian scholar who with a better background than I have can work them into something closer to the truth.

But what about our methodological test? Many facts not listed in Table 4.1 have been woven into the discussion to support various points of the analysis, but have all the facts we listed in advance been accounted for? Table 4.2 provides an answer. It shows that practically all of the 26 observations listed in advance can be understood in terms of one or more themes. There is one partial exception—the first fact listed in the Table as the "crowding of public spaces." Though this may be explained in part by Theme 7, the unwillingness to interfere with people for the sake of public order, that is not the whole story.

Beaches in India and America fill up very differently as people arrive. In America individuals typically arrange themselves as far as possible from any other individuals or family groups on the beach; if one flies over a beach in a helicopter, he observes a series of evenly spaced dots. In India, on the contrary, if there is one man on the beach and another arrives, he goes over to join him, until as more and more later arrivals are added, a knot of humanity can be observed from a plane. Why? None of our seven themes really explains this behavior very well, yet it is characteristic of Indian culture. Even in a country village where there is plenty of room, people crowd their shops

Table 4.2–Classification of observations in Table 4.1 by themes in Indian culture

1. Giving and exchange are central in the universe.
   7, 9, 25
2. Worship the divine source of every material gift (spirit over matter).
   3, 6, 11
3. Attain merit by giving.
   12, 13, 14, 15
4. Giving becomes a mode of expression for power needs in the struggle for moral worth.
   4, 5, 16, 17, 18, 19, 21
5. Power aspects of sharing resources may be managed by renunciation, rules, requests, and reasoning.
   4, 5, 8, 10, 22, 24, 26
6. Work is a form of giving or service to others.
   19, 20
7. No one should be prevented from representing God (the Divine source) in his own way.
   2

Apparently not covered by any of the themes.
   1

together to create a marketplace characterized by the noise and confusion of close human interaction. They actively like to be close together in a way that is often incorrectly attributed by Western observers to poverty or overpopulation. When I first wrote about it this fact seemed to me to fit under none of the themes I had isolated.

Some time later, I discovered an odd fact reported by experimental social psychologists working with American college students (Freeman, 1971, Ross *et al.*, 1973). Because they were interested in the effects of "over crowding" on morale, physcial comfort, etc., they arranged to have subjects spend some time (up to 20 minutes) talking in groups in very close quarters. Men, they found, were upset by the crowding, and rated themselves and others more unfavorably under crowded conditions. But the reverse was true of women; they *liked* themselves and others better in groups where people were closer together. They felt, in short, the way Indians do who also like "overcrowding" and being physically close to others. So after all, this "odd" previously unassimilated fact turns out to be an independent confirmation of our central hypothesis that the traditional female role is centrally valued in Indian culture. What is particularly impressive, at least to me, is that no one could accuse me of having chosen this fact in the first place to confirm the hypothesis, since I frankly did not understand how it could fit the thematic analysis I was making, and said so in print.

One final point about the analysis: it should be obvious, but perhaps it ought to be stressed, that I have attempted to avoid evaluative remarks throughout. Nothing that I have said should be interpreted to mean that I believe this aspect of Indian culture is good or that aspect bad. My overwhelming conviction after doing several national character studies (1963a, 1963b) like this is that the so-called "defects" of a culture, often as seen by its own members, arise nearly always from an excess of its "virtues." Thus, self-sacrifice and tolerance would doubtless be acknowledged in nearly every culture as important virtues. They become handicaps for certain purposes in India only when they are practiced to an extreme seldom reached in other societies.

The Problem of Modernization

One way in which cultures tend to be judged in the 1970's is in terms of whether their value systems promote or impede economic and social progress as that is defined in these days. Without attempting any ultimate value judgments, one can still legitimately ask the extent to which the themes just described will interfere with rapid economic progress. Many have argued of course that Indian values are obstacles to development: the stress on otherworldliness, the lack of a concern for concrete achievements, the social discriminations built into the caste system that prevent upward mobility, etc. do not seem compatible with a rapidly growing industrial society. Yet on this point, based on my own experience, I would urge caution. To begin with, we have been describing a traditional culture pattern in a kind of abstract, ideal, or extreme form. There must be millions of Indians—certainly I know personally dozens of them—whose thinking and acting are influenced by this traditional ideal-typical pattern only slightly if at all, and then only in marginal ways. Even if one assumes these values are antithetical to rapid modernization, there are probably enough Indians who do not share them to bring about changes in the country.

My specific reason for being doubtful about the braking influence of traditionalism lies in research results we obtained in our efforts to promote an achievement orientation among businessmen in Kakinada and Vellore. In our training courses we studied intensively the traditionalism of the participants. By interviews and questionnaires we attempted to find out what their attitudes and practices were on a whole range of issues in the areas of religion, family caste, eating habits, work attitudes, etc. We then classified the men as to whether they were very traditional or very modern in their attitudes and practices. The traditional men, for instance, said that they went on religious pilgrimages, refused to eat meat or kill diseased cows, consulted gurus or astrologers regularly, would not eat food prepared by a member of a lower caste, would arrange a marriage for their daughters, believed that there was little use in human effort because fate determined the outcome of all human activities, etc. We then followed the men for two years after our motivation training and discovered which ones became unusually active and which ones did not. To our surprise, in view of all the previous writing on this subject, there was no relationship between traditionalism and becoming more active in business after training in achievement motivation —supposedly a very Western, "modern" concept (McClelland & Winter, 1969). For every modern man who changed, there was an orthodox Hindu who also changed. Both men actively contributed to the economic development of their city and India; traditionalism did not seem to be any particular handicap. How can we understand such a result?

One must remember, as Kluckhohn and Strodtbeck (1961) make clear, that every culture has dominant and substitute or variant value orientations. While countries in the West may at the present time be achievement-oriented, at a secondary level of importance they are also service-oriented. Even though India has stressed non-violence, the Ksatriyas have traditionally been supposed to be strong and fearless in battle. Thus in training these businessmen, we were dealing probably with the group in all of India that was most achievement-oriented to start with, at least in the sense that they were already in business, an achievement-oriented occupation. This is not to say that they individually had high needs to achieve, but at least they recognized that they were in the kind of occupation where results of efforts could readily be measured and checked for an improvement. Thus it was probably easier to talk to them in terms of the concepts of the course than it would have been to other groups —say, government clerks, where it is by no means so obvious that improved performance leads to better functioning of an office. So one might argue that economic development depends on the extraordinary activities of a small fraction of the population —the entrepreneurial fraction —and that there are enough men in India now with an orientation toward achievement to promote rapid economic development, if their latent energies are mobilized. While the dominant tendency may be to see work as the power-oriented service described in Theme 6, there are enough people who view it differently to bring about economic development.

More than this, however, even the traditionalism among some

members of this group did not prevent them from becoming active in a way that they *might* have regarded as self-seeking and immoral. Value patterns of the sort described are not rigid and inflexible, we learned, but can be reinterpreted in ways consistent with change. The courses stressed over and over again, for example, the fact that training in achievement motivation would benefit not only them individually in their businesses, but also their communities, India as a whole, and even the entire world as they showed the way for others to follow. By improving their businesses, they were *making a contribution* to employment, income demand, and ultimately economic growth. In apparently doing something for themselves, they were doing a great deal for others. Because we were able to link an achievement orientation with an altruistic conception of providing services to others, we succeeded in enlisting the wholehearted cooperation of these businessmen. They probably would not have been excited by a course stressing selfish gain, nor would they have been moved by appeals solely to altruistic giving. It was the combination of these two motive systems that seemed to be effective. Certainly these attempts to make Indian businessmen more achievement-oriented ran into no insuperable obstacles from traditional value themes in Indian culture.

More difficulty may arise in attempts to use power to control the behavior of some for the benefit of the whole. This is a problem that every modern state must solve, but a particularly difficult one for Indians. The prescribed way—by public self-sacrifice as in the Gandhian fast—has proved remarkably effective on occasion, but it seems hardly likely to lead to an orderly and regular exercise of authority. Indians will have to find some way of reconciling the use of authority for the public good with their traditional values. The problem is a difficult one, and I hope this essay has suggested why it is. My own conviction is that once the problem is seen more clearly—perhaps as it has been explained above—Indians will find a way of reinterpreting the problem in traditional moral terms. Some kinds of calculus of greater and lesser damage to the life force might work: in terms of modern knowledge a diseased cow or diseased dog may be responsible for the death of hundreds or even millions of other animals (manifestations of the life force). Or one might argue that it is wrong to permit any casual, material manifestation of the divine to go its own way, completely unhindered. Such an attitude represents a fixation on a particular materialistic form that is antithetical to the fundamental belief that spirit is more important than matter. Thus, one actually worships the divine spirit better if one prunes its material manifestations to let the light shine through or even in some cases destroys a particular manifestation (e.g., a diseased cow), so that the divine may manifest itself again in a purer material form. As Krishna reminded Arjuna, in a certain ultimate sense there is no such thing as killing. The Atman is the only reality.

More probably a solution will result from the external pressure exerted by an international value system with its insistence that a country, particularly a large one, try to be a "great power." In conventional terms this means playing power politics in a conventional way and exerting a Stage III type of aggressiveness in foreign affairs, including the willingness to make war, as India did recently in helping dismember Pakistan. As noted in Chapter 8, India has the high power drive and the high sense of control usually associated with expanding bureaucracies or growing empires. In the political sphere, her traditional reservations about interfering with others seem likely to be overcome fairly rapidly as she acts more and more like a great power, though they will probably continue to promote considerable freedom in religious and personal life for some years to come.

Notes

1. The substance of this chapter has been previously published as "Some Themes in the Culture of India" in A. R. Desai (Ed.), *Essays on Modernization of Underdeveloped Societies.* Vol. II, Bombay, Thacker and Co., 1971. Here it has been revised and expanded to include references to the framework for analyzing the power motive used in other chapters.

2. Throughout this paper, I have relied heavily on information gathered in a field study of a North Indian village, sponsored by Drs. John and Beatrice Whiting as part of a systematic comparative study of six cultures. Publications include Minturn and Hitchcock (1963) and Whiting, Whiting, and Longabaugh (1974). But the Whitings carefully insist that their findings are based on studies of 38 households in Khalapur, U.P. and can be generalized to other groups in India or to India as a whole only with extreme caution.

3. He does not note that this idea is common also in other cultures. As recently as the 1930's the official handbook of the Boy Scouts of America also warned that loss of semen led to loss of manliness —as a way of warning boys against masturbation.

PART C

EXPRESSING POWER

LIVING IN the village of Tepoztlan, Mexico, in the summer of 1960 turned out to be critical for my understanding of the assertive dimension of the need for Power. I was of course unaware of it at the time; I was there to find the peace and quiet necessary to finish my study of the need for Achievement, in *The achieving society*. The fact that I was in Mexico seemed of secondary importance to the central task of writing my book. But events kept intruding in my life, many of them to be stored away to develop into ideas about power much later. Mexicans kept celebrating by shooting off rockets and singing; yet they also kept talking about death and violence. How could I help noticing and being puzzled?

What I subsequently worked out as an analysis of Mexican character is reported in the following chapter. Mexican violence, it turned out, is a kind of *self*-assertion characteristic of a Stage II expression of the power drive in an extreme form. Although the violence looks like a Stage III attempt to influence, it is actually a violent affirmation of the self and thus the most elemental form of the assertiveness mode. I have referred to it as the Icarian mode, follow-

169

ing Professor Murray's lead (1955), after Icarus who aspired so high that he fell like a Mexican rocket.

Timothy Leary was living not far away from us in Cuernavaca and we saw each other often; we had become friends first in Italy and later at Harvard. One day he told us in great excitement about the visions he had had from eating a magic mushroom (containing psilocybin) obtained from a curandera (a native healer) in the mountains. We must come and take it right away so that we too could experience at first hand the glory of existence and penetrate deeply into the meaning of life and death. We never did, since by accident the cook had dried the essential principle out of the mushrooms in the oven, but this was the beginning of his bizarre crusade to turn first his psychologist friends, then all Americans, then the whole world on to the power visions induced by psychedelic drugs like LSD (Leary, 1967). In my struggles to keep up with his expanding empire-building fantasies after we both returned to Harvard, I learned a lot about how power visions (Chapter 6), particularly if they are expressed as a revolt against established authority, can breathe fire into a social movement. I also learned something at first hand about charisma, since Tim Leary had a remarkable ability to charm those who came near, to exude a warmth and radiance that made others feel strong in his presence. These experiences contributed to my thinking about power motivation and leadership (Chapter 7). But since the drug movement was an organizational failure even at the time, I began to wonder about why some movements fueled by a power vision failed and others led to great, highly organized empires. It was such wondering that finally led to the research reported here and in Chapters 8 and 9, which deal with organized assertiveness.

Richard Alpert, a former student and a colleague at Harvard, was also in Mexico that summer. He was charming, intelligent, and witty. He looked after us and our children, and became fascinated by Leary's drug experiences. He followed Tim for awhile, dropping out of academic life for the drug movement, but eventually he found his way to a high spiritual power vision in India. In the end it was his voyage of discovery and my struggle to understand him that enabled me to write Chapter 6; I saw the power vision as a return to Stage I intimacy, which at its best ultimately leads the person back into the world at a Stage IV level, shorn of the aggressive competitiveness of Stage III.

Inevitably all of these struggles turned my attention to ultimate religious questions like the meaning of life and death. I began to see that the world's major religions were concerned at their very core with problems of power — how to deal with man's power, whether to encourage or control it, and how to deal with God's power or the external forces shaping man's destiny. In the end I was led to contrast Eastern and Western religious orientations toward power and finally to discover some of the origins of war and conflict in the motivational dynamics that Christianity seems at times to encourage (Chapter 9).

All in all, it was an eventful summer. Then were sown the seeds that later developed into understandings of various modes of traditional masculine assertiveness as a source of strength. These in turn fleshed out the abstract descriptions of Stage III and Stage IV expressions of the need for Power.

THE ICARUS COMPLEX: TRADITIONAL MEXICO

THE NIGHT we arrived in Mexico our friends began to regale us with stories of death. They knew many such tales and enjoyed telling them. For instance, one of our friends said that he (or a friend of his, I was never sure!) was driving on a main street in Mexico City in the third car stopped at a red light. When the light turned green, the first car stalled in trying to start. The man in the second car blew his horn — not such a surprising act after all — but what happened next certainly *was.* The man in the first car got out of his car, pulled out a gun, shot the man in the second car dead, and drove off.

Or, to illustrate what the Mexicans thought of the Spaniards, we were told about the master of ceremonies who, in introducing the speaker of the evening, mistakenly referred to him as Señor Cortez. For this error he was punished by the gods and died of a heart attack that same evening. No one even today, even by mistake, can honor the Spanish conqueror of Mexico without suffering the consequences!

Just before we arrived there had been a dramatic incident at Teotihuacan, the great pyramids south of Mexico City where the Aztecs had performed their ritual human sacrifices before the Spanish conquest. Two women tourists from the United States had been killed on top of one of the pyramids on the very spot —we were told mysteriously and with some glee —where Aztecs used to perform their rites of human sacrifice. In this case the agent of death was the son of a Latin American diplomat who was just learning to fly and had decided to buzz the top of the pyramid which, as usual, was covered with tourists. Going in a little too close, he killed the two women. The facts seemed not especially mysterious, but in Mexican imagination as we heard the stories, there were reverberations of present events echoing past events, and a kind of fascination with death and talking about death that is not common in my experience elsewhere in the world.

The point came closer to home when one day my wife arrived back at Tepoztlan from a marketing trip to Cuernavaca without the car. She had had a minor accident on the way back and had been forced to abandon the car in the care of our fifteen-year-old son and hitch a ride home. I saw the problem as something of a nuisance and wondered how I could possibly borrow a car or a horse or any means of transport to go back and get our car to town, in view of the almost complete absence of motor vehicles in Tepoztlan. But Don Manuel, a kind of major domo at the house in which we lived, was obviously upset. At first I was unable to understand why, partly because my Spanish was inadequate to the excitement of the occasion. Finally I pieced together what he was telling me. Just a little while before, two women tourists had had a flat tire in that exact same spot and "had been murdered, Señor, for the rings on their fingers. The people in that village are dangerous, Señor. They are not to be trusted." Well, we safely retrieved our car and our son, who confessed only to a few tremors at being surrounded by dozens of hungry-looking Mexicans staring at the car and the food inside as he sat on the hood playing with his slingshot. But the image of death lying ever present just around the corner stuck with us.

Then there was the day we looked into the field just outside our courtyard and discovered our youngest son, age six, playing "sacrificio" with some Mexican boys from the village. Since he was the youngest in the group and perhaps because he was whiter, like the youths especially prepared for the sacrifice by the Aztec priests, he would lie stretched out on a bier. Then one of the Mexican boys would stand over him raising a stone "ax" high over his chest and at a signal, plunge it into his heart; symbolically he would rip open his chest, pull out his heart and hold it up to the sun, after which the lifeless body would be rolled down the nearby "cliff." The game proved endlessly fascinating to all the participants. They played it over and over again.

Symbolic sacrificial death. The past in the present, even here in a Nahuatl village which had become Spanish speaking only in the previous thirty or forty years. Perhaps it should not have come as a surprise after all this, although it certainly did, to discover that Mexicans often "eat" their dead relatives on the Day of the Dead. They buy a skull made out of candy, have a name written on it, and eat it. Again the fascination with death and the past in the present.

I kept thinking, "I'm a psychologist; I ought to be able to explain all this." But instead I kept working on *The Achieving Society*.

And that wasn't all that was happening. One morning, which I shall never forget, my wife and I were awakened suddenly at six A.M. by a couple of rockets going off outside our window on the first floor. As we struggled awake enough to see what calamity had befallen us, we heard Las Mañanitas being sung, accompanied by guitars, outside our window. Looking out, we discovered that four of the Mexicans who worked around our house were happily serenading us at the top of their voices. Not quite sure what we were supposed to do under the circumstances, we decided it was best to stay in bed and look happy, which we did without difficulty. Later we found out that one of the girls had gone to some trouble to find out my wife's first name so that they could serenade her on her name day. The outstanding quality of this episode was the extent to which they enjoyed it. They were having the time of their lives. They had surprised us, and they had made us and themselves happy.

Although the so-called fiesta pattern has often been described as a key element in Mexican culture, I had never been prepared for the extent to which it permeates everyday life. It seemed to me that it was somebody's name day almost every day of the summer we lived there. There were always *cohetes,* "skyrockets," going up to celebrate something. Our sons found the rockets so cheap for people with American money and so glorious—partly because they couldn't set them off in the United States—that they once decided to have a real festival of rocket firing. And they did. They set off skyrockets almost continually for five hours. We thought it might cure them of their fascination, but it didn't—and it pleased the Mexicans immensely.

Rockets and songs were not all there was to Mexican enjoyment of life. There was also a lot of what can only be described as "horse play." After reading Oscar Lewis, (1958, 1961) one gets the impression that Tepoztlan is a grim place where people suffer a good deal. Perhaps they do, but if you walk through it on any given day, you will hear a tremendous amount of laughter and see a lot of chasing and hacking around to which Lewis doesn't give much space in his books.

More and more the Mexicans began to seem like a people of contradictions. They were obsessed with death, yet threw themselves into life with unusual vigor. They lived in closed family compounds in the villages, or in vecindades which could be locked up in the cities; yet they loved to swarm into open plazas for market days or fiestas. They hated the Spaniards, and yet there were some Spanish character-istics they secretly admired. They had produced great artists like Orozco and Rivera whose murals we were seeing, and yet oddly enough these same artists had been leaders in the Mexican Revolu-tion. Why should artists be agents of social reform? That had certainly never been true in the U.S. or in England. Can one make psychologi-cal sense out of all these phenomena?

After I left Mexico my interest in it was further stimulated by two books. One was *The Children of Sanches* by Oscar Lewis, an account of the lives of a lower-class Mexican, Jesus Sanchez, and his four children, as narrated by themselves for the tape recorder and edited by Lewis. There is a live documentary quality to the book that almost makes the reader feel as if he himself had experienced the things they describe. The hopes, the fears, the impulsive actions, the regrets, the marital entanglements, the joyous drunken parties—they are all there to be enjoyed and experienced as if they were part of one's own life.

The other book was *The Labyrinth of Solitude* (1950) by Octavio Paz, without doubt one of the great books of the twentieth century, perhaps of all time. Only when I got into it did I begin to understand the essence of Mexican character, though, oddly enough, Paz is a poet, not a psychologist. Yet to me he seemed a better psychologist than most psychologists, because we have developed a trained incapacity to understand complex human experiences if they do not fit our con-structs developed out of watching white rats run through mazes.

Lewis and Paz supplement each other. Without Lewis's accounts, Paz's imaginative reconstructions might seem too fanciful to have any bearing on everyday life. Without Paz, Mexican lives might not make much sense, any more than our experiences in Mexico made any sense to us at the time. I shall attempt here to use them both to give a more systematic account of Mexican national character, adding to them another source that I found eminently useful in discovering the main themes in Indian character—children's stories. The stories were

)ks used in the second grade in Mexican

is analysis of Mexican national character
confirmed, that its focal point is a conflict
illing the Stage I experience of power and
power. The resolution of the conflict is
tion (Stage II) against the pull back of Stage
empted break out (Stage III) of the closed
ch ollowed by a *fall* back into Stage I intimacy,
symb nd reunion.

The maternal source of life and strength. Children's stories have much in common all over the world. Many are based on Aesop's fables, Mexican stories being no exception. Sometimes the way a traditional fable is retold reveals something about national character, but the most significant clues are hidden in stories that seem strange or that employ unusual imagery. A striking story in the Mexican collection is entitled "I Know a Game which is Better." A little boy is talking to his mother and tells her how the people who live up there in the clouds and those who live in the waves are tempting him to go away and play with them, but he answers always, "Momma wants me to be at home by night, how can I leave her and go?" The story goes on, "And they sing, laugh, and go away. But I don't care, Mommy, because I know a game much better than that; I will be the waves and you will be a shore, and I will roll and roll to break myself against you and no one in the world will know where we are." The story depicts an extremely close relationship between the mother and the son. There are tempters without, but he should stay at home and get his fun playing with her and being warm and secure in her presence. As noted in Chapter 2, this is characteristic of men with a Stage I power orientation.

Paz puts it this way: "The Mexican woman has a sort of hieratic calm . . . the man circles around her, courts her, sings to her, sets his horse (or his imagination) to performing caracoles for her pleasure. Meanwhile she remains behind the veil of her modesty and immobility . . . there is a cosmic analogy here: woman does not seek, she attracts, and the center of attraction is her hidden, passive sexuality. It is a secret and immobile sun" (1950, pp. 37–38). If statistical confirmation of the importance of the mother is needed, Diaz-Guerrero (1961) reports that 95% of Mexican men sampled stated that they loved their mothers more than anyone else.

Of particular interest in Paz's description is the fact that he uses the image of the sun to describe female strength, for in another unusual story we learn about a healthy boy who wants to do something for his poor, weak sister. "Their mother was so poor, that she owned nothing at all on earth, and she was not able to give Maria the sunlight she needed." So Juan decides to go look for some sunlight on a hill and bring it back in a can for his sister. He lets the sun into his can, closes it carefully, and starts home; but passing through a forest he is overcome by curiosity and opens the can to see if the sun is still there—alas, it is not. He sits down and cries. A little girl elf comes out of the grass and tells him to cheer up and to go farther up the mountain to the top, where His Majesty the Sun will give him a piece of his robe. This time he fulfills his mission. The sun gladly gives him a piece of his robe to cure his little sister. When he takes it home, his sister jumps up from her bed and says, "How nice, how very nice the sunlight is!"

Without Paz's clue we might be hard put to explain this story, but once we equate femininity with a "secret sun" we can explain it readily. Since the little girl is weak, she is lacking in her essence—the "sunlight which fills the house with happiness and warmth." Her brother decides to help her out, but the first time he makes the mistake of looking at something which is supposed to be secret. Encouraged by the little girl sprite—the essence of femininity—he succeeds in helping his sister the second time by not looking. What is made clear symbolically is that it is the brother who helps provide and protect the sister's femininity.

This theme comes up over and over again in the daily lives of the *Children of Sanchez*. The brothers are always trying to protect their sisters against what they regard as improper advances by other men, even though the sisters seem to be enjoying themselves. The issue is particularly poignant for poor Roberto, who has the misfortune actually to fall in love with his half-sister Antonia. Males have a special role in bringing out the sun, the warmth, in femininity, but brothers have an even more special role—they cannot become personally involved.

Paz finds evidence of this imagery among the Chamula, a people who live in the southernmost state of Mexico, Chiapas, where they have remained relatively untouched by modern developments. A Chamula, Juan Pérez Jolote, talks about the image of Christ in a church in his village and explains what it means to him and his people, ". . . the sun began to grow warm after the birth of the Child-God, Señor San Salvador, who is the son of the Virgin" (Paz, 1950, p. 107). As Paz sums it up, "Before the birth of Christ, the sun—eye of God— did not give warmth." He finds in it a version of the ancient Mexican creation myth. Again one sees the link between the sun, warmth, creation, femininity, and the fact that the male activates the whole sequence. Yet the first and strongest attachment of the Mexican male to a woman is to his mother. Recall how the children's story put it very simply: "I will be the wave (the active principle) and you will be a shore (the immobile sun) and I will roll and roll to break myself against you. And no one in the world will know where we are."

The intimacy of the relationship between the son and his mother is summed up in the shrine of the Virgin of Guadalupe, the most sacred shrine in all of Mexico. Hundreds of pilgrims visit it daily throughout the year. Everyone knows its story. Over four hundred years ago Don Diego, a simple peasant working in the fields, climbed to the top of a small hill where he was astonished and awed by a visit from the Virgin Mary. She spoke to him and asked him to build her a church there. When he went to the bishop to tell his story, the bishop was skeptical and insisted that he bring proof that he really had seen the Virgin Mary and not imagined her. Don Diego went back and spoke again to the Virgin asking her help. She instructed him to hold up his tilma (the tunic he was wearing) while she filled it with flowers to be taken to the bishop. The bishop was not overly impressed with the flowers until Don Diego delivered them to him and let his tilma drop. There, clearly impressed on the cloth, was an image of the Virgin. The bishop, now convinced, gave instructions to have the first church built, using the extraordinary image of the Virgin on Don Diego's tilma as the center of the shrine.

Over the hundreds of years since, larger and larger churches have had to be built to accommodate the thousands of pilgrims who visit the shrine daily. The tilma image of the Virgin is still there, undiminished by time, possessed of great power to convey benefits and relieve suffering. Mexicans often pray to the Virgin for help and promise that if help is given, they will walk on their knees across the huge courtyard or further to give thanks to the Virgin. The power of the image is further attested by the fact that a bomb set off below it by a revolutionary in the 1920s destroyed parts of the altar and twisted a large metal cross into a corkscrew, but left the image untouched. In recent years, with the advent of modern photography, someone had the idea of photographing the face of the Virgin and greatly enlarging the photograph. There in one corner of her eye is a clear image of Don Diego, just as it would appear if in fact he had been standing in front of her when she impressed her image on his tilma. In the anteroom adjoining the shrine there is a picture of Don Diego taken from historical records to compare with the image in the Virgin's eye as seen under a magnifying glass, and there is also a scientific demonstration to show that people talking to each other are reflected in each other's eyes.

Of interest to the psychologist is not so much whether Don Diego "actually" saw the Virgin, but the imagery used to capture the essence of the most sacred relationship in all of Mexico. It is man's relationship to the holy mother, his guide, benefactor, protector. He is a reflection in her eye. The image sums up man's relationship to his mother or by extension to women in general in Mexico. It is a relation close and intimate enough to give a reflection. Man is active, doing things; woman is passive, reflecting. He sees himself through her eyes, finds his identity, so to speak, through her, a theme to which we will return.

The children's stories also contain cautionary tales about the dangers of breaking up the intimate, cozy bond between mother and children. The mother hen keeps warning her twelve chickens that they must not go away from her because there is a wicked fox who will catch them or a horrible sparrow hawk who will grab them with his strong claws and eat them. One day one of the little male chicks, saying he wants to see what there is farther away, goes despite his mother's warning calls to come back. The fox catches him, and he calls "peep-peep" for his mother, but it is too late and the fox eats him up. Or in another case, a rabbit has a cozy house where he is visited by a fox who asks to be let in for a moment because it is cold outside. The rabbit lets him in but then the fox says, "We cannot both stay here because the house is very small. You have to get out." And the rabbit went out crying. In other words, if you leave the coziness of home you are apt to get hurt, and if you let somebody into that cozy place, you may be put out yourself.

The conclusion is clear: in the prevailing myths, images, symbols and stories of Mexico, the mother-son tie is pictured as central, all-important. The image is not at all one of dependency in the literal sense of the child hanging on the mother; rather, the mother, like the holy Virgin, strengthens, supports, protects, and heals. She provides safety, security, and strength.

Talk and Transformation of Reality. This focus on Stage I power behavior prepares us for another Mexican characteristic—the love of talk. As we saw in Table 2.4, men with a Stage I power orientation are not only fixated on their mothers, but they describe themselves as "interruptive talkers," for whom psychological states of mind have a special reality. Mexicans use talk endlessly to recreate reality.

The theme is a strong one in the children's stories. When the rabbit is thrown out of his house by the fox, he asks various other animals to help him get the fox out of there. The donkey, for instance, promises to teach the fox a lesson and runs over to order him out. The fox simply answers that if he comes out, he'll eat the donkey, which scares the donkey away. Finally the rabbit enlists the support of the cock. He goes over and starts singing outside the house at the top of his voice, "I have a gun right here to kill the fox, cock-a-doodle do. If the fox doesn't go out at once, I'll kill him with one single shot, cock-a-doodle do." The fox was so frightened that he ran away and never came back again. The fox wasn't macho enough, like Roberto, to call the cock's bluff and tell him to go ahead and shoot. For it was a bluff; that is the important point to note. The cock didn't have a gun, but he managed to convince the fox that he did, which was just as good as having one.

How talk can deceive is neatly illustrated for children in a funny story about a man who taught a parrot to say "No doubt about it." That was all the parrot could say. One day a man came in to buy the parrot, and the owner said the price was $80.00. The prospective buyer thought that was pretty steep and so he turned to the parrot and asked him, "Are you worth $80.00?" "No doubt about it!" answered the parrot. The man was so pleased that he bought him and took him home, only to discover that the parrot couldn't say anything else. "I was very foolish when I wasted so much money!" he said. "No doubt about it!" the parrot exclaimed, and "this time he was right."

In still another story talking plays a key role.

"One day while fishing the fisherman caught a beautiful big fish, which on being pulled out of the water began to talk, saying:

"'I pray you, kind fisherman, to spare my life. Though I look like a fish, I am a prince who has been bewitched. Let me live in this lake.'

"I'm going to let you go,' the good man answered, 'not because I'm sure you're a bewitched prince, but because I would be revolted to eat such a learned fish that can even talk.'" The fisherman recognizes that talk can often be used to dissemble, but he is also revolted by the thought of eating something that talks. Obviously talking has a special significance for Mexicans.

It is part of the horse play we mentioned earlier. People get carried away into half-believing their own stories as they tell them more and more dramatically. The Mexican playmates of our children loved to try to fool others into believing things that they ended believing themselves. Once they were up in the mountains and heard a strange sound. One of the Mexican boys said half-seriously that it was a leopard coming towards them; but soon they all heard it and fled from the by now clearly audible pursuit in the brush. Or one of the maids convinced our sons that there was a movie in the village that night, and they were to get their money and walk to the village with her to see it. Halfway there she stopped, laughing, and told them that it was all a joke and there was no movie. Mexicans love an expert story teller. Lewis describes Manuel, one of the children of Sanchez, as a fluent and dramatic story teller ". . . whose story perhaps more than others loses a great deal in transcription and translation because he is a born actor with a great gift for nuance, timing, and intonation. A single question would often elicit an uninterrupted monologue of forty minutes" (1961, p. xxi).

Paz provides a perceptive summary: "The Dissembler pretends to be someone he is not. His role requires constant improvisation, a steady forward progress across shifting sands. Every moment he must remake, recreate, modify the personage he is playing, until at last the moment arrives when reality and appearance, the lie and the truth, are one. At first the pretence is only a fabric of invention intended to baffle our neighbors, but eventually it becomes a superior, because more artistic, form of reality." We have here a clue as to the reason why Mexican art has played such an important role in social revolution and reform. It is by art that one transforms "reality" into something else. Transformation by thought is what is meant when psychoanalysts talk of omnipotence of thought as typical of the oral character, or our Stage I power-oriented individuals. They too not only like to explode in talk, they also value highly the "rich internal world of ideals, of sensitive feelings and reverie" and sometimes feel even natural objects possess human qualities. The fit between Mexican character and our empirical understanding of the Stage I power orientation is very close.

It is one thing to argue that infants in all cultures experience power at an early age in a Stage I manner. It is another to note that a particular culture chooses to collaborate and stress the importance of this theme in myth and symbol in ways that cannot help but continue to influence the way a person experiences power.

Aloneness and Self-protection. The stress on Stage I intimacy often brings with it warnings about the dangers of the outside world, always somehow tempting. The little boy is tempted to run away and play with the people in the clouds, but he decides to stay home and play with mommy. The little chick who leaves his mommy is eaten. What happens when the person is more or less forced to go out in the world and leave that intimacy? Paz puts it simply, "We are alone. Solitude, a source of anxiety, begins on the day we are deprived of maternal protection and fall into a strange and hostile world" (1950, p. 80). So what does one do? Again Paz answers eloquently: "The Mexican . . . shuts himself away to protect himself: his face is a mask and so is his smile. In his harsh solitude, which is both barbed and courteous, everything serves him as a defense: silence and words, politeness and disdain, irony and resignation" (1950, p. 29).

Strangers to Mexico are often outraged by this stubborn defense of privacy. D. H. Lawrence, in his *Mornings in Mexico* (1927), tells a story typical of the experience of many visitors, including our own. "On the bottom of the plaza is a shop. We want some fruit. 'Hay frutas? Oranges or bananas?' —'No, Senor.' —'No fruits?' —'No hay!' —'Can I buy a cup?' —'No hay" . . .

"(No) hay means *there isn't any,* and it's the most regular sound made by the dumbbells of the land.

"We go up the Street of Independence. They've got rid of us from the plaza. Another black hut with a yard, and orange trees beyond."

"'Hay frutas?'

"'No hay.'

"'Not an orange, or a banana?'

"We go on. *She* has got rid of us. We descend the black rocky steps to the stream, and up on the other side, past the high weeds. There is a yard with heaps of maize and a shed, and tethered bullocks; and a bare-bosomed, black browed girl.

"'Hay frutas?'

"'No hay.'

"'But yes! There are oranges—there!'

"She turns and looks at the oranges on the trees at the back, and imbecilely answers:

"'No hay.'

"There is a choice between killing her and hurrying away."

Why should she say there is no fruit when there is fruit? Because the outside world is dangerous. People are not to be trusted, particularly strangers, gringos at that, who are asking for strange things at a strange time in a strange place, in a strange way. When Diaz Guerrero asked his large sample of respondents (1961) if you can trust people, 68% of them said, "No." The children of Sanchez said into Oscar Lewis's tape recorder over and over again that you cannot trust people. They take advantage of you. The best strategy is to play it safe by not doing anything; but if you do get involved, you must *make yourself invulnerable to deception and attack.* It is a Stage II build-up of strength. See Tables 8.1 and 8.2. Manliness (being macho) "is judged according to one's invulnerability to enemy arms or the impacts of the outside world. Stoicism is the most exalted of our military and political attributes" (Paz, 1950, p. 31). Roberto, one of the children of Sanchez, was describing a fight he got into: "and so we mixed it up, but rough . . . all of a sudden, he pulled a gun and threatened me. I don't scare when I see a weapon. Instead of getting scared and backing off, I go absolutely blind mad and try to beat them to a pulp.

"He said, 'Today you die, you son of a whore.'

"'Let's see about it. Anybody can pull a pistol . . . that's easy . . . But it's something else again to shoot it . . . You've got to have guts'" (p. 372).

Fortunately for Roberto, his opponent did not have guts enough to shoot, but the revealing part of the episode was that Roberto, who was *macho,* is showing the kind of invulnerability to enemy arms that Mexicans prize most.

The Mexican as Paz points out, can defend himself against invasion of privacy by disguising himself. He wears masks, pretends he's someone else, or pretends he's no one. Paz tells of knocking at a house door. The servant girl answers from inside without opening the door, and he asks her who is there. She answers, "No one, Señor, just me." Not perhaps such an unusual event except that it reflects a well-known literary tradition in which Don No One, an empty, meaningless nobody, is a key figure.

More fascinating is the attempt to be someone else, to be at least somebody special. Paz points to the Mexican love of fancy dress, to the "delight in decoration, carelessness and pomp," which characterizes festive occasions. When we were serenaded in our beds on my wife's name day, the house servants were daringly and dramatically dressed. They transcended themselves in song. In short, they were not house servants at all at that moment, but serenaders. Paz reminds us that the Pachucos, the Mexican-American forerunners of the hippies, brought this method of displaying individuality to America, and he was writing in 1950, long before the love of strange and wonderful clothes had caught on among American youth. "The Pachuco," he said, "actually flaunts his differences. The purposes of his grotesque dandyism and anarchic behavior is not so much to point out the injustice and incapacity of a society that has failed to assimilate him, as it is to demonstrate his personal will to remain different" (1950, p. 15).

At the theoretical level, this is a precise way of stating how a person feels strong who has chosen a Stage II approach to experiencing power. He has learned to assert his individuality, his autonomy, by his stubbornness or by decorating himself.

Mexicans, it is clear, have a big investment in the Stage II as well as in the Stage I mode of experiencing power. Stage II behavior seems almost a reaction to or an extension of problems encountered in Stage I; the intimacy of Stage I proves so overwhelming that a Mexican must assert his autonomy by rejecting all institutional pressures, in the typical Stage II fashion (cf. Table 2.5). The male Mexican is also under pressure to become assertive (Stage III), "to be a man" in the Spanish cultural tradition.

So far we have spoken only of the defenders of privacy and intimacy. What about the attackers? How are they perceived? Who are they and whence do they come? As Paz makes clear, aggression is practically defined as invasion of privacy, as ripping someone open so that he feels exposed and defenseless. Even looking at someone can be taken as an invasion of privacy; again the symbolism of the eye is crucial. "A mere glance can trigger the rage of these electrically charged spirits" (Paz, 1950, p. 29). According to Roberto, the fight mentioned earlier began this way, "I was drinking and turned around. He stood there looking at me, so I looked at him, very natural, right? I didn't say a thing to him and he didn't say a thing to me. We just looked at each other. Well, that's how the tique began, as we say in Mexico." They were challenging each other with a duel of the eyes to open up. In the Mexican game of sacrificio that our son was playing, the same symbolism is apparent. To attack, to kill, to destroy is to open up, to rip open.

The person who dares the most in these combats is the true macho. Paz finds that the feeling of all this is best expressed by the slightly obscene verb "chingar" which is "to do violence to another. The verb is masculine, active, cruel: it stings, wounds, gashes, stains. And it provokes a bitter, resentful satisfaction" (Paz, 1950, p. 77). With the world so full of "chingones" (big fuckers) who are out to do each other in, to prove the other person weak and helpless, no wonder there is suspicion and mistrust. "The chingon is the macho, the male: he rips open the chingada, the female, who is pure passivity, defenseless against the exterior world . . . One word sums up the aggressiveness, insensitivity, invulnerability and other attributes of the macho: power. It is force without the discipline of any notion of order: arbitrary power, the will without reins and without a set course" (Paz, 1950, p. 81).

In terms of our theoretical scheme Paz refers to an impulsive expression of the power drive, uncontrolled by inhibition. It is an insecure, ambivalent Stage III attempt to be assertive and not at all a disciplined display of force. The contrast will become clearer in

Chapter 8. Previously we pictured the man circling around the passive feminine sun, singing to her, courting her. Now he is raping her, ripping her open. How are we to account for this darker side of the male image? Is he trying to get back in or trying to prove how male he is because of a feared weakness?

Protest Masculinity. Whiting and his associates have developed a theory of protest masculinity in a variety of sociological and anthropological studies which could account for the impulsive aggressive behavior of the Mexican macho. (See Harrington and Whiting, 1972.) Cross-culturally an intimate mother-son tie is usually associated if the culture is patriarchal, with severe initiation rites for the sons when they reach adolescence. Mother-son intimacy is defined by these researchers as the mother and child sleeping together while the father sleeps elsewhere, and the father being generally absent through the imposition of a post partum sex taboo for at least a year after the birth of the child. Under such conditions, Whiting and his collaborators argue, the male child tends to identify with its mother, because the mother is perceived as controlling all-important resources and the child wants to be like whoever it is who has all the power to give him what he wants. If such a boy also lives in a society where males are important, as defined by patrilineality, then his attachment to his mother and his identification with her have to be symbolically broken by a severe initiation ceremony to make sure he assumes a male identity. "If the identity conflict were not resolved, boys would retain behaviors inappropriate to the society's adult male role" (Harrington and Whiting, 1972). If all of these conditions obtain —that is, if there is primary cross-sex identity because of an intimate mother-son tie and if the culture is strongly male oriented, but there is no initiation ceremony to force adoption of the new male behavior —then exaggerated masculinity of the macho type may occur as a form of defense against underlying feminine traits. In other words, if sons who have been brought up exclusively by their mothers live in a very masculine society, they may have to assert their masculinity loudly and violently because deep down underneath they are really feminine in orientation.

Beatrice Whiting (1965) uses this theory to account for a number of studies showing that delinquency and personal crime are associated with broken homes, on the grounds that the boys have been brought up by their mothers almost exclusively and have developed tough macho behavior to defend against underlying femininity. Bacon, Barry and Child (1963), for example, demonstrated that in a carefully selected sample of forty-eight cultures theft and personal crime are more common in societies which have polygamous mother-child households, associated with mother-child sleeping arrangements and infrequent contact between male infant and his father. B. Whiting checks out the hypothesis in detail on the six cultures that she and her husband systematically studied in order to get comparable data on parent and child behavior. "In comparing the six societies," she notes, "it seems clear that more cases of assault and homicide occurred in Nyansongo and Khalapur than in any one of the other four societies. This conclusion is based on the total reported cases of assault and homicide which involve people known by name to members of the primary social unit." Nyansongo is the name for a group of Gusii in East Africa, and Khalapur is a Rajput town in north India. The other four cultures included the Mixtecan barrio of Juxtlahuaca in the state of Oaxaca, Mexico, a barrio of Tarong in the Phillipines, a group of families in Okinawa, and another group in a small town in New England. The Mexican group is of interest to us, although one might question whether Mixtecans are in any way representative Mexicans; but one might wonder whether any particular group of Mexicans is typical of the whole, since the nation is such a conglomerate of partially assimilated Indian cultures.

As would be predicted from the hypothesis, Whiting observed that the sons in Nyansongo and Khalapur spent most of their time with their mothers and seldom saw their fathers, as compared with sons in the other four societies. In Nyansongo (Africa) if a man is a polygamist, he builds a separate house for each wife, visits each one in turn, often sleeps in a separate hut of his own, and does not visit the wife while she is nursing a baby. If he is a monogamist, he divides the hut into two sections, one of which belongs to himself exclusively. In Khalapur (India) the Rajput woman is in purdah (which means that she has to stay behind the mud walls of the courtyard and cannot visit in town) until her children are grown up and married. She never sleeps or eats with her husband; the men sleep in a separate place. When he does visit his wife at night, "they repair surreptiously to a deserted part of the courtyard or to one of the unused rooms"; usually he does not visit his wife at all until she is through nursing her child. In all the other societies the men and women spend much more time together, eating together and often working together. There the little boy has an opportunity to identify with someone of his own sex, namely his father. Where he lacks that opportunity, according to the Whitings, and yet where the male role is clearly important, as in

Nyansongo and Khalapur, then he develops protest masculinity, which, according to the Whiting theory, explains the higher crime rates in these two societies.

Some of these conditions clearly hold in Mexico; male dominance is widely accepted there, and so is the son's intimate tie to the mother. In Juxtlahuaca the father, for example, always eats before his wife and children. As Diaz Guerrero (1961) says, the structure of the Mexican family is founded on two fundamental principles: 1) the indisputable supremacy of the father, and 2) the necessary and absolute self-sacrifice of the mother.

The trouble with the theory is that in Juxtlahuaca and elsewhere in Mexico the son has the opportunity to identify with his father as much as with his mother, since there are always males around. Oscar Lewis' case histories also make this clear. It is not just that Jesus Sanchez is the stable family figure in the lives of his children, rather than their various mothers; it is also that in the various permutations and combinations of marital arrangements, there always seems to be some father figure around with whom a young boy can identify. The theory is not put to a test in this instance, because the Mixtecans appear not to be involved in much personal crime or to be macho. "Within the Mixtecan barrio, fights over women and the beating of adulterous wives were the only type of conflict which informants mentioned as occurring frequently. However there were no such fights during the field work (which took place over about a year's time). Moreover, A. Kimball Romney was with an informant when the latter discovered his wife in bed with another man. The aggrieved husband shrugged his shoulders and walked around the block and there was no subsequent beating or violence."

Are the Mixtecans more pacific than other Mexicans? Or can it be that Mexicans are not so violent in fact as they say they are? Possibly they fear violence so much that they talk endlessly about the few actual murders, giving a visitor the impression that murders are in fact common. Certainly they fear violence and children are told they will die if they get angry and then eat; the stories of actual knife fights and the like among the children of Sanchez suggests that perhaps not all of it is just talk. The truth may lie somewhere between the exaggerated talk of violence and the apparent lack of it in Juxtlahuaca.

For the theory, however, there is still a problem, if we accept any appreciable degree of personal violence as characteristic of the Mexicans; and in fact we must accept it. The rate of death by murder and other external causes (leaving out disease, accidents and suicides) in Mexico was reported in the U.N. Demographic Yearbook to be about

45 per 100,000 inhabitants in 1969. The figure is 2 for Japan, which ought to have comparability to the data for Okinawa in the Whiting sample, 2 for the Philippines and 10 for the United States (although it is doubtless lower in New England). Although it is not possible to get reliable estimates of murder rates in Africa or India, figures from the Poona and Bombay corporations and Delhi suggest that the comparable figure is at least 12 to 18 for India. The available figures strongly suggest that crimes of personal violence are not only higher in India, as B. Whiting argues on the basis of her evidence, but also in Mexico as compared with the Philippines, Okinawa and the United States. Perhaps the Mixtecans are an exceptionally pacific group of Mexicans, but the data presented in Table 5.1 below from the Whitings (1973) do not bear this out. Recorded there on the bottom line is the average frequency of assaults from older boys recorded in the behavior observations from the six cultures. Once again, three of the groups appear to be considerably higher in assault behavior than the other three, and they are exactly the same three groups that other statistics suggest might be high in violence. And the Mixtecans are highest of all!

What then are we to make of the hypothesis of protest masculinity, which seems not to fit the Mixtecans or the Mexicans in general? They do seem to be violent, yet they live with their fathers. A slight modification of the hypothesis, however, to bring it more in line with the mode of experiencing power encouraged by the culture, fits the results rather better. One difficulty with the cross-sex identity hypothesis is that it never makes clear what the word "identity" means. Exactly what is it that the son identifies with in his mother? Is it that he wants to look like her, dress like her, use her speech patterns? Almost certainly not. The most likely possibility is that he would want to *act* like her. The most important thing she does for him is to give him support (typical feminine sharing behavior). Since that is her mode of making him feel powerful, it is the way in which he perceives her to be powerful. If he wants to imitate her, he will try to act like her by giving support and approval to others. Figures have accordingly been collected from the report by the Whitings and Longabaugh (1974) for presentation in Table 5.1 to show how frequently young and old boys and girls display behavior coded as *gives support and approval*.

The notable point about these results is that the young boys from the three cultural groups on the left of the table (the high personal violence cultures) show much higher frequencies of giving support and approval (median = 7.5% of acts) than the three cultures on the right (the low violence societies) for which the median percentage of such acts is around 2.5%. In the case of the Gusii (Africa) and Rajput

Table 5.1—Means of proportions of acts* by children from various cultures

| | | Higher Personal Violence | | | Lower Personal Violence | | |
		Nyansongo (E. Africa)	Khalapur (India)	Juxtlahaca (Mexico)	Orchardtown (U.S.A.)	Taira (Okinawa)	Tarong (Philippines)
Gives	Young boys	10.0%	5.2%	7.6%	1.2%	2.5%	4.8%
Support	Old boys	3.8	1.4	4.0	2.9	5.5	7.3
and							
Approval	Young girls	7.8	2.1	10.0	1.6	7.7	6.9
	Old girls	8.6	6.3	11.6	5.3	7.9	10.9
Assaults	Old boys	2.1	2.8	5.4	1.3	1.9	1.6

*Means of proportion scores for each child (the frequency for an act type divided by the total acts of all twelve types performed by him).

(India) the young boys even show more of this behavior than the young girls do. In this sense they show cross-sex identity, because giving support and approval is clearly sex typed behavior which older girls in every one of the six cultures show more often than the older boys in the same culture. See the next to bottom line in Table 5.1. The only differences for the Mixtecans is that this type of intimate supportive behavior is of very high frequency *both* for boys and girls so that the young boys remain "properly" sex typed because they show a little less of it than the young Mixtecan girls do.

But in the three high-violence cultures, the young boys must stop behaving in this way if they are to become properly masculine; and by the time they are older, the boys all display marked drops in what we would call Stage I giving behavior, the behavior that imitates what mothers do for them. It is indeed as if they were trying to reduce sharply their feminine type behavior and replace it with more masculine assaultive behavior (see bottom line of Table 5.1). In low violence cultures, on the other hand, the older boys become somewhat more apt to give support and approval, presumably because they have never shown what the culture defines as feminine behavior, even when very young.

The differences between this explanation of protest masculinity and the Whitings' are: (1) that it specifies what cross-sex identity means—adopting what we have called a Stage I form of power behavior (giving); and (2) that it relies less on mother-son sleeping arrangements or the absence of the father to explain why young boys grow attached to feminine behavior early in life. In the case of Mixtecans, and presumably the Mexicans generally, neither sleeping arrangements nor father absence could explain the high frequency of supportive behavior shown by young boys. Rather, this kind of intimate sharing behavior is strongly supported by the symbol systems of the culture, in myth, song, and story. The holy mother-holy child image, we contend, has a strong hold on the imaginations of even the poorest Mexicans. Babies, considered holy, become sinful only as they grow older; indeed, if they die in infancy, as so many do, they are supposed to go straight to heaven. Thus if they are holy, they are expected to act holy—both the little boys and the little girls to an unusual degree if the figures in Table 5.1 are to be believed—by loving others, giving them support and approval. In Chapter 4, we showed that Indians also idealize a Stage I type of feminine giving, so that we need not be surprised to discover that the young Rajput boys imitate their mothers in a high rate of supportive giving. Although we do not know as much about the symbolic representation of mother-baby intimacy among the Gusii, we do know that mother and child are unusually close. The point is that father absence and mother-baby sleeping arrangements are external signs that the culture places a very high value on mother intimacy or Stage I power behavior, but they are not the only evidence for such a value, nor even the most direct evidence; that is better obtained from learning what goes on in the heads of the people concerned, as for instance in their mythology.

Furthermore while the patriarchal image puts strong pressures on the Mexican boys to abandon feminine ways, they have a particular historical reason for not wanting to identify with responsible male authority because they think of fathers as Spaniards who conquered and raped their Indian mothers. Even though fathers are around, therefore, they cannot identify unambivalently with them, as boys could in another culture. In short, it is not father absence that reinforces mother-son intimacy in Mexico as much as it is ambivalence towards male authority in the culture.

What then do we conclude from this excursion into theory? Why are Mexican men so likely to erupt suddenly into violence, often after long periods of stubborn withdrawal or silence? The theory says only in more systematic form exactly what Paz and the children's stories have been saying. For the male, the powerful intimacy of Stage I gives way to the stubborn individuality of Stage II, because of the cultural stress on male dominance; but he resents the change and forever sees the world as threatening the sense of intimate power he gained early in life. He defends himself against these threats, often more projected than real, as long as he can, in all the varieties of wonderful ways described earlier. His first defense is to change reality, to see everything as psychological, the product of the mind (Stage I power behavior). Then he builds up his armor, trying to take refuge in silence, in masks, and "aloneness" (Stage II power behavior). When the pressure to break out continues, he at last gives in, somewhat desparately, half-suspecting, half-hoping that he will die in the attempt, because death will bring a return to that lost intimacy with his mother. To a true disciplined Stage III assertiveness he cannot go on, partly because of the pull of Stage I and partly because he cannot easily identify with male authority.

The Meaning of Death. Now the Mexican fascination with death suddenly makes sense. The symbolism of the *cohete* is clear. The rocket soars up to a glorious peak, explodes and dies. Violence is total *self-assertion* (Stage II). Total *self*-assertion means rupture of total intimacy (Stage I), which is the source of life and strength; so total *self*-assertion is, by psychological definition, death. Or is it? At some deeper level complete violence means loss of self. In the madness or ecstasy of the moment the person loses himself. So violence represents both an affirmation of self and a return to intimacy with the mother, whom he had not wanted to leave anyway. Empirical confirmation of this interpretation can be found in Chapter 8.

Paz puts it this way: "Death is present in our fiestas, our games, our loves and our thoughts. To die and to kill are ideas that rarely leave us. We are seduced by death. The fascination it exerts over us is the result, perhaps, of our hermit-like solitude and of the fury with which we break out of it . . . When we explode . . . we graze the very zenith of life. And there at the height of our frenzy, suddenly we feel dizzy: it is then that death attracts us" (1950, p. 58). Or again, "murder is still a relationship in Mexico, and in this sense it has the same liberating significance as the fiesta or the confession . . . Through murder we achieve a momentary transcendence" (p. 60–61).

This "ecstacy of violence" can be felt by all people. For the Mexican it has a special attraction because he has such a strong pull to transcend himself, at the very moment when he is asserting himself, to return to an earlier state of intimacy. He is torn, in short, by strong pulls toward both Stage I and Stage II experiences of power. Violence, ending perhaps in either his own death or in that of another, has the unique quality of apparently being able to satisfy both goals at once. It asserts the self and transcends the self at one and the same time. There is nostalgia for death, a sorrowfulness even in fiestas, which, Paz reminds us, supports the notion that the Mexican, through his explosions, is seeking something further back. In eating the candied representation of his friends he is expressing that nostalgia, the desire for transcendence and intimacy through an act of violence.

Perhaps all this seems too poetic to convey the feelings of an ordinary Mexican. Let's put it in simpler terms. The average Mexican watches with satisfaction as the rocket takes off and soars into the air. He identifies with its power and glory, its breaking away from mother earth. But in his identification with its soaring power, there is always the knowledge that it will fall back to earth, its power spent. And he feels there is a "rightness" about that too—that power goes before a fall.

We hear it in the words of one of the children's stories. "A conceited duckling was swimming on the tranquil pond of a farm. 'Oh' he said, 'I am a distinguished duck; I can swim, I can run, I can fly . . . quack, quack.' He then compares himself to a fish and says to him 'You can swim but you can neither fly nor run like me,' and he passes proudly by." Then he points out that he can swim and fly which the rabbit cannot, and run and swim which a bird cannot. But finally the wise old owl hoots him down by pointing out that each of the animals he's compared himself with can do what he does better than he can. "Then the conceited duckling lowered his head, and went back to the pond, very much ashamed." The picture shows the duck looking at his image in the pond. The duck started taking off like a rocket; self-assertiveness and pride are qualities one should have. Remember the cock who with his big bluff scared the fox out of the rabbit's home. But that tale also ends in a fall.

Another story repeats the theme even more literally. "The swallow was the last of the birds made by the creator. When she came into the world all the other birds knew how to make their nests, and everyone of them had one, so the swallow couldn't see how they were building them." She asked the linnet how to make the nest, and the linnet started to explain, but every time she described a process like finding some twigs and crossing them, the swallow interrupted, "Oh, I know that already." Finally the linnet gave up, saying, "Well, if you know, why do you ask me?" and went away. "And the swallow was left alone with her half-made nest and no other bird wanted to show her how to finish it." The moral is clear: if you are a conceited smart aleck, you will end up without a nest. If you are too self-assertive (Stage II), no one will help you, and you will end with none of the intimate satisfactions of Stage I (no nest). One way to describe this conflict is to say that one soars up in conceit and then falls back to Stage I.

The Eye and the Mirror. For Paz death often appears as a mirror, "which reflects the vain gesticulations of the living" (p. 54) or generally "Mexican life" (1950, p. 58). He also pictures the Mexican as an adolescent looking at his reflection: "As he leans over the river of his consciousness, he asks himself if the face that appears there, this figure in the water, is his own" (1950, p. 9). And as consciousness contemplates itself in the water, "both mirror and I at the same time," it "strips itself naked and turns in upon itself, loves itself, falls into itself: a tireless death without end" (1950, p. 63).

We know something of the importance of this symbolism of the eye looking at itself in a mirror from the story of Don Diego and the Virgin at the shrine of Guadalupe. Looking can also be hostile. Eyeing another opens him up. The sun, sometimes seen as the eye of God, is linked to feminity both in Paz and in the children's stories. A similar symbolism is reported in *Five Families* by Oscar Lewis among the poor in Mexico City. Inés is a medium who has spiritual powers and works in a Temple of Light, where there is the following arrangement: "Against one wall of the room stood a green staircase of seven steps, each with a thick candle and a vase of flowers. The top step held a crucifix and four votive candles arranged in the form of a cross. Tacked on the wall above was a triangular picture of a woman's eye from which rays emanated." A woman's eye, represented like the sun, is used to picture Inés' power to heal or to reflect directly God's power transmitted through her (Lewis, 1959, p. 159).

How are we to understand this symbolism? Why is the eye so important to the Mexican? What is significant about looking at oneself in the mirror, or as a reflection in another person's eye?

The Icarus Complex. Looking at oneself in a reflection reminds us of Narcissus, the Greek youth who fell in love with his image in the pond, or the image of conceit in the Mexican children's stories of the duck preening himself in the pond. The image always seems to contain within it elements of rising (pride, self-conceit, narcissism,) and of falling (losing all in the water). Professor Murray discovered an undergraduate whom he named Grope who combined these themes in a distinctive way. Grope had extraordinary fantasies of flying which had elements of exhibitionism in them. The higher he flew, the more people looked up to him; he was the cynosure of all eyes. "The upward thrust of desire," Professor Murray commented, "may also manifest itself in the convection of tall pillars and towers, of high peaks and mountains, of birds —high flying hawks and eagles —and of heavenly bodies, especially the sun. In its most mundane and secular form, ascensionism consists of a craving for upward social mobility, for rapid and spectacular rise of prestige" (Murray, 1955, p. 631). In our terms, ascensionism is an expression of the power drive (Stage II). It shows us a person engaged in an extreme form of asserting his independence of earthly ties, narcissistically insisting on his autonomy. But Grope's fantasies also included falls, descension, undesirable terminations of his high-flying adventures.

Narcissism, rising, flying and falling make up the three central elements of what Professor Murray called the Icarus complex after the boy in Greek mythology who flew so near the sun on his wings of wax that the wax melted and he fell into the sea. In Grope's case there were also three secondary concerns: 1) Urethral eroticism—seeing sex in urinary terms as in fantasies of urinating on women from the sky; 2) craving for immortality; and 3) depreciation of women, seen as objects for exploitation. Ogilvie (1967), who carried Murray's work further, described three other cases who showed these six features of the Icarus complex: another undergraduate; the well-known artist Marc Chagall; and Perry Smith, the murderer whose fantasies and actions are so vividly described by Truman Capote in the book *In Cold Blood* (1965).

Perry's ascensionism was well developed. Not only did he often have dreams of glory in which he was the famous Perry O'Parsons on center stage before a cheering audience; he had a recurrent dream of being carried up, up and away by a parrot. When he was in a California orphanage run by nuns, he was often whipped for wetting his bed. "It was after one of these beatings, one he could never forget ('She woke me up. She had a flashlight, and she hit me with it. Hit me and hit me. And when the flashlight broke, she went on hitting me in the dark.'), that the parrot appeared, arrived while he slept, a bird 'taller than Jesus, yellow like a sunflower,' a warrior angel who blinded the nuns with its beak, fed upon their eyes, slaughtered them as they 'pleaded for mercy,' then so gently lifted him, enfolded him, winged him away to paradise" (1965, p. 93).

Other aspects of his complex were equally apparent: "Time rarely weighed upon him, for he had many methods of passing it . . . among them, mirror gazing. Dick had once observed, 'Every time you see a mirror you go into a trance, like. Like you was looking at some gorgeous piece of butt. I mean, my god, don't you ever get tired?' Far from it; his own face enthralled him. Each angle of it induced a different impression. It was a changeling's face, and mirror guided experiments had taught him how to ring the changes, how to look now ominous, now impish, now soulful; a tilt of the head, a twist of the lips, and the corrupt gipsy became the gentle romantic." "Since childhood, for more than half his 31 years, he had been sending off for literature ('Fortunes in Diving! Train at home in your spare time. Make big money fast in skin and lung diving. Free booklets . . .'), answering advertisements ('Sunken treasure! 50 genuine maps! amazing offer . . .') that stoked his imagination swiftly and over and over enabled him to experience: the dream of drifting downward through strange waters, of plunging toward a green sea-dust, sliding past this scaley, savage eyed protector of the ship's hulk that loomed ahead, a Spanish galleon, —a drowned cargo of diamonds and pearls, heaping caskets of gold" (1965, pp. 16–17). The reality of his experiences put some flesh and blood on the abstract psychological concepts of Narcissism (mirror gazing), ascensionism, descensionism, desire for fame and immortality, and depreciation of women revealed in the other portions of the case history.

All this reminds us of some of the key images characteristic of Mexican culture: narcissism (looking at one's reflection), ascensionism (rising up like a rocket, sun imagery), and descensionism (obsession with death and exploding like a rocket). If Mexican culture is Icarian, it is appropriate to discover that one of the children of Sanchez, Roberto, the most macho, also has a well developed Icarus complex. "I have always wanted to be an aviator; . . . when I played with my friends, the game was always aviation. To make it more real, I would lower my goggles and go up on the roof to run there like a plane. Or I would go running around the courtyard. I'd tie ropes to the water pipes and make a swing. That was my airplane and I really felt as if I was flying. That was one of my dreams. Whenever a plane flew by, even to this day, I keep watching it, wanting to fly one someday. My head was cracked open because I wanted to fly" (Lewis, 1961, p. 67). In other words, in one of his flying simulations he fell and cracked his head open.

In more general terms he put his feelings about his ascensionism-descensionism this way: "Never in my whole life did I feel there was anyone who paid attention to me. I have always been sneered at . . . belittled. I always wanted to be something in life, do whatever I felt like and not have to take orders from anyone. I wanted to make a kite of my life and fly it in any field." He also had the classic problem of the Icarian. "I had a real problem. I always wet the bed, right up to the age of 9 or 10. They called me the champion bed-wetter in the house" (p. 61). With women he never got on very well because he felt they would betray him.

Ogilvie (1967) has increased our understanding of the Icarus complex by testing for its generality in various cultures of the world. He collected an average of 14 folk tales from each of 44 independent cultures (for a total of 355,000 words). With the objective of discovering if the key themes in the Icarus complex tended to occur together in the folk tales of a particular culture, he developed word lists characteristic of a variety of psychological themes but in particular for the several elements in the Icarus complex—ascend, descend, fire, water, immortality, and narcissism. A computerized system of content analysis (*The General Inquirer,* see Stone, *et al.,* 1966), coded the frequency with which words of each type appeared in a collection of folk tales from a given culture. Then the word list frequencies for each culture were intercorrelated for the sample of cultures to see if a high frequency of *ascend* words went with a high frequency of *fire* and so on. He performed the analysis twice on the two halves of the folk tales to make sure that his results were not just chance. In both cases he factor analyzed the resulting correlation matrix and discovered a factor upon which four of the Icarus complex variables loaded highly—ascend, descend, fire, and water. "The variables 'time (long)' and 'stay' were included in the dictionary as possible measures of a concern with immortality. They, too, appear in this cluster. The variable that is missing from this cluster is narcissism. It is not known whether its absence should be attributed to extremely weak measures of its expression or to 'real' lack of relationship." In short, Ogilvie found support for the conclusion that certain key elements in the Icarus complex tended to co-occur in folktales from various cultures. Thus there seems to be a universal cluster of themes, not peculiar to a few individuals, or to the poetic imaginings of a great writer like Octavio Paz, or to a psychologist like Professor Henry Murray.

Having confirmed the existence of the Icarus complex cross-culturally, Ogilvie went on to search out other characteristics of societies high in Icarianism. Some of his findings are particularly relevant here: the high Icarian societies produced high word counts on the variable *sensation.* "Twenty-seven of the 41 words defined by 'sensation' denote the use of visual capacities (for example, gaze, look, perceive, stare and watch)." These are the very words that at this concrete level are used to describe narcissism or looking at one's reflection in the water or in the mirror. Given the limitations of computerized content analysis, it is not possible to check easily whether the use of these words is associated with looking at one's reflection, but it is not a wild leap of the imagination to assume that looking is an essential part of narcissism. The remaining 14 words out of the 41 in this list which were more common in high Icarian societies included references to smelling, hearing, and touching—in other words, to sensory "inputs." In terms of our theoretical scheme, they signify a Stage I orientation in which the primary source of stimulation (or strength) comes from without (mother-baby intimate contact).

Low Icarian societies scored higher on words from the following lists: *denotative sex* (words like copulate, embrace, love, and hug);

aggressive act (abuse, argue, blame, nag); *communication* (ask, discuss, inform, reply); and *affiliation* (friend, help, and phrases like "thank you"). As Ogilvie points out, what these word lists seem to have in common is an *interpersonal* dimension. It would not be stretching their meaning too far to conclude that many of them refer to interpersonal influence, which in terms of our theoretical scheme refers to a Stage III form of the expression of the power motive. Low Icarian societies, in short, have passed beyond narcissistic forms of expressing the power drive to interpersonal attempts at feeling powerful by influencing others. Such findings, it is comforting to note, independently confirm the utility of the scheme for classifying modalities of power motivation as well as our interpretation of Mexican character.

In another computerized content analysis of the same folk tales (see McClelland *et al.*, 1972) it was decided to get a rough measure of Icarianism in another way, by simply counting the number of sentences in which *both* upward and downward expressions appeared. In most cases the words involved were "up" and "down," as in the sentence, "He went up the river and came down" or "It went up in the air and fell down." The frequency with which this "Icarian" theme occurred in the folk tales of a culture was significantly correlated with non-lineal methods of calculating descent in the culture ($r = .34$, $N = 44$, $p < .05$). To put it the other way around, cultures low in Icarianism counted descent in the more common patrilineal way, whereas in high Icarian societies, the mother's descent line was more important.

Ogilvie, who had obtained similar findings for his measure of Icarianism, pointed out —correctly, in our opinion that the implication is that the mother is more important in high Icarian societies. This too confirms our analysis of Mexican culture and also of the source of Icarianism, since we contend that mother intimacy (Stage I) is of crucial importance in both instances.

One other correlation also confirms the importance of women: the significant relationship ($r = .46$, $p < .05$) between the up-down measure of Icarianism and the institution of couvade, in which the husband shows many of the same physcial symptoms as the wife when she is pregnant and gives birth to a baby. He may have symptoms of morning sickness during pregnancy, or even go to bed as his wife does after she delivers the baby. Whiting and others have used this as an index of cross-sex identity, but in our terms it signifies simply the great value the culture places on the mother and on her method of giving resources to others.

To sum up, Icarianism is an impulsive effort to escape from a strong mother fixation in Stage I via a Stage II act of self-affirmation;

yet it is so exaggerated and self-glorifying that it seems suicidal in intent, as if the person would destroy the self and return to Stage I intimacy. We promised an explanation some time ago, of the meaning of the eye and the mirror, of the proof that Don Diego saw the Virgin by the discovery of his image reflected in her eye. The curious fact about looking at yourself in a mirror or in the water, or in the eye of your mother is that you are *simultaneously* affirming your existence and non-existence. You show off, affirming yourself (Stage II), but at the same time you realize you are not really there: you are merely a reflection of someone else. You exist only in the eye of the beholder. Thus the image captures the essence of self-affirmation—not really self-affirmation but reflection from another, where a Stage II act simultaneously re-affirms a Stage I intimacy. You can drown yourself in the other.

Masculine Identity. What about the father? Nothing has been said about his role in the life of Icarians. Why doesn't the young boy identify with paternal authority and want to grow up to be like his father, in the classic picture presented by Freud of the passing of the Oedipus complex? That it might be due to father absence seems not to be true in the Mexican case, as we have seen. Paz provides us with a convincing explanation of Mexican ambivalence about paternal authority: he points out that Mexicans think of themselves consciously as a product of the rape of Indian women by Spanish conquista-dores—hijos de la chingada, sons of the violated Mother (1950, p. 86). The Spanish adventurers, they believe, defeated the Indians by treachery, by seducing Indian women like Dona Malinche, the mis-tress of Cortez, who helped him get inside the defenses of the city of Mexico. When he had used her, however, he deserted her. So the Mexican grows up hating the Spanish conqueror, his father. Remem-ber the strange story about the man who died of a heart attack from mistakenly calling someone Cortez. There are no statues to Cortez in Mexico City; the hero is the Indian defender of the City, Cuauht-emoc. The Mexican has no male patriarchal figure with whom he can identify without ambivalence. "Among the numerous patron saints of the Mexicans, there are none who resemble the great masculine deities . . . there is no especial veneration for God the Father in the Trinity. He is a dim figure at best" (Paz, 1950, p. 82).

Yet at the same time Mexico is a Spanish culture in which the patriarchal myth is strong. The Mexican secretly *admires* the Spanish father at the same time he hates him. Thus he is in a quite different position from the East Indian male, who also has a strong mother tie;

unlike the Indian, the Mexican has a strong pull to the masculine assertive modes of Stages III and IV —to an exercise of responsible male authority in the family, for instance. For the Indian, the female mode (sharing) is centrally valued; for the Mexican it is valued and rejected, ambivalently, for masculine assertiveness. It seems highly unlikely that with such a value system Mexico could ever have a female head of state, as India has today.

Some of the Mexican ambivalence about authority appears to be at work among young Americans in the early 1970's. Their favorite reading is an Icarian fantasy, Jonathan Livingston Seagull, about a seagull who develops his flying speed to the point where he leaves the flock, cracks the sound barrier, and becomes one with God. Why should they take such pleasure in this rather simple story at this time? Like the Mexicans, young Americans in the 1960's developed an intense ambivalence about "responsible" masculine authority because of their widespread conviction that it had led to an immoral Vietnam war and oppression of blacks, women, and others. Since the mother-son tie is also strong in American life, the failure of the father identification promotes —as it does in Mexico—a *self*-assertiveness, designed to express a Stage II autonomy, but which in its ultimate form destroys the self and permits the person to return to the intimacy of Stage I.

The picture we have been painting of Mexican men makes them appear pathological; they end by seeming immature, arrested in development, tortured by emotional attachments, and beset by conflicts in identity that prevent full maturity. But in Mexico Icarianism develops often in creative ways, or perhaps not at all in most men. The children's stories suggest that both Paz and we may have overstressed this lack of a strong father image; a number of them picture the father as the patrón, the stable responsible provider who looks after those in need. Among Spanish Americans, at least, as Kluckhohn and Strodtbeck (1961) demonstrate convincingly, this relationship is central. In one children's story a little boy is told by his mother to go buy some bread. When he objects and tries to get out of it, his father says, "OK, kids, since today is Sunday, I can play a little with you. We'll make believe that you are the parents and I am your son. What do you want me to do?" "Go and buy the bread!" the boy exclaims triumphantly. But the father asks, "Who is going to give me the money?" and this teaches the kids a lesson. They realize their father is always the unprotesting provider and ashamedly they quickly go for the bread.

In another story, the father returns from a trip and has a tender reunion scene with his children. He brings with him a poor little orphan boy whose mother has died in a flood. When he explains to the other children that since the child has no father and no mother, the family should help him, everyone agrees that the father has done right. In *The Children of Sanchez* Jesus Sanchez continually looks after, not only his own children, but all his grandchildren when necessary as they are brought home to him from various marital entanglements. Perhaps he is not typical of his environment, but he comes through as a strong patriarchal figure who cares.

Ross and Glazer (1970) have reported a rather surprising finding about Mexican American families. In an attempt to find out why some boys from poor backgrounds turned out well, whereas others turned out to be delinquents, they chose some "bad" boys and some "good" boys, originating from the same neighborhoods and presumably exposed to the same crime rates, values, and so forth. Among blacks, they found that the presence of a stable mother figure in the home was crucial; far more of the delinquent black boys came from homes without such a stable mother figure. The presence or absence of the father made no difference in the delinquency rate of black sons. The reverse was true, however, of the Mexican-American boys. Far more of the delinquent chicanos came from homes in which there was no stable father figure. If there was a stable father figure, the boy was more likely to grow up normally. Perhaps this is just a way of emphasizing that most Mexicans do, of course, grow up normally identifying with their fathers. We have stressed the other strains in Mexican character because they lend it the unusual flavor Paz describes, and because they help us to understand the unfolding of the power drive.

While Mexicans may feel caught in the labyrinth of narcissistic solitude—the labyrinth that Daedalus built, the vivid symbol of con-stipated closed-upness—they escape and fly out of it in a special way. Their very Icarianism makes them experts at psychological self-exami-nation; and self-examination is a prelude to art. Art in such hands becomes the instrument of social revolution and the means to helping all of civilization examine where it is and where it is going. It is no accident, in short, that Mexican artists were leaders in the Mexican revolution. Their Icarian fantasies enabled them to picture vividly a better life to be attained by the revolt of the masses against the elite, and to set it up as a symbol for which people could struggle. Their concern clearly moved beyond Stages I–III in expression of the power drive and directly into Stage IV, in which the person sees himself as the instrument of some higher moral authority that brings order and strength to the people. To men like Diego Rivera Marxism meant precisely that.

At an even profounder level, Paz uses the Mexican experience to call us all to a more mature realization of the varieties of power experiences; modern man, he reminds us, also needs to break out of being a total prisoner to the controlled assertiveness of Stage III —the principled, orderly assertion in which technological development, time as succession, and empire-building are all. (See Chapter 8.) "Man, the prisoner of succession, breaks out of his invisible jail and enters living time . . . Myth and fiestas, whether secular or religious, permit men to emerge from his solitude and become one with creation . . . Then time will cease to torment us with doubts, with the necessity of chosing between good and evil, the just and the unjust, the real and the imaginary. The kingdom of the fixed present, of perpetual communion, will be reestablished" (p. 211). Although this may grow out of a Stage I power orientation, it reaches beyond Stage III authoritarianism to a higher level of maturity, in which the ego is again lost or merged (Stage IV). Here is no pathological fixation on the security of mother love characteristic of a driven Icarian, who is not free because he does not understand what is happening to him. Rather, this is the mature realization of a power in the universe that transcends the ego and its endless self-serving games. Perhaps, above all, we who are bound to the disciplined technological, bureaucratic society of Stage III need to be recalled to *experiencing* the elemental creative source from which all our feelings of power originally derive.

VISIONS OF POWER:
RAM DASS, BLACK ELK, AND THE
BOOK OF REVELATION

OCCASIONALLY AN individual life is so ordered that it illustrates vividly a particular mode of expression of the power drive. An example is the power visions reported throughout recorded history. Such visions, often occurring in response to some personal or social crisis, are vivid and dramatic, even supernatural in character; that is, a person experiences manifestations of power that do not belong to the natural order of things and that do not originate in the self. Often he then actively pursues them, by some form of self-discipline, even though he recognizes that he cannot produce them by an act of his will. In such ways he begins to transcend the critical issue in power experiences as to whether their source is in the self or outside the self.

In terms of our theoretical scheme, the power vision is a special type of behavior involving aspects of three stages in development. It may begin as an attempt to understand or develop the self (Stage II).

When power experiences first break through, they often have the quality of a Stage I enhancement of the self. But typically the person then sees his visions as of value for others and he seeks to become a channel through which divine power is provided to others (Stage IV). In a sense, the power vision is an alternative style which bypasses to Stage IV the more common competitive-assertive mode of Stage III to be examined in the next two chapters. As such it deserves careful study.

In our time, changes in the life style of a psychologist, Dr. Richard Alpert, provide an excellent opportunity to study the power vision at work—both its nature and its impact on the individual. Alpert's story is interesting for a number of reasons. To begin with, he is a psychologist, and it is particularly fitting that psychologists—who usually express their power drives by studying other people—should themselves become the object of study. It is significant also that Dr. Alpert had his power vision in India, a country whose value system we have analyzed in Chapter 4 in terms of a Stage I orientation of the power need. Studying Alpert's life will not only illustrate further how the Indian system works, but will also shed light on how the power need expresses itself in the American value system, and why that American system seemingly forced him to go elsewhere for his vision.

We shall be concerned, in short with how and why Richard Alpert, Ph.D., was transformed into Baba Ram Dass, an Indian-style mystic and spiritual teacher. For evidence we have his own account of his life and his reasons for change in his popular book, *Be here now* (1971). I personally have the advantage, in addition, of having known him well as a student and as a colleague in the days before his transformation.

What is his story in brief? He was born into a wealthy, powerful Jewish family living in a suburb of Boston, Massachusetts. His father was an influential lawyer who was one of the founders of Brandeis University, an institution with the ambitious goal of becoming a top flight Jewish-sponsored non-sectarian institution of higher learning on a par with Harvard University. Like the young Gautama Buddha, Dick Alpert had all the material advantages that wealth could provide plus the knowledge that his family and their connections were in a position to give him powerful assistance in any career he chose. Although his father tried to force him to go to medical school because medicine seemed to provide a greater opportunity for a successful career, he chose to be a psychologist. In fact, I helped him pursue his goal by providing him a research assistantship at Wesleyan University in the early fifties when his father had said he would not finance graduate study in psychology. From Wesleyan he went on to Stanford University for his Ph.D. and then returned to a position on the teaching staff at Harvard University—which gave him considerable satisfaction since he had been unable to gain admission to Harvard as an undergraduate. At that point his career in psychology looked very promising. He sums it up as follows:

> In 1961, the beginning of March, I was perhaps at the highest point of my academic career. I had just returned from being a visiting professor at the University of California at Berkeley: I had been assured of a permanent post that was being held for me at Harvard, if I got my publications in order. I held appointments in four departments at Harvard: the Social Relations Department, the Psychology Department, the Graduate School of Education, and the Health Service (where I was a therapist). I had research contracts with Yale and Stanford. In a worldly sense I was making a great income and I was a collector of possessions.
>
> I had an apartment in Cambridge that was filled with antiques, and I gave very charming dinner parties. I had a Mercedes-Benz sedan, and a Triumph 500 cc motorcycle and a Cessna airplane and an MG sportscar and a bicycle. I vacationed in the Caribbean where I did scuba diving. I was living the way a successful bachelor professor is supposed to live in the American world of "he who makes it." I wasn't a genuine scholar, but I had gone through the whole academic trip. I had gotten my Ph.D; I was writing books. I had research contracts. I taught courses in human motivation, Freudian theory, child development. (Ram Dass, 1971).

At this point he started taking first psilocybin, then LSD and other hallucinogenic drugs in collaboration with another psychologist, Dr. Timothy Leary, also at that time at Harvard. Although Alpert took them at first in the genuine spirit of scientific inquiry, their effect on him personally was so powerful that he began to feel they might provide meaning to a life which, though successful, had come to seem empty to him. As he put it, even after five years of psychoanalysis he was still a neurotic who was seeking something that was more honest, real, and fulfilling than the academic career he was pursuing. Eventually, therefore, he abandoned his position as a psychologist in the "establishment" in order to spend full-time exploring varieties of drug experiences and setting up environments where people could take drugs without being persecuted by society. After six years of this, he still felt that he had not found what he was looking for. No matter how "high" he became on drugs for periods of time, he always "came down." He was still the old, sad, disillusioned Richard Alpert.

Following the lead of others in the counterculture, he went to India in 1967 to see if he could find there someone who "knew," who could guide him to a more satisfactory life. Eventually he ran across a guru (spiritual teacher), Maharaj-ji (Neem Karoli Baba), who had extraordinary psychic powers. In his first visit, Maharaj-ji demonstrated to Alpert that he could read his mind, that he knew things about what he had been thinking that Dick believed he could not possibly know. He told Alpert, for instance, at this first meeting that his mother had died of "spleen trouble" the previous year—something that Dick couldn't figure out how he could possibly have known. "The guy I was with didn't know all that stuff, and I was a tourist in a car, and the whole thing was just too far out. My mind went faster and faster and faster . . . and then I felt like what happens when a computer is given an insoluble problem; the bell rings and the red light goes on and the machine stops. I burned out its circuitry . . . its zeal to have an explanation. I needed something to get closure at the rational level and there wasn't anything. There just wasn't a place I could hide in my head about this.

"And at this same moment, I felt this extremely violent pain in my chest and a tremendous wrenching feeling and I started to cry. And I cried and I cried and I cried. And I wasn't happy and I wasn't sad. It was not that kind of crying. The only thing I could say was it felt like I was home, like the journey was over. Like I had finished."

This conversion experience was the beginning of his transformation. He stayed with the Maharaj-ji's entourage for many months, learning about Hinduism and Buddhism, but more particularly learning to practice the disciplines of meditation and yoga. He learned to go without speaking for months, using a chalk board to write messages even in the center of Delhi, to sit in meditation in a small white room devoid of decoration, to go without food for days, and wander around India as a barefoot sadhu. In the end he changed his way of life entirely—his name, his clothing, above all his worship of the rational mind. His guru took over the direction of his life and after a couple of years ordered him to return to America to tell his story.

Balding on top with a full bushy beard, he created something of a sensation when under his new name he reappeared in the synagogue in Newton, Mass., garbed in a long white Hindu "dress" with beads around his neck. Even more, he created a stir in the counterculture. Thousands of young people flocked to hear his story. He returned to Harvard to speak. The lecture room was jammed with four hundred people and more trying to get in. He started talking at 7:30, sitting cross-legged on a table in the dark with a candle and a picture of his guru facing him. He was still talking six or seven hours later. His audience had kept him there all that time, questioning him, demanding to know more about his experiences; and this was the same sophisticated Harvard audience that ordinarily can hardly stick out the fifty-minute lecture. The story was the same everywhere he went on university campuses. Students flocked to him to see if he had the answers they were seeking. He wrote a book about his experiences, *Be here now,* which as of today has sold more than 300,000 copies, although it was not printed, advertised, or distributed by a regular publishing house. Obviously he was speaking to some need among American students, and paradoxically he became better known and more influential on the American university scene than he would have been had he remained a traditional academic psychologist.

How are we to understand what happened to him? On the surface his life is full of paradoxes. He was trained in and fully accepted the Western tradition of rational scientific inquiry. Particularly as a psychologist, and a therapist at that, he was well aware of the ways in which the mind could invent all kinds of experiences to achieve its unconscious aims. Yet after his transformation he was the follower of an Indian mystic, someone he described as a little old man in a blanket who was both nobody and everybody to him. How could a trained, disciplined, Western scientific mind come so completely under the sway of a non-rational, spiritual, Indian guru?

Or consider other paradoxes: Richard Alpert had enjoyed all sorts of material possessions; Ram Dass had none. He accepted no royalties from his book or money from his father. At one point his guru even ordered him not to carry money because he had such a hang-up about it and ought to learn to live without it. Richard Alpert was trained as a specialist in human motivation; he studied initially with me. He knew all about achievement motivation and made a specialty of studying achievement anxiety. Yet as Ram Dass he accepted the Hindu-Buddhist belief that desire is at the root of all suffering and that therefore the ultimate goal of life is to give up desire and all motivated striving.

As his former mentor in the field of motivation, I couldn't help wondering if he was trying to tell me something. Why did he feel it was so important to give up motivation? As Richard Alpert, all who knew him agreed he needed above all the approval of his friends. Unusually sensitive to the opinions of others, he generally tried to please people and make them happy. Yet first in his promotion of the use of psychedelic drugs, and later in his Indian transformation, he seemed to go out of his way to earn disapproval. Though we had been close friends, he broke completely with me in pursuing his drug experiences. To adopt Indian ways, he dropped out of a serious scientific career for which he had been long prepared. He seemed completely "weird" to many of his family and friends. What could explain these radical transformations? He liked to dramatize things, as he himself admits, and his life during this period was full of a drama that brought him the attention of a fairly large audience. But he seems to have gone to unusual lengths if he was just out to get attention. We still need to explain, moreover, why he chose this particular form of dramatic behavior rather than some other. And finally, his appeal to young people indicates strongly that his particular trip must have a significance beyond a purely idiosyncratic desire to get attention.

Suppose we look at his life in terms of the scheme we have been using for describing the various expressions of the power need. The first thing we note is that his need for power is very strong and, second, that he found a variety of means for expressing it. Some of his behavior seems characteristic of a Stage I power orientation; for instance, he reports that he ate a lot, particularly when he was an adolescent. "In the old days, like many of you (I suppose) I was a good oral-type person. You open the refrigerator and you can't stuff your mouth fast enough! Everything turns you on. And I'll have a little of that! And there's some ice-cream—there's some cole slaw; butter'd go good with the ice-cream. Oh boy!" In response to his anxiety during his appointment at Harvard in the early sixties he also says he "ate more."

Though in Chapter 2 we reported no direct evidence that men with a Stage I power need ate more, as theory would lead one to expect, it is at least interesting that they did drink more milk ($r = .10$, $p < .10$, in the expected direction). More significantly, Alpert as a psychologist, psychoanalytic patient, and therapist showed the fascination with fantasy and a rich inner world of feeling that characterizes such men. See Table 2.3. He also liked to talk a lot, to share his inner thoughts and feelings with others, to check over his car or plane very carefully, just as they do.

Another of his major characteristics may fit here: he liked to help others, to nurture them. He loved to do things for people, particularly children. He was a kind of godfather to our twin sons—a magical godfather. It gave him great pleasure to provide them with new and wonderful experiences, to take them up to his family farm where they could tear around the lake in his speedboat or play the slot machines all night long; or he would give them a ride in his airplane with the additional thrill of landing in the fairway of the Alpert private golf course. When we were going on leave to spend the spring in Italy in 1958, he delighted in arranging that the private car of the President of the New Haven Railroad (his father's car) should be put at our disposal to take us from Boston to New York. It was particularly exciting and memorable occasion for us and our children, since the car had formerly belonged to J. P. Morgan and was fitted out in a style suited to one of the biggest business tycoons of them all.

In talking about his relationship to Tim Leary during their mutual exploration of psychedelic drugs, Dick summed up his role succinctly this way: "I'll help him with pleasure 'cause he's that great a being. And I'd help raise money and run the kitchen and clean the house and raise the children . . ." Such words define typical female nurturant role behavior, which tends to be associated among the men studied in Chapter 2, if at all, with Stage I power-behavior. In general, power-oriented men do not report liking child care of children at any stage of life, but if their *relative* preferences for children are obtained (by standard scoring judgments within subjects), those with a Stage I power orientation prefer "babies, little and helpless, nice to hold, feed, and make happy." The correlation of .16 (p < .10 in the expected direction) gains added significance from the fact that nearly all other correlations in this area are negative. On the other hand, it may simply be that Alpert's power motivation expressed itself through the typical feminine nurturant style (see Chapter 3) because of sex identity problems. He was more comfortable, as we shall see in a moment, behaving as a nurturant woman than as a competitive man. It is scarcely surprising in the light of all this to learn of his struggle with homosexuality. In American society, unfortunately, sex-role confusion creates problems both consciously and unconsciously, and they were part of the reason why he sought in various ways for relief from tension and anxiety.

Alpert also showed many characteristics of a Stage II power orientation. He generally controlled well any outward expression of anger. He refused to seek personal help from his parents. (See Table 2.5). He tried to get out of institutional responsibility. His struggle for autonomy, his attempts to break away from the dependence on an outside source of power characteristic of Stage I, led him more than once to dramatic displays of independence. I was, as I have said, the means by which he broke away from his father's influence. Later he broke from my influence in much the same way by following Tim Leary. Still later he broke with Tim. In all these instances he showed a strong ambivalence about guidance from another, on the one hand being attracted to it (Stage I) and on the other, feeling the necessity to break with it (Stage II). As we shall see later, he solved this problem in his relationship to his guru by transforming the nature of power in the relationship. The point here is to recognize that his continuing rebelliousness against authority represents a strong Stage II orientation.

His disillusionment with scientific knowledge is another sign of a Stage II expression of the power need (Table 2.3). After all, there were many young psychologists at Harvard and elsewhere in Richard Alpert's position, none of whom felt the same degree of disillusionment. What bothered him so much? He puts it this way, "Something was wrong. And the something wrong was that I just didn't *know*, though I kept feeling all along the way that somebody else must *know* even if I didn't. The nature of life was a mystery to me. All the stuff I was teaching was just like little molecular bits of stuff but they didn't add up to a feeling anything like *wisdom.*" Or again, "There was still that horrible awareness that I didn't *know* something or other which made it all fall together. There was a slight panic in me that I was going to spend the next forty years *not knowing,* and apparently that was par for the course" (italics mine).

Looking for knowledge in others, he realized that Tim Leary had "an absolutely extraordinary intellect. He really *knew* a lot." His despair after all his drug experiences he described in terms of their not giving him the wisdom for which he was searching-the ultimate secret of life. And then when he went to India he met a young American who was wearing Indian holy clothes, and "I had the feeling I had met somebody who *knew.*" With knowledge goes power. "I see that he is very powerful, so extraordinarily powerful . . ." And what brought about his spiritual transformation when he met Maharaj-ji was that he suddenly realized Maharaj-ji had supernatural powers of knowing.

Our interpretation of all this is that, like all men with a Stage II power orientation, he wanted knowledge in order to control things better, particularly to predict the future. But scientific knowledge, reason, he found totally inadequate to the purpose, just as they do. Hence he sought the all-powerful knowledge in the "ground of being" that lies behind all surface manifestations. Since Maharaj-ji was in that place he knew everything that went on anywhere.

In Stage III expressions of the power need, he was something of a Don Juan, seeking sexual experiences with a variety of women and men, drinking a lot, feeling many neurotic symptoms, and having to lead various double lives to protect himself, just as the men in Table 2.6 report. Above all, he collected valuable possessions, as we have seen. Owning things, as in Chapter 2, can build feelings of strength and security (Stage II) or it can be for a love of display (Stage III); whatever the reason, Alpert was strongly oriented in this mode. "I . . . collected more possessions, collected more appointments and positions and status . . . I was the boy who made it. I was a professor at Harvard and everybody stood around in awe and listened to my every word . . . I had an empire . . . with two secretaries and many graduate and undergraduate research assistants."

Notice that he describes even his students and his knowledge as possessions. Although he saw himself as a typical middle-class Jewish neurotic achiever, his goal was not "achievement" in the technically correct sense of wanting to do a better job regardless of whether one is noticed or not (see McClelland *et al.*, 1953). To him a research contract was not an opportunity to find out something new, but a kind of prestige possession with which to impress people and increase his reputation (Stage III). His primary goal was power, not achievement. Even his various social roles he saw as possessions which he could lose. During his first experience with psilocybin, he says, "I saw a figure standing about eight feet away, where a moment before there had been none. I peered into the semi-darkness and recognized none other than myself, in cap and gown and hood, as a professor. It was as if that part of me, which was Harvard professor, had separated or dissassociated itself from me." He thought it was interesting that he could lose that part of himself. "Well, I worked hard to get that status but I don't really need it." Later he lost other aspects of himself until he found even his body dissolving, and that frightened him. "Doing without professorness or loverness, or even Richard Alpertness, O. K., but I did NEED the body." It alarmed him greatly to realize that if everything was a possession, he might *lose* everything.

He avoided the competitive assertiveness characteristic of Stage III, although we failed to pick it up with the questions asked in Chapter 2. Dick really didn't like competitive sports and didn't participate in them much, either in school or afterwards. While other young men in his circle would enjoy a competitive game of tennis or handball, he preferred scuba diving or learning to fly his own plane. But most strikingly he reports that "though I had been through five years of psychoanalysis, still, every time I lectured, I would get extraordinary diarrhea and tension." It has been found, in Winter's book (1973) and also in three independent samples from the Harvard Summer School, that men choosing a teaching career are significantly higher in *n* Power. Our hypothesis is that lecturing represents a Stage III orientation in the sense that the teacher is directly trying to influence his students or exert his power over them. Thus the significance of Alpert's report is that trying directly to influence others caused him tremendous anxiety.

Although he does not say it in so many words, there is indirect evidence in his autobiography that the implicit competition with his colleagues for advancement in academia also bothered him. It is almost as if he feared success. At one moment he says that "the keys to the kingdom were handed to me," and then a little later that he was in panic about his success and the meaninglessness of it all. When he was in his early twenties, he was made special assistant to his father, then President of the New Haven Railroad. There he had all sort of power over men with years of experience in railroading. The experience frightened him so much that he had to arrange quickly to get someone appointed in his place to still his anxiety.

Horner (1972) has labeled this paradoxical reaction the "fear of success." It is common in women who fear that if they stand out in any way they will be punished or rejected. In Dick's case, we know he liked to please other people; he cared greatly for the good opinion of others. If he were successful in the competition with his peers, however, or if he bossed others, they would scarcely be likely to continue loving him. Success in competition meant increasing the possibility of rejection and dislike; he could no longer please everybody. More than that, he had the example of his father always in mind; his father he saw as someone who had been tremendously successful but who had paid in his view a terrible price in unhappiness. He preferred earlier stage outlets for his power drive.

Finally, there was very little evidence of Stage IV power behavior; he was not an organization man. Like most psychologists, he was oriented more towards individuals than towards groups. He was not conspicuously loyal to some higher authority, organizing things on its behalf, or serving it gladly. Rather he saw organizing, which he did well, as a means of self-development or promoting his own career rather than as doing the will of some authority beyond himself.

In summary, then, we have the picture of a man whose power drive is strong and fixated at Stage I and II levels with some forays into Stage III. Such forays were not, however, expressed at the Stage III level in male competitiveness, which in turn should develop into losing one's self for a higher cause (Stage IV). Why did he find his adjustment so unsatisfactory? Dick explained the problem very well; the difficulty with power in possessions is that possessions do not last. They lose their importance, rust, and decay. You soon discover that you can't "hold on" to anything for very long—not even to the prestige of being on the Harvard faculty, getting a research contract, or being on an important committee. Cessnas, speedboats, and Mercedes Benz sedans, beautiful women, even LSD highs—all lose their charm in time. Under the influence of psilocybin Dick felt that even his social roles were aspects of an identity that he might lose. Thus for the sensitive person, the modes of satisfying his power drive have built-in sources of dissatisfaction, the more so if, as in Dick's case, there is also an ambivalent yearning to return to a Stage I dependence on a strong external power.

What is the solution? If the problem becomes acute enough, it may be resolved by what has traditionally been called the power vision—an abrupt and dramatic *re-experiencing* of power as it courses through you, not as a thing to get and possess through your own efforts. To understand Dick's power vision, and his spiritual experience in general, more fully, let us first examine some classical power visions as they have been reported elsewhere.

Black Elk's Power Vision

To sort out the most general features of a power vision, we need to go outside the particularities of any given time, place, and culture. Let us begin with the vision of an old Sioux medicine man, Black Elk, who told it to John Neihardt, in 1931. To start here has several advantages. Since power visions are considered normal among American Plains Indians, when young men have them, they pay more attention to them, remember them, elaborate and use them throughout their lives. Thus the main features of a vision are likely to come through in simpler and bolder relief than when it is essentially a private, somewhat scarey "hallucination" in a culture which scoffs at such things. In addition, Black Elk had his power vision first in 1872, when he was nine years old, before he or his tribe had had any contact with white men or Christianity. Thus we can be sure that, if we find features in it that also characterize visions in our culture, the similarity cannot be due to cultural borrowing, but must instead be due to the psychic unity of mankind—the tendency of men everywhere to react in similar ways to similar situations. Finally, Black Elk's vision itself is both clear and elaborate. It provides in rich detail the material necessary for a thematic analysis.

Black Elk first had his vision when he was nine years old (Neihardt, *Black Elk Speaks,* 1932, 1972, hereafter referred to as BES). From the beginning he realized that it was designed to give him power, to help him face the winds of life. He kept it secret from others, partly because he was afraid they would think he was crazy, and partly because secrecy is one of the ways to enhance the power of information (see Chapter 3). Although he had never felt he was able to tell all of his vision to anybody, he gave as complete a description as he could to Neihardt because by that time he felt that he had somehow not lived out the implications of his vision and he wanted to save it for other men to use.

As a boy he felt sick one day, his legs hurt, and he heard voices saying, "Hurry! Come! Your grandfathers are calling you!" He saw a cloud coming for him with two spirit men who lifted him up to the heavens, where he saw not only the earth beneath but many strange and wonderful things. He met his old grandfathers, the basic powers in the universe, who bestowed on him various gifts of power for the benefit of the Sioux nation, which he saw in his vision would undergo great troubles in the future. He saw that with the powers he had been given he would triumph in the end; his people would be well and happy. The oldest grandfather dismissed him with these words, "Grandson, all over the universe you have seen. Now you shall go back with power to the place from whence you came" (BES, pp. 37–38). As soon as his vision ended, he "awoke" and was told that he had been unconscious for twelve days. Although he soon got well, he kept having flashbacks to his power vision from time to time, as his people wandered about hunting the buffalo and being chased and often killed by the white man who was gradually destroying the Indian way of life.

Finally when he was seventeen years old, he felt desperately that the powers were calling him and that he must do something, but he did not know what. Ram Dass reports feeling the same way when he was young. It is as if some power is trying the use the person (Stage I), who, however, is caught up in Stage II, thinking *he* must somehow know and decide what he is to do. Later the person learns to lose the sense of ego control in doing the will of higher powers. Black Elk dealt with his problem at the time by telling some of his vision to an older medicine man, who arranged to have it enacted in real life just as Black Elk had seen it. Black Elk felt strengthened by this great ceremony, as did all the people who participated in it. They discovered after going through these visionary enactments further that he had powers for healing the sick; but he still could do nothing for his people as a nation, as the white man systematically slaughtered the buffalo herds and drove the Sioux into smaller and smaller reservations. He even joined a circus for a while and went to Chicago, New York and Europe in order to learn something of the white man's magic, and try to find some way of coping with the destruction of his nation. In the end nothing worked, and because he had failed to help his people, he felt that somehow he had missed the true implications of his vision. Yet he still felt the vision itself was valuable and therefore told it to Neihardt.

With this overview of the function of the vision in his life, let us go back and examine it in more detail. Table 6.1 has been prepared as a kind of outline or guide to the vision: on the left side are listed the various thematic characteristics of the vision; concrete illustrations of these characteristics are provided on the right side. First he experienced the messenger voices which called him to come. Indeed he heard them on occasions before his vision actually took place.

The vision itself begins with a spiritual trip up into the heavens. "I could see my mother and father up yonder and I felt sorry to be leaving them. Then there was nothing but the air and the swiftness of the little cloud that bore me and those two men still leading up to where white clouds were piled like mountains on a wide blue plain, and in them thunder-beings lived and leaped and flashed" (BES, p. 19). He experienced many natural phenomena—rainbows, strong winds, thunder and lightning; but above all he had clear visions. He saw the future of the Sioux nation and the difficulties it would be facing. To face these difficulties he was assisted by various divine helpers—the spirit men who took him up, a bay horse which he rode, but above all the six grandfathers, who represented for him the great spirits or powers of the world. The oldest spoke to him, "Your grandfathers all over the world are having a council, and they have called you here to teach you." "His voice was very kind but I shook all over with fear now, for I knew that these were not old men, but the powers of the world." " . . . Behold . . . the thunder-beings! You shall see, and have from them my power; and they shall take you to the high and lonely center of the earth that you may see. . . ." (BES, p. 22).

As this passage suggests, Black Elk was in tremendous awe of the powers he met. He completely lost the power of choice or decision, but was literally taken and shown things. He had surrendered himself to higher authority. His compulsion to do something that the grandfathers wanted him to do grew on him afterwards until it produced a crisis when he was about seventeen. "I was sixteen years old and more, and I had not yet done anything the grandfathers wanted me to do, but they had been helping me. I did not know how to do what they wanted me to do. A terrible time began for me then . . . I was afraid to see a cloud coming up; and whenever one did, I could hear the thunder-beings calling to me: 'Behold your grandfathers! Make haste!'

Table 6.1—Black Elk's Power Vision

"With Your power only can I face the winds"

Thematic characteristics	Special features
1. The messenger voice	"Hurry! Come! Your grandfathers are calling you."
2. The spiritual trip	Up to the heavens amidst winds, thunder, lightning and a rainbow where he could see the future on earth.
3. Divine helpers	Grandfathers, Great Spirit, Powers of the world, spirit men, horses.
4. Surrender of self to spiritual authority	Loyalty to the vision. He had to act on it.
5. Dangers, threats to be faced	The blue man, sickness and death, fighting, the nation's hoop is broken.
6. The gifts of power	Four kinds of horses
I. Health, relief from suffering	North, white horses, cleansing wind (white goose wing), healing herb
II. Wisdom, foreknowledge	East, sorrel horses, daybreak star of understanding, pipe of peace
III. Supernatural strength	West, black horses, cup of water to make life, bow to destroy
IV. Generativity, compassion	South, buckskin horses, flowering stick and nation's hoop.
7. The spirit guided life Evidences of:	
I. Healing	Curing sick people, not I who did it.
II. Wisdom, foreknowledge	Advance knowledge of significant events.
III. Supernatural strength	Controlling storms, protection against bullets.
IV. Generativity, compassion	All life is holy. Unable to help his nation, as promised.

. . . the crows in the day and the coyotes at night all called and called to me; 'It is time! It is time! It is time!' Time to do what? I did not know" (BES, p. 134). When the tribe enacted his vision, he was relieved, because he felt that at least he had done something that higher authority wanted him to do.

The dangers and threats to be faced by him and his people were experienced vividly in his vision. "Something terrible was there. Flames were rising from the waters and in the flames a blue man lived. The dust was floating all about him in the air, the grass was short and withered, the trees were wilting, two-legged and four-legged beings lay there thin and panting, and wings too weak to fly." Repeatedly he had visions of extreme suffering: "I entered the village . . . and the place was filled with moaning and with mourning for the dead. The wind was blowing from the south like fever, and when I looked around I saw that in nearly every tepee the women and the children and the men lay dying with the dead" (BES, p. 28). "When the people were getting ready to begin the fourth ascent . . . and I looked down . . . they were thin, their faces sharp, for they were starving. Their ponies were only hide and bones. . . ." "The people were camping yonder at the top of the third long rise. It was dark and terrible about me, for all the winds of the world were fighting. It was like rapid gunfire and whirling smoke, and like women and children wailing and like horses screaming all over the world" (BES, pp. 32–33). In many of these instances he was able to restore his people to health by the magical powers that had been given him.

What were these gifts of power? In Black Elk's vision they were associated with four different types of horses and the four points of the compass (outlined in Table 6.1). The first grandfather, represented by a troop of black horses, gave him the gift of supernatural strength symbolized by a cup of water, which is "the power to make live," and a bow, "the power to destroy." When he swooped down and killed the horrible blue man he had the cup of water in one hand and in the other the bow, which turned into a spear with which he stabbed the blue man's heart.

We have listed this gift of strength in Table 6.1 as 6.III to draw attention to the remarkable coincidence between Black Elk's vision of the four gifts of power and our scheme for showing the four levels of the power drive. "The power to make live or destroy" is clearly a Stage III power expression in which a person acts strongly on others. Similarly the other gifts to be described represent the other three stages: health is Stage I; knowledge is Stage II; and generosity and compassion are Stage IV. Although the relationship between the two schemes is coincidental, since my analysis of the stages of power was developed long before I had read Black Elk's account, it is further testimony to the universal applicability of a scheme that fits so well the various gifts of power as described in a non-Western source.

The second grandfather, represented by a troop of white horses from the north, gave him the power to heal and relieve suffering by means of a healing herb and a white goose wing, symbolizing the cleansing wind (BES, p. 139). The gift of health, as we have seen, is strongly associated with Stage I, with the intake of substances which, like mother's milk, strengthen and heal.

The third grandfather, represented by a troop of sorrel horses from the east, gave him the gifts of wisdom and foreknowledge symbolized by the daybreak star of understanding and the pipe of peace. "Then the daybreak star was rising, and a voice said: 'It shall be a relative to them; and who shall see it, shall see much more, for thence comes wisdom; and those who do not see it shall be dark'" (BES, p. 29). The desire for wisdom is the most universal attribute of a Stage II expression of the power need, as we noted in the case of Richard Alpert.

The fourth grandfather, represented by a troop of buckskin horses from the south, gave him the gift of generativity and compassion as symbolized by the flowering stick and the nation's hoop. "Behold, the living center of a nation I shall give you, and with it many you shall save." "And I saw that in his hand he was holding a bright red stick that was alive and as I looked, it sprouted at the top and sent forth branches and on the branches many leaves came out and murmured and in the leaves the birds began to sing. And then, just for a little while I thought I saw beneath it in the shade the circle villages of people and every living thing with roots or legs or wings, and all were happy." "It shall stand in the center of a nation's circle" (BES, p. 24). The flowering stick signifies the power to make his people grow and prosper and be happy. A little later he spoke of the nation's hoop as broken, for he knew Sioux society was breaking up, that the people were no longer thriving like a living thing. Once again the parallel to our scheme is close. Black Elk is defining here what we have called generative power, the Stage IV expression of the power drive, which is associated with organizations and collective leadership.

Black Elk makes one other point of general significance about these gifts of power. In enacting his vision, young women, virgins, were given an important role. "One of the virgins carried the flowering stick, another carried the pipe which gives peace, a third bore the herb of healing, and the fourth held the sacred hoop; for all these powers together are women's power" (BES, p. 178). He seems to be saying, in short, that health, wisdom, and generativity (the flowering stick and the sacred hoop) belong primarily to women, whereas he makes clear elsewhere that the gift of strength (the bow to destroy and the cup of water "to make live") is primarily associated with men. We have found evidence of this same sex role differentiation in Chapter 3 and will have occasion to refer to it again. If there is indeed a natural affinity of the sexes for these different types of power expression, then it is easy to see why a culture stressing strength and competitiveness (Stage III) might be particularly frustrating to women. They would feel neither respected nor valuable in the exercise of the kinds of power that come naturally to them. This may be part of the reason for the unhappiness of many women in the United States today.

Another way to look at a power vision is to see whether it endows the individual with the powers it promises. Did Black Elk benefit from the gifts of power he received in his vision? He showed evidence of three of those four types of power. He discovered fairly early that he had power through prayer and through invoking his vision, to cause storms to come up (the Stage III gift of strength). "As we fled east, a thunder cloud came from the west behind us, and I knew it was coming to protect us . . . I knew better than ever now that I really had power, for I had prayed for help from the grandfathers and they had heard me and set the thunder-beings to hide us and watch over us while we fled" (BES, p. 133). Again, when the whole village enacted his vision in the horse dance, a storm came up. "The hail and rain were falling yonder just a little way from us, and we could see it, but the clouds stood there and flashed and thundered, and only a little sprinkle fell on us. The thunder-beings were glad and it had come in a great crowd to see the dance" (BES, p. 143).

Neihardt reports that after Black Elk as an old man had completed telling his story, he expressed a wish to go once more to Harney Peak, where he had first had his vision when young, in order to recall it once again and to invoke once more the Great Spirit, his Grandfather. Neihardt arranged the trip and reported it was "a bright and cloudless day, and after we reached the summit the sky was perfectly clear. It was a season of drouth, one of the worst in memory of the old men" (BES, p. 232). Black Elk, dressed and painted as he was in his great vision, invoked the spirits of his grandfathers, as he had done all through his life; but this time in a "thin, pathetic voice with tears running down his cheeks because he had accomplished so little for his people." He spoke: "Again, and maybe the last time on this earth, I recall the great vision you sent me. It may be that some little ruler of the sacred tree still lives. . . . Hear me, not for myself but for my people . . ." Then Neihardt goes on to report that "we who listened now noted that thin clouds had gathered about us. A scant chill rain began to fall, and there was low, muttering thunder without lightning. . . . For some minutes the old man stood silent, with face uplifted, weeping in the drizzling rain. In a little while the sky was clear again." His power to influence the weather remained to the end.

Black Elk also reported that his sacred bow protected him from bullets. In the final fight called "The Butchering at Wounded Knee," when white cavalry shot up the nearly defenseless Sioux, he dressed himself as in his vision. He rode "out alone on the old road that ran across the hills to Wounded Knee. I had no gun. I carried only the sacred bow of the West that I had seen in my great vision" (BES, p. 218). With some others he rode over a ridge to charge a group of soldiers who had been holding his relatives at gun point. "The soldiers who were guarding our relatives shot at us and then ran away fast, and some more cavalrymen on the other side of the gulch did too. We got our relatives and sent them across the ridge to the northwest where they would be safe. I had no gun, and when we were charging I just held the sacred bow out in front of me with my right hand. The bullets did not hit us at all" (BES, p. 218–220). Later he says he relaxed and, thinking he was out of danger, put down his bow, at which point a bullet seared his abdomen knocking him off his horse. Although the evidence that he had supernatural strength would not stand against determined skepticism, he certainly believed he had it, and others who knew him believed it too.

Much more evident was his power to heal, (Stage I). After he had gone through various ceremonies enacting his vision, and was recognized as a man of power, a father came to him to ask a cure for his son, who had been sick a long time. Black Elk says that he was uncertain as to whether he could do it, but he wanted to and he prayed hard for help. He drummed, chanted, and enacted various rituals for some time, and "while I was doing this I could feel the power coming through me from my feet up, and I knew that I could help the sick little boy." "I was so eager to help the sick little boy that I called on every power there is" (BES, p. 170). Finally, "putting my mouth to the pit of his stomach, I drew through him the cleansing wind of the North. I next chewed some of the herb and put it in the water, afterward blowing some of it on the boy and to the four quarters. The cup with the rest of the water I gave to the virgin, who gave it to the sick little boy to drink." Then he had the virgin help the boy stand up to walk through the circle of the four quarters, and although he was very weak, he was able to complete the circle. The next day the boy was better, and soon he got well.

From then on Black Elk was much in demand as a medicine man and had many cures to his credit. "And many I cured with the power that came through me. Of course it was not I who cured. It was the power from the outer world and the visions and ceremonies had only made me like a hole through which the power could come to the two-leggeds. If I thought that I was doing it myself, the hole would close up and no power could come through" (BES, p. 174). Thus he says clearly what all healers who have had the power vision conclude: that it is not they who do the curing, but some power beyond themselves that courses through them into the sick person.

Black Elk was known as a wise man, but his reputation derived in large part from the fact that he often could foresee what was going to happen (Stage II power). Neihardt reported that when he first went to see the old man, who lived all alone at the end of a road, he found him standing outside his cabin as if expecting a visitor. His son commented that he had the impression that the old man knew they were coming.

Black Elk had noticed this power in himself when he was growing up. Once when he was with his family in Canada searching for game in the deep snow, he said, "Father, I have heard a coyote say that there are bison on the bit of ridge west of us, and that we shall perceive two people over there. Let us get up early. By this time my father had noticed that I had some kind of queer power, and he believed me" (BES, p. 128). They started off at dawn the next day and eventually stumbled across two horses dim in the blowing snow beside some bushes. With them they found an old man and a boy very cold and hungry and discouraged. As they were talking, the snow haze opened up a little and they saw seven buffalo walking by. They killed them and brought home plenty of meat for the hungry Sioux.

It was helpful visions like these that gave him the reputation of being a seer and wise man. He also reports occasions when he had warning visions—feelings that meant something terrible was going to happen. He had such a feeling that kept him up all the night before the butchering at Wounded Knee. On more than one occasion he sensed before anyone else that hostile Indians were about to attack his band, and he used his knowledge to help them escape injury.

He himself felt that he had not properly used his fourth gift of power—the power to help his people grow and prosper (Stage IV organizational power). "You see me now a pitiable old man, who has done nothing, for the nation's hoop is broken and scattered. There is no center any longer, and the sacred tree is dead" (BES, p. 230). As an individual, however, he did feel the compassion and oneness of all living things that is a part of the gift of generativity. Once when he was still a boy and out shooting with the other boys, he began thinking about his vision. "I felt foolish and tried to make myself think that it was all only a dream anyway. So I thought I would forget about it and shoot something. There was a bush and a little bird sitting on it; but just as I was going to shoot, I felt queer again, and remembered that I was to be like a relative with the birds. So I did not shoot" (BES, pp. 42–42). On another occasion when he was eleven, the boys were all trying to hit some swallows with stones, and "it hurt me to see them doing this, but I could not tell them. I got a stone and acted as though I were going to throw but I did not. The swallows seemed holy." His dream was that all the four-leggeds and the birds and the two-leggeds would live together in harmony, and that all would thrive. Yet he was able to use this gift of power only a little at the personal level. He failed at the societal level, because of hostile forces, largely the greed and superior firepower of the white settlers over which he had no influence.

The Christian Power Vision

The white culture that was pressing in upon Black Elk's people also had its power vision. It is a central part of the Christian faith, which most of these whites professed, and it led some of them to go as missionaries to the Sioux to try to convert them to Christianity. The vision is represented of course by the story of the life of Christ, the Divine Helper, as told in the New Testament; but the *Book of Revelation* presents it in a style more like that of the vision reported by Black Elk. Let us look at the *Book of Revelation* to see if the dramatic power vision reported there has the same thematic elements we have found in Black Elk's vision.

Revelation is a strange book. It reads like a dream—or, more precisely, like the experiences of someone who has just taken LSD or some other psychedelic substance. It is full of bizarre visual images—of dazzling thrones and angels, of horrible beasts and tortures. Difficult to understand in terms of ordinary interpretations of reality, it has led to considerable confusion among theologians who have tried to make sense of it. From the psychological point of view, however, its thematic content is fairly easy to understand. John, a disciple of Jesus Christ, reports the vision to seven Christian churches in Asia Minor whose members are being persecuted by Roman officials. His purpose is clearly to encourage them, to help them remain loyal to the church despite their sufferings. The whole first section of the book reports a message received directly from Jesus Christ stating unequivocally that He is planning to come again quickly. His followers, therefore should remain loyal, because when He comes He will reward them and punish forever those who do not believe in Him.

After reporting these words from Christ, John begins in Chapter 4 of *Revelation* to tell of his great vision. He is taken up to heaven, where he sees what is going to happen in the future. He meets four horsemen and various angels who represent the powers of God. The servants of God—Christian believers—are protected (sealed) against the terrible plagues, tortures and disasters which are going to overtake mankind. The horrors of these terrible times ahead are described in graphic detail. Christ, the Lamb, comes and conquers the evil powers that thrive in the world, e.g., the beasts, and Babylon, mother of harlots. The devil is chained and a new heaven and a new earth—a new Jerusalem—appear in the vision, representing the final triumph of Jesus Christ, who again promises that he is coming quickly. So far as thematic characteristics are concerned, the vision has many similarities to Black Elk's. Table 6.2 has been prepared to highlight these similarities by using the same framework we employed to analyze Black Elk's vision.

Once again, the first event reported is the messenger voice. John hears a voice calling to him to listen or to go and look; repeatedly throughout the vision he hears voices calling him just as Black Elk did. "And the first voice which I heard was as it were of a trumpet talking with me; which said, Come up hither, and I will show thee things which must be hereafter" (4:1). "And the voice which I heard from heaven spoke unto me again, and said, Go and take the little book . . ." (10:8). He too experiences spirit men accompanied by storm signals. "And I saw another mighty angel come down from heaven, clothed with a cloud: and a rainbow was upon his head, and his face was as it were the sun, and his feet as pillars of fire" (10:1). The imagery (clouds, rainbow, fire) is almost exactly the same as Black Elk used, as it is also in the vision of the final day of judgment: "There were lightnings, and voices, and thunderings, and an earthquake, and great hail" (11:19).

John also meets all sorts of divine helpers, representing the power of God. He sees twenty-four elders by the throne of God, just as Black Elk sees his grandfathers. God Himself is not directly described but His power is referred to again and again as reflected through the acts of His angels and of course particularly through Jesus Christ. Jesus appears in various forms, as the Lamb who feeds the people (7:17), by whose sacrificial blood His followers overcome the enemy (12:11), and as a successful warrior. "And I saw heaven opened, and behold a white horse; and He that sat upon him was called Faithful and True, and in rightousness he doth judge and make war . . . and the armies which were in heaven followed him upon white horses, clothed in fine linen, white and clean. And out of his mouth goeth a sharp sword, that with it he might smite the nations . . . and the beast was taken . . . and the remnant was slain with the sword of him that sat upon the horse" (19:14–15, 20, 21). The description is very like Black Elk's vision of the destruction by a sword of the wicked blue man who was laying waste the earth and its people.

A key theme in John's revelation is that people must be loyal to Christ, and surrender themselves to the Lord's spiritual authority.

Table 6.2-The Christian power vision in the Book of Revelation

Thematic characteristics	Special features
1. The messenger voice	"The first voice which I heard was, as it were, of a trumpet." (4:11)
2. The spiritual trip	"Come up hither and I will show thee things which must be hereafter." (4:1) Winds, thunder, lightning, rainbows."
3. Divine helpers	24 elders, Lord God Almighty; Jesus Christ, the Lamb, angels, horses.
4. Surrender of self to spiritual authority	"Redemed among men are those which follow the Lamb whithersoever He goeth." (14:4)
4. Dangers, threats to be faced	The beast (13:1–7, 11). Babylon, mother of harlots (17:6). The Devil (8–9: 16), Death, sickness, pain, burning, drought.
6. The gifts of power	
I. Health, relief from suffering	The pale horse, whose rider is suffering, hunger, and death. "And God shall wipe away all tears from their eyes." (7:17)
II. Wisdom, foreknowledge	The black horse, the pair of balances, fair prices (6:6). "The bright and morning star." ". . . to testify with you those things" (22:16). "The little book," "sweet in thy mouth." (10:8–9)
III. Supernatural strength	The white horse, a bow to conquer (6:12), a sword (19:11–15), the water of life. (22:17)
IV. Generativity, compassion	The red horse, power to kill one another (6:4). The tree of life . . . "and the leaves of the tree were for the healing of nations." (22:2).
7. The spirit guided life	
I. Healing	Peter heals Tabitha. (Acts 9:37–41).
II. Wisdom, foreknowledge	"Ye are wise in Christ." (I. Cor. 4:10).
III. Supernatural strength	Peter freed from prison, Paul by an earthquake. (Acts 16:26)
IV. Generativity, compassion	"And the greatest of these is charity." (I. Cor. 13:13).

"And I heard a voice from heaven saying unto me, Write, Blessed are the dead which die in the Lord henceforth; Yea, sayeth the spirit, that they may rest from their labors" (14:13). Those who surrender their will to the Lord shall rest and be easy. They shall also be saved from death and destruction. "And I saw another angel ascending from the east . . . and he cried in a loud voice to the four angels, to whom it was given to hurt the earth and the sea, Saying, Hurt not the earth neither the sea, nor the trees, 'til we have sealed the servants of our God in their foreheads" (7:2–3). Those who are sealed, who "follow the Lord whithersoever he goeth," are saved for the new Jerusalem.

John sees the horrible dangers to be faced by his people even more vividly than Black Elk does. When the Seventh Seal is opened, he predicts that all manner of plagues will be visited upon the earth. Hail and fire will come down and burn up the trees and the green grass and turn a third of the sea into blood, killing the creatures in it and the ships that sail upon it. The waters will become bitter and the men who drink them will die. A plague of locusts will arise which will torment men since they have breastplates of iron and tails like scorpions with stings that can hurt a man for five months. Horses will come breathing fire and brimstone and kill a third of all men living (Chapters 8–9). Although John does not see a terrible blue man, he does observe a beast rising up out of the sea "having seven heads and ten horns" like unto a leopard "with the feet of a bear, the mouth of a lion and the power of a dragon" (13:1–2). Riding on the beast is a woman "drunken with the blood of the saints, and with the blood of the martyrs of Jesus", Babylon the great, "the mother of harlots and abominations of the earth" (17:5–6). But the people with the power of the Lord, those who are loyal and faithful to Him, shall overcome the beast and the city of Babylon represented by the woman, just as Black Elk in his vision overcame the blue man. An angel shall "bind for a thousand years" the Devil and Satan as representatives of the evil forces which had beheaded the witnesses for Jesus (20:2, 4).

Here again, the psychological situation is similar to Black Elk's. In his case the beast was the white man who was destroying his people. The power vision gave him confidence in ultimate triumph, just as John's power vision was to give him and the Christian church confidence that it would ultimately overcome the persecutions of the Romans and those who followed other gods.

Let us next take a look at the gifts of power that are conveyed to John. As in Black Elk's vision, the powers are described as coming from the four corners of the earth (the four points of the compass) and are represented by four horsemen. The horse imagery is elaborated less in John, however, which is not surprising since he was speaking for a people who were not nearly as oriented towards horses as the Plains Indians were. So we have to look elsewhere in the book for the powers the Lord confers. In this search we are helped by the symbols Black Elk associated with each of these powers; several of them turn out to be the same.

John sees a pale horse (6:8) and a rider, clearly representing suffering, hunger, and death. The Lord's first gift of power is relief from suffering. Those that serve him day and night "shall hunger no more, neither thirst anymore; neither shall the sun light on them, nor any heat. For the Lamb which is in the midst of the throne shall feed them, and shall lead them unto living fountains of waters; and God shall wipe away all tears from their eyes" (7:16–17). This is classic Stage I power imagery. Missing from this description is Black Elk's healing herb and cleansing wind, although there is a reference to wings. When the mother of Jesus was persecuted by the dragon, she was "given two wings and a great eagle, that she might fly into the wilderness" where she was safe (Chapter 12:14). Eagle wings were important symbols of power to Black Elk also.

In John's revelation, the Stage II concern for increased wisdom seems to be represented by the black horse whose rider carried a pair of balances (6:6). Although the passage is somewhat obscure ("A measure of wheat for a penny . . .") its import seems to be a concern for fair pricing. A fair bargain is certainly a key symbol of wisdom to the Jews, although not to the Sioux. More directly comparable are several references to the morning star which to John as to Black Elk, represents understanding. Jesus promises that he who is loyal to the end shall not only rule nations, "I will give him the morning star" (2:28). Elsewhere he explains his meaning. "I, Jesus, have sent mine angel to testify unto you these things in the churches. I am the root and the offspring of David, and the bright and morning star" (22:16). In other words, I, who know all these things and who have explained them all to you, am the morning star: the morning star represents wisdom and foreknowledge.

The Jews, from whom the Christians derived, were also a people of the book. They could, and did, write, whereas the Sioux did not. Thus for John the "little book" is a symbol of the foreknowledge given to him in his vision of what will happen. The angel, who gives him the book of knowledge when he asks for it, warns him that it will be sweet in his mouth but bitter in his belly, and he finds that it is so (10:8–10). At first, in other words, foreknowledge seems a wonderful thing, until one discovers what terrible things are going to happen.

Supernatural strength, the power over life and death, is for John the Stage III gift of power, as it is in Black Elk's vision. "And I saw, and behold a white horse: and he that sat on him had a bow; . . . and he went forth conquering, and to conquer." Once again we find the bow as a symbol of strength, and again, as in Black Elk's vision, it turns into a sword which vanquishes the enemy (19:11–15). The lord also conveys the power of life. "And he that sat upon the thrones said . . . I will give unto him that is athirst of the fountain of the water of life freely" (21:5–7). The image of the cup of water or the water of life (22:17) is the same in the two visions.

The fourth gift of power is represented negatively by the fourth horseman who represents the power to destroy peace and to kill. This power is different from the power of conquest represented by the first horseman since it refers to internal struggles among family, neighbors, and friends. It is therefore the opposite of compassion for one another and the prosperity of a nation. The Lord also conveys the gift of the tree of life, which is just like the image of Black Elk's flowering stick. "And on either side of the river was there the tree of life, which bare twelve manner of fruits, and yielded her fruit every month: and the leaves of the tree were for the healing of the nations" (22:2). This passage makes clear that the final gift of power is for organizations of people (the nations), just as the flowering stick was for building the sacred hoop of the Sioux nation. In the new Jerusalem, as in heaven, men and beasts will live peaceably together; in his vision John sees a lion, a calf, a man, and a flying eagle all together around the throne of God (4:7). "And all the beasts gave honor and glory to the Lord who had created all things." The experience is not unlike Black Elk's when he saw all living things gathered in harmony together as creations of God or of the central powers in the universe.

The visions of Black Elk and John seem remarkably similar. A spirit voice calls. The person is lifted up to heaven where he foresees the future; warned to surrender himself to the spiritual authority, he is given divine help in the form of four particular types of power which he can use to overcome the many dangers foreseen as threatening him and his people in the future. These four gifts of power resemble the four stages in the expression of the power drive which we have derived from quite different sources. Some of the details of the visions are similar, such as the heavenly displays (rainbows, clouds, thunder and lightning), the four corners of the earth, the spirit men, the water of life, the morning star, the tree of life, and the four horses—which happen also to be of the same four colors, black, white, red, and grey. The colors of the horses, to be sure, are not associated with the same gifts of power; but it is worth mentioning that Winter (1973) has reported the colors black and red (two of the colors of the horses) to be associated with a heightened need for power. He did not check unfortunately to see whether white and grey are also symbolic of the need for Power. The skeptic may argue that since horses come in a limited number of colors, the choice is not wide, but one might answer that neither visionary saw spotted or dappled horses taking part in the pageant of power.

Such arguments, however, are largely beside the point because it is obvious not only that the two visions do differ in important respects but that these differences arise from the values in the two cultures of the visionaries themselves. Since the Jews valued book learning and fair bargains, it is not surprising to find these elements more elaborated by John than by Black Elk. Our point is that an individual who has a vision experiences a similar sequence of events representing the means for gaining power, and overcoming difficulties. He gets the same four different varieties of power simply because there are four major types of human power that can be attained by those who have a heightened need for Power. Although the particular imagery the visionary uses will be shaped by his cultural experience, he will be influenced even here by a number of universal natural phenomena, such as the way water makes a plant grow. Thus similar images, such as water as the symbol of life, tend to be used by individuals from unrelated cultures.

As to the effects of the Christian vision on those who experience it, and its effectiveness in giving them powers such as Black Elk's, we cannot be sure in the case of John himself; but there is ample evidence in the New Testament that other disciples had such powers. Jesus spent much of his time healing others, even those who were apparently dead (Stage I). He had almost complete foreknowledge (Stage II) of what was about to happen to him in Jerusalem when he was crucified. He demonstrated supernatural strength (Stage III) in walking on the water, turning water into wine, or casting out demons. And his compassion (Stage IV) as represented by the Sermon on the Mount is one of his outstanding characteristics. "Inasmuch as ye have done it to the least of these, ye have done it unto me." Or, "Suffer the little children to come unto me."

In varying degrees his disciples are also reported to have had these powers. Peter was put in prison and chained between two soldiers. An angel of the Lord came to him, struck the chains from his hands and led him out of prison (Acts 12:6–10). Paul and Silas were also delivered from an inner prison where their feet had been fastened in stocks. After praying and praising God, "Suddenly there was a great earthquake, so that the foundations of the prison were shaking: and immediately all the doors were opened, and everyone's bands were loosed" (Acts 16:26). The disciples could also heal. A certain disciple named Tabitha who was full of good deeds, became sick and died, "whom when they washed, they laid her in an upper chamber." Peter was called in; he sent the weeping widows out of the room where she was lying, "kneeled down and prayed; and turning him to the body said, Tabitha, arise. And she opened her eyes: and when she saw Peter, she sat up" (Acts 10:40).

The disciples also knew things that ordinary people did not. Since Jesus had explained everything to them, they knew what was going to happen not only to him but to the world, as laid out in the book of Revelation. "Henceforth I call you not servants; for the servant knoweth not what his Lord doeth: but I have called you friends; for all things that I have known of my Father I have made known unto you" (John 15:15). They also received practical guidance in everyday life, as Black Elk did, as to the consequences of a contemplated action. Paul was forever getting into trouble by preaching Christ in the synagogues to the Jews. They became so angry with him in Corinth that he must have wondered if it was safe for him to stay in that town. "Then spake the Lord to Paul in the night by a vision, be not afraid, but speak and hold not thy peace, for I am with thee, and no man shall set on thee to hurt thee: for I have much people in this city" (Acts 18:9–10). And Paul stayed in Corinth preaching successfully, and he was not harmed.

The early Christians were urged to be compassionate, to be charitable and loving at all times. The best known expression of this ideal is the thirteenth chapter of Paul's first epistle to the church at Corinth. "And though I have the gift of prophecy, and understand all mysteries, and all knowledge; and though I have all faith, so that I could remove mountains, and have not charity, I am nothing. And though I bestow all my goods to feed the poor, and though I give my body to be burned, and have not charity, it profiteth me nothing" (I Corinthians 13:2–3). In other words, no matter how many good things I may do, unless I do them in the spirit of love, compassion, or charity, they are not meritorious.

Modern Christian Power Visions

All of these are events of a long time ago, and perhaps they were built up in the telling to bolster the case for Christianity. Are those who have the Christian power vision today affected by it in the same ways? Apparently they are. Consider the case of R. D. Cronquist, pastor of Coniah Chapel, a fundamentalist evangelical Christian group in Chula Vista, California, which calls itself the Body of Christ. Of a relatively simple background, like the early disciples, he did not have much education. While he worked in the San Diego navy yard, he engaged in part-time preaching. In this respect he was like dozens of other Christian evangelists preaching to a tiny group in southern California. Over a period of time, as he read his Bible daily and increased his devotion to the Lord, he began to feel more and more vividly the presence of God, who spoke to him from time to time and asked him to do things.

He is a visionary mystic in much the same sense as John was, who reported his visions in the Book of Revelation; in fact, the Book of Revelation is one of R.D.'s (as he is called) favorite books. Eventually the Lord called him to give up his job and to preach fulltime, although, as he admits, he was very reluctant to do so and was not at all sure he had heard correctly, because he didn't know where the next dollar was coming from. But the Lord was right: money seemed to appear whenever he needed it, and his message appealed powerfully to a group of young people, many of them from middle-class families who had dropped out in one way or another, often becoming involved in the process in the drug culture.

Coniah Chapel was, when I visited it in the early 1970's, a vital growing institution which had attracted two to three hundred people, most of them in their twenties. They attend church services four nights a week for two and a half to three hours. The members of the Body sing gospel songs, speak aloud in tongues often for as long as twenty to thirty minutes, and listen to a sermon by one of the brothers or by R.D.—an exposition of some Biblical text in traditional Christian terms. The message is clear: everyone should submit his will totally and completely to the authority of Jesus Christ, our Lord and Savior. They believe that other churches have fallen away from the vitality of the early Christian message as represented quite literally in the Bible, and they try to practice early devout Christianity as closely as possible. After each service, there is usually a period of healing in which various elders with the gift, aided by others, lay hands on someone who is in trouble and pray that God will release him or help him. If R.D. is present, he is the central figure in these healing ceremonies.

One evening I asked R.D. if there were any instances in which these efforts to heal had proven successful. He said, Oh yes, of course there were, and cited a number of instances; but he cautioned me to remember that it was not he who did the curing, but the Lord operating through him. He used almost the same words as Black Elk. Like Black Elk also, he is himself an impressive person with the look of one who has seen visions and could have a powerful influence on people; yet in telling stories about instances of healing that he personally observed, he is humble and humorous. One anecdote he told illustrates particularly well how these experiences happen to him.

He had been preaching the gospel in Mexico and was driving alone back towards the border, when a message came to him strongly from the Lord that he was to go to the "El Alamein" hospital in the town through which he was passing. So far as he could recall, he had never heard of such a hospital; he certainly did not know where it was. Obedient to the call, however, he inquired and discovered that there was such a hospital, and found his way to it. Once there, he was still not at all sure of what he was supposed to do. As he put it, the message from the Lord is not always entirely clear and what you have to do is follow it as far as you can. So he mingled with the crowd and went into the hospital, trying to get a further insight as to what he was supposed to do. In the end, he stood in each doorway on the first floor, trying to get a message as to whether he was supposed to go into that room and pray for the patient inside. But having done this in every doorway on the first floor, he still had no lead; he repeated the process on the second floor and the third floor, still with no further indication of what he should do. He was about to give up, thinking that he must have got the message from the Lord wrong, when he noticed that one corner of the third floor consisted of two rooms locked and barred as if they were prison cells. In one room there were a lot of Mexicans and in the other he saw an American walking around. He went up to speak to the American, thinking that it might be here that he was called; as he did so, he noticed another man lying as if drunk or asleep on a bed. When he asked the American who the other man was, he said he knew neither who he was nor what was the matter with him. He had been lying like that, unconscious, unmoving, ever since he, the American, had been put in the room some thirty-six hours earlier.

R.D. then realized that the Lord had called him there to pray for this sick man, and he felt a strong urge to go in immediately and do so. The American told him, however, that no one was allowed in there, but that the Mexican guards standing nearby had the key. Then R.D. reports what for him was a remarkable phenomenon: he found himself going up to one of the guards and speaking to him in Spanish asking to be let into the room. He also understood the man's replies in Spanish, although he claims that he really doesn't speak Spanish and can't understand it ordinarily. The guard told him that no one was allowed in there without the permission of higher authorities, but that the other guard had the key. So again, R.D. spoke to the other guard in Spanish, asking to be let into the room. The other guard explained to him that he could not let him in, at the very moment, as R.D. reports it, that he was taking the key out of his pocket and unlocking the door. R.D. went immediately to the side of the sick man and discovered that he was not just asleep but unconscious; he felt his pulse, which was very weak, and decided that all he could do was pray for God to heal him, which he knelt and did. After a time, he felt released from the duty God had laid on him, and got up. Nothing happened. The man did not stir. So he left the room, noting, as he went out, that he could no longer understand what the Mexican guards were saying to him. He returned to his car and drove on to his home in southern California, wondering what it was all about, and thinking that sometimes the ways of God are truly mysterious.

He had more or less forgotten about the episode when, about five months later, a man came up to him after he had been preaching to a large gathering and asked him if he had ever seen him before. R.D. looked at him and said no, he didn't recall ever having seen him, but that, of course, he met a lot of people in the course of his work. The man then told him that he had saved his life, that he was that sick man in the cell in the hospital in Mexico. Not long after R.D. had left, he woke from his stupor, very weak, but clear in his mind. From talking with the other American in the room, he had learned about R.D.'s visit. What had happened was that in the days before R.D. found him in the hospital, he had been having a series of what appeared to be epileptic fits in which he would fall to the ground unconscious, bleeding and foaming at the mouth. At first the Mexican police authorities had assumed that he had taken massive doses of drugs of some kind, but when his condition seemed to get worse and worse, they had taken him out of jail where they had put him to recover, and sent him to the hospital. There he had fallen into the coma in which R.D. had found him, and apparently the medical authorities also had been unable to do anything for him. Being of clear mind again, after R.D.'s intercession, he was able to explain to the Mexican authorities what had been wrong with him. When he was let out of jail, he found that his sister had sent him some money from Kansas so that he was able to go back to California. Apparently he had been unwell for some time before the final crisis, and had been wandering around in a dazed state unable to care for himself. In the five months since his recovery, however, he had had no recurrence of his attacks, and had been able to go back to work and lead a normal life.

R.D. told the story in a simple, matter-of-fact way, much as one would describe a trip taken to the mountains. He saw nothing particularly miraculous about it, since, as he put it, the Lord was more real to him than most people, and he knew the Lord was capable of healing in this way through those who opened themselves totally to him as R.D. tried to do.

Particularly noteworthy, however, is the fact that the account sounds so much like the stories of healing in the New Testament. Just as when Peter healed Tabitha, the person healed was unconscious and presumably unaware that he was being prayed over. Thus it is difficult to explain the result as a "faith cure," as psychologists are wont to do. What is also important is that R.D. insists, as Black Elk and the disciples did, that he himself has no particular power, that it is *God* who heals working through him. In fact, he warns against the use of the Lord's name as a kind of magic formula in an effort to cast out demons, citing the example given in Acts of the sorcerers who tried it and ended up having to run away naked. One has to really *experience* the power, not just call upon it or name it.

This episode illustrates how a modern Christian visionary has received the promised gifts of supernatural strength (R.D. got into the prison, could speak and understand Spanish) and healing (the man with epileptic fits was cured). R.D. also told instances in which foreknowledge had been granted as to what was going to happen. Some eleven years earlier, he had gone to Los Angeles to see Brother Stevens, another Christian mystic, to ask for guidance as to what he should do with his life. Brother Stevens told him of a vision he had of a chapel R.D. would build on a certain piece of ground. He described buildings that were already on the ground, including a house and a shed, and the general layout of the property, just as if he had really seen it. The vision meant absolutely nothing to R.D. He knew of no such property, and certainly the vision had no relation to the tiny room in which he was conducting services at the time. Although he told the vision to a number of people, it seemed to have no meaning to anyone.

Nine years later, his sister-in-law, who was connected with a real estate firm, came in great excitment to tell him that she had just seen a property newly come on the market that matched in every detail the vision Brother Stevens had had so long ago. A man had died, and his property had to be sold quickly to settle his estate. Since R.D. realized that Brother Stevens' vision meant he must build a chapel on this property, he got an option on the property and immediately set to work to raise money to buy it. Through what he regarded as a miracle, since his congregation was by no means well-to-do, the money arrived in bits and pieces to buy the property, available at a price much below what it was worth in that part of California.

Love, fellowship, and compassion are key characteristics of R.D. and the Body of Christ. They love one another, they help one another, they are constantly together. As one elder put it in a sermon "you are to be servants of the Lord in bearing one another's burdens.

Drink not of your own cup, but of each others' cups." They bless each other whenever they meet. And unlike some evangelical Christian groups, they are unwilling to condemn those who do not belong to their particular circle of Christians, because, as R.D. puts its, you can never be sure what instrument the Lord will use.

Richard Alpert's Power Vision

The Christian power vision has had a strong revival in the United States today, particularly among young people, many of whom are from middle class backgrounds and have had at least some college education. The Body of Christ is by no means an unusual phenomenon. There are dozens of other groups of "Jesus freaks," as they are sometimes called, commonly made up of formerly alienated young people who had found power, release, and joy in the Christian vision. These groups have founded churches, set up Christian communes, published newspapers like *Right On* that have the character of underground newspapers with the important difference that they are Jesus-oriented. Evangelical Christianity is growing in the United States everywhere. Its churches are growing in membership, its periodicals are increasing in circulation, at the very moment when the more traditional liberal Christian journal, *The Christian Century,* is losing circulation. The Methodist Church, the mainstream American Protestant denomination, is also declining in numbers, though the more evangelical Southern Baptist Convention is increasing in membership. Some of the reasons for this evangelical Christian revival will be discussed in Chapter 9.

To be noted here is the fact that the Christian vision appeals precisely to the same alienated intellectual group to which Richard Alpert belonged. Since he was of Jewish background, it would not have been easy for him to buy into the Christian power vision, although some young Jews have, and have formed a group which they call Jews for Jesus. He had not only the personal reasons for seeking a power vision described earlier, he was subject to the same social influences that led young people everywhere to reach out for a power vision. They had been called to a war on racism, poverty, and on war itself—all of which wars require, in our terms, Stage III or Stage IV expressions of the power drive. The very notion of "war" on something requires that one seek aggressively to destroy or do away with something (Stage III). At the same time, one is acting on behalf of some higher principle (Stage IV). When in the late 1960's, all of these wars seemed to be unsuccessful, the heightened power drive of the young people sought an expression in some other modality—particularly in the Stage I modality, for which drug experiences and religious power visions are prime examples. As in Black Elk's time, and as in Palestine at the time Christianity started, the young people in American in the late 1960's felt oppressed. Their power drives were aroused (see Chapter 9), and yet they seemed to be singularly unsuccessful in expressing them in ways in the real world that would bring about the end of oppression. So their power drive sought some other outlet—the power vision.

A direct method is available for checking this hypothesis. To anticipate the next chapters, concern for organizational leadership and crusades for social justice are associated with a high power need when it is combined with a concern for discipline, estimated through a measure of inhibition also obtained from fantasy. If what we have just argued is true, therefore, it should follow that America was high in n Power and Inhibition in the late 1960's—which Chapter 9 demonstrates to be true. People high in n Power and Inhibition should also have more power visions, as also turns out to be true among the subjects tested in Chapter 2. We asked them in the questionnaire whether they had ever had a definite experience of "the presence of God", "being 'at one with nature,'" communicating psychically "with someone not present, dead, etc." or being healed by a "spiritual or religious healer." For those high in inhibition, n Power was associated with the number of such experiences reported, significantly for the men ($r = .41$, $n = 34$, $p < .05$) and nearly so for the women ($r = .21$, $n = 38$, $p < .10$ in the predicted direction). Why should this be true? Perhaps the keen desire to bring about organizational or social change, particularly when it is blocked or one is anxious about expressing aggression, leads one to search actively for those sources of power that will best justify assertiveness and provide a greater feeling of the strength needed to bring the change about.

In Richard Alpert's case, as in the case of a significant number of other young people, he found his vision not in Christianity, but in Hinduism and Buddhism. He experienced his saving vision in India. The fact should not surprise a reader who has examined the earlier chapter on themes in the culture of India. A psychological analysis of popular and religious stories in India reveals that frustration or anxiety over expressing aggression is one of the prime movers behind the formulation of Hindu and Buddhist thought. The central notion is that personal desire is the cause of all suffering and that in order to attain the ultimate goal of peace or nirvana, one must give up attachment or desire. One must give up the *self* as the source of power motivation (Stages II and III in our terms). It is significant that this lesson is driven home in the episode (cited in the chapter on India) in the Bhagavad Gita in which Arjuna was anxious about going to war with his kinsmen—anxious about being aggressive, a Stage III expression of the power drive, just as we discovered Dick Alpert was. The answer Krishna gave him was that he must fight without attachment, give up the impulse to be aggressive as coming from the self and yet still do his duty, what he *had* to do.

In Buddhist teachings also it is clear that the sensuous craving which is the primary source of suffering involves what we would call Stage III expressions of the power drive (self acting on others). For instance, here is a passage from the Sutta-Pitaka (discourse collection), the earliest record of the teachings of Buddha in the Pali Canon.

> "Verily, due to sensuous craving, conditioned through sensuous craving, impelled by sensuous craving, entirely moved by sensuous craving, kings fight with kings, princes with princes, priests with priests, citizens with citizens; the mother quarrels with the son, the son with the mother; father with son, son with father; brother with brother, etc. Thus, given to dissension, quarreling, and fighting, they fall upon one another with fists, sticks or weapons. And thereby they suffer death or deadly pain.
>
> And further, due to sensuous craving, people break into houses, rob, plunder, pillage whole houses, commit highway robbery, seduce the wives of others . . . And further, people take to the evil way in deeds, word, and thought . . . they fall into . . . a state of suffering . . . This is the misery of sensuous craving, the heaping up of suffering in the future life, due to sensuous craving."

We have here, in short, a list of various ways in which a person can be aggressive and express his power needs at a Stage III level, and they are all considered to be bad and to constitute the fundamental cause of suffering. The Five Precepts central to Buddhist philosophy are: not to take life, not to steal, not to commit sexual misconduct, not to lie, and not to get drunk. Again, these are all Stage III power-related acts, and religious thinking in India seems designed particularly to escape performing such acts. This situation corresponds exactly to the personal problem faced by Richard Alpert, as well as to the social problem many American young people felt when their aggressive acts to bring about a better world seemed to lead only to increased suffering and disillusionment. It is not surprising that the Indian solution to this problem appealed to Alpert: it exhorts man to give up sensuous craving (meaning largely aggressive urges, Stage III) and to seek union with the divine ground in Nirvana (a Stage I or Stage IV power vision).

We have had to speak here of course in a very general, over-simplified way about Indian religious thinking, which is obviously complex and interpreted in various ways by hundreds of scholars over centuries. Our particular concern here is the way in which Alpert and his associates perceived Indian religion and expounded it in their book, *Be here now*. What they have done is stick fairly closely to standard Buddhist teachings, themselves derived from earlier Hindu teachings, although Buddhists sometimes say they are not religious since they do not believe in God. To this doctrine Ram Dass and his friends added some elements from Hinduism, and some fairly idiosyncratic ideas that seem to have been drawn from their own experience or from western culture. The result is syncretistic, although it does not deviate greatly from standard Indian religious teachings, as Ram Dass was instructed in them in Maharaj-ji's ashram and elsewhere.

Let us use once more the framework we developed to analyze Black Elk's vision, and sort out different aspects of Dick's Alpert's vision. Is the framework applicable? To a remarkable extent it is: it enables us to make sense out of his many and varied experiences, even though technically he did not have any one vision as reported by Black Elk or John. Nevertheless, the format of his power "trip" or power experience turns out to be similar to that of the other two visionaries.

Table 6.3 has been prepared to show in more detail how his experiences fit the analytic framework we have been using. We refer to it as the Ram Dass vision because, like Saul of Tarsus, to signify that he was a new man, he accepted a new name given him by Maharaj-ji after his conversion. As he has recognized, his drug experiences clearly prepared him for the trip he eventually took. They opened his eyes to strange and wonderful sights, sounds, and feelings in much the same way as the visions of Black Elk and John prepared them for the subsequent message. Since in the cultures from which they came, it was normal for people to have visions, they paid close attention to them, remembered them, and kept re-experiencing them afterwards. In the culture of academic psychology to which Richard Alpert belonged, it is definitely abnormal to have visions: they are considered to be hallucinations produced by mental disorder. Therefore one should be ashamed of them and, if they are persistent, go to a psychiatrist to be cured of them. Thus the only practicable way to have a visionary experience in the West is to take the drugs that produce it. As Ram Dass' teacher, Hari Dass Baba, pointed out, in the materialistic West it is perhaps necessary to have a material object like an LSD pill to produce a genuine spiritual experience. Of course the Westerner knows that his experiences are brought on by a pill rather than by a spiritual force, but the experiences themselves are so overwhelming that they convert people to an appreciation of the tremendous power of the not-self, that which is not under conscious control—call it what you will. It opens their eyes to the narrowness of the band of phenomenal experiencing that most people live in all their lives, and prepares them for psychic experiences that lie outside that band. In this sense Dick Alpert's drug experiences prepared him for his spiritual trip. Bruce Smith (1973) has in fact collected empirical evidence to support the notion that those who continue taking LSD as opposed to other drugs are those who feel a tremendous surge of power from *outside* themselves during their best trips.

The trip proper begins again with messenger voices. They came in two forms. One was Bhagwan Dass, the tall, blond, young American who had become completely Indianized in dress and habits, and who lived as a kind of wandering Indian holy man. Dick somehow felt Bhagwan Dass "knew," that he was extraordinarily powerful, and that he himself should follow this man, becoming like him and living like a Sadhu also, without shoes, medicines or any of the comforts to which a wealthy Western traveler is accustomed. Eventually, Bhagwan Dass turned out to be a messenger who had picked Alpert up to take him to his guru, Maharaj-ji; but at the time, Dick felt only that he had to follow him.

During their travels the second call came, this time from Dick's mother, who had died the year before. He was out under the stars at night urinating when he looked up and suddenly experienced the presence of his mother. "It's very, very powerful, and I feel great love for her, and then I go back to bed." It reminded him of an earlier experience when he had had "a vision of her one night, when I was going to bed. I saw her up on the ceiling and I was wondering whether to go to India or go on to Japan, and she had a look that was the look of 'You damned fool—you're always getting into hot water, but go ahead, and I think that's great.'" He felt that there was a spiritual being underneath her middle-class respectability which was in effect saying "Go, Baby." He also reported that several times he had had a fantasy, while taking drugs, of a woman's voice telling him to proceed.

He then goes up to this "lovely, lovely place" in the foothills of the Himalayas—"clouds cover a beautiful green valley"—where he meets Maharaj-ji and observes what is to him a very strange scene of Maharaj-ji's devotees, crying, kissing his feet, and feeding him. Maharaj-ji demonstrates that he knows about Dick's thoughts under the stars about his mother the previous night and also about how she died. Somehow this demonstrates to Dick conclusively in the emotional sense that there is a spiritual world of tremendous power outside of himself. This was something the drug experiences had never been able to do for him because, as he puts it, "After all, under the influence of a chemical, how do I know I'm not creating the whole thing?" But he knew he was awake then, he hadn't taken any chemicals, and yet here was a man knowing things that he just couldn't figure out that anybody could have told him. Later on Maharaj-ji was to demonstrate over and over again his psychic powers to know what was passing in Dick's mind or in other people's minds, and to influence what happened to them.

So Maharaj-ji becomes his major divine helper, his guru, although he also gets help from Bhagwan Dass, from Hari Dass Baba, who is the intellectual teacher in Maharaj-ji's entourage, and from Munindra, a Buddhist meditation teacher in Bodhgaya, the place where Buddha received enlightenment under the Bo-tree. Although Hari Dass Baba has taken a vow of silence, he is a "spit and polish" teacher who knows many languages, and who instructs Ram Dass daily in "Raja Yoga," with simple metaphor and brief phrase. The divine mother is for Ram Dass also a spiritual helper. "The divine mother which is nature! Which is you! Which is all of this! Which is the whole physical plane!" (*Be Here Now,* Part 2, p. 48).

One of the main things Ram Dass learned in his spiritual journey was to surrender the ego. "What are you giving up? A hollow little trip that's good for another forty years at best. You're giving it up for eternal union with pure energy and pure light, because the rainbow means you no longer die. Because if there was no you, no ego, you can't die. You are part of all patterns of energy" (*Be Here Now,* Part 2, p. 20). In another place he puts it this way: "If I am a potter, I make pots. But *who* is making the pots? I am not under the illusion that I am making the pots. Pots are. The potter is. I am a hollow bamboo" (2:54). At a more mundane level, all of his major decisions are made for him by his guru. He tells his father that he'll go back to India when his guru says he's to come back. He has surrendered himself to Maharaj-ji because Maharaj-ji represents "the universal guru, a level of consciousness, a frequency of vibration, a connection to another plane" (p. 62). He is so in love with him or the principle he represents "that I would do anything that he would ever ask of me." And to the extent that Ram Dass is spiritually attuned, "he's right here now."

The dangers and threats to be faced are internal psychological states rather than external threats of war, hunger, and oppression. But

Table 6.3—*The Ram Dass Power Vision*

	Special features
Thematic characteristics	
1. The messenger voice	Vision of his mother on the ceiling, under the stars. "Go, baby."
2. The spiritual trip	LSD visions of heaven and hell, trip to India, "clouds, beautiful green valley, lovely place, foothills of the Himalayas."
3. Divine helpers	Bhagwan Dass, Maharaj-ji, Hari Dass Baba, Munindra, etc.
4. Surrender self to spiritual authority	"Total surrender, there's no more you, you're part of it all." "I'm going back to India when the guru says I'm to come back." Love, serve, remember God.
5. Dangers, threats to be faced	The births, the deaths, the suffering, despair, alienation, decay, desire, anger, greed, lust, fear.
6. The gifts of power	SAT CHIT ANANDA (total existence, knowledge, bliss).
I. Health, relief from suffering	Get free of desire . . . Be here now, the stillness, the calmness, the fulfillment, exhilaration, the divine dance.
II. Wisdom, foreknowledge	The witness, the highest chakras: wisdom (the third eye) and full enlightenment.
III. Supernatural strength	"You become ALL energy." "As one increases the one-pointedness of mind, one gains more and more powers (siddhis)."
IV. Generativity, compassion	"Compassionate feelings of the brotherhood of the spirit with all other beings."
7. The spirit guided life	
I. Healing	Getting straight, help for the dying.
II. Wisdom, foreknowledge	My guru knew everything in my head, whether "I liked it or not."
III. Supernatural strength	Siddhis: overcoming drugs, physical powers.
IV. Generativity, compassion	Vegetarianism. "You make many people laugh, feed children."

the suffering is nevertheless real if you are not enlightened. Beauty withers, the fear of death plagues us. "Lame, halt, blind, dying, . . . we're all dying at this moment. Your body is disintegrating before your very eyes." "It is attachment, desire which causes births, deaths, and suffering" (2:38). The divine mother also has her fearful aspect, as represented by the Hindu goddess Kali. "Look at how much she can teach. Her tongue dripping blood, a circle of skulls around her neck. A dagger in one hand, giving birth in the other, the whole process of nature" (2:51). She teaches us that death, as well as birth, violence as well as peace are part of it all.

By what gifts of power will dangers and suffering be overcome? The promise, or goal, is Sat Chit Ananda: total existence, total knowledge, total bliss. Here again we have the classic four gifts of a power vision; total existence breaks down into being one with all energy (the gift of strength, Stage III) and into compassion (Stage IV), since everyone shares in the same existence. Knowledge is the gift of wisdom (Stage II), and bliss is the gift of health or relief from suffering (Stage I).

The first gift in the spiritual journey is spiritual health (Stage I), or relief from suffering caused by desire. Ram Dass quotes with approval Buddha's four noble truths: that life always has in it the element of unfullfillment or suffering, such as birth, old age, sickness and not getting what you want; that the cause of suffering is desire, and the way to end the suffering is to give up attachment and desire; and that there is an eight-fold path for getting rid of desire, which includes such things as watching your thought, speech, and action, watching your calmness, getting free of attachment (2:35–40). If the disciple succeeds, he will be enlightened. He will realize that "nobody's going anywhere, nobody is coming from anywhere, we're all here . . . doing Lila Rasa, the divine dance, we're dancing and dancing and dancing" (2:81).

Maharaj-ji has the gift of healing, as R.D. does or as Black Elk did. In one case he cured a painful knee joint which had resisted treatment simply by blowing on it. In another case he apparently cured in a few hours a case of pneumonia that the doctor had said would keep the person in bed for at least a week.

The gift of wisdom (Stage II) is described in several ways. Perhaps it comes first as "witness." You develop the capacity to observe yourself doing different things. "You realize that you play many roles in the course of a day . . . and that *who you are* from moment to moment changes. There is the angry you and the kind you, the lazy you, the lustful you . . ." (3:67). If your goal is to get rid of desire, "the *work* is to break these identifications by making each of these 'you's' objects" (3:67). The witness is not evaluative. It simply observes you doing things and helps you break your attachment to them.

In a higher form, wisdom is represented by the sixth and seventh Chakras, or focal points of psychic energy in the body. As you transcend the three lower Chakras which have to do with the self— with survival, sexual gratification, and ego power, you gradually rise to the fourth through seventh Chakras, which transcend the ego. You lose your lower selfish desires and realize that attachment is what "keeps men caught in the illusion of separateness" (3:86). You understand what the rational mind can provide explanations for but beyond this you have experienced an intuitive understanding of "how it all is." Then, if you know it all and yet realize that you can't know it all, but can only *be* it all, you have penetrated through to the final stage of enlightenment. Since at this stage, you are in union with everything, you know everything that is going on and this presumably is the explanation for how it is that Maharaj-ji, who is at this stage, is able from time to time to report what is happening all over the universe, including in other people's minds.

As you advance on your spiritual journey, purifying mind and body, you gain more and more powers (*Siddhis,* Stage III) . . . "if you are interested in powers, you will get them. That's the trouble! . . . if you want wealth, wealth will be yours." The problem is that if you gratify these desires with the new powers you have, you increase the hold that those desires have over you and slow down your journey into the light (*Be Here Now,* Part 3, p. 50). Extraordinary powers you will have, but you must be careful to use them only in the service of some higher spiritual authority, not for ego enhancement, like the *Sadhu* "who lifts a hundred pound bag of sand with his penis." Ram Dass reports that Hari Dass Baba, who is small and exists on very little food intake each day, can exert a physical force, as in moving a rock, that seems way out of proportion to his size and physique, because he is so "one pointed" in exercising his psychic energy.

The gift of compassion (Stage IV) is associated with the fourth Chakra. An important gift, it is central to Ram Dass's teaching. You should develop compassion for all other beings. "Whether in a sexual embrace or in a business or social contact, the only feeling towards the other person would be one of "us-ness," of brotherhood." "Keep converting every relationship into one of compassion. Keep a compassionate model uppermost in your consciousness at all times. Every time you slip back into one of the lower *Chakras,* don't pity yourself or damn yourself. Merely redefine the situation in terms of the fourth

Chakra . . . in terms of compassionate love for all beings." He calls to mind vividly the example of Christ. "Do you think that when Christ is lying there and they're nailing the nails in, he's saying, 'Oh man, does that hurt!'? He's probably looking at the guy who's nailing him with *absolute compassion.* He understands why the guy is doing it, why he's got to be doing it, because that's the way it is, but he may ask 'Am I he who is being pained?' No! That's the thing. Once you know that, then: pleasure and pain, loss and gain, fame and shame, are all the same. They're all just happening." We're all just part of the same process.

Perhaps enough has been said to demonstrate that the four gifts of power Ram Dass is promised on his spiritual journey are much the same four gifts of power promised in other power visions. And, as we have also indicated, the powers seem to be conferred on those who take the spiritual journey seriously. As to healing powers, Ram Dass has been able to straighten out with his family and friends the broken relationships that had resulted from his extensive experiments with drugs. Many young people come to him for help, and are helped. He is drawn particularly to work with people who are dying and seems able to reduce suffering. Maharaj-ji has the gift of foreknowledge, and there is some evidence that to some degree other devotees have it too. Both Bhagwan Dass and Ram Dass are back in the United States as of the present writing. Since they each travel around a good deal, it is impossible to know where either one will be at any particular moment, and they cannot keep in touch with each other by letter or telephone. One night Ram Dass was coming to our house for a kind of ceremonial reunion of family and friends. That afternoon, Bhagwan Dass showed up unexpectedly and of course was invited to stay for dinner. Ram Dass was overwhelmed and delighted to meet his spiritual guide, but not overly surprised that he "knew" about the occasion, though told by no one. To outsiders it was a happy coincidence; to those involved it was no more a coincidence than that Black Elk knew when people were going to visit him, or that Paul knew he would be unharmed if he stayed in Corinth.

Devotees develop extraordinary powers (Siddhis), which they usually do not use. When he was young, Maharaj-ji received wide attention in the press in India for stopping a train. He was thrown out of first class by an Englishman for not having a ticket, although gurus normally did not need tickets. He went and sat in meditation under a nearby tree, but the train would not start up again. For three hours they tried without success to discover the reason. Finally the engineer, who was a religious man, noticed Maharaj-ji sitting under the tree and asked who he was. When told what had happened, he said they had better put Maharaj-ji back on the train. When they did, the train started.

On another occasion, a demented Indian came into Maharaj-ji's presence carrying a small bird in his shirt pocket with a stake through its heart. The bird seemed completely dead. Maharaj-ji screamed at the man, had the bird brought to him, took out the stake, gave the bird to an attendant saying "Give it water," and the bird flew off.

Ram Dass is nervous still about expressing this kind of power himself, just as in the old days. He spent some time with another Indian guru, Swami Mukhtananda, who promised to share with him his special secrets on how to acquire vast wealth and power. Even though Ram Dass observed Mukhtananda employ these powers and even felt the beginnings of employing them himself, he ran away in the end from these dreams of glory back to Maharaj-ji, who he feels will protect him from doing anything really wrong like pursuing personal power.

The practical manifestations of compassion take the form often of vegetarianism, or refusal to eat animals killed in violence, and love of being with people and making them happy. In Ram Dass's case, it seems that Maharaj-ji was right when he said somewhat enigmatically that Ram Dass liked to make many people laugh and to feed children. He has devoted his life since his spiritual journey to those two goals— to making people happy, and to nurturing and helping the young. By what right can we say, however, that Ram Dass has received gifts of power when on every other page of his book he cautions the would-be devotee against seeking power through spiritual means? The whole goal is to surrender the ego, to transcend the third Chakra which represents the lust for power. He points out that it is dangerous even to try to help others, to help suffering people, because you become the giver and the other person becomes the receiver. In other words, as we pointed out in the chapter on India, giving can easily become a power trip because the giver has more of something than the receiver has. Greed is the near enemy of loving kindness. Ram Dass points out that "many of the greatest minds in history have gotten caught in this trap of wanting to be God and at the same time to retain their separate identity. They are caught because they still have energy attached to the third Chakra, the desire for ego power. And to be God is obviously the ultimate power trip" (3:86). Is this what we are accusing Ram Dass of?

Not at all. The difficulty is largely semantic. According to our classification, ego power is what we have been calling Stage II and

Stage III experiences of power, in which the self is the source of the power. What we are saying then is not very different from what he is saying. He is trying to give up attachment to Stages II and III, and to experience instead what we have been calling Stages I and IV, power that originates outside the self and flows through the self leading to health or enlightenment (Stage I) or compassion for others (Stage IV). This shift in emphasis is illustrated by a story Ram Dass likes to tell about the time he got annoyed at all the American seekers who had come to be around Maharaj-ji. He felt they were insensitive. They bothered him. He decided he hated them all and wanted neither to see nor to talk to them ever again. Indeed he threw a plate of food at one of them. Maharaj-ji called him over to ask if something was the matter. Ram Dass said that he couldn't stand adharma (bad conduct) in others and himself, that Maharaj-ji had told him to "love everybody and speak the truth," but how could he do both if the truth was that he didn't love everybody? Maharaj-ji consoled him, looked straight in his eyes: "we cried together; he fed me milk, told me to take food. Then I realized that he was telling me who I would be when I finished being who I think I am." The message seems to be, if you are angry at someone (Stage III), eat (Stage I). Shift from the self as a source of power to some other source of strength. Don't be what *you* think you are; be what God makes you. It is as if a traditional Jewish mother were helping Ram Dass.

We are now in a position to understand more fully the reasons why Ram Dass's spiritual journey into Indian religious life satisfied his personal needs. Hindu and Buddhist religious teaching is designed to handle the two problems which were central for Richard Alpert: that possessions are impermanent, that they decay, just as the body decays; and that Stage III aggression or competitiveness is fraught with anxiety, leading inevitably to hatred, quarreling, fighting, killing, and guilt. The answer is to renounce totally the self as a source of power, to give up ego striving, and to return to a Stage I type of power orientation, where the individual becomes one with and is strengthened by spiritual forces outside himself, but of which he is also a part. In India, as elsewhere, but perhaps particularly in Jewish culture, Stage I is symbolized at the concrete level by the giving of food or by the partaking of something from outside the self which strengthens the self.

This resolution of the problem has several other advantages. The person needs no longer feel guilty over past aggressions against others. There is no past, there is no future, and there is no reparation for past misdeeds. Instead, you "get straight" here and now with all those people whom you have had trouble with in the past. *Both* of you submit to the realization that you are part of some greater process. It's all just happening.

Alpert's sex role difficulties are also overcome. Compassionate giving, which is a central part of his new role, comes naturally to him and he no longer need feel less adequate as a male for such behavior. Anyway, sex role distinctions are wiped out at the highest level of realization since they represent a polarity which cannot be part of the ultimate formless world.

His relationship to Maharaj-ji deals neatly with the ambivalence Ram Dass formerly felt about authority figures. On the one hand, someone seems to have complete power over him, deciding what he should do, programming his consciousness; yet on the other hand, he can say that when he is with the guru, "there's nobody home" (*Be Here Now,* 2:60). The guru is part of him, or he and the guru are part of something else. "The guru is the way into this perfect center, to going into the inner place . . . Maharaj-ji is not further away from you at this moment than the thought you are thinking now and: if you are capable of completely stopping this thought or: transcending it, or: being centered from the inside behind it, he and you would be one" (BHN, 2:64). Ram Dass owes obedience to the guru as a representative of that inner place. The obedience is not always literal because he sees Maharaj-ji's often arbitrary orders as primarily educational, designed to help him with his spiritual work. "He is for me the eyes I can't see with yet. He once told me not to touch money, and I at first took him literally and had other people carry money for me. Then it came clear to me that it was the touch of money he wanted me to be concerned about; he wanted me not to be attached to it." " . . . When the correct manifestation of the guru for you appears, you'll know it with *all your heart.* It is surrender which is no surrender. It is inevitable and totally compelling" (BHN, 3:6).

In this way he reconciles both his positive and negative feelings about authority and no longer is caught in the trap of having to rebel against authority; even his rebellions are part of Maharaj-ji's teachings. Also the guru has female as well as male attributes. He gives and supports as a mother does. One can cry in front of him without shame. Yet he can also order one about as a father does. To Alpert, as we have seen, it was important to find a vision in which his mother's power could be acknowledged along with his father's. It is characteristic of Indian religions to see power as more female than in Judeo-Christianity. The female principle—Shakti—represents energy whereas the male principle—Brahma—evokes the image of the mindless, or formless one. (See also Chapter 5.) Even statues of the Buddha became feminized, so that in the end the image is really sexless.

Finally, Ram Dass' vision resolves the alienation felt by so many young people when their efforts to bring about a better world immediately fail. They can continue to work for that better world. As Ram Dass says, "If it is your karma, do it! But do it without attachment. Don't worry if you're succeeding or not. Thus if you don't succeed, at least you're spared the frustration of failure. You realize that it is all part of some divine plan of which you are somehow a part. 'Not my will, but thine be done.'"

The individual learns to live with the paradox that man's conscious function is to alleviate suffering; yet to realize he cannot end suffering since it is built into the very nature of existence. So one can feel no frustration at not ending suffering while continuing to act to avoid an increase in suffering.

Values and Limits of Power Visions

The virtues of power visions are self-evident. They deal effectively with the problems that originally bothered Buddha—the problem of suffering that arises from desire, the fear of death or non-being, and the impermanence of the material world (in Pali, dukkha, anatta, and anicca). Ideally through meditation and other techniques, one is able to experience union with the ultimate ground of being and to recognize desire, the ego, and material possessions as transitory and unimportant. One transcends them. In our psychological framework, the individual is released from the self as an origin of powerful acts and experiences submission to a power beyond the self. In a culture like the contemporary American culture, such an orientation has particular value, since Americans tend to overstress the self—the importance of self-reliance, of self-actualization, of making right choices for which the individual will be held accountable. In the end, particularly under the influence of psychoanalysis and clinical psychology, the whole world becomes simply a projection of the self. There is scarcely any reality at all beyond the person. Everything is in the eye of the beholder. The obligation of the beholder to construe the world correctly is overwhelmingly oppressive. Freudianism, as represented by the hard work of psychoanalysis, is a grim burden for the self to bear since its aim is for the self to reconstruct its picture of the world and to maintain at all times control over the world or at least over one's perception of it. To be overwhelmed by the world, to lose control, is to be sick. This is obviously a partial view, an exaggeration of the importance of the self in the scheme of things. The power vision comes as a healing, vital experience of that which is beyond the self. It is, as Eric Fromm put it years ago, an escape from freedom, but a necessary escape from total reliance on the self as a measure of all things.

The limits of the power vision are equally apparent. It does not deal directly with problems of action and social organization; if it becomes the overwhelmingly dominant form of expression of the power need, it can even draw attention away from these problems. Black Elk found that his power vision was of little assistance in helping his people prosper as a nation. Personally it made him more effective, particularly in healing people, but as a means of helping to save his Sioux nation as had seemed possible, it was a failure. The same can be said of the Christian power vision in the early days after Jesus' death. It helped many people individually, but as a group they continued to be martyred and persecuted. John's vision promised that Jesus was to come quickly and straighten things out in the Day of Judgment. Yet He failed to come, at least in the worldly sense, and the church was left to solve the problems of action and social organization in other ways. Ram Dass' vision makes no promises about producing a better social order. It is oriented towards individual rather than social salvation.

The vision itself should be the key to a better social order. "If you could stand back for but a moment you could see that if man were more conscious from moment to moment he could transcend most of the difficulties he now faces: poverty, war, pollution, neurosis, disease." Great! But how? The idea seems to be that right feelings *solve* serious organizational problems. The rest is a question of detail to be worked out by those whose karma it is to do such things. The vision itself is essentially blank on *how* people are to be *organized* to manage the causes of suffering better. The emphasis is more on the removal of suffering than on acting effectively to remove the causes of suffering, which are there always anyway. There is no objection to a person's trying to eliminate causes of suffering, of course, so long as he loves everybody (3:59), but there is also no explicit advice or assistance on just how to go about such things.

The result of not facing such problems appears to be an unexpected amount of tension and dissension in communities organized along these spiritual lines, unless they are under the absolute authority of a single leader. Ram Dass recommends forming communities that will worship together and try to practice the procedures he discovered on his spiritual journey. Though he speaks particularly of the Lama Foundation in New Mexico which he helped organize along these lines, it has so far not been notably successful as an *organization* which removed the causes of suffering. For a time, indeed, it was more than usually torn with dissension.

The power vision appears to be most effective in a society already well organized in a ritually prescribed way, as in traditional India. The problem of career choice, for example, is not serious in a society organized according to a caste system in which every person at birth knows what he is going to do. Right action is also not hard to determine in a traditional society where such things are carefully prescribed. These are serious problems, however, in an open society where young people do not know what they are supposed to do just from the accident of their birth in a caste system, nor are they very clear about what constitutes sexual morality, about whether it is all right to take drugs or not, or to live together without getting married, etc. In traditional Indian society all of these matters were governed by explicit rules.

Furthermore, the power vision works best in a social organization that is hierarchically arranged and run by one supreme authority, whether at the level of the ashram or of the nation state. In such situations, organizational matters are taken care of by a simple chain of command, and there is no necessity for committees to plan what should be done, for discovering methods of sharing power to make decisions at various levels, and so on. Although such organizations have an appealing simplicity, and often produce high morale, modern organization theory shows their limitations for accomplishing many tasks. We will return to a discussion of these matters in Chapter 8. At the very least, the history of such institutions in Southeast Asian countries suggests that they breed violence at the top, as one leader after another is forced out to make way for another.

The root of the problem is a partial or inadequate analysis of human motivation by Indian spiritual leaders. Because desire is the cause of suffering, they recommend renouncing desire. At times they seem to mean *all* desire, including the desire to be compassionate towards others; but clearly in practice, and in most of the examples they give, they mean conscious, ego-oriented desire, or what we have been calling Stage II or III expressions of the power need. The impulse to do good is to be renounced only if it arises from pride or ego satisfaction. There are many desires, however, as we have shown in Chapter 1, that do not involve the self either as the source or the object of the action undertaken. Even among religious Indians, at the practical level, there are obviously good desires. How would monks, Sadhus, or gurus be supported otherwise? The impulse to make gifts to gurus is obviously meritorious, so long as it is not consciously done to attain merit. The desire to seek Nirvana is also worthy. The Buddha's last words were said to be "Strive on heedfully." The desire to become like Buddha is worthy, as is the desire to avoid violence and killing.

Eastern religious psychology has a variety of ways of dealing with such apparent contradictions. One of the most common is that there are and always will be less developed souls who keep the world moving because they have not yet transcended ego desires. A better approach seems to be to make a more complete analysis of human motivation, to understand that there are several different ways of expressing the desire to be strong, not all of which involve the self as a source or object of striving. One may feel strong by submission to spiritual authority (Stage I), or one may attempt to express this divine love in practical love for others (Stage IV). To live on the partial and inadequate analysis of human motivation made in Indian philosophies of religion, is hazardous, to be ignorant of the different ways in which the power motive expresses itself. Ignorance, as these same philosophers point out, can only cause confusion, and confusion causes despair and suffering.

It seems better to accept *all* aspects of human motivation, to understand them both conceptually and through experience. Nowadays this goes under the name of "motivation training" (McClelland and Winter, 1969). A person learns to recognize a power motive. He discovers how strong his own is and learns what it feels like to express it in various ways, including giving up self and being totally dependent on another's authority. He learns to feel the transitoriness of possessions and reputation, to feel the excitement, say, of winning or losing. He also learns that there are other human motives that have nothing to do with power—like the happiness of just being with other people (the need for Affiliation) or the satisfaction of doing a job well or efficiently, whether anyone else knows about it or not (the need for Achievement). In a sense, motivation training seems to be the exact opposite of what Indian religious psychologists recommend. They say: give up your motives, avoid situations which give rise to them, suppress them if they do arise, or try to develop or maintain a concentration on detachment, extinction, and death so that desires do not come to mind (Nyanatiloka, 1952, pp. 50–51). Motivation training says: embrace your motives, experience them in all their aspects in the safety of a training situation. Become aware of alternative courses of action. Find what is most appropriate for you and your life situation and realize above all that this discovery is *not* just a matter of conscious choice, but is a joint product of conscious planning and forces outside your control, including spiritual authority, the world situation, your own past history, and the present situation (the law of Karma). It would clearly be a mistake to discard the insights gained by Eastern psychologists, and not to use the techniques of meditation and concentration they have developed over the centuries. These techniques can even be regarded as precursors of motivation training, in the sense that they too are methods of making people aware of their desires and of changing and transcending their ties to the ego. To be complete and adequate, motivation training (self-knowledge) must incorporate the virtues of mysticism and the power vision along with the techniques of conscious planning already so highly developed in the West.

POWER MOTIVATION AND ORGANIZATIONAL LEADERSHIP[1]

As WE have reviewed the vicissitudes of the power motive in its various stages, it may seem to be inevitably linked to extraordinary phenomena, from sacrificial giving and mystical visions to Icarian explosions. It is also, however, the basis for more ordinary phenomena such as organizational leadership, particularly when it is combined with a high sense of control and a Stage IV level of maturity. This and the next chapter will deal with what power motivation does to and for societies and individuals in its more evolved and organized stages.

I first ran into the problem of organizational leadership when I was studying the need to Achieve, the need to do something better than it has been done before. As the investigation advanced, it became clear that this need to Achieve (*n* Achievement) was one of the keys to economic growth; men who are concerned with doing things better become active entrepreneurs and create the growing business firms that are the foundation stones of a developing economy (McClelland,

1961). Although some of these heroic entrepreneurs might be regarded as leaders in the restricted sense that their activities established the economic base for the rise of a new type of civilization, they were seldom leaders of men. The reason for this is simple: *n* Achievement is a one-man game that need never involve other people. Boys who are high in *n* Achievement like to build things or to make things with their hands, presumably because they can tell easily and directly whether they have done a good job. A boy who is trying to build as tall a tower as possible out of blocks can measure very precisely how well he has done. He is in no way dependent on someone else to tell him how good his performance is. So in the pure case, the man with high *n* Achievement is not dependent on the judgment of others; he is concerned with improving his own performance. As an ideal type, he is most easily conceived of as a salesman or an owner-manager of a small business, in a position to watch carefully whether or not his performance is improving.

Motives Needed for Management

While studying such men and their role in economic development, I ran head on into problems of leadership, power, and social influence, with which *n* Achievement clearly did not prepare a man to cope. As a one-man firm grows larger, it obviously requires some division of function and some organizational structure. Organizational structure involves relationships among people, and sooner or later someone in the organization, if it is to survive, must pay attention to getting people to work together, or to dividing up the tasks to be performed, or to supervising the work of others. Yet a high need to Achieve does not equip a man to deal effectively with managing human relationships. For instance, a salesman with high *n* Achievement does not necessarily make a good sales manager. As a manager, his task is not to sell, but to inspire others to sell, which involves a different set of personal goals and different strategies for reaching them.

I shall not forget the moment when I learned that the president of one of the most successful *achievement*-oriented firms we had been studying scored exactly zero in *n* Achievement! Up to that point I had fallen into the easy assumption that a man with a high need to Achieve does better work, gets promoted faster, and ultimately ends up as president of a company. How was it possible for a man to head an obviously achieving company and yet score so low in *n* Achievement?

At the time I was tempted to dismiss the finding as a measurement error, but there is now little doubt that it was a dramatic example of the fact that stimulating achievement motivation in others requires a different motive and a different set of skills from wanting achievement satisfaction for oneself.

For some time now, research on achievement motivation has shifted in focus from the individual with high *n* Achievement to the climate that encourages him and rewards him for doing well (Litwin and Stringer, 1968). No matter how high a person's need to Achieve may be, he cannot succeed if he has no opportunities, if the organization keeps him from taking initiative, or does not reward him when he does. As a simple illustration of this point, we found in our research in India that it did no good to raise achievement motivation through training if the trained individual was not in charge of his business (McClelland and Winter, 1969). Even though a person might be "all fired up" and prepared to be more active and entrepreneurial, he could not do much if he was working for someone else, someone who had the final say as to whether any of the things he wanted to do would in fact be attempted. In short, the man with high *n* Achievement seldom can act alone, even though he might like to. He is caught up in an organizational context in which he is managed, controlled, or directed by others. To understand better what happens to him, we must shift our attention to those who are managing him, to those who are concerned about organizational relationships—to the leaders of men.

Since managers are primarily concerned with influencing others, it seems obvious that they should be characterized by a high need for Power, and that by studying the power motive we can learn something about the way effective managerial leaders work. If A gets B to do something, A is at one and the same time a leader (i.e., he is leading B), and a power-wielder (i.e., he is exercising some kind of influence or power over B). Thus, leadership and power appear as two closely related concepts, and if we want to understand better effective leadership, we may begin by studying the power motive in thought and action. What arouses thoughts of being powerful? What kinds of strategies does the man employ who thinks constantly about gaining power? Are some of these strategies more effective than others in influencing people? In pursuing such a line of inquiry in this area, we are adopting an approach that worked well in another. Studying the achievement motive led to a better understanding of business entrepreneurship. Analogously, studying the power motive may help us understand managerial, societal, or even political leadership.

Negative View of the Need for Power

One striking difference between the two motivation systems is apparent from the outset. In American society in general, individuals are proud of having a high need to Achieve, but dislike being told they have a high need for Power. It is a fine thing to be concerned about doing things well (*n* Achievement) or making friends (*n* Affiliation), but it is reprehensible to be concerned about having influence over others (*n* Power). Even the vocabulary behavioral scientists use to describe power relations is strongly negative in tone. If one opens *The Authoritarian Personality* (Adorno, *et al.*, 1950), one of the major works dealing with people concerned with power, one finds them depicted as harsh, sadistic, fascist, Machiavellian, prejudiced, and neurotic. Ultimately, many claim, the concern for power leads to Nazi-type dictatorships, to the slaughter of innocent Jews, to political terror, police states, brainwashing, and the exploitation of helpless masses. Even less political terms for power than these have a distinctively negative flavor—dominance-submission, competition, zero-sum game (if I win, you lose). It is small wonder that people do not like being told they have a high need for Power.

The negative reactions to the exercise of power became vividly apparent to me in the course of our recent research to develop achievement motivation (McClelland and Winter, 1969). In the course of our work we conceived of possible ways to increase motivation through short intensive courses. At first people were interested and curious. It seemed an excellent idea to develop a fine motive like *n* Achievement, particularly among under-achievers in school or relatively inactive businessmen in underdeveloped countries. But most people were also skeptical. Could it be done?

It turned out that many remained interested only as long as they were skeptical about our ability to change motivation. As soon as it became apparent that we could indeed change people in a relatively short period of time, many observers began to worry. Was it ethical to change people's personalities? Were we not brainwashing them? What magical power were we employing to change an underlying personality disposition presumably established in childhood and laboriously stabilized over the years? Once these questions were raised, we became aware of the fundamental dilemma confronting anyone who becomes involved in any branch of the "influence game." He may think that he is exercising leadership—i.e., influencing people for their own good—but if he succeeds, he is likely to be accused of manipulating people. Although we thought of our attempts as benign, and were a little proud of ourselves—after all, we were giving people a chance to be more "successful" in business and at school—yet we soon found ourselves attacked as potentially dangerous "brainwashers."

To some extent, ordinary psychotherapy avoids these accusations because the power of the therapist seems to be relatively weak. Therapy does not work very well or very quickly, and when it does, the therapist can say that the patient did most of the work himself.

But consider the following anecdote. Johnny was a bright but lazy sixth-grade student in math. His parents were concerned because he was not motivated to work harder, preferring to spend his evenings watching television; thus they were delighted when psychologists explained that there were some new techniques for developing motivation to which they would like to expose Johnny. Soon after the motivation training regime began, they noticed a dramatic change in Johnny's behavior. He never watched television, but spent all of his time studying, and was soon way ahead of his class in advanced mathematics. At this point, his parents began to worry. What had the psychologists done to produce such a dramatic change in their son's behavior? They had wanted him changed, but not *that* much. They reacted very negatively to the power the psychologists seemed to have exercised over him.

This experience was enough to make us yearn for the position of the detached-scientist or consulting-expert so vividly described by John Gardner in *The Anti-Leadership Vaccine* (1965) as the preferred role for more and more young people today. The "scientist" ordinarily does not directly intervene—does not exercise power—in human or social affairs. He observes the interventions of others, reports, analyzes and advises, but never takes responsibility himself. Our research had led us to intervene actively in Johnny's life, and even that small, relatively benign exercise of influence had led to some negative responses from the "public." My own view is that young people avoid socio-political leadership roles not so much because their professors brainwash them into believing that it is better to be a professional, but because in our society in our time, and perhaps in all societies at all times, the exercise of power is viewed negatively. People are suspicious of a man who wants power, even if he wants it for sincere and altruistic reasons. He is often socially conditioned to be suspicious of himself. Since he does not want to be in a position where he might be thought to be seeking power in order to exploit others, he shuns public responsibility.

The Two Faces of Power

Yet surely this negative face of power is only part of the story. Power must have a positive face too. After all, people cannot help influencing one another; organizations cannot function without some kind of authority relationships. It is necessary and desirable for some people to concern themselves with management, with working out influence relationships that make it possible to achieve the goals of the group. A man who is consciously concerned with the development of proper channels of influence is better able to contribute to group goals than a man who neglects or represses power problems and lets the working relationships of men grow up without supervision. Our problem, then, is to try to understand two faces of power. When is power bad and when is it good? Why is it often perceived as dangerous? Which aspects of power are viewed favorably, and which unfavorably? When is it proper, and when improper, to exercise influence? And finally, are there different kinds of power motivation?

It will not be possible to answer all of these questions definitively, but the findings of attempts to arouse the power motives as reviewed in Chapter 1 will help us understand the two faces of power better.

When power motivation was aroused, students thought more often about people having strong impact on others. This was true not only for student candidates for office awaiting election returns, but also for student experimenters who were about to demonstrate their power over subjects by employing a winning strategy in a competitive game that they had been taught beforehand (Uleman, 1966).

What surprised us greatly was the discovery that drinking alcohol also stimulated similar power thoughts in men. This finding was one of those happy accidents that sometimes occurs in scientific laboratories when two studies thought to be unrelated are proceeding side by side. When we began studying the effects of social drinking on fantasy, we had no idea that alcohol would increase power fantasies. Yet we immediately found that it increased sex and aggression fantasies; and one day it occurred to us that certain types of exploitative sex and certainly aggression were instances of "having impact" on others, and therefore could be considered part of an *n* Power scoring definition. We later found that drinking alcohol in small amounts increased the frequency of *socialized* power thoughts while in larger amounts it promoted thinking in terms of *personalized* power. We began to notice that these two types of power concern had different consequences in action. For instance, Winter found that some college students with high *n* Power scores tended to drink more heavily while others held more offices in student organizations. These were not, however, the same people. A student with high *n* Power either drank more heavily or he was a club officer, though he was usually not both, possibly because heavy drinking would prevent him from being elected to a responsible office. In other words, Winter identified alternative manifestations of the power drive—either heavy drinking or holding office. Later we found that the orientation of the power thoughts of these two types of people was quite different.

Those with a personal power concern (p Power) wrote stories in which the hero was engaged in a struggle to win out over an active adversary. Life was pictured as a "zero-sum game" in which "if I win, you lose" or "I lose, if you win." The law of the jungle ruled; the fittest survive by destroying their adversaries. Men with high p Power tend to drink more liquor, collect more "prestige supplies" (like convertibles or Playboy Club keys), prefer man-to-man competitive sports, and display more impulsive aggressive actions (like making hostile remarks to storekeepers, yelling at someone in traffic, or getting into a physical fight), provided the norms of the man's social groups permit it. They display what we define in the next chapter as the "conquistador" motivational pattern characteristic of men high in *n* Power and low in Inhibition. The style of these men involves a kind of man-to-man competitiveness in which they want most of all to dominate or win out over someone else.

Men with socialized power concern, on the other hand, seem to have more hesitation about expressing power in a direct interpersonal way. Their stories are characterized by thoughts of exercising power for the benefit of others (altruistic power), and by feelings of greater ambivalence about the exercise of personal strength, the realization that most victories must be carefully planned in advance, and that every victory means a loss for someone. All this was not surprising because the s Power (socialized power) scoring definition had been obtained by examining the stories of men high in Power motivation and also high in Activity Inhibition, as represented by the number of times the word "not" appeared in their stories, usually as a way of blocking an action. These men had a need for Power together with a strong inhibitory sense that could well lead to a disciplined expression of the power need useful in social leadership. We will find again in the next chapter that high Power plus high Inhibition (represented also by the s Power score) is central to organizational effectiveness, particularly when *n* Affiliation is also low.

At the level of action, men with high s Power scores seemed

interested in impersonal influence situations such as teaching (see Winter, 1973), and of most importance for our present interest, they were more apt to move into leadership positions in various social organizations (McClelland *et al.*, 1972). Why should men of this type be more likely to be organizational leaders? How does their power orientation better suit them for political leadership than that of men interested in personal dominance?

The Meaning of Charisma

Again a clue came from an unexpected source. It is traditional in the literature of social psychology and political science to describe a leader as someone who is able to evoke feelings of obedience or loyal submission in his followers. A leader is sometimes said to have charisma if, when he makes a speech, for example, the members of his audience are swept off their feet and feel that they must submit to his overwhelming authority and power. In the extreme case they are like iron filings that have been polarized by a powerful magnet. The leader is recognized as supernatural or superhuman; his followers feel submissive, loyal, devoted, and obedient to his will. Certainly this is the most common description of what happened at mass meetings addressed by Hitler or Lenin. As great demagogues they established their power over the masses who followed loyally and obediently.

Winter set out to find exactly, by experiment, what kinds of thoughts the members of an audience had when exposed to a charismatic leader (Winter, 1967). He wanted to know if the common analysis of what was going on in the minds of the audience was in fact accurate. Some time after John F. Kennedy's assassination Winter exposed groups of business-school students to a film of his Inaugural Address as President of the United States. There was no doubt that this film was a highly moving presentation of a charismatic leader for such an audience at that time. After the film was over, he asked them to write imaginative stories as usual, and contrasted the themes of their stories with those written by a comparable group of students after they had seen a film explaining some aspects of modern architecture. Contrary to expectation, he did not find that the students exposed to the Kennedy film thought more afterwards about submission, following, obedience, or loyalty. Instead, the frequency of power themes in their stories increased. They were apparently strengthened and uplifted by the experience; they felt more powerful, rather than less powerful or submissive.

This suggests that the traditional way of explaining the influence of a leader on his followers has not been entirely correct. He does not force them to submit and follow him by the sheer overwhelming magic of his personality and persuasive powers. To see the situation thus is to interpret effective leadership in terms of the kind of personalized power syndrome described above; leadership has been discredited in this country precisely because social scientists have often used this personal power image to explain how the leader gets his effects. In fact, he is influential by strengthening and inspiriting his audience. Max Weber, the source of much of the sociological treatment of charisma, recognized that charismatic leaders obtained their effects through *Begeisterung,* a word which means "inspiritation" rather than its usual translation as "enthusiasm."[2] The leader arouses confidence in his followers. The followers feel better able to accomplish whatever goals he and they share. There has been much discussion of whether the leader's ideas about what will inspire his followers come from God, from himself, or from some intuitive sense of what the people need. Whatever the source of the leader's ideas, he cannot inspire his people unless he expresses vivid goals which in some sense they want. Of course, the more closely he meets their needs, the less "persuasive" he has to be; but in no case does it make sense to speak as if his role is to force submission. Rather it is to strengthen and uplift, to make people feel that they are the origins, not the pawns, of the socio-political system (deCharms, 1968). His message is not so much: "Do as I say because I am strong and know best. You are children with no wills of your own and must follow me because I know better," but rather, "Here are the goals which are true and right and which we share. Here is how we can reach them. You are strong and capable. You can accomplish these goals." His role is to make clear which are the goals the group should achieve, and then to create confidence in its members that they can achieve them. John Gardner (1965) described these two aspects of the socialized leadership role very well when he said that leaders "can conceive and articulate goals that lift people out of their petty preoccupations, carry them above the conflicts that tear a society apart, and unite them in the pursuit of objectives worthy of their best efforts."

The socialized type of leadership is not characterized by the primitive methods of trying to win out over adversaries or to exert personal dominance. In their thinking about the power motive, social scientists have been too much impressed by the dominance hierarchies established by brute force among lower animals. Lasswell and other political scientists have described all concern with power as a defensive attempt to compensate for a feeling of weakness. At best this describes the personalized face of the power motive, not its socialized face—and even at that, we can only say that the personalized power drive *perceives* the world in defensive terms, not that it originates as a defense. Personal dominance may be effective in very small groups, but if a human leader wants to become effective in large groups, he must rely on more subtle and socialized forms of influence. He is necessarily more interested in formulating the goals toward which groups of people can move. If he is to move the group toward achieving them, he must define the goals clearly and persuasively, and then be able to strengthen the will of the individual members of the group to work for them.[3]

Some further light on the two types of power orientation is shed by our experience in offering achievement motivation development courses for business leaders in small cities in India. When we began to succeed in these efforts, some observers began to wonder whether we were coarsely interfering in people's lives, perhaps spreading some new brand of American imperialism by foisting achievement values on a people that had got along very well without them. The reaction was not unlike that just described, in which an outsider seeing a leader sway an audience concludes that he must have some mysterious power over the audience. Did we have a similar kind of *power over* the Indian businessmen who came for motivation training? Were we psychological Machiavellians?

Helping Followers Feel Powerful

We never thought we were; nor, we are certain, did the businessmen perceive us as very powerful agents. How did we manage to influence them? The course of events was very much like the process of social leadership described by John Gardner. First, we set before the participants certain goals which we felt would be desired by them—namely, to be better businessmen, to improve economic welfare in their community, to make a contribution in this way to the development of their country as a whole, to provide a pilot project that the rest of the underdeveloped world might copy, and to advance the cause of science. These goals ranged all the way from the specific and personal—improving one's business—to improving the community, the nation, and the world. While a selfish appeal to personal power generally has not been as effective as an appeal to important social goals via increased personal power, the goals we presented were objectives that interested the businessmen we contacted.

Second, we provided them with the means of achieving these goals. The courses in achievement motivation development, we explained, were designed to make them personally better able to move quickly and efficiently towards these objectives. We offered new types of training in goal setting, planning, and risk taking which research had shown would help men become more effective entrepreneurs. No one was pressured to undergo this training or pursue these goals. If there was any pressure exerted, it was in the eyes of the outside observer noting the effects of our "intervention"; it was not in the minds of the participants at the time.

Third, the major goal of all of our educational exercises was to make the participants feel strong, like original movers rather than pawns. Thus we insisted that the initial decision to take part in the training sessions must be their own, and that they not come out of a sense of obligation or a desire to conform. In fact, we depicted the training as a difficult process, so that a high degree of personal involvement would be necessary to complete it. During the training, we never set goals for the participants, but let them set their own. We made no psychological analyses of their test behavior, which we might have kept for our private diagnosis or presented to them as evidence of our superior psychological knowledge. Rather we taught them to analyze their own test records and to make their own decisions as to what a test score meant. After the course they set up their own association to work together for common community goals. We did not even provide them with technical information about the various types of new businesses they might enter, but let them search for it themselves. We had no fixed order of presenting course materials, but constantly asked the participants to criticise the material as it was presented and to direct the staff as to what new types of presentations were desired.

Thus, in our ceaseless efforts to make the participants feel strong, competent, and effective, we behaved throughout the entire experiment like effective socialized leaders. We expressed in many ways our faith in their ability to act as initiators and to solve their own problems. In the end many of them justified our faith. They became more active, as we expected them to, and once again validated the ubiquitous psychological findings that what you expect other people to do, they will in fact tend to do (Rosenthal and Jacobson, 1968). Furthermore, we have good evidence that we succeeded only with those businessmen whose sense of personal efficacy was increased. This demonstrated the ultimate paradox of social leadership and social power: to be an effective leader, one must turn all of his so-called followers into leaders. There is little wonder that the situation is confusing not only to the would-be leader, but also to the social scientist observing the leadership phenomenon.

Maturity, the Need for Power, and Leadership

Now let us put together these bits and pieces of evidence about the nature of interpersonal power, and see what kind of picture they make. The negative or personal face of power is characterized by the dominance-submission mode: if I win, you lose. It is more *primitive* in the sense that the strategies employed are learned early in life, before the child is socialized enough to learn more subtle techniques of influence. In fantasy it expresses itself in thoughts of conquering opponents. In real life it leads to simple and direct means of feeling powerful—drinking heavily, acquiring "prestige supplies," and being aggressive. It does not often lead to effective social leadership for the reason that such a person tends to treat other people as pawns. People who feel that they are pawns tend to be passive and useless to the leader who gets his satisfaction from dominating them. Slaves are the most inefficient form of labor ever devised by man. If a leader wants to have far-reaching influence, he must make his followers feel powerful and able to accomplish things on their own.

The positive or socialized face of power is characterized by a concern for group goals, for finding those goals that will move men, for helping the group to formulate them, for taking initiative in providing means of achieving them, and for giving group members the feeling of competence they need to work hard for them. In fantasy it leads to a concern with exercising influence *for* others, with planning, and with the ambivalent bitter-sweet meaning of many so-called "victories." In real life, it leads to an interest in impersonal conquests, in politics, and in holding office. It functions in a way that makes members of a group feel like initiators of action rather than pawns. Even the most dictatorial leader does not succeed if he .has not instilled in at least some of his followers a sense of power and the strength to pursue the goals he has set. This is often hard for outside observers to believe, because they do not experience the situation as it is experienced by the group members. The outsider, who notices only the success or failure of an influence attempt, tends to believe that the leader must have "dominated" because he was so effective, whereas in fact direct domination could never have produced so large an effect.[4]

Our theoretical analysis suggests that p Power represents an earlier stage of maturity than s Power. What light do the data collected in Chapter 2 shed on this point? They make it clear, first of all, that p Power is not Stage III power and s Power Stage IV power, as one might reasonably infer from the descriptions given so far. Rather p Power appears to be an undisciplined (and probably earlier) form of Stage III power and s Power a disciplined and later form of Stage III power. If we categorize either the men or the women in the Chapter 2 sample as high in *n* Power and either low or high in Inhibition, we find that the average Stage scores of these two categories of people differ only for Stage III. As Table 8.1 in the next chapter shows, men and women high in *n* Power are significantly higher on Stage III scores, than those low in *n* Power; but those high in *n* Power and also Inhibition (both men and women) are higher still. For men and women combined, the mean Stage III score for the high *n* Power, high Inhibition group is 1.56 (N = 57) and for the high *n* Power, low Inhibition group it is .86 (N = 88). The difference is highly significant (p < .001). This finding suggests that s Power (high *n* Power, high Inhibition) represents a more socialized or fully developed Stage III expression of the power drive, but it is not accompanied in these subjects by a higher Stage IV score. Since we have become accustomed to thinking of people with a Stage IV power orientation as organizationally minded (Table 2.7), this seems confusing at first. One must remember that the measures employed here are slightly different: there is no *direct* measure of s Power in the Chapter 2 sample. For what it is worth, our best guess is that the sequence of development of power orientations in relationship to leadership goes as follows:

Table 7.1–Relation of power motivation and inhibition to maturity and leadership potential

Maturity levels		*Leadership potential*
Stage I	1. Low power motivation	Not assertive enough (Stage III) to provide good leadership, except in certain situations.
Stage IIIa	2. High power motivation Low inhibition	The "conquistador," p Power, personal dominance pattern, particularly if *n* Affiliation is also low. See Table 8.4 below.
Stage IIIb	3. High power motivation High inhibition	The imperial motivation pattern, particularly if *n* Affiliation is also low. Ruthless, efficient organizing tendencies. Shades into altruistic s Power which shades into
Stage IV	3. High power motivation High inhibition High Stage IV scores	Selfless leadership, efficient organizing tendencies.

In Table 7.1 we have shown how Stage IIIa is related to p Power and Stage IIIb to s Power, which may shade over into a Stage IV leadership style.

It is also important to remember that we are dealing here in ideal types and that there are many variations in the kind of power motivation that is best adapted to various leadership roles. The distinction between personal and socialized power was helpful to us because it enabled us to distinguish two ways of exercising assertiveness in a social situation; but there is by no means a simple one-to-one correspondence between a high s Power concern and effective leadership in all situations or a high p Power concern and ineffectiveness in the leadership role. Although no empirical study has been done on the problem, it seems reasonable, for example, that effective leadership of a labor union local or a tank unit in battle may require the combative style of man-to-man influence we have found characteristic of p Power or the concern for personal dominance.

Nor should we make the mistake of assuming that all leadership positions require high power motivation. Litwin and Siebrecht (1967) have shown that ideally an integrative manager in a large organization is not excessively high in power motivation. If he were, he would spend too much time influencing and not enough time integrating conflicting viewpoints. The successful man in this position typically has a balanced motivational profile—with moderately high power, affiliation, and achievement motivation scores. Donley and Winter (1970) have shown, furthermore, that not all U.S. Presidents were high in power motivation. These authors scored achievement and power motivation in Presidential inaugural addresses from Theodore Roosevelt to Richard Nixon and demonstrated fairly conclusively that relatively inactive Presidents like Coolidge and Eisenhower were low in both motives. Dynamic active Presidents, on the other hand, like Franklin Roosevelt, John Kennedy, and Lyndon Johnson tended to be high in both. Men in our society are often put in positions of political or organizational leadership, even though they lack the motives that would have led them to seek the office or to be very active in it once they get it. (See also Browning, 1968.) As women need more personal assertiveness to develop the Stage IV maturity required for office, men may need less (see Chapter 2).

In real life many leaders balance on a knife edge between expressing personal dominance and exercising the more socialized type of leadership. They show first one face of power, then the other. The reason lies in the simple fact that even if the man is a socialized leader, he must take initiative in helping the group he leads to form its goals. How much initiative he should take, how persuasive he should attempt to be, and at what point his clear enthusiasm for certain goals becomes personal authoritarian insistence that those goals are the right ones whatever the members of the group may think, are all questions calculated to frustrate the well-intentioned leader. If he takes no initiative, he is no leader. If he takes too much, he becomes a dictator—particularly if he tries to curtail the process by which members of the group participate in shaping group goals. There is a particular danger for the man who has demonstrated his competence in shaping group goals and in inspiring group members to pursue them. In time both he and they may assume that he knows best, and he may almost imperceptibly change from a democratic to an authoritarian leader. There are, of course, safeguards against slipping from the more socialized to the less socialized expressions of power. One is psychological: the leader must thoroughly learn the lesson that his role is not to dominate and treat people like pawns, but to give strength to others and to make them feel like originators of ideas. If they are to be truly strong, he must continually consult them and be aware of their wishes. *A firm faith in people prevents the development of the kind of cynicism that so often characterizes authoritarian leaders.* A second safeguard is social: democracy provides a system whereby the group can expel the leader from office when it feels that he no longer properly represents its interests.

U.S. Leaders Viewed with Suspicion

Despite these safeguards, Americans remain suspicious of the leadership role for fear of its becoming a vehicle of the personal use and abuse of power. Students do not aspire to leadership roles because they are sensitive to the negative face of power and suspicious of their own motives. They know, furthermore, that in a position of leadership, they will be under constant surveillance by all sorts of groups, ready to accuse them of the personal abuse of power. Americans probably have less respect for authority than any other people in the world. The reasons are not hard to find. Many Americans originally came here to avoid tyranny in other countries. We have come to hate and fear authority in many of its forms because of its excesses elsewhere. As a nation, we are strongly committed to an ideology of personal freedom and non-interference by government. We cherish our free press as the guardian of our freedom because it can ferret out tendencies toward the misuse of personal power before they become dangerous to the public. In government, as in other organizations, we have developed elaborate systems of checks and balances which make it difficult for any one person or group to abuse power. In government, power is divided three ways—among the executive, the legislative, and the judicial branches. In business it is divided among management, labor, and owners; and in the university, among trustees, administration, and students. Many of these organizations also have a system for rotating leadership to make sure that no one acquires enough power over time to be able to misuse it. A Martian observer might conclude that as a nation we are excessively, almost obsessively worried about the abuse of power.

Under such conditions it is incredible that any leadership at all can be exercised. Consider the situation from the point of view of a would-be leader. He knows that if he takes too much initiative—or perhaps even if he does not—he is very likely to be attacked by some sub-group as a malicious, power-hungry status-seeker. If he is in any way a public figure, he may be viciously attacked for any misstep or chancy episode in his past life. Even though the majority of the people are satisfied with his leadership, a small vociferous minority can make his life unpleasant and at times unbearable. He knows too that he will not be the only leader trying to formulate group goals. If he is a Congressman, he has to work not only with his fellow Congressmen, but also with representatives of independent sources of power in the executive branch and the governmental bureaucracy. If he is a college president, he has to cope with the relatively independent power of his trustees, the faculty and the student body. If he is a business manager, he must share power with labor leaders. In addition, he knows that his tenure of office is likely to be short. Since it is doubtful that he will ever be able to exert true leadership, there seems little purpose in preparing for it. Logically, then, he should spend his time preparing for what he will do before and after his short tenure in office.

Under these conditions why would any promising young man aspire to be a leader? He begins by doubting his motives and ends by concluding that even if he believes his motives to be altruistic, the game is scarcely worth the candle. In other words, the anti-leadership vaccine, which John Gardner speaks of, is partly supplied by the negative face that power wears in our society and the extraordinary lengths to which we have gone to protect ourselves against misused power. It is much safer to pursue a career as a professional adviser, assured some continuity of service and some freedom from public attack—because, after all, one is not responsible for decisions—and some certainty that one's motives are *good,* and that power conflicts have to be settled by someone else.

How to Develop Leaders

How can immunity against the anti-leadership vaccine be strengthened? Some immunity surely needs to be built up if our society is not to flounder because of a lack of socialized leadership. Personally, I would concoct a remedy composed of one part changes in the system, one part rehabilitation of the positive face of power, and one part adult education. Let me explain each ingredient in turn.

I feel least confident in speaking about the first one, because I am neither a political scientist, a management expert, nor a revolutionary. Yet as a psychologist, I do feel that America's concern about the possible misuse of power verges at times on a neurotic obsession. To control the abuses of power, is it really necessary to divide authority so extensively and to give such free license to anyone to attack a leader in any way he likes? Doesn't this make the leadership role so difficult and unrewarding that it ends by appealing only to cynics? Who in his right mind would want the job of college president under most operating conditions today? A president has great responsibility—for raising money, for setting goals of the institution that faculty, students, and trustees can share, for student discipline, and for appointment of a distinguished faculty. Yet often he has only a very shaky authority with which to execute these responsibilities. Such authority as he has he must share with the faculty (many of whom he cannot remove no matter how violently they disagree with the goals set for the university), with the trustees, and with students who speak with one voice one year and quite a different one two years later. I am not now trying to defend an ineffective college president. I am simply trying to point out that our social system makes his role an extraordinarily difficult one. Other democratic nations—Britain, for example—have not found it necessary to go to such extremes to protect their liberty against possible encroachment by power-hungry leaders. Some structural reform of the American system definitely seems called for. It is beyond the scope of this paper to say what it might be. The possibilities range all the way from a less structured system in which all organizations are conceived as temporary (Bennis and Slater, 1968), to a system in which leaders are given more authority or offered greater protection from irresponsible attack. The problem deserves serious attention. If we want better leaders, we will have to find ways of making the conditions under which they work less frustrating.

The second ingredient in my remedy for the anti-leadership vaccine is rehabilitation of the positive face of power. This paper has been an effort in that direction. Its major thesis is that many people, including both social scientists and potential leaders, have consistently misunderstood or misperceived the way in which effective social leadership takes place. They have confused it regularly, we have pointed out, with the more primitive exercise of personal power. The error is perpetuated by people who speak of leaders as "making decisions." Such a statement only serves to obscure the true process by which decisions should be taken. It suggests that the leader is making a decision arbitrarily without consulting anyone, exercising his power or authority for his own ends. It is more exact to think of an effective leader as an educator. The relationship between leading and educating is more obvious in Latin than it is in English; the word *educate* comes from the Latin *educare,* meaning *to lead out.* An effective leader is an educator. One leads people by helping them set their goals, by communicating widely throughout the group, and by taking initiative in formulating means of achieving the goals, and finally, by inspiring the members of the group to feel strong enough to work hard for those goals. Such an image of the exercise of power and influence in a leadership role should not frighten anybody and should convince more people that power exercised in this way is not only not dangerous but of the greatest possible use to society.

My experience in training businessmen in India has led me to propose the third ingredient in my formula for producing better leaders—namely, psychological education for adults. What impressed me greatly was the apparent ease with which adults can be changed by the methods we used. The dominant view in American psychology today is still that basic personality structure is laid down early in life and is hard to change later on. Whether the psychologist is a Freudian or a learning theorist, he believes that early experiences are critical and shape everything a person can learn, feel, and want throughout his life span. As a consequence, many educators have come to be pessimistic about what can be done for the poor, the black, or the dispossessed who have undergone damaging experiences early in life. Such traumatized individuals, they argue, have developed non-adaptive personality structures that are difficult, if not impossible, to change later in life. Yet our experience with the effectiveness of short-term training courses in achievement motivation for adult businessmen in India and elsewhere does not support this view. I have seen men change, many of them dramatically, after only a five-day exposure to our specialized techniques of psychological instruction. They changed in the way they thought, in the way they talked, and in the way they spent their time. The message is clear: adults can be changed, often with a relatively short exposure to specialized techniques of psychological education.

The implication for the present discussion is obvious. If it is true, as John Gardner argues, that many young men and women have learned from their professors that the professional role is preferable to the leadership role, then psychological education offers society a method of changing their views and self-conceptions when they are faced with leadership opportunities. The type of psychological education needed will of course differ from the more simple emphasis on achievement motivation. More stress will have to be laid on the means of managing motivation in others. More explanations will have to be given of the positive face of leadership as an educational enterprise. Participants will have to be provided with a better idea of how to be effective leaders. These alterations are quite feasible; in fact they have been tried.

Repeatedly we have discovered that leaders are not so much born as made. We have worked in places where most people feel there is not much leadership potential—specifically, among the poor and dispossessed. Yet we have found over and over again that even among people who have never thought of themselves as leaders or attempted to have influence in any way, real leadership performance can be elicited by specialized techniques of psychological education. We need not be pessimistic about possibilities for change in adults. *Real leaders* have been developed in such disadvantaged locations as the Delmarva peninsula of the United States, the hills of Kentucky (McClelland, Rinesmith, & Kristensen, 1975), the black business community of Washington, D.C., and the relatively stagnant small cities of India. Thus I can end on an optimistic note. Even if the leadership role today is becoming more and more difficult, and even if people are tending to avoid it for a variety of reasons, advances in scientific psychological techniques can to some degree provide society with the techniques for developing and socializing the effective leaders who will be needed for the well-being of the world of tomorrow.

Notes

1. This chapter is a revision of a paper originally presented at Albion College, Albion, Michigan and published under the title "The two faces of

power" in the *Journal of International Affairs,* 1970, 24 (1), 29–47. Copyright by the Trustees of Columbia University. Permission to reprint is gratefully acknowledged to the Editors of the Journal. It was intended as a commentary on the lack of leadership in contemporary America noted by John Gardner in his paper "The anti-leadership vaccine", (1965 Annual Report, The Carnegie Corporation of New York).

2. For a fuller discussion of what Weber and other social scientists have meant by charisma, see Samuel N. Eisenstadt, *Charisma, institution building, and social transformation: Max Weber and modern sociology.* Chicago: The University of Chicago Press, 1968; also Robert C. Tucker, The theory of charismatic leadership. *Daedalus,* 1968, (97), 731–756.

3. To be sure, if he is a gang leader, he may display actions like physical aggression which are characteristic of the personalized power drive. But to the extent that he is the leader of a large group, he is effective because he presents, by personal example, objectives that they find attractive, rather than because he can keep many people in line by threatening them.

4. Why is a successful influence attempt so often perceived as an instance of personal domination by the leader? One answer lies in the simplifying nature of social perception. The observer notices a change in the behavior of a group of people, and he can single out one or two people as leaders in some way involved in the change. He does not know how the leaders operated to bring about the change since he was not intimately involved in the process. As a result, he tends to perceive the process as an instance of the application of personal power, as founded on a simple dominance-submission relationship. The more effective the leader is, the more personal power tends to be attributed to him, regardless of how he has actually achieved his effects.

THE EMPIRE-BUILDERS

EVEN THE casual tourist viewing the extensive ruins of ancient cities cannot help wondering what motivated men in certain times and places to build great empires. What is astonishing about such monuments to man's past efforts is the energy and organization needed to put them together. Even today, centuries later, the aqueducts the Romans built are impressive. They extend for miles over valleys and deserts, beautifully engineered to provide an even flow of water to thousands of acres of land. The aqueducts are only one sign of the organizing genius of the Romans. They built roads all over Europe, North Africa, and England. They devised an elaborate legal system, much of which is still in use. They organized a superb army which controlled vast territories for centuries at a time when communications were slow and difficult.

The Romans were by no means the only effective empire builders whose monuments still remain to remind us of past glories. Visit Monte Alban in the hills of Oaxaca, Mexico and you will see the ruins of a city that rivals anything Rome built. Or observe the marvelous walls and buildings put together out of huge blocks of fitted stone by the Aztecs in Cuzco or the Incas in Macchu Picchu. Since remnants of the Aztec empire were still present as Europeans arrived, we have more or less contemporary accounts of how well organized it was.

Or contemplate for a moment the task of building the huge Peacock palace in Anuradhapura, the ancient capital of a kingdom in Ceylon. One can get an idea of its magnitude from looking at the 1600 granite pillars, twelve feet in height, which supported the first floor. It was reported by contemporary chroniclers to have had nine stories, to have contained a thousand rooms, and to have housed three thousand monks. It was only one of dozens of elaborate structures, remains of which are still visible at the center of a city of some two to three million people, the hub of an empire which lasted for centuries. Here as in the case of Rome or Egypt, success depended upon energy and organization. All of the plains of northern Ceylon had been turned into a vast series of paddy fields for growing rice through an elaborate irrigation system. Huge ponds or tanks were constructed by closing off streams with earth dams to collect water during the rainy season, and to allow it to run out through irrigation channels to supply thousands of small paddy fields with water during the dry season. In the centuries after the civilization disappeared, the irrigation system fell into disuse, the people were killed off by malaria—possibly because they ate the fish in the ponds which formerly had eaten the mosquito larvae. By the seventeenth century the whole area was an uncultivated, uninhabited wilderness. See Knox (1681). One cannot help wondering why.

Why did some people at one point in history suddenly have the energy to construct all those dams, irrigation channels, and paddy fields, and eventually those great urban monuments? And why at some later period did the impulse to maintain such a system, which would have required less effort than to build it, die out and leave everything in ruins? Historians are not particularly helpful. Though they know that such things happen, they usually attribute the rise of civilization to some fortunate combination of external circumstances, such as a technological discovery or an able ruler, and its fall to an unfavorable combination of circumstances such as internal dissension or invasion from without.

External events like an able king or an invasion may precipitate change, but they are seldom the root cause of the change. The causal role of kings, for example, either for good or evil, has been exaggerated in the popular mind, probably because kings can easily be identified with a period of imperial expansion or decay. It is sometimes supposed that a ruthless, or inspiring, able king forces his people, let us say, to construct an elaborate irrigation system by making slaves out of them. The empire then is seen as a product of one man's will and abilities. He orders his assistants to do certain things on the pain of royal displeasure. They in turn pass the orders down through a chain of command ending with a mass of slaves who do what they are told for fear of the consequences if they don't. Systems of this sort have often, in fact, been set up in history. On the hill at Mihintale at the end of the eight-mile sacred way from the center of Anuradhapura, stands a stone tablet erected by a king who tried to maintain his empire in just this way. He granted land to his people on conditions that they give him half of their crops and that they provide so many days of work on public projects during the year. The interesting point is that this arrangement was put into force toward the end of the civilization, not at its beginning. When the empire was getting underway, the king is said to have paid the people who worked on the great irrigation projects. In some real sense they *wanted* to do what they were doing; they were not forced into it. As Galbraith has pointed out, slavery has always been one of the poorest ways of motivating people to work effectively.

What then did motivate people to organize empires? Our study of power motivation has given us a clue to the answer. Individuals are interested in political organization and are good at it if their power motivation is of the socialized type (s Power). The s Power scoring system was derived by examining the qualitative characteristics of power themes written by men who were high in power motivation and also high in Activity Inhibition. According to the evidence of the previous chapter, men who are high in the need for Power and also in the need for control or order, tend to think in terms of expressing power on behalf of others rather than for themselves. This altruistic concern is abstract, concerned with needs of the system, not the particular needs of an individual. Ever since Max Weber first made the point so clearly, social scientists have argued (cf. Parsons, 1967) that for a bureaucracy to function efficiently, it must be governed by the norm of universalistic justice. Individuals must be treated "fairly"— that is, equally in terms of the rules of the system—rather than in terms of their particular needs or their ties with officials operating the system. In psychological terms, the need for Affiliation must be low, because *n* Affiliation is the motive that leads people to care about the happiness of particular others. It places the well-being of individuals above the well-being of the system.

Empire building, in short, is the symptom of a state in which the need for Power and the need for control are both very strong, and the need for Affiliation is weak. Such an interpretation makes good sense. Almost any historian would argue that the Romans had a strong need for Power as well as a passion for discipline that curbed self-interest and particularistic treatment of others on the basis of personal ties. Similarly, the greatest empire of modern times, built up over three centuries by the British, is popularly supposed to have arisen out of the energies and ambitions of great men and the iron self-control which they and their troops displayed. What can the psychologist add to this understanding? Details. Clarification. Expansion. Measurement. Because the conventional wisdom or popular psychology appears to have been on the right track, it does not follow that it can explain the full story. Let us try to examine our hypothesis carefully and in more detail.

The Link Between Motives and
Stages of Maturity

In order to understand why a certain combination of motives may help build empires, it is helpful to observe where individuals with very different motive combinations stand on the average with respect to the various levels of ego development established in Chapter 2. The question might be reformulated this way: Why do individuals—either men or women—in the course of their natural development become interested in doing things that build strong and expanding organizational structures? At what point in the developmental sequence are they most likely to develop such interests?

Certain hypotheses can readily be formulated from data already presented. From the correlations reported in Appendix Table 2.3 on the miscellaneous sample of adult men and women tested, it appears that high need for Power both in men and women is associated with Stage III, the phallic or assertive stage. *N* Affiliation is more positively associated with Stages I and II, and if anything it is negatively correlated with Stage III. A reasonable inference would be that the empire-building motive might develop out of the phallic stage when normally *n* Power is high and *n* Affiliation is low. Among some peoples at certain times and places, one might suppose, a strong need for control also develops, which when added to a high *n* Power and low *n* Affiliation produces the combination of motives leading to strong organizations. At the moment we do not know why this sometimes happens. In the next chapter we will speculate that the rather unstable motive combination of high *n* Power and high *n* Affiliation may encourage the development of religious reformist orientations; such people often insist on self-control, which may in time create the motive complex responsible for empire building. To know where and how in the developmental sequence the motive complex is most likely to occur would be advantageous; then historians could be guided accordingly in their search for those social factors that might have produced the motivational changes preliminary to empire building.

Our view of the historical process is quite straightforward. All individuals at all times and places proceed through the developmental sequence described in Chapters 1 and 2 at varying speeds and to various levels. Some may continue to be oriented predominantly towards Stage II; a number of individuals in our samples of adult men and women remained thus oriented. More may go on to Stages III or IV. For historical or cultural reasons, the majority of individuals in a particular group (or nation) may reach Stage III with a strong need for Power, a weak need for Affiliation, and a strong need for control. If this happens, they are likely to act in ways that produce effective organizations which often expand into empires, given a large enough population base from which to operate.

Table 8.1 presents in more concrete form some of the information needed to check the hypotheses under consideration. It shows

Table 8.1–Mean maturity stage scores for various motive combinations (men and women combined, N = 200)

	N	Stage I Intake Mean	SD	Stage II Control Mean	SD	Stage III Assertion Mean	SD	Stage IV Generativity Mean	SD
A. Low *n* Power	55	1.07	1.0	.86	.9	.26	.5	1.60	1.3
B. High need for Power[a] and high *n* Aff.[b]	73	1.16	1.2	1.41	1.1	.96	1.2	1.93	1.3
C. High *n* Power,[a] low *n* Aff. low Inhibition	43	.72	1.0	1.21	1.0	1.00	1.1	1.56	1.1
D. High *n* Power,[a] low *n* Aff. high Inhibition[c]	29	.86	.9	1.00	1.0	1.79	1.3	1.76	1.4

p values (from t tests)
Group B vs. C	<.05							
Group B vs. D			<.08		<.001			
Group C vs. D					<.001			

a. Score of 3 or more
b. Score of 2 or more
c. Score of 2 or more

the mean stage scores for adult individuals with various combinations of motive scores. Most of the people in this sample, as we have noted, are predominantly oriented towards Stage IV, but our interest here is in the relative importance of earlier stages among the various subgroups. Consider first Group A, those low in need for Power. They tend to be somewhat higher than Groups C or D in Stage I (Intake) orientation, but above all they are significantly lower in Stage III orientation ($p < .001$ as compared with any of the three high n Power groups). Group B, those high in need for Power and high in need for Affiliation, though also high in Stage I scores, are particularly high in Stage II scores; from this one might infer that this motive combination develops most naturally out of or in combination with a Stage II interest in control, just as low n Power is more associated with the earlier stage of intake orientation. Groups C and D, the individuals with high n Power and low n Affiliation tend to be somewhat less oriented towards Stage II and more oriented towards Stage III. Particularly is this true for Group D, which is of main concern to us here—those high in n Power, low in n Affiliation, and high in inhibition. They score significantly higher in Stage III orientation than any of the other three groups. They are more assertive or intrusive in their approach to life.

These various stage and motive orientations translate into actions which would or would not build strong organizations. The men and women in Group A, who are low in n Power with a stronger Stage I orientation, seem to lack the self-confidence and assertiveness necessary to organize effectively. See Table 2.3. The men report that they seldom get into arguments. They do not dare to discuss with others such intimate matters as their love lives and their pressures at work ($r = .26$, $p < .05$). These are Freud's vital themes of "Lieben und Arbeiten." They frequently go back to check on whether their living quarters are locked and in order. They alone among men say that they like looking after children ($r = .25$, $p < .05$) and they strongly endorse the dictum that reason should rule the world, presumably because they do not feel they have the strength otherwise to have their way. The women low in n Power say that their parents taught them to be nice to others ($r = .22$, $p < .05$) rather than to actualize themselves ($r = .25$, $p < .01$). They do not join as many organizations ($r = -.23$, $p < .05$) nor do they attempt to build themselves up through physical exercise or dieting, to take special care of their appearance, or to collect credit cards which expand their power. One can hardly imagine such men or women acting in ways that would end by producing a great empire.

The Personal Enclave Power System

Of somewhat greater interest here is Group B, those who are high in *n* Power as well as in *n* Affiliation. Although they have the power motivation to produce an assertive life style, they are oriented primarily around the pre-phallic stages of development; they see the self rather than others as the primary target in any attempts to feel powerful. They would seek to feel more powerful either through searching for powerful influences from the outside (Stage I), or through self-control (Stage II). Mexicans represent the ideal case, for Mexico's stories for children collected for *The achieving society* score high in *n* Power (standard score = +1.20), high in *n* Affiliation (standard score = +.62), and low in Activity Inhibition (standard score = −.51). (See Appendix Table 8.1, which includes the motive scores for children's stories from *The achieving society* and also the same measure of inhibition used for stories of individuals—namely the number of times the word "not" appears in the stories, as an indicator of the extent to which there is a concern over controlling action. These Activity Inhibition scores were standardized for both the 1925 and 1950 samples of countries and will be referred to throughout this chapter.)

The themes in Mexican culture, which have already been analyzed in Chapter 5, center on the notion that one can build a closed circle of intimate personal relationships which will protect one from threats and dangers in the outside world. Inside this shelter one feels warm, strong, safe. Outside he feels exposed, lonely, threatened by unknown attackers. When he is brave against threat, he is "macho".

As one might expect, Italy is one of the few other countries whose stories display the same motivational profile (Appendix Table 8.1). Italian stories also build on the same central theme of security in the home. In one typical story, two little boys run away from home because they are jealous of the attention their mother is bestowing on their newly arrived baby sister. Alone in the dark, they are frightened and have a "vision of a peaceful home, of the light that is turned on on the table, of the white tablecloth—of the good smells that come from the kitchen—the voice of their mother." Their guardian angel leads them home and their mother is overjoyed to see them. "They put down their small bundles. It is true they are big children, but the arms of the mother are so warm, they feel so strong, tight around." In the Italian stories as in the Mexican, the main themes deal with maternal support, with the need for security and self-protection, and with the dangerous consequences of self-assertion when it results in leaving the security of home. Although in the Mexican case, one may break away with a certain exuberance like a soaring rocket (being daring or macho), in the end the rocket dies and returns home to earth.

One of the questions that always arises in analyzing themes in children's stories is whether they bear any connection whatsoever with what individuals actually do in real life. To find out in the present instance, we identified those men and women who had the same motive combination as appeared in the Mexican and Italian stories— high *n* Power, high *n* Affiliation, and low Inhibition—and checked to see whether they reported actions and preferences reflecting the same views of the world as appeared in the children's stories. The results are recorded in Table 8.2, in the form of correlations between a composite motive score and answers to various items on the questionnaire administered to adult men and women, as reported in Chapter 2. To obtain the composite score, each motive score was standardized and those with a low *n* Power score excluded from the sample; we were interested only in those with a relatively high *n* Power. Among those remaining, if *n* Power and Inhibition scores are subtracted from the *n* Affiliation score, then those subjects should score highest who are high in *n* Affiliation relative to *n* Power (which is at least moderately high) and low in Inhibition. In other words, they are high in *n* Power, high in *n* Affiliation and low in Inhibition. Such people are more likely to report that they do the things listed in Table 8.2 than are those who score lower in *n* Affiliation and higher in inhibition while remaining high in *n* Power.

To a surprising degree the correlations confirm expectations. While the particular items of correlation differ for men and women, with only one or two exceptions they correspond rather well to the themes already identified in the children's stories. Both men and women feel the need for obtaining strength from external sources (Stage I). They pray more often; the men report that they are more likely to go to a minister or priest for personal help; the women state that the inspirational power of religion appeals to them because of "its ability to provide an important source of strength to deal with life." The women also list more other women who have been strong sources of inspiration to them.

Both men and women also seem to seek security in close personal ties; both report that they share more private information with their mothers. The men are fond of babies and school-age children, and even list people among their precious possessions. The women's feelings for close personal ties are expressed exclusively in their tendency to share their feelings and other private information more

Table 8.2—Characteristics associated with the "personal enclave" motivational pattern (High n Power, High n Affiliation, Low Inhibition)

	Correlation of [n Affiliation – high n Power[a] – Inhibition] with	
	Among men (N = 71)	Among women (N = 74)
A. *Importance of strength from external sources*	r	r
Prays more often	.30*	Prays more often .23†
More likely to go to minister or priest for personal help	.31*	Religion for inspirational strength .23+
		Female figures strong source of inspiration .26*
B. *Security in close personal ties*		
Shares more with mother	.23+	Shares more with mother .17
Likes babies better	.25*	Shares feelings more .25*
Likes school age children better	.35*	Shares sex life more .29*
		Few secrets .26*
Lists people as precious possessions	.24*	
C. *Be ready for trouble* (threats from outside)		
Travels less alone in new places	.33**	Travels less alone in new places .15
Yells less at people in traffic	.28*	Holds down a power job now .26*
Plays checkers or chess less	.28*	Has walked off on husband on a social occasion .23+
D. *Death as a friend*		
As a compassionate mother	.28*	As a compassionate mother .26*
As a murderer (castration metaphors)	–.13	As a murderer –.18

†p < .10, *p < .05, **p < .01
a. score of 3 or more

with friends and family members. Except for talking more with their mothers, the men build their personal ties in an external way, the women in a more internal psychological manner.

They seem also to feel that trouble waits in the outside world. Both sexes say they travel less alone in new places. The men say they are less likely to yell at people in traffic, presumably because they are afraid of retaliation, and they don't expose themselves to defeat by playing games of strategy like checkers or chess. The women seem to take a more assertive stance in warding off trouble. They are more likely to hold down power jobs at the present time and to report that they have walked out on their husbands on a social occasion. Unfortunately there were no items in the questionnaire that tested directly what might be called the Icarian mode—the tendency to look upon assertive breaking away as exciting but ultimately both dangerous and self-destructive.

The section of the questionnaire on the death metaphor, however, turned up an odd fact. Both sexes agreed that death as "a compassionate mother" was a more appropriate metaphor than any of the others. They disliked more than average the castration metaphors of death as a murderer. The striking part about this finding is that it is direct empirical support for the theoretical view advanced in Chapter 5 to the effect that Mexicans view death more positively than might be expected. At times, indeed, they seem to court death when they are being macho, or to think of it with nostalgia. Our interpretation was that death for them represents a return to the mother. Though they may break away from home and soar like rockets, in the end they fall back to mother earth and find in death a desired reunion with the compassionate mother they have left. It is seldom that one gets the chance to confirm in such a concrete empirical way a clinical or theoretical interpretation seemingly "far out" or speculative. To a surprising degree, in fact, all the correlations in Table 8.2 confirm the overall picture obtained from the analysis of Mexican culture—surprising particularly when one recalls that these are the relatively few correlations out of some 200 that reached significant or near significant levels.

Individuals with a strong power need, and high *n* Affiliation, particularly if they also have low Inhibition, try to build a kind of personal enclave which gives them a feeling of warmth, strength, and security. For them the family often becomes a kind of fortress; inside it they feel safe, and the whole outside world they view as potentially threatening. They get inspiration from the mother or religious sources, and their attachment to family members is their security and their strength. That such an orientation does not promote the building of strong organizations outside the family is easy to see. Social scientists have for a long time explained that the "familism" of countries like Italy prevents the development of loyalties to larger entities such as the State. Furthermore, the importance of family ties prevents officials from serving in bureaucracies in the universalistic manner; they tend to "play favorites," dealing with family members and friends in particularistic ways that undermine the system of universalistic justice required by well-functioning organizations. Now we understand better from the motivational point of view why this family orientation occurs in the first place and why it is difficult for such people to function well in an organization. Their goal is still primarily that of Stage I and Stage II: they want to feel strong personally. Since they do not want to influence other people, they are not willing to make the adjustments necessary to do so. Rather, they devote their energies to building a personal enclave that will make them feel strong.

What about India? According to our analysis in Chapter 4, it represents a culture traditionally oriented towards the pre-phallic stages, particularly Stage I in which the mother as giver of strength and resources is the model. Here the motivational profile for the children's stories collected around 1950 does not fit expectations. It is high in *n* Power, slightly below average in *n* Affiliation, and above average in inhibition; it fits the imperial pattern which we will be discussing in a moment rather than the maternal Stage I orientation expected. This suggests that modern India may have moved away from its traditional orientation towards the empire-building pattern. Some political observers would agree that it is becoming organizationally more efficient and that it has behaved more like a great power in recent years—in the way, for instance, it decisively entered the Civil War in Pakistan. It intervened to save the persecuted and oppressed Bengalis, to be sure, but in so doing it acted as imperial nations like Britain have typically behaved in the past.

Nevertheless, we would have to continue to argue that in traditional Hinduism and in Buddhism, one of its important by-products, the primary orientation is towards Stage I and secondarily towards Stage II. The primary goal of both stages is to feel strong personally, not to influence others. In both religions the primary concern is with individual, not social, salvation. Hence, Hinduism and Buddhism have not promoted the building of great organizations or empires, except during periods when other motivational combinations have temporarily been dominant. In fact, the archetypical Indian organization is the ashram, something like a group of children (disciples) gathered around a mother figure (guru) to provide them with divine inspiration (milk). In Sri Lanka today, the three main themes in a standard sermon are: "the Buddha is like a mother; the dharma (doctrine) is like milk; the sangha (the brotherhood of monks) is like milk-drinking children" (Gombrich, 1972). Ashrams are not the stuff out of which empires have been built.

The Empire Building Motivational Syndrome

So far we have just been clearing the ground, so to speak, to understand why Group A, low *n* Power, and Group B, high *n* Power plus high *n* Affiliation do *not* lead to building strong organizations or empires. Why, in contrast, should the combination of high *n* Power, low *n* Affiliation, and high Inhibition apparently work so well? We have made a general case but we need to know in much greater detail just how it works, how the motive pattern shapes the norms which build effective organizations, and how it predisposes individuals to act in ways that strengthen organizations.

It will be helpful to describe in more detail the ideology of effective organizational systems and to look at themes in children's stories from countries noted for their organizing capacity. Just as we found Mexican, Indian, and Italian stories helpful in understanding how "mother power" social systems work, we may now find an examination of the ideology of patriarchal systems relevant. There can be no doubt about it: effective empires have most often employed patriarchal imagery to gain the understanding and devotion of their members.

What are the elements in the patriarchal scenario that promote organizational effectiveness? Let us begin by reviewing the patriarchal authority system as pictured in the Bible because it is so familiar and because it has been so influential in Western cultures, including Western psychology. Jehovah is the ideal father—all powerful, loving, but stern. He rewards His people if they obey His commandments and punishes them fearfully if they do not. His sons, like father Abraham, the prophet Isaiah, or Moses are His representatives on earth. They never act on the basis of their own authority but always on the basis of His authority. The ideal relationship to His authority is, as Jesus put it, "Father, not my will, but Thine, be done." This means of course, that a person must be willing to give up not only his own ego, his own sense of personal power, but also even his life, as Jesus did, to be obedient to higher authority in the system. To question this authority is to question the system itself.

There are four key psychological themes in classical patriarchal ideology. First, the individual gets power by *submission* to higher authority. By accepting the father's authority and joining with it, he gains all the power of the authority itself. By becoming an official representative of that power, he too as an individual has power. Second, the individual must show *self-control*; he must curb his selfish impulses. He must obey God at all times in all ways. Doing anything on his own is a sign that he has not accepted completely the authority of the Father. Third, he must be willing to *sacrifice his interests* for others that the whole system may prevail. The ultimate test of whether a person has abandoned self-interest is whether he is willing to do something that actually costs him something. He may be asked even to sacrifice his life, as in the story of Jesus. People must be willing to die that the system may prevail. Fourth, the theme of *justice* is prominent. If a person gives up his assertiveness and submits to the Father's will, he will get his just rewards. God, the Father, operates a divine "payback" system which rewards those who do His will and punishes those who disobey Him. In Christianity, as we noted in discussing the Book of Revelation, the individual may not get his just reward in his lifetime, but he will be rewarded in heaven. Personal sacrifice for the authority of the system, in short, will bring a just reward to the individual. On the other hand, the person who disobeys will be punished. Otherwise he who does obey the Father may feel he has sacrificed himself in vain.

These four themes—power through submission, self-discipline, sacrifice for others, and justice—are an intrinsic part of the patriarchal power myth in its Judaeo-Christian form, and perhaps in all forms. They represent a complex but coherent world view which explains how the individual gains power by subordinating his will to the will of the group, how his personal aggressiveness can be sublimated into serving others in the in-group and attacking those outside it, and how he is rewarded for serving the public good and punished for not doing so. Obviously the patriarchal ideology has not always led to building empires. It is not even regularly associated with a high need for Power. In fact, in a sample of twenty-two preliterate cultures the correlation between patrilineality versus all other lineage systems and the need for Power scores obtained from folk tales is an insignificant $-.29$. At the individual level the correlation between father identification and n Power in men is also negative and insignificant. ($r = -.08$, data from sample described in Chapter 2.) Yet when the motivational pattern is right for whatever reason, the patriarchal ideology provides ready justification for building, and for expanding, effective organizational structures. If an individual's power need is strong, he apparently realizes it can be best served by linking up with a powerful collective will and an authority figure at the top. If his inhibition score is high, he is ready to discipline himself, or even sacrifice himself for others in order to achieve collective power. If his n Affiliation is low, he is readier to enforce a universalistic code of justice in which people are rewarded in terms of what they do for the system rather than in terms of their personal needs or ties to officials in the system. In a well-functioning organization each person must be treated alike, that is, fairly. He must not be able to obtain special privileges through his personal relationships with superiors or, when the shoe is on the other foot, provide favors for his friends. The ideal of universalistic justice within the system as a whole must be paramount.

There can be no doubt that when the motive combination was right, the core values in the ideology of patriarchal authority have led to some of the strongest organizations and most expansive empires in history. Patriarchal values were strongly present in the Roman empire, various Christian empires, and the spread of Islam. They provide the moral basis for all effective military organizations in which the authority of the supreme commander (father figure) at the top is delegated down the chain of command; in which every subordinate knows that he must obey rigid controls on his personal freedom so as to act and be ready to sacrifice his life if necessary for the good of the system; and in which distributive justice is a paramount value. Every man must be rewarded in terms of his performance of his duty and punished for not doing his duty.

The Black Muslims

The way in which such values work to create an effective organization is difficult to appreciate fully in the abstract. We need an example—and a living example at that, because our ideas about such shop-worn instances as the Roman empire or the British empire are so stereotyped and encrusted with tradition that we have a hard time seeing in psychological terms what happened. The development of the Black Muslim movement in America in the 1950's and 1960's will serve our purposes admirably.

All would agree that the nation of Islam, as the Black Muslims called themselves, developed a highly efficient organizational structure. Why and how? By this period in American history many blacks and liberal whites had begun to accept the fact that the black population in the United States had for centuries been an oppressed underclass, a kind of internal colony ruled by white authority. As more and more black people understood this, they rejected white authority as morally illegitimate, even in terms of its own standards, because it systematically deprived blacks of equal rights to education, jobs, health, and even in some cases to life itself.

What can a group do when it discovers that it is governed by an illegitimate authority? It can give up, so to speak, by "copping out" of the system as far as possible. Many black individuals took this route, becoming alienated outlaws, anarchists, or hedonists. Another option is to try to change the white power structure or to infiltrate it in such a way as to change it from within. Many blacks chose this approach. But what Elijah Muhammad did was more radical and more organizationally effective. He created a whole new moral authority that legitimated black power. He began by constructing an elaborate new history of the human race to prove that the white man is the devil. Original man was black, and he had "built great empires and civilizations and cultures while the white man was still living on all fours in caves. The Devil White Man down through history, through his devilish nature, had pillaged, murdered, raped, and exploited every race of man not white" (Malcolm X, 1966, p. 162). The Black Muslim learned, in other words, that white authority was morally illegitimate and that black authority was morally superior and should be obeyed. Its supreme representative was the father figure, Elijah Muhammad, who delegated his authority to his ministers to interpret his divine revelations. Submitting to his authority and joining the Nation of Islam would bring to blacks the power that they have been denied by whites. As Malcolm X put it, "That devil white man does not want the honorable Elijah Muhammad stirring awake the sleeping giant of you and me and of all our ignorant, brain-washed kind here in the white man's heaven and the black man's hell . . ." (p. 210).

The first theme associated with organizational effectiveness was clearly present: gain individual power by submitting to a supreme morally legitimate patriarchal authority. The second and third themes were also key elements in the movement. Joining the Nation of Islam involved extensive *self-discipline* and *sacrifice for others,* for the welfare of the group as a whole. Members had to give up pork, tobacco, liquor, narcotics, and had to follow daily, weekly, monthly and yearly rituals as detailed as those described in the Old Testament for Jews. "There was none of the morning confusion that exists in most homes. Wilfred, the father, the family protector and provider, was the first to rise. 'The father prepares the way for his family,' he said. He, then I, perform the morning ablutions. Next came Wilfred's wife, Ruth, and then their children, so that orderliness prevailed in the use of the bathroom. 'In the name of Allah, I perform the ablution' the Muslims said aloud before washing first the right hand, then the left hand. The teeth were thoroughly brushed, followed by three rinsings out of the mouth. The nostrils were also rinsed out thrice. The shower then completed the whole body purification in readiness for prayer" (Malcolm X, p. 193). Members gave up their old personal identities and adopted new names. They learned new methods of greeting each other. Prayers were prescribed for certain times of the day. Each night was set aside for a different Muslim function. At certain times of the year all Muslims gathered together and went in trains and busses to Chicago for mass meetings. Discipline in the movement was very strict. Members were sentenced to isolation for disobeying ritual prescriptions and were even ordered to keep silent, as Malcolm X himself finally was for disobedience. A visible sign of all this emphasis on power and discipline was the corps of guards known as the Fruit of Islam; it consisted of men especially chosen for their magnificent physiques and trained to perfection in military drill.

Yet the man who was responsible for the exercise of all this authority, Elijah Muhammad, was described as a "gentle, sweet, little brown man who had spent seven years on the run and three and a half years in prison, put there by the devil white man" (p. 210). His gentleness and devotion to his people were a model for the personal sacrifice demanded of his followers. Yet he understood well that to build a successful stable organization or "empire" it is essential to demand personal sacrifice, to build a network of rituals to control personal impulses, and to promise power through identification with superior moral authority.

He also invoked the fourth theme in the patriarchal cluster. He promised *justice*—justice at last for the black man. Elijah Muhammad "showed us how his teachings of the true knowledge of ourselves would lift up the black man from the bottom of the white man's society and place the black man where he had begun, at the top of civilization" (Malcolm X, p. 197). The devil white man's civilization was condemned to be destroyed by Allah. The supreme moral authority represented by Islam will see to it that the bad people—the whites—are punished, and the good people—the blacks—are rewarded. In other words, all the discipline and personal sacrifice are justified as they normally are in patriarchal ideology, on the grounds that in time they will bring each person his just reward. The long-term success of the Nation of Islam will depend, as in the case of all such movements, on the degree to which blacks generally can accept the moral leadership of Elijah Muhammad and the new interpretation of the history of mankind which legitimates that authority. Most educated blacks cannot accept his authority, but for those who can, he has skillfully employed the four key themes in the patriarchal power myth to build an effective organization with high morale. In so doing, he has demonstrated once again the effectiveness of the patriarchal power complex of ideas for empire building.

Patriarchal Power in Stories for Children

Next, we can pick out nations whose children's stories score high in the empire-building motivational pattern—high *n* Power, low *n* Affilation, and high Inhibition. (See Appendix Table 8.1, which is based on the research reported in *The achieving society*.) They turn out to include Germany, Russia, and the People's Republic of China, countries that stand among the first in the world measured by the effectiveness of their state bureaucracies. Thus we gain added confidence that our hypothesized motivational pattern is associated with the building of well-disciplined organizations. It is instructive to see how the key values in the patriarchal power complex are expressed in stories; the values become more real, alive, and understandable than in the abstractions we have so far presented. It is possible, furthermore, to observe variations in the way the four main patriarchal themes are expressed—variations important for understanding how a particular country organizes itself and for demonstrating that a given theme does not always have to be expressed in exactly the same way. Let us consider stories from Germany.

Theme A. Submit to get power from collective authority. The German stories for 1950 include one that makes this point dramatically. Called "The Dispute of the Parts of the Human Body," it begins: "When God created man he gave a task to every part of the human body. Thus man lived rightly and happily as God had intended, and every part of his body did its duty. But once it happened that the parts got into a quarrel concerning the question which one of them deserved the greatest honor." Each one argued that it deserved the most honor: the eye because it had to see before the foot or hands could move, the ear because it gets guidance as to what other parts should do, the mouth because without the food that it takes in, the others could not live, the brain because it guides the other organs, and so on. "But now all of them rebelled and talked cross-wise, saying that they were above the brain, for they perceived things first, and then only did the brain come in and make use of them like a master. They no longer wanted to be his slaves . . . the quarrel lasted for days, and the body lost more and more of its energy because the mouth did not eat, the eyes did not see, the ear did not listen, the nose did not smell, the hands and feet were at rest, the brain sat aside grumbling."

The lesson by now is clear. Every individual must do his part, submit to the needs of the whole system, or it will perish and all will suffer. The heart finally brings them to their senses by reminding them that no part of the body could exist without its nourishing support. "I am the first and the noblest as you all depend on me. But I need you just as much as you need me to exist. I sustain you but at the same time I am your servant . . . everyone should do his duty so that everyone may live." Notice that as always in this value system the most powerful person recognizes that his power must not be used for selfish ends but for the good of others (s Power).

The image of supreme authority here is not a male father figure—a fact which emphasizes the point made earlier: we may use the term "patriarchal power" as a kind of shorthand, with some historical validity, but in technical psychological terms, it is necessary only that a supreme authority be recognized, not that it be identified with the father.

Theme B. Self-control. In the German stories, self-control is described in the context of overcoming fears. In one such story Peter is a little boy whose mother has just tucked him into bed and put out the lights for the night. All of a sudden he noticed a moving black shape in the corner by the window. "He was very frightened. He could see it quite plainly. It went forward, it went backward, it moved this way and that way. He trembled with his whole body. He could not call his mother." Finally mastering his terror, he jumped out of bed and ran across the room and "reached with both his hands into the dark shadow which was still moving back and forth." He discovered that it was just his bath towel, and he was very pleased that he had not cried for his mother like a small child.

Theme C. Sacrifice self for others, be altruistic. These themes are very common in the German stories. In a typical tale, a little girl is out searching for water during a disastrous drought. She falls asleep, and when she awakes, finds that her pitcher is magically filled with water. Although she is very thirsty, she decides that there might not be enough for her mother and hurries home to give her the water first. On the way she gives some to a poor little dog, and the pitcher magically turns to silver. When she tries to give the water to her mother, the latter refuses on the ground that she is about to die anyway and it would be better for the daughter to drink. Then the pitcher changes from silver to gold. The girl is now at last about to drink when a poor wanderer appears at the door asking for water; she gives it to him, and seven magnificent diamonds appear on the pitcher. There can be little doubt in the mind of the reader of this and other similar stories that altruism is one of the greatest virtues.

Theme D. Authority enforces justice. In the German stories there is much concern that justice be done in the form of punishing the mistreatment of others. In one tale, for instance, a man notices that a poor dog with a sore foot is running painfully alongside an empty butcher's wagon; he stops the butcher and shames him into taking the dog into the wagon. In another, the king of a certain city hangs a bell which the people are to pull whenever they need a judge to settle a dispute. The rope breaks and is replaced by a rope of straw. To everyone's astonishment, a poor half-starved horse eats the rope and pulls the bell, whereupon they discover that the horse has been maltreated by the duke, its owner, because it is old and useless. The judge shames the duke into taking better care of his horse. Or again, a violinist shopkeeper overcharges a poor foreigner; an innkeeper notices it and with the help of a strict judge forces the shopkeeper to pay the money back. In all of these cases justice is done, but individuals must take initiative to make sure that bad behavior is punished. Good behavior tends to be somewhat miraculously rewarded, as in the case of the girl whose pitcher turns to silver and gold.

Behavior of Individuals with the Imperial Motivational Pattern

With a better understanding of the themes governing strong organizations, we can now search for their presence in the responses of individuals who are characterized by the imperial motivational pattern—high *n* Power, low *n* Affiliation, and high Inhibition. Using the sample of adult men and women studied in Chapter 2, we discarded those low in *n* Power from the sample. We then subtracted the *n* Affiliation score from the *n* Power score to measure the extent to which *n* Power was higher than *n* Affiliation, and correlated this resultant score with various responses to the questionnaire among those who were high or low in Inhibition. In other words, our basic argument formulated from Table 8.1 is that both of these groups (Group C and Group D) are oriented more towards Stages III and IV than they are towards Stages I and II. They both have a more phallic or assertive orientation, but the point of major interest is how Inhibition directs assertiveness into actions characteristic of the four themes of the ideological system based on patriarchal authority. In Table 8.3, therefore, actions correlated with high *n* Power > *n* Affiliation are grouped under the themes they seem to represent. To show the input of Inhibition on such relationships, the correlations for Groups C and D are shown side by side.

The very first line of correlations in Table 8.3 illustrates the point nicely. When *n* Power is at least moderately high, and higher than *n* Affiliation, people tend to be more "institution-minded" if their Inhibition score is above the median, but not if it is below. Men with this combination of motives are more likely to have joined organizations if their Inhibition score is high and significantly *less* likely if their Inhibition score is low. Among women the same tendency appears not as a tendency to join more organizations, but as a tendency to be

Table 8.3—Personal characteristics associated with the imperial motivational pattern (High n Power[a] over n Affiliation, high Inhibition [b])

Among Men	Correlations of High n Power – n Aff. when Inhibition is		Among Women	Correlations of High n Power – n Aff. when Inhibition is	
	High N = 29	Low N = 42		High N = 28	Low N = 46
A. *Respect for institutional authority*					
Joins more organizations	.25†	– .35*	Elected to more offices	.33*	.05
Psychiatrist preferred for personal help	.29†	– .11	Accepts institutional responsibility	.37*	– .11
Taller	.26*	– .12	More inspirational males than females	.44**	.01
Parents *less* preferred for personal help	.42**	– .13			
Few individuals admired, as inspiration	.26†	.15			
B. *Discipline and self-control*					
Work is enjoyable	.41**	.03	Work is enjoyable	.20	.05
Feelings kept to self	.31†	– .12	Work is not boring	.40**	.01
Dislike child care	.36*	.00	Income kept to self	.27†	.10
Controlled anger	.25†	.15	No lies told	.40**	.04
C. *Sacrifice self for others, altruism*					
Share $10,000 gift with charities	.23	– .32*	Share $10,000 gift with friends	.36*	.07
Parents taught sociocentric virtues	.30†	– .24	Volunteer to look after children	.27†	–.05
			Parents taught egocentric virtues	.31	.20
			Owns more credit cards	.38*	.04
			Lists people as precious possessions	.48**	.02
D. *Concern for just reward*					
Argues frequently	.39**	.22			
Metaphors for death as murder more appropriate	.27†	.01	Metaphors for death as murder more appropriate	.30†	.20
Stage III (Phallic) score in Maturity Scale	.22	.33*	Stage III (Phallic) score in Maturity Scale	.30†	.38*

†p < .10, *p < .05, **p < .025, in the predicted direction
a = Score of 3 or more, b = Score of 2 or more

elected to more offices within such organizations. Other items listed under Theme A tend to confirm the hypothesis based on our prior analyses that the people with this motivational pattern show more respect for institutional authority. The men would go to a recognized expert for personal help—a psychiatrist—rather than to their parents, who would be less formally qualified to help them. They also tend to list fewer individuals as sources of personal inspiration, presumably because they see authority as coming not from individuals but from institutions. Oddly enough, they are also taller than the average; does this mean that their natural advantage in height predisposes them towards hierarchical institutions, or supreme authorities?

Women with the imperial motive combination state more explicitly that they enjoy feeling "part of an organization like my church, or where I work because it makes me feel more useful or more significant" and that "people regard me as a very responsible person. I volunteer for jobs that need doing in an organization and see they are properly done." Unlike the men with the same motive patterns, they list more individuals as being personally inspiring; but since the individuals are males rather than females, we are free to infer that they are accepting the institutional superiority of men to provide such inspiration for women, in the classic patriarchal pattern.

Both men and women with the imperial motivational pattern show the expected concern for *discipline* and *self-control* (Theme B, Table 8.3). The men report that they are likely to find their work enjoyable; the women agree, at least to the extent of saying that it is not boring. Shades of the Calvinist work ethic! They *like* to work. I was delighted to come across this finding, because for years people have been mistakenly interpreting my studies of achievement motivation as meaning that people with high n Achievement represent the Protestant work ethic. They don't. They like to do things more efficiently and get out of work. Apparently it is people with high n Power, low n Affiliation, and high control who like to work for its own sake because it is a form of self-discipline.

The men show other signs of this interest in self-control. They keep their feelings to themselves (disclose less about themselves to others); they control their admittedly aggressive impulses; and they particularly dislike looking after children, presumably because children often are so undisciplined and need to be controlled. The women keep information about their income to themselves and are strict with themselves in not telling lies to anyone about anything.

The expected *altruism* (Theme C) shows up unambiguously only in one item. The men are more apt to say that if they were given

$10,000 they would share some of it with charitable organizations, whereas the women would share it with friends. In either case they would not keep it all themselves but give some of it away, just as the little girl in the German story shared her precious water with others. The result is more impressive when we note that men with high n Power and low n Affiliation in whom control is low are significantly *less* likely to give money away. As might further be expected, the men with the imperial motive combination claim that their parents taught them to be kind and friendly to others, whereas women are more likely to say that they volunteer to take care of children even when they do not have to. The puzzles in this list are the claims by women that their parents taught them more egocentric virtues; that they own more credit cards; and that they tend to put down people's names as personal possessions—all of which are hard to fit under a concern for altruism. Perhaps one can argue that women who develop their talents or their credit do so because they feel they then have more to offer to others. Also they may think of people as possessions because they want to *serve* them. This line of reasoning would make the opposite trend for the two sexes consistent by showing that for a man to be altruistic, he must be trained to overcome his sex-typed assertiveness, whereas for a woman to serve others, she must overcome her sex-typed passivity.

Unfortunately the questionnaire did not elicit responses directly reflecting a passionate concern for justice (Theme D). One might infer that the tendency of men with the imperial motive pattern to argue frequently (Table 8.3) means that they have a strong concern for the rights and wrongs of situations, which makes them contentious. Unfortunately no similar trend appeared for women with this motive syndrome. A reasonable case might be made, however, for interpreting their preferences in death metaphors as concern for a just reward. Both sexes felt that the castration metaphors—those dealing with death as murder—were relatively more appropriate. Put another way, they see death as unfair, as a kind of murderous termination of life. The argument gains added weight in the light of the Christian insistence that there is life after death. Sacrificing oneself for the group is justified in terms of Christian or other patriarchal ideologies on the ground that one will be ultimately rewarded, if not in this life, at least in the next. Death is a sensitive issue, because it may often seem to terminate a person's life before there is a chance for a just reward. If one does not believe strongly in an afterlife—as is probably the case with most of the individuals in our sample—then death to those with this orientation is particularly likely to seem an unfair outcome for the expectations one has built up out of working so loyally for the "system."

Theme D appears clearly to be related to what social psychologists have called "Belief in a Just World" (Heider, 1958; Lerner, 1970). Rubin and Peplau (1973) have developed a set of items to measure this attitude such as: "People who get lucky breaks have usually earned their good fortune" and "People who meet with misfortune often have brought it on themselves." Students who scored high on this attitude scale tended not to feel sorry for other students who got low draft numbers in the national lottery, presumably because they somehow "deserved" them. What links their findings to our hypothetical syndrome is the fact that among students "Just World scores" were significantly correlated with belief in an active God—"a Being beyond ourselves who takes an active part in the affairs of man" and with reported frequency of church attendance. They infer, as I have here, that belief in the presence of an active God, as in Western religions, helps "to instill the belief that the world is a just place" (1973, p. 89). It is unfortunate that I did not run across their attitude scale in time to include it in the questionnaire.

Although the measures of the four themes are not as consistent from one sex to the other, or as much on target in some cases as one would like, there are four items that present a coherent and vivid picture of the organizational work ethic. They are: either joining organizations for men or being elected to offices in them for women; liking to work; either giving money away to charity for men or to family and friends for women; and feeling keenly the injustice of dying. These measures were accordingly combined into an overall "organizational ethic" index by converting the score on each to a standard score (mean = 50, SD = 10) and summing them, using the appropriate alternatives for men and women for the first and third measures. As one would expect, those individuals, both men and women, with the imperial motivational pattern scored significantly higher on the organizational ethic index (mean = 52.2) than those who were high in n Power and low in n Affiliation but low in Inhibition (mean = 49.5), the difference being significant at the .05 level. Those who were high in n Power and also in n Affiliation scored even lower (mean = 49.1). In other words, those whose power motivation goes into building a personal enclave, score lowest on items indicating a strong devotion towards work in an institutional system, where one can sacrifice himself for others and get his just rewards.

In contrast, it is not difficult at all to see how people with the imperial motivational pattern act in ways that build strong organizations. They like to be in them, to work for them. They like to work. They share with others out of a sense of obligation to the system. Their concern with justice inclines them to deal with people even-handedly in terms of the system norms or rules rather than in terms of their personal likes or dislikes. One should recall that they also display the kinds of assertiveness that we found in Chapter 2 to characterize men and women with high *n* Power; the men more emotionally assertive, and the women more concerned with building up their resources to serve others. Thus overall we have a picture of men and women who could easily build empires.

The Conquistador Motive Pattern

By way of contrast, let us look at the characteristics of the men who are high in *n* Power, low in *n* Affiliation, but also low in Inhibition. They too behave in an imperious manner, but their assertiveness is neither disciplined nor channeled through organizational structures. As shown in Table 8.4, they fight more, drink more, and boast more about their sex lives. When asked to list stressful events in their lives, they do not recall many for which they could be held personally responsible. They tend to score higher in both the fantasy and action measures of Stage III phallic assertiveness, as discussed in Chapter 2. They actively reject institutional responsibility. They join fewer organizations; they report that they do not enjoy feeling part of an organization and are not regarded as responsible people doing work for an organization. Nor do they feel any obligation to share money with charities. In short, they behave like "tough guys," miniature war lords or "conquistadores." Women with this motivational pattern are also tougher. They report that they get into more arguments, that they are more likely to deliberately break things or slam doors, that they actively dislike children of school age, and share less information about their private lives with family and friends.

The male pattern should not be confused with being "macho" in the Mexican sense. The true *macho* may fight but only out of desperation and defiance, or the desire to protect himself against threats, knowing all along that he is courting death. His actions stem from the motivational pattern of personal security described in Table 8.2. The terminology has been confused in this area because the term "macho" has been introduced into the English language to mean the kind of masculine toughness and phallic assertiveness described in Table 8.4.

Table 8.4—*Personal characteristics associated with the*
Conquistador motivational pattern in men (High n Power over
n Affiliation, low Inhibition)

	Correlations of high n Power − n Affiliation among men low in inhibition (N = 42)
A. *Phallic assertiveness*	
More frequent physical fights reported	.23†
Maximum consumption of any alcoholic drink higher	.27*
Talks more about sex life	.25†
Doesn't recall distress for which he was responsible	.28*
Scores higher on Stage III (Phallic) score on Maturity Scale	.33**
Scores higher on any alternative in male Stage III cluster of actions (promiscuity, drinking, lying, collecting valuable objects)	.35**
B. *Rejects institutional responsibility*	
Joins fewer organizations	.35**
Rejects institutional responsibility	.33**
Would not share $10,000 gift with charity	.32*

†p < .10, *p < .05, **p < .025 in the predicted direction

Even though Mexican-Americans often use the term in that sense, their songs, as Tomás Pérez (1974) has shown, reflect the influence of Texan frontier toughness as much as the true Mexican feeling of desperate defiance.

The men with the conquistador motivational pattern make good feudal lords or perhaps daring tank commanders, but they are difficult to organize into any kind of a system. They establish their personal authority through sheer force if they are skillful, as in the traditional Spanish patrón system. Thus it is not surprising to discover that the Spanish children's stories show this pattern both for the 1925 and the 1950 period. The stories from Iran for the 1950 period show the same pattern. In both countries power has traditionally been in the hands of semi-independent chieftains who ruled within the limits of their domain. The only way a strong state system of government can be built up in such a society is through the imposition of force from an even bigger "chief" or dictator at the center; once he establishes his authority, he can command loyalty from the lesser chieftains in the same way they get it from those who serve them. The notion that some individuals have a natural right to rule is characteristic of the conquistador mentality and is reinforced by stories about loyalty in both countries.

In Iran, for example, textbooks include a story of the extreme faithfulness of a dog. "One day a villager goes to the city and sells his goods. He ties his money in a bag on the back of his horse and starts off for home with the dog following faithfully behind. Suddenly the dog runs in front of the horse, barking and carrying on so wildly that the man cannot proceed. He tries to calm or control the dog, is completely unsuccessful, decides the dog must be mad, and finally cuts his throat with much regret. The dog keeps barking, but more and more feebly, and the man rides on and leaves him. Finally he looks back and sees that the dog is dead, but also that his bag of money is missing. It had fallen off; the loyal dog had kept trying to call it to his attention even though it meant in the end that he was killed for his act of devotion. The master is very sad and touched by such extreme loyalty, as presumably is the child who reads the story" (McClelland, 1963).

To build a strong organization, this kind of personal loyalty to a particular master must be transferred to the system. In the children's stories, such a transformation appears usually to be associated with an increase in the Inhibition score, leading to the imperial motivational pattern if power motivation remains high at the same time. In discussing the above story from Iran, for example, I pointed out that similar stories in Turkey place loyalty in the context of doing one's duty to one's country. A boy of thirteen in the fury of a gun battle at sea slips and drops a shell overboard. His father, the master of the ship, is furious and whips him. The boy bravely does not protest but jumps into the sea to retrieve the shell. "Like the faithful dog, he is willing to sacrifice his life for his master, but the context is different: the father's anger and the boy's sacrificial loyalty occur in time of war, when a whole nation is involved." And the greater devotion to the system in the Turkish than the Iranian stories is reflected in the fact that the Turkish stories score well above average in Activity Inhibition.

The case of the People's Republic of China is also instructive in this regard. (McClelland, 1963). In 1925 its stories for children reflected the war lord or conquistador pattern present in Table 8.4

(high *n* Power, low *n* Affiliation, low Inhibition); indeed the country was very nearly anarchic with independent feudal chieftains running separate domains. By the 1960's however, under Communist rule, the children's stories revealed the same high need for Power and low need for Affiliation, but the index of control and discipline had risen well above the world average (see Appendix Table 8.1), producing the imperial motivational pattern characteristic of the men in Table 8.3. How was this accomplished ideologically? The stories themselves make it clear. In traditional China, filial piety was the supreme virtue (cf. Solomon, 1971). Children were taught to be loyal to their particular masters beginning with their fathers who in turn were loyal to their masters, the local landlords or ruling chieftains. Chairman Mao and the other Communist Party leaders set out to transfer this loyalty to the system, or more particularly to the Communist Party. To accomplish this end they stressed the four themes in the imperial motivational pattern previously discussed: obedience to supreme authority, self-sacrifice, service to others in the party, and justice, particularly through punishing landlords for their past misdeeds.

In a typical story, on a very cold night a soldier peeks into a shed on a farm where a general is resting. He observes the general take off his coat and put it over the sleeping guard, who is "shrunk up like a shrimp" because of the cold. The soldier is so moved by what he sees that he runs and gets his own blanket and insists that the general take it, even though the general refuses it for a long time. Then the soldier goes back to bed. "Although one blanket was taken away and I felt a little cold, my heart was very warm. Gradually I fell asleep and I felt warmer and warmer as the night passed. The next morning I woke up and was surprised to see the blanket which I had given the general was over me."

Authority is benevolent and self-sacrificing, but ordinary workers must sacrifice themselves for the good of the whole too. A girl is working in a biochemical laboratory when a fire starts among the chemicals and spreads towards some sodium which would explode and destroy the factory and injure many people. The girl heroically throws herself on the flames to keep them from spreading to the sodium. Though she succeeds, in the process she burns herself so badly that she dies. "Although she died, her noble spirit and her heroic image of sacrificing herself for the sake of others will remain alive in the heart of the people!"

Whatever else one may say about the system of government in the People's Republic of China, all would have to agree that it has greatly increased in the efficiency with which it controls the lives of its citizens. By the late 1950's the motive combination and thematic content of Chinese children's stories were exactly what produces strong, efficient organizational systems, according to all the evidence we have been able to assemble so far.

Leaders with the Imperial Motive Combination

Individuals with the imperial motive combination behave in ways to produce strong organizations. Nations with the imperial motive combination appear to have strong efficient governing systems. But there is a missing link in the analysis. How are the concerns of individuals transformed into organized systems? Obviously the leadership or management style should provide a connection between the two. What kind of leaders do men with the imperial motive combination make? How are they viewed by the people who work for them? Can they inspire loyalty and devotion to the system? Or could it be that, even in imperially oriented countries, the leader with some other motivational pattern—say with more of an affiliative concern for people—would be more successful in mobilizing people to work for the system? Perhaps even a more domineering type of leader with the conquistador motive pattern would be more effective, whatever the motivational profile of his constituency.

Some preliminary evidence relevant to these questions has been assembled by Winter and Stewart (1975), who have scored the inaugural addresses of American Presidents from Theodore Roosevelt to Richard Nixon for n Achievement, n Affiliation, and n Power. Though they suspected that these speeches were not, strictly speaking, personal documents like the stories a person writes for normal motive assessment, they found that their motive levels predicted surprisingly well the administrative style of each President while he· was in office. The men high in n Power and n Achievement were dynamic, activist Presidents like Theodore Roosevelt, Franklin Roosevelt, John F. Kennedy, Harry Truman, and Lyndon Johnson. Those with low n Power and low n Achievement were notably less active, like Taft, Harding, Coolidge, and Eisenhower. They found in addition that the most inspiring Presidents like Franklin Roosevelt were also low in n Affiliation, just as our analysis suggests. While Winter et al. did not score for Inhibition, it seems reasonable to infer that Franklin Roosevelt's speeches would have scored high on this variable also and that consequently he would have represented the classical imperial motive combination—high n Power, low n Affiliation, and high Inhibition. Certainly he was regarded by the majority of Americans during his lifetime and by historians since as one of the most successful, charismatic U.S. Presidents.

More precise evidence along these lines comes from the study of the motivational profiles of top managers in a large American corporation. At least three subordinates of each of them were given a climate survey in which they were asked to report in detail on how things were going in their offices (see Litwin and Stringer, 1968). The climate survey is scored for six dimensions: the amount of *Conformity* that a subordinate feels is required, e.g., the number of rules and regulations that have to be obeyed; the *Responsibility* that he feels he has to make his own decision; the *Standards* that he thinks are set for his performance; the *Rewards* that he either receives or fails to receive for his work; the *Organizational Clarity* of his unit—whether he knows what he is supposed to do or not; and the *Team Spirit* in his unit.

The scores on Organizational Clarity and Team Spirit were combined to give a rough and ready measure of morale. Out of forty-nine top managers tested, subordinates of twenty-six reported above-average morale and subordinates of twenty-three reported below-average morale. Of the twenty-six managers in charge of high-morale units, 88% had higher *n* Power than *n* Affiliation scores as contrasted with only 30% of the managers of lower-morale units. In nearly every case the *n* Power scores were also high; most of the managers tended to have high *n* Power in terms of the norms for a miscellaneous sample of men taking the same test. With amazing consistency, in short, the managers with high *n* Power and low *n* Affiliation produced higher morale in their subordinates, who reported that things were well organized in the office and that they were proud to belong to that organization. The difference is highly significant statistically ($\chi^2 = 17.4$, $p < .001$). The finding is surprising also in view of all that has been written by psychologists like McGregor (1960) and Argyris (1970) about the faults of authoritarian managers and their lack of concern about the people who work for them. On the surface at least it looks as if the better managers were greatly concerned with power and not very much concerned for the welfare of individuals. If this is, as it seems, the very pattern of the much maligned authoritarian manager, how can such men produce better morale?

Fortunately, the picture-story tests for twenty of these managers could be retrieved for further scoring. First they were scored for Inhibition, so that we could separate out those showing the various motive combinations under consideration in this chapter. With two exceptions the results are presented in Table 8.5 according to the format followed in Table 8.1. Not enough of these managers were low in *n* Power to form a separate low *n* Power group (Group A); and every one of the managers in whom *n* Affiliation was greater than *n* Power also scored high in Inhibition, which suggests that the personal enclave personality types (high *n* Power, high *n* Affiliation, and low Inhibition) do not end up in top management.

The climate-survey scores for the three groups of managers in Table 8.5 add several new pieces of information. If we look first at the morale scores—Organizational Clarity plus Team Spirit—we observe that it is above all the five managers with the "imperial" motive combination to whom their subordinates give the highest marks. These managers produce significantly greater scores on Organizational Clarity and Team Spirit. If their *n* Power is greater than *n* Affiliation but they have low Inhibition (the "conquistador mentality"), they produce higher Team Spirit, but Organizational Clarity suffers—as indeed we would expect if they have less concern with discipline.

Somewhat surprisingly, the subordinates of the men with the imperial motive combination also report feeling a greater sense of personal responsibility and less compulsion to obey regulations than the subordinates of men with other motive combinations. How can this be? The very term, "imperial" suggests that such managers would run things with an iron hand. But such an interpretation involves a fundamental misunderstanding of how the effective leader of a strong organization works. He develops loyalty to the *system*, not to himself. If he must rely on rules to insure conformity, he is in a sense keeping power in his own hands and relying less on the loyalty of his subordi-

Table 8.5—Impact on organizational climate of various motive combinations in managers

Mean climate Scale scores from three subordinates for each manager

	N	Conformity Mean	Responsibility Mean	Organization Clarity Mean	Team Spirit Mean
Group B *n* Aff. > high					
n Power, high Inhibition	7	16.8	10.7	10.4	12.4
Group C High *n* Power > *n* Aff.					
low Inhibition	8	15.7	12.8	11.9	15.7
Group D High *n* Power > *n* Aff.					
high Inhibition	5	13.4	13.6	13.5	15.6
	Groups				
p values by Mann-	B with C		$p < .10$		
Whitney U tests	B with D	$p < .01$	$p < .05$	$p < .01$	$p < .01$
	C with D	$p < .05$		$p < .05$	

nates to the system. Such a manager, in other words, does not trust his subordinates; he has to have rules to keep them in line. These managers, according to Table 8.5, are characterized not only by the usual high *n* Power but more often by either high *n* Affiliation or by low *n* Affiliation plus low Inhibition. Once more it is the men with the imperial motive combination who come out as the best leaders. They make their subordinates feel strong and responsible, bind them less by petty rules, help produce a clear organizational structure, and create pride in belonging to the unit. The findings in Table 8.3 help explain how they do it. Such managers themselves like to be part of organizations, they find their work enjoyable, are capable of sacrificing themselves for others, and are concerned for distributive justice—all characteristics that should and apparently do create system loyalty and high morale among the people they are leading.

Yet there is still reason to worry about these men. Are these not the characteristics possessed in high degree by major dictators like Adolph Hitler and Josef Stalin? Are we merely endowing authoritarian leaders with pleasanter, nicer-sounding personality characteristics? In one sense we are. The theoretical psychological question is: What motive combination in a leader is most likely to produce the best organized and most efficient organization? Identification of the motive combination carries no guarantee that a leader with it will develop the capabilities of a system for morally desirable ends. The facts imply only that he is the kind of person most likely to be able to develop the capabilities of the system. It is for this reason that we have termed the motive combination "imperial," even though the term has a negative connotation in many contexts. It means only that a man with such a motive profile will tend to build an empire, whether for good or ill, in the sense of strengthening and expanding whatever organization he leads.

In terms of developmental stages, he is a man who has reached what in the previous chapter we called Stage IIIb. He can mobilize institutional loyalty, the discipline of hard work, self-sacrifice for the group, and a passion for justice, perhaps because he feels all these values himself. As such he is a "mover and shaker," but unless he matures to a still higher stage, his empire building remains an extension of his ego (Stage IIIb).

What about the Group D top managers in Table 8.5? Are they egotistic empire-builders, exponents of McGregor's generally disapproved theory X? Their subordinates think not, but perhaps they have been duped. The managers' stories, scored for the various stages in the Stewart Maturity Scale (with the results shown in Table 8.6) shed

Table 8.6—Mean Maturity stage scores for various motive combinations among senior managers

	N	Stage I Intake Mean	Stage II Control Mean	Stage III Assertion Mean	Stage IV Generativity Mean	Maturity Scale score Mean
Group B. High n Power and high n Aff.	7	2.43	1.43	.43	2.71	2.48
Group C. High n Power, low n Aff. low Inhibition	8	1.38	1.50	1.75	2.13	2.77
Group D. High n Power, low n Aff. high Inhibition	5	1.00	.80	2.20	4.60	3.15
p values by Mann-Whitney U tests		Group B with C p < .05 B with D p < .01			C with D p < .05	p < .05

some light on the question. As expected, Group B, those with high *n* Affiliation and high *n* Power, scored higher on Stage I (intake) and lower on Stage III (assertion) than those with the imperial motive combination. Just as in Table 8.1 for men and women in general, those with what we have been calling the conquistador motive pattern (Group C) tend to score higher in Stage II and Stage III. What is new and striking is that while all the groups tend to be highest in Stage IV generativity, it is those with the "imperial" motive pattern in this sample who score markedly higher than the other two groups on this characteristic. It is worth recalling what this means in terms of the associated action characteristics presented in Chapter 2. Such men are more willing to join in organizational efforts, as we already know; they share more with their wives, they are willing to seek expert help when they need it. They seem to amass fewer possessions. Note also that the five managers with the imperial motive pattern (Group D), score much higher on Stage IV than do men in general with the same motive pattern (see Table 8.1). Some selective factor, therefore, has been at work in their rise to positions of top leadership. They have the motive profile of strong leaders, but they also have the maturity to make them wise rather than egotistic leaders. Thus the Stage IV generativity score on the maturity scale might be considered a rough check on whether the leadership of men with this motive combination will be "imperious" or effective and wise.

The Imperial Motive Combination and System Capability

One final piece of evidence is needed to complete the chain of reasoning that explains the rise of great, well-organized empires in terms of a particular motive combination. We have shown how high *n* Power, low *n* Affiliation, and high Inhibition are linked to later stages in social emotional maturity and to characteristics in individuals and leaders promoting strong organizations. Stories for children from well-organized countries with the imperial motive combination contain themes that are also reflected in actions of individuals with the imperial motive combination. Where is the evidence, however, to demonstrate that all this appropriate activity by individuals leads to greater system capability for nation states? It is possible to look for that evidence by studying the system capability of modern nations with various motive combinations, but first it is necessary to explain what is meant by system capability, so that we can get a measure of it.

Modern political and sociological theorists speak of the capability of an organizational system in the sense of the extent to which it can organize and pursue "effective collective actions in the attainment of the goals" of the collectivity (Parsons, 1967, p. 300). Almond and Powell (1966) refer to the extractive capability of the political system, for example, which "refers to the range of system performance in drawing material and human resources from the domestic and international environment. The capability to obtain such resources underlies the other capability, and it limits or expands the possibilities of obtaining various goals for the system and for the society" (p. 195). They are speaking, then, of the extent to which a system can mobilize resources, as represented, for example, by "the amount of resources which flows into the government at various levels." Their point is that obviously systems vary in the extent to which they effectively mobilize, control, and distribute resources to the people in the system. At one extreme is the band of individuals with little or no *system* capability above and beyond what each individual decides to do on his own. At the other extreme is a highly organized system of government which extracts great resources from its members and uses them to control or service individuals or groups, or to defend the society against attack from another system.

Russett *et al.* (1964) have published a number of political, economic, and social indicators on contemporary nations; two of them appear related to system capability in the sense just defined and are available on a number of the countries for which we also have motive scores in *The achieving society.* The indicators are: "expenditure on defense as a percentage of gross national product" (GNP), and "private consumption as a percentage of gross national product." The two indexes in a sense measure opposite ends of the same continuum, which runs from low to high mobilization of resources for the system. A country that spends a high percentage of its GNP on defense or the military establishment, in other words, is obviously mobilizing more of its people's resources for a system goal. On the other hand, a country that allows a large percentage of its GNP to go for private consumption is less mobilized to pursue system goals.

Standardized motive scores and those on Activity Inhibition are available in Appendix Table 8.1. The system capability indexes for countries with various motive combinations are assembled in Table 8.7 in the familiar format necessary to test the hypothesis. The United States has been included in the upper right quadrant, even though technically its level of n Affiliation in 1950 in the children's stories was slightly higher than its n Power. The reason is that more complete

Table 8.7—Expenditures on defense (1959–60) and private consumption (1950's) among countries with the imperial vs. other motivational combinations

		Low Inhibition[1] % of GNP			High Inhibition % of GNP	
Group	Country	for defense[2]	for private consumption[3]	Country	for defense	for private consumption
High n Power > n Affiliation	Belgium	3.0	71.1	(The Imperial Syndrome)		
				Argentina	2.6	68.6
	Canada	4.4	63.5	China	3.6	68.6
	Finland	2.0	60.5	Denmark	2.6	68.6
	Iran	5.6		W. Germany	3.8	58.7
	Italy	3.0	68.2	India	1.9	62.0
	Mexico	.7	79.4	Iraq	8.2	
	New Zealand	2.2	65.8	Pakistan	3.9	
	Spain	2.2	74.1	Switzerland	2.9	63.2
	Taiwan	12.3	70.8	USSR	10.4	55.8
	U. So. Africa	.8	66.6	U.S.	9.6	63.7
	Mean	3.62	68.9	Mean	4.95	62.9

Country			Country		
Australia	2.7	63.9	Austria	1.5	65.2
Chile	2.8	82.4	Bulgaria		69.7
France	5.9	67.0	England	6.7	66.7
Hungary		72.9	Greece	5.1	77.8
Netherlands	4.0	60.0	Ireland	1.4	75.9
Norway	3.5	60.0	Israel	6.3	72.0
Portugal	3.2	77.8	Lebanon	2.4	
Sweden	4.7	61.9	Japan	1.6	59.5
Syria	4.9		Poland		69.8
Tunisia	1.8		Turkey	2.4	76.9
			Uruguay	1.0	70.4
Mean	3.72	68.2	Mean	3.16	70.4

1. 45 or fewer "nots" in a sample of 21 children's stories. See Appendix Table 8.1.
2. From Russett, B.: et al. (1964), Table 23, median for whole sample = 2.70.
3. From Russett, B. et al. (1964), Table 48, Median for whole sample = 69.75.

data, assembled and reported in the next chapter, show that *n* Power was definitely higher in the United States for the time period under consideration (see Figure 9.4). As predicted, countries in the upper right hand quadrant, with the imperial motive combination in their popular literature, score on the average higher in the percentage of GNP devoted to defense and lower in the percentage allowed for private consumption than do countries with the other three categories of motive combinations. The countries oriented more towards power and control than affiliation mobilize more resources to spend on military functions, as one would expect if such a motivational orientation is the foundation of empire building. They spend nearly 5% of their GNP on the average on defense, which is nearly significantly higher than the average 3.5% spent by other countries (diff. = 1.45, t = 1.33, p < .10 in the predicted direction).

Such an "imperial" motivational pattern does not necessarily lead to military expansion if, for instance, the country is small as in the case of Switzerland; but it is interesting to observe that the three major powers in 1950 did show this pattern (the U.S., Russia, and China). Of course major power status is partly accorded to a country because of the percentage of its gross national product allocated to the military. Thus, at the present time Japan is not ordinarily listed as a major "power" since its defense establishment is small. So the linkage appears to be: the imperial motive combination leads to mobilizing resources for the system, which can then increase its military capability which, if the nation is also large, leads to great-power status.

The more general measure of system capability—% GNP available for private consumption—even more strongly supports the hypothesis that the imperial motive combination leads a country to mobilize resources out of private hands for the system's use as a collectivity. All seven of the countries in the upper right quadrant allow less expenditure for private consumption than the median for all countries. In contrast, only 13 of the 26 countries in the other three quadrants allow less than the median to be spent on private consumption. The difference is highly significant (by Mann Whitney U-test, p < .001 in the predicted direction). In other words, the countries with the imperial motive pattern allow citizens to spend less of the GNP themselves, because the governments have mobilized resources for purposes of the system. Such countries spend more on guns and allow less to be spent on butter.

It is possible to go one step further and single out those countries which spend both more on guns and less on butter. As shown in Table 8.8, countries with the imperial motivational pattern behave *only* in

Table 8.8—Classification of countries by various motive combinations and national expenditures on defense and private consumption

	"Imperial" motive pattern High n Power, Low n Affiliation High Inhibition	Other motivational patterns
High expenditure on defense, low expenditure in private consumption	Argentina Denmark West Germany Iraq Switzerland USSR U.S.	Australia Canada England France Italy Netherlands Norway Sweden
Other expenditure patterns		Austria Belgium Chile Finland Greece Ireland Israel Mexico Japan New Zealand Portugal Spain Taiwan Turkey U. So. Africa

$\chi^2 = 6.86$, $p < .01$

this way. No imperial country for which both indexes are available shows any other expenditure pattern. There are, to be sure, some countries with other motivational patterns which show high expenditure on defense and low expenditure on private consumption; most of them, however, show a different expenditure pattern, and the over-all difference in Table 8.8 is highly significant. One cannot escape the conclusion that there is a strong association between the imperial motive pattern and the mobilization of resources for system capability, as reflected in spending more on guns and less on butter. So far as these measures go, therefore, they strongly support the chain of evidence accumulated in this chapter, leading to the conclusion that great empires tend to be organized by people with a strong need for Power, a low need for Affiliation, and a heightened need for discipline and control. As individuals and as leaders they act in ways that build strong and expanding organizations. When such people dominate the scene in a particular nation state, it tends to develop into a great power or empire if it has the requisite population base.

Generative Power and Organizational Effectiveness

Now, however, we are in trouble. Authority systems based on the imperial motive pattern have been shown to promote organizational effectiveness, but they are often notoriously ruthless. They may suppress individual freedom at home and start wars abroad to expand or maintain their influence, as we shall see in the next chapter. The only alternatives so far presented have been orientations towards Stage I and Stage II power, and these seem to be associated with organizational ineffectiveness. Isn't there some way to have organizational effectiveness without the negative characteristics of imperial authoritarianism? What motivational pattern would be associated with such organizations?

It would be helpful if we could find such organizations to study. Many social theorists and profound religious thinkers have argued that they cannot be found, that there is an intrinsic contradiction between organizational perfection and individual fulfillment. Efficient organizations necessarily thwart self-actualization—or so the argument goes. It may be possible for a man to be moral, but he necessarily has to live in an immoral society. An old fable reports that God and the Devil were out walking one day when God suddenly stooped over and picked up something which he hid in his hand. The Devil asked him what he had there, and God replied that he had found the truth. "Let me organize it," said the Devil.

Many young people are fleeing organizations throughout the world today because of their conviction that there is no way for an organization to be strong and to promote growth among its members at the same time. They retreat to the Stage I and II position that all they can hope to do is perfect their own lives. Organizations—a better social order—will just have to "happen" spontaneously as a natural byproduct of enlightened individuals. They do not believe that organizations can *produce* enlightenment. This is probably an overreaction. Even the alienated younger generation might recognize that some families on occasion have promoted growth among their members or that an agriculture community may have organized itself in ways to produce more food for everyone, all of which contributes to the well-being of individual members of the community. Yet the problem is real at both the theoretical and the empirical level.

Practically speaking, one can think only of small-scale religious communities that have managed to operate effective organizations on a non-imperial basis. The early rule of Pennsylvania by the Quakers might be considered a case in point. They tried to establish a "Holy Experiment," a colony in Pennsylvania to be run according to Quaker religious principles, which were distinctly anti-patriarchal and pro-democratic. In Quakerism there is no chain of command, not even a religious leader who has special sacred or secular authority. Instead a meeting of members is held to conduct business directly under God's inspiration. No votes are taken, but the "sense of the meeting" is determined so far as possible by the clerk after a matter has been discussed for some time. Since Quakers had renounced war and violence, the colony was no threat to its neighbors, even though it was well run internally.

But the experiment was short-lived. It worked as well as it did only so long as those who lived in the colony accepted the ideology that supported this form of government. When other settlers moved in, they wanted arms to fight the Indians which the Quakers felt they could not in conscience provide. So they ultimately abandoned their attempt to govern the colony. This does not mean of course that Quaker principles of government through decisions by "bands of brothers" (boards of directors and the like) disappeared from the American scene. They have continued indeed to be effective in many organizations and at least one sociologist (Digby Baltzell, 1974) believes they are still at least as influential in America as the patriarchal principles of government promoted by the Puritans in New England. Recent influential treatises on how businesses should be governed, such as McGregor's emphasis on democratic management (Theory Y), seem to hark back to the Quaker emphasis on a group of equals collectively making a decision. Such a type of authority seems to be close to the kind of generative power characteristic of the Stage IV expression of the power drive. For example, Quakers believe that out of the conflict of different opinions over a course of action comes not a compromise but a creative new idea as to what to do. The image is close to the one behind the notion of generative power which implies the coming together of two independent beings—a mother and a father to produce another independent being, a child.

Perhaps the Quaker system of government worked as well as it did as a system because many of its members had attained what we have identified as the Stage IV or generative power orientation. That is, they may have had the imperial motive combination which made them good organizers in trying to produce the kingdom of God on earth, but the motives expressed themselves in action through the medium of mature people. The right motive combination, in other words, will produce the good society, if the people who have it are themselves mature: vice versa; an organization governed along these lines will help produce more mature people. The situation is reminiscent of what we discovered about the five top executives who were high in the imperial motive combination. They were also high in Stage IV generativity (as shown in Tables 8.5 and 8.6) and they tended to create a climate in which their subordinates were glad to work because they felt less hemmed in by regulations and more responsible and knew what they were supposed to be doing. One can argue that the climate created by the managers not only reinforced their own motive dispositions but also helped create maturity in others. Five individuals are a very small sample on which to build the case for an ideal society, but their example is instructive in our quest to avoid the dangers of authoritarian efficiency on the one hand and democratic anarchy on the other.

It is worth reviewing in this connection once again the dispositions of people high in *n* Power and also mature. Suppose we set their characteristics as shown in Table 2.7 over against the themes in the traditional authoritarian organization as we discovered them in the Bible or German children's stories. The traditional ideology teaches that one must submit to a supreme authority. Those high in generative *n* Power believe that one should join a group and rely on *expert* help. It is not as if they have given unconditional surrender to one supreme authority; rather, they show a willingness to follow the advice of whatever authority is appropriate to the task at hand. In both cases, there is a real surrender of the ego. Those high in generative power do not feel at all that they personally have to know everything or understand everything. They are willing to follow the lead of the group, to which they surrendered some personal autonomy when they joined it.

The traditional ideology stresses discipline, self-sacrifice for others, and personal justice. Among those high in generative *n* Power, there is an indication of the same concern for personal justice among women, but little else to suggest a concern in the same areas. Instead one finds an emphasis on sharing, particularly with an intimate like one's husband or wife, on taking responsibility for strangers, and accumulating fewer possessions. Remember also that men seem to attain generativity more easily if they abandon some of their traditional assertiveness, and women if they abandon some of their traditional dependency.

One is tempted to speculate that individuals high in generative power may be less ego-oriented, as in fact they ought to be according to theory. The reason then that they are less interested in self-discipline, sacrificing for others, and personal justice is simply that *they have less self to discipline, sacrifice or save from injustice.* Traditional organizational ideology, which according to our argument develops out of Stage III assertiveness, sees the self as an all-important source of power. In the usual imperial motive combination, therefore, the self is first built up as tremendously important, and then *forced*, as it were, to yield to the system. But the person high in generative *n* Power does not have such a strong ego to sacrifice or discipline. He has abandoned the ego's attachments; in the Buddhist sense he feels more "part of the flow." When he joins an organization, he is sharing or merging, not surrendering. When he gives, he is sharing, not sacrificing, himself. Though all the great religious teachers like Jesus or Buddha have tried to explain this state of mind, which could be taken as a kind of ideal of psychological maturity, neither the common man nor psychologists have found it easy to understand or believe in it. In psychoanalytic terms, a man who abandons his ego, is simply allowing his actions to be dictated by his unconscious drives and his super ego.

Yet there is a difference; and our findings suggest what it is. A man in the earlier stages of development may be driven by unconscious forces, but if he attains Stage IV, all of his earlier hang-ups have been worked through and become conscious, so to speak. He has lived through the stage of dependency, taken control of his life, developed his egoistic assertiveness, and then abandoned it after realizing its ultimate unimportance. But he cannot abandon it before he develops it. He cannot lose himself before he has some sense of who he is. Once he has attained this sense in Stages II and III, he should go on to an even higher level of maturity in which his participation in building better organizations out of his motivational needs will be essentially ego-less. The self is no longer in need of strengthening. If the leaders and participants in such organizations are at that stage of development, then one need not fear that the organizations will turn into ruthlessly authoritarian empires.

Admittedly such an interpretation goes beyond our empirical findings. Since the connection between a certain motive combination and empire building has been so well established, however, it has seemed worth trying to develop the picture of the way things are into a picture of the way they ought ideally to be.

CHAPTER 9

LOVE AND POWER: THE PSYCHOLOGICAL BASIS OF WAR

OUR INVESTIGATION of modes of expression of the need for Power has led us to examine its effect on the way organizations and even political systems behave. The next logical step in the inquiry is to ask: what happens to the way an organization functions as the power orientation of its members or leaders varies over time? In Chapter 8, we discovered that modern nations strongly oriented towards power and control tend to mobilize more resources from the people for use by the state. We captured, so to speak, the motivational orientation of a nation and observed its effect across nations at a given moment in time. Yet such a comparison inevitably raises questions as to how nations got that way. Why are some more power-oriented than others? Did they become power-oriented in response to external events like the necessity to behave as "big powers" in a world of competing nations or did their power orientation lead them to act like or become a big power? Or even more critically, how can we be sure that the motivational orientations are the really important factors in the situation? Perhaps they just reflect other economic or political realities that basically determine whether a nation happens to extract large resources from its people for military or other purposes.

One way to try to get answers to questions like these is to examine how changes in motivational orientations in a country over time relate to historical events in that country. For example, do increases in the measured need for Power in the United States precede, accompany, or follow wars? If they precede wars regularly, we have some basis for arguing for a motivational determination of history. If they accompany or follow wars, we might prefer a Social Darwinian interpretation of history in which we conceive of an event as calling forth the kind of motivation needed to cope with it. If there is no regular association of motivational trends with historical events, we may conclude that the cross-national relationships we have found are accidental results of the operation of other factors as yet unidentified.

Power Motivation in English History from 1500–1800

In *The achieving society* (1961), I reported historical studies demonstrating that increases in achievement orientation in a number of nations at different time periods preceded more rapid rates of economic growth. Chief among these studies was an analysis of *n* Achievement levels in English plays, street ballads, and accounts of sea voyages over a 300-year period from roughly 1500–1800. A simple way to begin examining the role of power motivation in a nation's history seemed to be to code this same material for *n* Power and for *n* Affiliation, since, as reported in Chapter 8, it is the relationship of these two motives that is particularly relevant for organizational behavior.

Accordingly, an undergraduate at Harvard, Michael Giliberto, searched out the same English sources Bradburn and Berlew (1961) had used for the study of *n* Achievement. Unfortunately their records were not precise enough for him to score exactly the same pages from each source, but he was able to take comparable excerpts from the same plays and books of ballads used in the previous study. The accounts of sea voyages he omitted, partly because of the pressure of time and partly because they seemed relevant to the economy rather than to the political system. All the excerpts were scored blindly (without knowledge of the historical period to which they belonged) by expert coders for need for Power and need for Affiliation (see Winter, 1973, and Atkinson, 1958, for coding definitions).

The results are reported in Figures 9.1 and 9.2 below. The basic unit of measurement is the number of times scoreable Power, Affiliation, or Achievement thoughts or images occur for each sample of 100 lines of text (approximately 1,000 words). For each time period a number of samples of 100 lines in length were drawn from different works of fiction by different authors and the average number of power or affiliation images per 100 line unit was computed for each time period. These averages and the sources on which they are based are given in Appendix Table 9.2. If more than one sample was drawn from a given author, each was from a different play. Every effort was made to make sure the sample of material to be scored was representative of the time by choosing a reasonably large number of authors, the best known for their period, and by scoring material from their most popular plays. The street ballads were also for the most part known to be popular since they were part of an oral tradition in which such ballads were sung often in public at the time they were recorded. More detailed explanations of how popular literature is sampled and scored are given in Appendix 4, in the hope that historians may be encouraged to employ this method as an additional tool in their attempt to understand historical events.

Giliberto had no strong hypotheses as to what to expect except that he thought the two new motives scored would probably be related to religious and political events. That turned out to be the case. Let us begin by examining levels of power motivation in the "masses" and the "classes," or among the lower and upper orders of English society. It seems reasonable to assume that street ballads reflected the sentiments (feelings, motivations) of the lower orders better than the plays, which in turn should reflect the motives of the elite, for whom they were so often produced. If we make this assumption and plot the curves for the two classes separately as in Figure 9.1, we get some interesting and understandable results.

A crucial issue in English history at the beginning of this period was the power of the king versus Parliament. Historians have been impressed by the fact that the early Tudor kings, and particularly Henry VIII, succeeded in consolidating the power of the king and the aristocracy, and in creating a nation state in which strong centralized authority was vested in the monarchy. Subsequently the "people" (as opposed to the monarchy) struggled long and hard and eventually

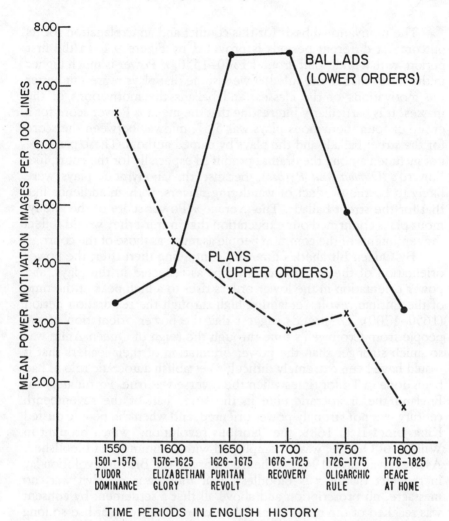

Figure 9.1—Power motivation levels in lower and upper classes: England 1500–1800

successfully to gain and hold onto power as represented by the authority of Parliament. From the time of the Puritan revolution onward, the English kings and the aristocracy never seemed to exercise the absolute power of many European monarchs. Although they attempted to revive arbitrary authority, as at the time of James II, the people (meaning what we would call the middle classes) seemed always able to collect themselves and defeat autocratic rule when necessary.

The motivational basis for this conflict and an explanation for its outcome at different periods is provided by Figure 9.1. In the first period, with a mid-point around 1540–1550, n Power is much higher in the rulers than in the ruled, if we assume that plays represent better the motivations of the classes, and ballads the motivations of the masses. It is particularly interesting that the mean n Power score for a group of four anonymous plays was 5.57, midway between the score for the street ballads and the plays by named authors. These plays are not included among the dramas produced especially for the court, like Edward's *Damon and Pythias,* because the anonymous plays were likely to be the product of wandering players, with an audience like that for the street ballads. The average n Power score of the anonymous plays confirmed our expectation that in spirit they would reflect the sentiments of the common people as much as those of the court.

By Queen Elizabeth's time and continuing thereafter, the power orientation of the upper orders drops as reflected in the plays, and power orientation in the lower orders rises to a high peak at the time of the Puritan revolt, remaining high through the restoration period (1650–1700). The trends suggest that the power orientation of the people from Cromwell's time through the reign of Queen Anne was so much stronger than the power orientation of their leaders that it would have been extremely difficult to establish autocratic rule as had been done in Tudor times when the reverse was true. Fortunately for England the aristocratic elite in the latter half of the seventeenth century was not strongly power oriented, and when the people ousted King James II in 1688, the "glorious revolution," which brought in William of Orange, was accomplished with a minimum of bloodshed. As Trevelyan says (1942), "The true glory of the British revolution lay in the fact that it was bloodless, that there was no civil war, no massacre, no proscription and above all that a settlement by consent was reached of the religious and political differences that had so long and fiercely divided men and parties. The settlement of 1689 stood the test of time." It stood the test of time, in motivational terms, because power motivation levels in both leaders and led dropped off significantly from 1700 on. What is more, the continued greater power orientation of the lower orders seemed to serve as a psychological guarantee that parliament would continue stronger than the king's party (representing the upper orders) to the end of this period in history. There is a suggestion of a rise in power orientation in 1730–1770 for the elite, which would correspond to the dominance of the Whig and Tory oligarchy and the brief attempt by the Georges to return to personal rule, but one should beware of over-interpreting small and insignificant shifts in the trend line.

It is worth noting also that by 1800 general power orientation in England was at its lowest ebb since the measures start in the early 16th century. This places a somewhat different light on the relative peaceableness of Britain at home and abroad in the early 19th century. Trevelyan (1942) argues that because the victory over Napoleon at Waterloo restored the balance of power, there "was no call for us to fight in order to prevent the conquest of Europe by a single nation and its vassals." He also observes that there was relative peace at home fostered by prosperity and international security. Can we safely attribute all this peaceableness to external events? Might it not also be true that Britain was relatively peaceful at home and abroad because her level of power motivation was at its lowest since the 16th century? Thus the failure of Britain to expand politically or militarily on the continent may not have had directly to do with the balance of power or the victory at Waterloo, but may have arisen simply from a lower interest in power games. England was becoming absorbed in the excitement of the achievement game as played in the world of commerce and industry. See Figure 9.2, which shows that the *n* Achievement level was higher in 1800 than it had been at any time since 1500. We need to know more, of course, about why power motivation was so low in 1800, but at least we ought not to fall carelessly into the error of assuming that *n* Power was low because of a victory at Waterloo that occurred later, as Trevelyan's interpretation would suggest. Low power motivation preceded peace, not vice versa.

Figure 9.2 combines the scores for the two types of source material for *n* Power and for three types of material for *n* Achievement, as previously reported (McClelland, 1961). The street ballads unfortunately contained too little affiliation imagery to count, so that the *n* Affiliation curve is based exclusively on samples of texts from plays written in various time periods. One may legitimately question the comparability of these motivational indexes, certainly as to their absolute levels; but the shifts in a given index over time are less open to criticism and lead to some interesting interpretations of what was happening.

Compare first the shifts in the *n* Power and *n* Affiliation curves. In *The achieving society* (1961) high *n* Power combined with low *n* Affiliation has been associated among modern nations with dictatorships, with ruthlessness, suppression of liberty, and domestic and international violence. Looked at from this perspective there are only two periods represented in Figure 9.2, one around 1600 and the other around 1800, when Englishmen as a whole could feel safe from violence at the hands of some faction or group in power. Certainly there was violence in Tudor England towards the end of Henry VIII's

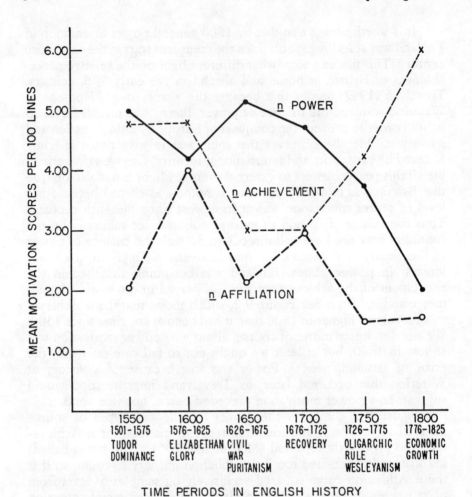

Figure 9.2—*Levels of concern for power, affiliation, and achievement in popular literature: England 1500–1800*

reign (what Trevelyan called a period of "senile, ferocious feudalism") and for the years thereafter until Elizabeth ascended to the throne. What is really remarkable about the Elizabethan period is that the motivational indicators all attest it must have been a good time to be alive, just as historians have always argued. Need for Affiliation had risen, n Power had dropped a bit, symbolizing an era of relative peace, and n Achievement had remained high, presaging some prosperity. Subsequently during the Cavalier and Roundhead struggles and civil war, n Power rose again and n Affiliation dropped sharply, indicating that this should have been a period of great violence and ruthlessness, as indeed it was. While *n* Power declined somewhat thereafter, so did *n* Affiliation; even in 1750 the gap between the two was sufficiently large to suggest that this was no time in English history to feel particularly safe from violence. As writers like Wearmouth (1945) have pointed out, working class offenders were regularly executed between 1740–1780 for even the most petty crimes such as "robbing John Burton of one shilling in a field near the city." Even a blind boy was condemned to death simply for being accused of breaking into a house with intent to steal. "The lower classes in the 18th century," Wearmouth concludes, "really longing in their hearts to emancipate themselves from distress, want, and famine, were repressed, beaten, and defeated by those who ought to have been their guides, philosophers, and friends. The hungry sheep looked up and were not fed; instead they were sent to the slaughter." Even allowing for some exaggeration on the part of an indignant Methodist, there is little doubt that the severe cruelties of the 18th century did not begin to abate until the early 19th century, when, as the curves in Figure 9.2 show, the need for Power and need for Affiliation were more nearly balanced.

Here perhaps the motivational indicators do little more than confirm what is already generally known about the periods in question. The fact that they do, however, tends to make one believe a little more in their validity, in the faithfulness with which they represent the sentiments of Englishmen at the time. It is always somewhat more interesting, however, to try to explain what happens later by what happens earlier, thus gaining some appreciation of the forces that bring about particular events. Southwood (1969) has reported in a study of contemporary nations that a rapid rate of economic growth appears to be followed by an increase in the need for Power. Those nations in his sample that developed rapidly economically between 1937–54 tended to have higher *n* Power scores in 1950 than nations that did not grow so fast ($r = .34$, $N = 40$, $p < .05$). The reason for this relationship is not yet understood, but it has occurred fairly often. Civilizations appear to develop first economically and then shift to an imperial, power-oriented phase. Perhaps it is as simple as that economic growth leads to the accumulation of wealth, and wealthy people decide to use money as power.

At any rate, I have shown in *The achieving society* that the rate of economic growth was significantly more rapid in England between 1600–1634 than it was earlier or later, and thus the rise in *n* Power in 1650 appears as an interesting confirmation of a generalization based on other instances. Here too, rapid economic growth was followed by a rise in *n* Power. Furthermore we would have to predict that the great rise in *n* Achievement from 1750–1800 (see Figure 9.2) would lead not only to the industrial revolution of Victorian England but later to a rise in *n* Power that would be the force behind Britain's 19th century imperial political expansion. Although unfortunately we cannot confirm this prediction directly, as we have no measures of *n* Power in Britain in the late 19th century, some indirect confirmation comes from the fact that even as late as 1925, when Britain was still something of an imperial power, the *n* Power level in its school textbooks was above the world average assessed at the time (McClelland, 1961).

Giliberto was particularly interested in the motivational dynamics for religious revivals or reforms. He wanted to know whether fluctuations in power motivation might be associated with periodic rises in the intensity of religious concern. In the period covered by Figure 9.2, there were two major religious revivals: Puritanism which reached its high point roughly in 1630–1670; and the Wesleyan revival, or Methodism, which swept the country about a century later (1740–1780). The only motivational shift preceding each of these events is a rise in the *n* Affiliation curve. Such a shift might account for a rise in religious fervor if we examine the consequences of the more nearly equal balance between power and affiliation resulting from these shifts.

Having *n* Power and *n* Affiliation in balance introduces a conflict in individual goals. Normally there is a negative correlation between the two motivational states (McClelland, 1961, p. 203 or Appendix Table 2.3): someone who is eager for power is *less* likely to be friendly with others. Occasionally, however, the two motives are present in about equal strengths, in an individual or in a society; when they are, Christian devotion might be one effective way of resolving the conflict and satisfying both somewhat contradictory concerns at once. The person with high *n* Affiliation typically feels lonely and in need of love, support, and friendship (Boyatzis, 1972). He wants to love and be loved. Normally, *n* Affiliation expresses itself in concern for good interpersonal relationships. But what if a person has an equally high *n* Power? Then he wants also to dominate, to have power and influence, to be important. The conflict becomes even more intense when he is *high* in both motives. If he becomes religiously aroused, however, a committed Christian, he can satisfy both goals. In Jesus he finds a personal Friend and Savior who heals his aching spirit and relieves his loneliness. In the words of popular nineteenth-century Christian hymns:

> "What a friend we have in Jesus   "I love to tell the Story
> All our troubles, griefs to bear"   or   of Jesus and His glory,
>   of Jesus and His love".

An individual can also have an increased sense of power by allying himself closely with the greatest power in the universe—God (Jesus and His glory)—and by becoming part of a "mighty army" of Christian soldiers marching onward to save the whole world. The Christian message has always appealed strongly to both the need for Power and the need for Love (or as we call it, Affiliation), from the time of Jesus to the time of John Wesley in the eighteenth century or Billy Graham in the twentieth century.

Another aspect of religious revival is that the human needs it satisfies also tend to promote a reformist zeal on behalf of the common man oppressed by power elites. Converts grow not only sorry for others, but so anxious to *save* them and the world that they become ruthless. In God's name they may start fighting others, as they did in England in the mid-seventeenth century. This in turn should go along with a *fall* in n Affiliation while n Power remains high or is accentuated. Note that such a decrease in n Affiliation occurred after the earlier rise around 1650 at the time of the Civil War and again around 1750 (Figure 9.2). It is as if people focus less on saving themselves (as in the high n Affiliation concern for personal salvation) and more on saving others or, as cynics would say, persecuting them if necessary for their own good. Thus the fanatical religious persecution that occurred after the original religious revival in Puritan England might well be the result of a fairly high n Power accompanied by a, by then, very low concern for being on friendly terms with other individuals.

Eventually, one supposes, a reaction sets in against so much "Christian" warfare, and people begin to feel sorry for the injuries caused to friends and relations or even strangers in the name of religion, and the concern for others (n Affiliation) may rise again as it did around 1700 in England. If n Power has remained high, as it had in England, this should set the stage for a new religious revival, as indeed happened in the subsequent Wesleyan movement around 1740–1780. Only this time, as a glance at Figure 9.1 will show, the increase in n Affiliation around 1700 should have had its greatest impact religiously on the lower orders—that is, on the "masses" whose power motivation was so much higher than that of the more educated elite. Methodism indeed had a stronger appeal among the "lower orders" than among the better educated and those better off financially. Certainly the rise in n Affiliation did not turn men of Dr. Samuel Johnson's class toward religion! In the earlier Puritan revival, on the other hand, religious fervor had been more general across all classes. Again our motivational hypothesis explains why: when *n* Affiliation rose around 1600, it interacted with *n* Power levels which were equally high among the masses (in the street ballads) and the classes (in the plays). (See Figure 9.1.)

Since the sequence of events is complex, Figure 9.3 has been prepared to show how motivational patterns tend to be associated with periods of religious reform and violence or with periods of peace, in a cyclical fashion. In the initial time period (1501–1575) *n* Power is very high, much higher than *n* Affiliation, resulting in a period characterized by violence or "ferocious feudalism" (represented by a shaded row in the figure). The internal warfare leads to a rise in *n* Affiliation in the next period, which then becomes associated with peace ("Elizabethan glory"). But high *n* Affiliation and *n* Power conflict, leading after a delay to a drop in *n* Affiliation, and re-introducing the gap between *n* Power and *n* Affiliation which ushers in a period of religious reform and warfare as the Puritans overthrow the monarchy. Once again increased violence leads to a rise in *n* Affiliation and initiates another cycle of peace (the Restoration), followed by the violence associated with the despotic rule of King George III and the American Revolution. The figure demonstrates how the motive changes follow each other and lead to war (shaded rows) or peace (unshaded rows) in a regular fashion. What it does not show very well is the exact connection in time between the drop in *n* Affiliation and the wave of religious reform. Since the intervals at which motive measures were taken are so large, it is not possible to be sure whether the *n* Affiliation drop precedes or accompanies religious reform. At the very least the sequences suggest a pattern worth further investigation.

By way of summary, let us list the points concerning power orientation in England that deserve further study:

1. A combination of high *n* Power and low *n* Affiliation is associated with or may lead to violence or warfare, as it did around 1550, 1650, and to a lesser extent 1750, in England. To connect this hypothesis with findings reported in the previous chapter, we need only infer that inhibition was also high; and we have here once again an instance of the imperial motivation pattern expressing itself in a ruthless attempt at empire-building. Other motive combinations, on the other hand, such as a low *n* Power, or high *n* Affiliation, or balanced *n* Power and *n* Affiliation are not associated with warfare.

2. As a possible explanation for the association just hypothesized, high *n* Power, unchecked by high *n* Affiliation, is expressed

HISTORICAL PERIOD	n Power > n Aff (gap)	LEAD TIME	MOTIVE CHANGES	LEAD TIME	SOCIAL EVENTS
1501-1575	HIGHER → FEROCIOUS FEUDALISM				TYRANNY
1576-1625	LOWER → ELIZABETHAN GLORY		RISE IN n Aff CONFLICT with n Pow		PEACE
1626-1675	HIGHER → CIVIL WAR		DROP in n Aff		DROP in n Aff PURITANISM, WAR
1676-1725	LOWER → RECOVERY RESTORATION		RISE in n Aff CONFLICT with n Pow		PEACE
1726-1775	HIGHER → OLIGARCHY RULE		DROP in n Aff		DROP in n Aff WESLEYANISM, WAR
1776-1825					PEACE

Figure 9.3—The relation of motivational trends, religious reform, and warfare England 1500–1800

more often as altruistic, idealistic power (s Power), the desire to save others regardless of their feelings in the matter.

3. Periods when n Power and n Affiliation are balanced are associated with religious reform or revival.

4. When n Power and n Affiliation are balanced, an unstable state of motive conflict occurs which is most commonly followed by a drop in n Affiliation earlier than in n Power; that in turn creates the conditions of hypothesis I above—high n Power and low n Affiliation leading to warfare.

5. Periods of warfare tend to be followed by a rise in need for Affiliation, which if it introduces a balance between n Affiliation and n Power, and n Power remains high, may start the cycle all over again.

These are important hypotheses. How can they be tested? Let us consider each one in turn.

The Motivational Pattern for Violence

Findings reported in *The achieving society* (1961) may be cited as further evidence for hypothesis 1, as already noted. They demonstrated that among nations in the modern period, a high need for Power, and low need for Affiliation in children's stories was associated with totalitarian regimes or "ruthlessness" (1961, p. 169). At the time of the research no direct attempt was made to measure the degree of political violence in such regimes; it was simply assumed to be higher.

Since then, several authors have obtained quantitative estimates of the degree of political turmoil, internal war, or political instability in various nations. Southwood (1969) has in addition suggestively shown that among forty nations, those that scored higher on a measure of internal war (based on amounts of guerila warfare, purges, revolutions, etc.) in the 1955–1960 period, tended to be those whose children's readers scored high in power motivation somewhat earlier, around 1950. His result is not a definitive test of the hypothesis, however, since he did not include a measure of the need for Affiliation. He also stressed, as have others (Feierabend & Feierabend, 1966), the part played by lack of opportunity or frustration of desires in producing political violence. In fact, he found that high need for Achievement in the children's stories combined with low opportunity for satisfying it was particularly likely to lead to political violence, even more than a high need for Power combined with lack of opportunity.

A more direct test of the hypothesis is provided in Table 9.1, using data on political instability published by the Feierabends (1966) and motive scores for nations from McClelland (1961). The measure of instability might better be called a measure of political violence, since "a general election is an item associated with a zero position on the rating instructions. Resignation of a cabinet official falls into the one position on the scale; peaceful demonstrations into the two position; assassination of a significant political leader into the three position; mass arrests into the four position; *coups d'états* into the five position; and civil war in the sixth position" (1966, p.252). In the lefthand column of Table 9.2 are listed those countries whose *n* Power scores are at least half a standard deviation higher than their *n* Affiliation scores in the 1950 children's readers. Only the extreme of the distribution of Power-Affiliation gaps is used because it seems reasonable to assume that for violence to occur the need for Power must be distinctly higher than the need for Affiliation. Also we have ignored the Inhibition score here since either the "imperial" (Table 8.3) or "conquistador" (Table 8.4) pattern seems likely to produce violence.

The relationship is as predicted by the hypothesis. Countries high in *n* Power and low in *n* Affiliation tend to score higher on the Feierabend scale of political violence than do countries whose power and affiliation orientations are more nearly balanced or tend in the other direction. One cannot bluntly argue of course that the power-affiliation gap *causes* political violence, because the two measures are taken more or less simultaneously and because it is impossible to disentangle the effect of lack of opportunity or economic frustration

**Table 9.1–Political violence among modern nations as a function of the
difference in standard scores for n Power and n Affiliation (from McClelland, 1961)**

	n Power −n Aff. >.5 (1950)	n Power − n Aff. <.5 (1950)
Politically unstable, violent	Argentina	Belgium
	China	Chile
	India	France
	Iraq	Hungary
Score of 422 or more (see	Iran	Italy
Feierabend and Feierabend,	Mexico	Japan
1966)	Pakistan	Lebanon
	Spain	Poland
	Turkey	Syria
	Russia	
	Union of S. Africa	
Politically stable, less violent	Germany	Australia
1955–1961	New Zealand	Austria
	Switzerland	Bulgaria
	Taiwan	Canada
		Denmark
		England
		Finland
		Greece
		Ireland
		Israel
		Netherlands
		Norway
		Portugal
		Sweden
		Tunisia
		U.S.A.
		Uruguay

$\chi^2 = 5.77$ p $< .05$

which powerfully affects the amount of violence in a country. For
example, every country in the top lefthand box in Table 9.1 is also
classified by Southwood as low in opportunity, as reflected in a low
percentage of children enrolled in secondary schools. On the other
hand, fourteen out of seventeen of the countries in the lower right-
hand box of the table have above average numbers of children in
secondary school. Thus as a number of authors have shown, low
opportunity, as measured in various ways, is associated with political
violence. Here it is also associated with the Power-Affiliation gap;
eleven out of thirteen (85%) of those high in *n* Power and low in
n Affiliation are low in educational opportunity, as contrasted with
eight of stwenty-six (31%) of those not showing such a Power-Afifila-

tion gap. ($\chi^2 = 10.21$, p $< .01$). The association between lack of opportunity and the Power-Affiliation gap is so strong that it is not possible to hold opportunity constant and see whether the combination of high n Power and low n Affiliation leads more often to violence under these conditions. Thus while it is encouraging to discover that our hypothesis is confirmed to the extent that the Power-Affiliation gap is associated with political violence, we cannot be sure whether this particular motive combination is the cause of the violence or the result of some other factors, particularly high systemic frustration. A more critical test of the causal hypothesis can be made only from a longitudinal study, which has in fact been carried out and will be reported below.

The second hypothesis, derived from the study of the motivational patterns of English history, concerns an explanation of why the combination of a high need for Power and low need for Affiliation should lead to violence. It predicts that if a high need for Power is unchecked by a need for Affiliation, the power need will express itself altruistically as a desire to save others. At first glance, such a prediction sounds paradoxical. Why does a high need for Affiliation not turn the power need in an altruistic direction? Doesn't altruism imply love of others and concern for their welfare? The paradox is more semantic than real, deriving as it does from a misunderstanding of how the need for Affiliation affects behavior. Individuals with a high need for Affiliation want to love and be loved. They don't want to save people; they want to spend time with them, appreciate them, enjoy each other's company. The need for Power, therefore—the desire to have influence or impact on another—in point of fact interferes with the affiliative need simply because pushing someone around is not the way to enjoy a friendly relationship. Thus it follows that only when the affiliative need is low can the power need properly express itself primarily as a desire to save or help other people in the abstract, not as particular friends. It is this abstract desire to save others that we have labeled the socialized power need (s Power). It may lead to violence, according to the hypothesis, precisely because it represents a strong urge to do what is good for people, regardless of what they may want. This was the form of power motive that justified imperial Christian nations like England in their intervention in countries like India and Ceylon to "save the natives" from poverty, suffering, internecine warfare, and worshipping savage idols. The empirical question is whether high power needs are expressed in terms of s Power more when the need for Affiliation is low than when it is high.

Appendix Table 9.9 reports three independent checks of this hypothesis. In each sample the mean s Power score is significantly higher among those high in *n* Power when *n* Affiliation is low than when it is high. The hypothesis is amply confirmed among eighth graders and college students, males and females, and individuals from different social class backgrounds.

The explanation is still incomplete. Why should a heightened s Power tend to be associated with violence? As a matter of historical fact, it has often been associated with violence, as various crusades in the name of religion or reforms on behalf of the people demonstrate. But what psychological or sociological mechanisms are involved? Can we shed any more light on how a motivational "state of mind" is converted into organized violence?

The findings reported on managers in the last chapter may prove helpful. Men with higher s Power, as we have seen, are likely to become leaders or officers in organizations. They are also the ones whose motivational pattern is imperial: high *n* Power, low *n* Affiliation, and high Inhibition. The behavior of managers with this motive pattern leads their subordinates to report that morale is high in the organization, that in particular Team Spirit and Organizational Clarity are higher than among subordinates of managers with other motivational patterns. Everyone knows what he is supposed to do when. The team works well together. Managers high in *n* Power, low in *n* Affiliation, and high in Inhibition (or high in s Power) are somehow able to create excellent organizational climates. They instill a sense of power in their subordinates and mobilize enthusiasm for working together and for the organization. Such a climate sounds ideal also for a political or military organization in which the measure of effectiveness is orderliness and the amount of loyalty and commitment to the organization which is aroused. Furthermore, as Table 8.3 demonstrated, even ordinary individuals with this motive pattern show the characteristics that lead to organizational effectiveness. They respect institutional authority, like to work, are willing to sacrifice themselves for the group and believe in a just world.

What we have uncovered then is the motivational pattern in leaders and followers that tends to build an effective, expanding organization with a strong in-group feeling. Such high in-group morale is regularly associated with hostility towards out-groups (see Adorno, *et al.*, 1950) and can readily erupt in violence if a provocation occurs. To understand why countries with the imperial motivation syndrome are violence-prone, therefore, we need only assume that they have a larger than usual number of people with this particular motivational pattern and that it predisposes them to build organizations with strong in-group spirit.

The line of reasoning is parallel to the one developed in *The achieving society,* in which I argued that if the popular literature of the country was particularly achievement-oriented, there would be a larger than usual number of individuals with high achievement motivation who would behave in an active entrepreneurial fashion, ultimately kicking off rapid economic growth for the country as a whole. What we have uncovered here is a motivational pattern that leads to organizational effectiveness and violence towards outgroups just as we uncovered there a motivational pattern underlying entrepreneurial performance. The imperial motive pattern is not the only one that leads to violence, as we will see in a moment, nor is organizational behavior the only possible way to explain the link between the motivational pattern in popular literature and collective violence; yet it does provide a way to understand the connection between the two phenomena.

Predicting War and Peace in American History

The remaining three hypotheses to come out of the study of motivational patterns in English history involve statements about sequences of events and therefore require a longitudinal study. So really does hypothesis 1 if we want to test whether a combination of high *n* Power and low *n* Affiliation *precedes,* and therefore causes collective violence at a later period. We decided therefore to check the findings of the English study against motivational trends in popular American literature from the founding of the Republic down to the present time (1780–1970). We would then be in a position once more to see whether the Power-Affiliation gap was associated with collective violence, whether Christian revivals were in turn connected with high levels of *n* Power and *n* Affiliation, and whether the sequences in shifts in these motive patterns followed some regular scheme. Since sequences were of particular importance, greater attention was paid to getting motivational measures representative of smaller units of time than in the English study. Specifically we wanted to get motive measures for each decade from 1780 to the present time, although we recognized the dangers of trying to pinpoint the popularity of a particular piece of literature in so narrow a time band.

What kind of literature could we code for motive orientation? To begin with, we had the samples of children's textbooks already collected and coded by deCharms and Moeller (1962). Although the series began only in 1800, we decided to code the same samples for *n* Power and *n* Affiliation, on the grounds that they had proven to be diagnostic of what was happening in the economic sphere in American history at different periods. DeCharms and Moeller chose selections from texts published in various decades; but since they were using a somewhat larger time unit than we had decided on, there are gaps in their series for 1810–1819, 1830–1839, 1860–69, and 1910–19. The complete list of these sources is given in Appendix Table 9.3. Unfortunately they could supply us only with pages from a shorter sample selected from the entire sample of pages they used, but they have demonstrated that the two samples give comparable results so far as achievement and affiliation motivation are concerned. The unit of measurement in this source is the page; the count is of the proportion of pages in a given decade which contain either achievement or affiliation or power imagery. To supplement their sample, the textbook pages scored in *The achieving society* for 1920–30 and 1946–1955 were added to the samples for the decades of the 1920's and 1950's respectively. The minimum number of pages scored for a given decade was 11, although most decades were represented by many more pages. Thus, figuring on 300–350 words to a page, the number of words of school text considered to be representative of a decade varied from approximately 4,000–9,000.

The next source was perhaps the most obvious. It consisted of bestselling or most popular novels for each decade from the 1780's through the 1960's, as reported for most of the time in Mott (1947). (The complete list of these novels is given in Appendix Table 9.4.) We were somewhat concerned about the representativeness of this sort of material, particularly in the early period, when only a rather small proportion of the total population must have read popular fiction. But, on the other hand, we thought that these selections would be representative of what the upper classes were thinking, they being the ones most likely to read such literature. They also would represent more what women were thinking, since studies have shown that, at least in recent times, more women than men read popular novels. This fact could of course be a disadvantage if we were predicting acts of violence or political acts and if these in turn were more likely to be undertaken by men. We felt, nevertheless, that the guaranteed popularity of the material more than outweighed the possible disadvantages of social class and sex bias.

The scoring unit here was a ten-line segment usually representing 100–125 words. *N* Achievement, *n* Affiliation, and *n* Power were scored as present or absent for each ten-line unit. A *selection* from the text consisted of 10 ten-line units or approximately 3–4 pages. If there were two novels from a given decade, ten selections were made from each, so that there were twenty selections or 200 ten-line units representing each decade. The number of words scored then was somewhat over 20,000 or more than double the number of words scored in the children's texts. This difference was considered justifiable since children's stories are condensed and to the point, whereas fiction contains a good deal more description that would not be scoreable.

The third source of popular literature was hymns published in the decade. These proved to be by far the most difficult source to date properly and to pinpoint as to popularity. So far as possible, hymns were chosen from books published by the major denominations such as the Methodists, Presbyterians, and Baptists. If no large denomination published hymnbooks during a particular decade, then general hymnbooks were chosen. Usually a hymn was assigned to the decade in which the book was published. This was no guarantee of course that the hymn was actually sung during that period (or any other period!); and in some cases the hymn was obviously composed at a much earlier period. Hymns by Charles Wesley, for example, have been popular among Methodists throughout the entire period under consideration. Famous hymns like "Abide with Me" or "Rock of Ages" were assigned to the year in which they were written. Such hymns were often chosen from L. F. Benson's collection, *Studies of familiar hymns* (1902). A complete list of sources is given in Appendix Table 9.5. In choosing hymns likely to be most popular and representative of the period under consideration, we were assisted by experts from the divinity schools in the Boston area.

The presence or absence of *n* Power, *n* Affiliation, *n* Achievement was noted for each ten-line unit, and 220 units were scored for each decade, or approximately 22,000 words.

All of the material was scored blindly in the sense that the coders did not know the hypotheses nor the period from which the material came. When the results were all in, the first question we asked was how the motive scores from different sources related to each other. One way to look at the question is to compare the average yield of the three sources for the three types of motivation. Unfortunately the method of scoring the children's texts was so different from that used for scoring fiction or hymns that it was not possible to compare the results directly. It is meaningful to compare, however, within any given source the relative importance of the three motives. From

Appendix Tables 9.6–9.8, it appears that children's texts are fairly evenly balanced for the amount of achievement, affiliation, and power motivation they express. In fiction, however, power motivation appears seven or eight times as often as achievement or affiliation motivations; even in hymns, power motivation appears twice as often as achievement or affiliation motivation. Such a stress on power motivation is not surprising, since the plots of novels usually center on power conflicts, and Christian hymns regularly celebrate God's power in the universe. Perhaps the only surprising part is that mention of affiliation is relatively infrequent in works of fiction. Since affiliation based exclusively on sex or kinship relations is not included in the affiliation scoring system, that may explain its comparatively low frequency in fiction.

Since the different sources were scored in different ways and each seemed to have a relatively unique pattern of emphasis on one motive or another, we thought it best to convert the raw motive scores for each source to standard scores which would be comparable from source to source. Accordingly, the motive scores for all sources were converted to the same scale in which the mean was arbitrarily set at 50 and the standard deviation at 10. These standard scores are reported for each decade on which information is available for each motive for each source in Appendix Tables 9.6–9.8.

Another way to look at the relation among the scores is to note whether leads or lags in motive scores appear in one source followed by another. For example, one might suppose that changes in religious conviction would influence motive patterns in hymns first, then spread to popular novels, and finally to children's texts. Hymns were chosen, indeed, as a source because of our concern to see whether motive changes occurred before, during, or after religious changes; we hoped we might pick up those leads or lags most directly in the hymns produced at the same time as the religious changes. A careful examination, however, revealed no regular leads or lags in motive scores from one source to another. It is true that for achievement motivation scores, the highs and lows coincide for hymns and texts 15 out of 18 times and 10 out of 13 times, respectively. And for some reason the n Achievement level of fiction *predicts* correctly n Achievement level thirty years later both for school texts (10 out of 12 times, $\chi^2 = 5.3$, $p < .05$) and hymns (13 out of 15 times, $\chi^2 = 8.1, p < .01$). It looks as if the authors of fiction are somehow leading the pack and injecting levels of achievement motivation into their novels in ways that influence compilers of hymns and writers of children's texts in the next generation. Yet none of the relationships is confirmed either for *n* Affiliation or *n* Power; and since they occur for only one of the motives, one can question whether the tendency of fiction writers to anticipate future levels of motivation is general.

Still another way to look at the relationships among the scores is to see whether highs and lows for any of the motives in a particular source coincide with the highs and lows for either of the other two motives in the same source. Here the findings are similar to what had been obtained in the study of individuals. Levels of expression of any one motive tend to be independent of or uncorrelated with the levels of expression of either of the other two motives. Highs and lows of each of the three motives tend to occur independently of each other for each source with one exception. So far as the children's texts and hymns are concerned, whenever power motivation is high in a given decade, affiliation motivation tends to be low and vice-versa, 12 out of 13 times for the texts, ($\chi^2 = 9.31$, p < .01), and 13 out of 18 times for the hymns, ($\chi^2 = 4.00$, p < .05). So far as these two sources are concerned, then, the general tendency already mentioned for power and affiliation motivation to conflict, and therefore not to be present in the same source at the same time, is confirmed here also. The inverse relationship does not hold for fiction, in which there is no significant correlation between *n* Power and *n* Affiliation by decade. Again, this is not hard to understand; the plots of popular novels often revolve around the conflicts between power drives and affiliative ties.

Our main objective is to get some combined estimate of each motive level for each decade in the period covered, so that we can compare these motive levels with other events in American history. None of the above findings provides a strong argument for weighting one source more than another. Though it is true that the children's textbook material is based on a much smaller number of pages than for the other two sources, nevertheless the raw mean scores suggest that, as we predicted, fiction and hymns contain more filler material which cannot be scored for any motive. So in the end, we adopted the simplest procedure. We averaged the standard scores for a given motive across all three sources for a particular decade.

Figure 9.4 plots these average scores (also presented in Appendix Tables 9.6–9.8) for *n* Power and *n* Affiliation at the mid-point of each decade from 1780–1970. An asterisk has been placed by each point which is based on only two sources (hymns and fiction); and a gap appears in the curve in the 1910–1920 decade because by accident sufficient material was scored for only one source for this period. Shaded in black in the figure are the time periods when the need for Power was at least moderately high, and higher than the need for

Affiliation. The question of special interest to us is whether these "black areas" regularly *preceded* outbreaks of war in the history of the United States, as listed along the time line at the base of Figure 9.6. Our hypothesis leads us to predict that they would, because we have regularly found that this motive combination represents an assertive, aggressive frame of mind. In the case of the United States, the frame of mind was almost certainly imperial also; at the two periods when we checked it, 1925 and 1950, the Activity Inhibition score in the children's stories was above the world average (cf. Appendix Table 8.1).

To a remarkable extent, then, this figure demonstrates what neither the study of English history or contemporary nations could show: when the need for Power is high and higher than the need for Affiliation in popular literature, a country is more likely to go to war *subsequently* than when these two motives are in some other relationship to each other. Generally speaking, with a few exceptions to be noted, the black areas in Figure 9.4 precede war, and the white areas precede peace. Let us consider the historical series in more detail.

The first dark area, when *n* Power is higher than *n* Affiliation, occurs in the 1795–1805 period. Towards the end of this decade Britain and France became engaged in the fierce Napoleonic wars, in the course of which they interfered with American shipping. Feeling in the United States ran high, particularly against the British, who continued to board American ships and impress American citizens (formerly British) into its navy. America's pride was aroused along with its desire to expand its territory into Florida and Canada. It declared war against Britain in 1812.

Figure 9.4 illustrates by means of a dark shaded area in 1795–1805, how a Power-Affiliation gap, may have set in motion an imperial spirit that would lead to a declaration of war in 1812 when the United States was sufficiently provoked. The struggle with Britain was pursued on land and sea for over two years. It ended with only one major victory for the Americans when Andrew Jackson overcame a strong British force in New Orleans, actually after the peace treaty had been signed. After the war, historians report, there was an era of good-feeling and increased unity in the young American republic. "Altogether, this ill-starred war did a great deal to make the republic more mature and more independent; to knit it together and to strengthen its character" (Nevins and Commager, 1966). The era of good-feeling is reflected in the motivational indexes; for the 1815 period *n* Affiliation appears higher than *n* Power.

By 1825 *n* Power had risen sharply and *n* Affiliation had dropped

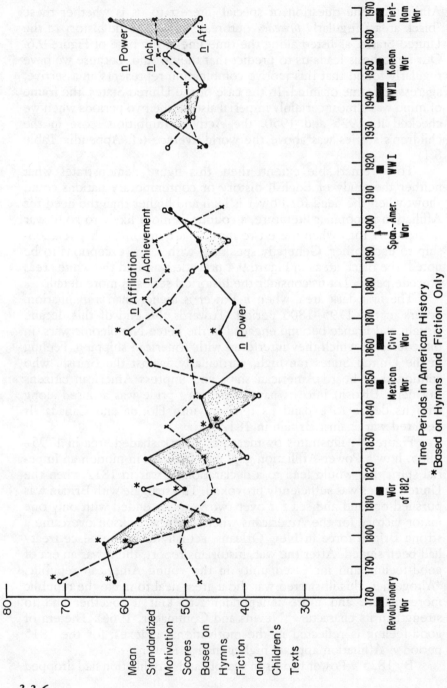

Figure 9.4—Levels of concern for power, affiliation and achievement in popular literature United States 1780-1970

precipitously, so that again a Power-Affiliation gap (reflecting an imperial, martial mood) characterized the American people. Once more—allowing time for this aggressive spirit to make itself felt in external events—we find that in the 1840's the Americans were engaged in an expansionist phase. They had largely destroyed the Indians and put the remainder on reservations, chiefly in Oklahoma, in the 1830's. They annexed Texas in 1845, took over the Oregon territory in 1846, went to war with Mexico in 1846, and acquired all of California, Nevada, Utah, Arizona, and New Mexico as a result.

The two motives were more nearly balanced in the mid-1830's forecasting a period of comparative peace in the 1850's. Again by 1845, however, power motivation was notably higher than affiliation motivation, creating a dangerous mood which erupted some fifteen years later in the bloodiest American conflict of all—the Civil War. It is worth pausing a moment here to examine in more detail what was going on, because it seems paradoxical that both at the time the Civil War actually started and just before (in the 1850's), *n* Affiliation was very much higher than *n* Power. How can it be argued that the country was in a mood for war at such a time? What explains the lag between the martial spirit of the 1840's and the outbreak of Civil War in 1861, a time when there was no sign of a martial spirit left in the popular literature?

A look at historical events in the 1840's and 1850's helps us understand the delay and the apparent paradox. Almost from the beginning, the country had been divided over the issue of slavery. The founding fathers like Washington and Jefferson had felt that slavery must go; but the South became so attached to it that when a storm over the issue arose in 1819, it was settled for a time in the Missouri Compromise under the pacific statesmanship of Henry Clay. It came violently to the fore again in the late 1840's, in a disagreement over whether slavery was to be allowed in the vast new territories taken from Mexico (California, Utah, Nevada, New Mexico, and Arizona). Southerners in the Congress openly stated that if the institution of slavery was not protected by the Federal government in the new territories, they were for disunion. Northerners argued just as fervently either for abolition of slavery everywhere, or for prohibiting its spread, or at the very least for not foisting it on a new territory if its legislature voted against it. Again with the strong support of the able but aging Clay a compromise was reached in 1850 and the outbreak of hostilities delayed.

Agitation by extremists on both sides continued through the 1850's; but if our scores for popular literature are to be believed, it did not create a general martial spirit, either then or in the 1860's since *n* Affiliation was higher than *n* Power. Rather our data suggest a generation gap or an elitist gap, in the sense that extremist leaders in both the North and the South carried forward their martial views, formed in the 1840's, and manipulated the country into a war in the 1860's. It is worth remembering that extremists on both sides had developed the moral fervor that characterizes high *n* Power and low *n* Affiliation and that is essential to working up the courage for collective violence. For the South the issue was freedom to live as it pleased; for the North, it was union and abhorrence of slavery. It is no accident that many of the Southern leaders, like Robert E. Lee, had been involved in the quick, overwhelmingly successful war against Mexico in the 1840's. They had learned, as had Northerners in their widespread support of the illegal underground railroad, that victories could be won by force; and they tried to apply this lesson in the battle over secession.

What evidence is there for making a distinction between the martial views of the extremist elites, which were formed earlier, and those of the general public, which by our measures seemed more pacific in the 1850's and 1860's? The voting pattern in the election of 1860 supports our argument. Lincoln won with a minority of the votes cast. He was considered at the time to belong in the extremist abolitionist camp, although even he did not propose to attack slavery where it existed. Even in the fourteen slave states, 124,000 more votes were cast for the two compromise candidates than for the secessionist Breckinridge. "The popular vote was unquestionably for the restriction of slavery, but also for union and peace . . . A careful analysis of the voting in some of the states in the deep South suggests that had the issue of secession been presented for a fair and open referendum, it would have been defeated" (Nevins and Commager, 1966, p. 245). Apparently this majority sentiment for peace and union is what was tapped by our motivation scores from the popular literature at the time. Yet the martial spirit of an earlier period lived on in leaders who, as a result of their passionate zeal either for abolition or secession, were in positions of sufficient power to plunge the country into war.

The time just before, during, and after the Civil War was a period when the need for Affiliation was much higher than the need for Power; according to our predictive model, that should have resulted in a period of relative peace from 1870–1890, as indeed happened. The next dark area occurs around 1895. While the lead time appears somewhat longer than on previous occasions, it correctly forecasts the entry of the United States into World War I in the 1910–1920 decade.

Once again we might wonder why a martial spirit in the 1890's is the driving force behind a major war occurring almost twenty years later. We must examine what happened in the interval. The major connecting links are: first, that in this period the United States became passionately and idealistically interested in reform to help the oppressed (the workingmen in the sweatshops, the slum-dwellers, prisoners, the insane); and second, it became convinced that it was a world power, and both could and should exert its influence for the welfare of mankind all over the world. We invaded Cuba to save the suffering people from the cruel Spaniards, assumed the "white man's burden" in taking over the Philippines, annexed Hawaii, intervened decisively in a quarrel between Great Britain and Venezuela, seized the Isthmus of Panama in order to build a canal for world trade, insisted on the Open Door in China, established "protectorates" in the Caribbean and elsewhere in Latin America under the umbrella of the Monroe Doctrine, took part in settling the Russo-Japanese war, etc. Much of this expansion of our influence abroad was justified on the moral ground that we were helping victims of injustice or mismanagement. But it took time for the martial spirit of the 1890's to express itself nationally in these many ways that were to convince us that we had a duty to fight a war to make the world safe for democracy.

As Donley and Winter (1970) have shown, Presidents Theodore Roosevelt and Woodrow Wilson, as representatives of the power elite, were both high in *n* Power as revealed by their inaugural addresses and men who did not hesitate to continue the imperial mood of the 1890's by their actions abroad. What the majority of the people felt, including younger leaders, is less clear: popular literature was high in *n* Power in 1900–10 but also in *n* Affiliation, and unfortunately we have no reliable data for the 1910–20 decade. Even if it were to reveal that the majority were not in a mood for war in 1917 (as in the parallel Civil War instance), a chain of events had been set in motion in the 1890's that made war inevitable given the extreme provocation of the sinking of American ships in 1917 by the Germans. During this time under the leadership of men in whom the imperial mood was dominant, the country had grown to think of itself as a world power with moral obligations that forced it to act on behalf of justice and democracy, when provoked, even if that meant going to war.

After World War I the lead time between motivational states and war or peace appears to get shorter. Higher *n* Affiliation than *n* Power in the 1920's was followed by peace in the 1930's; a dark area in the 1930's was followed by war in the 1940's. A "white" area after World War II was followed by the "Eisenhower peace" of the late 1950's; and the sharp increase in n Power and drop in n Affiliation late in the 1950's and early 1960's was followed by the Viet Nam struggle in the mid-1960's. At a first glance, the only two wars that the motivational indicators do not predict are the Spanish-American war of 1898, which was very short, and the Korean War beginning in 1950.

When one is looking for support for a hypothesis, however, it is dangerously easy to juggle with lead and lag times in such a way as to gloss over inconsistencies in the findings. Accordingly, Table 9.2 has been prepared in an effort to introduce enough precision into the forecasting model to make sure that it is given a proper test. In the period up to World War I, we have arbitrarily assumed that it would take about 15–20 years for an "aggressive spirt" (high n Power, low n Affiliation) to translate itself into war. Or more precisely, we have hypothesized that the motivational pattern plotted at the mid-point of a decade will translate itself into action (either war or peace) in the decade beginning fifteen years after this mid-point.

Thus the top of the table may be read as follows. The fact that n Affiliation is higher than n Power in 1785 (low Power-Affiliation gap) predicts that the decade beginning 15 years later, 1800–1810, will be a relatively peaceful or less violent period in American history. This prediction turns out to be correct: a white box (for predicted peace) occurs on the lefthand side of the line, indicating there actually was comparative peace in that decade. Next, the high Power-Affilation gap in 1795 predicts war in 1810–1820 (represented by a black box), which also turns out to be correct: the black box is on the right-hand side of the time line. And so on. This model for forecasting war and peace works pretty well, up to World War I. Of the thirteen predictions made, only one is clearly incorrect—for the 1820–1830 decade which was supposed to be violent and wasn't—and one other is doubtfully correct. The decade of 1890–1900 was predicted to be relatively peaceful, but the Spanish-American war occurred in 1898. Since this war was so short, lasting only about ten weeks, one may question whether this represents a serious flaw in the forecasting ability of the model. The outbreak seems rather an act of violence caused by economic consideration, which we will consider in another category in a moment. Even if it is taken as an incorrect prediction, 11 out of 13 of the predictions are clearly correct, yielding a number of hits which could hardly have risen by chance ($\chi^2 = 7.2$, $p < .01$).

After World War I, lead time clearly decreases. In Table 9.2 we have assumed, to be consistent, a very short lead time that yields four correct predictions and one incorrect—for the Korean War. We have assumed, in other words, that the predictions are for the decade starting at the midpoint of the previous decade when the motivational

Table 9.2—Predicting war and peace from population patterns in U.S. history

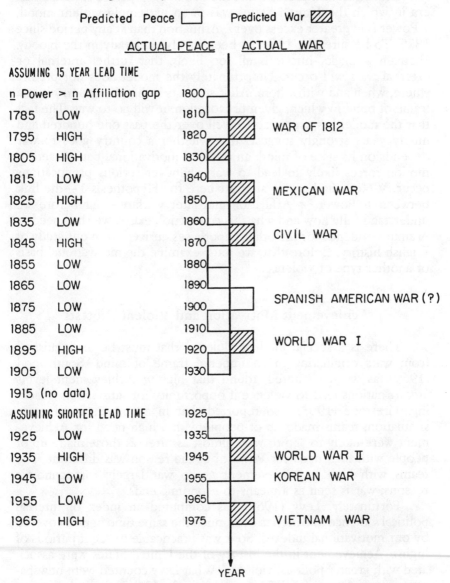

Predicted Peace ☐   Predicted War ▨

		ACTUAL PEACE	ACTUAL WAR
ASSUMING 15 YEAR LEAD TIME			
n Power > n Affiliation gap	1800		
1785	LOW	1810	
1795	HIGH	1820	WAR OF 1812
1805	HIGH	1830	
1815	LOW	1840	
1825	HIGH	1850	MEXICAN WAR
1835	LOW	1860	
1845	HIGH	1870	CIVIL WAR
1855	LOW	1880	
1865	LOW	1890	
1875	LOW	1900	SPANISH AMERICAN WAR (?)
1885	LOW	1910	
1895	HIGH	1920	WORLD WAR I
1905	LOW	1930	
1915 (no data)			
ASSUMING SHORTER LEAD TIME	1925		
1925	LOW	1935	
1935	HIGH	1945	WORLD WAR II
1945	LOW	1955	KOREAN WAR
1955	LOW	1965	
1965	HIGH	1975	VIETNAM WAR

YEAR

indexes are plotted. Thus a white area in 1925 predicts peace correctly
in 1925–1935; a dark area in 1935 predicts war correctly in 1935–
1945, etc. Only the very marginally white gap in 1945 incorrectly
predicts peace for the 1945–1955 period, when in fact we went to war
in Korea.

The model also predicts that the 1965–1975 period should be an era in which the United States was in an extremely violent mood: *n* Power is in greater excess over *n* Affiliation than at any period since 1825. To be sure, the U.S. has been involved already in the bloody Vietnam struggle, but it is all too likely that further internal or external wars will occur. Unfortunately the model does not predict where, when and with whom. All it suggests is that the country is in a frame of mind in which, given provocation, it will go to war. The fact that the model has predicted so well over the past one hundred and ninety years strongly suggests that whether a country goes to war depends on its state of mind: an imperial motivational pattern sets in motion forces likely to lead to war whenever serious provocations occur. We can find ample support here for Hypothesis 1—the link between *n* Power, *n* Affiliation and later warfare—but before we understand fully how and why this connection exists, we shall need to examine evidence for the other hypotheses derived from our study of English history. Before that, we must examine the motivational basis of another type of violence.

Achievement Motivation and Violent Protests

There is a special kind of violence that must be distinguished from wars originating in an imperial frame of mind.´ Southwood (1969), as we have noted, found that high *n* Achievement levels among nations lead to violence if opportunity for satisfaction is lacking. Firestone (1968) also reported that in an international game simulation, teams made up of people with a high need for Achievement were likely to "go to war" almost as often as those made up of people with high need for Power; but the reason was different. The teams with high *n* Achievement go to war largely for economic reasons; war is seen as a means to economic ends.

Fortunately, Levy (1969) has computed an index of internal political violence in America over much the same time period covered by our motivational indexes. So it was practicable to see if periods of high *n* Achievement in the history of the United States were associated with greater political violence. What Levy counted were newspaper reports of acts of political violence in the United States beginning with the decade 1818–28 and ending for 1959–68. To make the numbers comparable over this long time span, he of course had to correct in some way for the growing size and affluence of the United States; the country grew both in population and in the completeness of its news coverage. So he corrected his raw figures by dividing by the population of the country and by the number of pages in the newspapers. We have chosen the second correction as being more likely to affect directly the number of reports of political violence. Figure 9.5 plots Levy's index of violent political protest against our measure of n Achievement for the period 1820–1970. The mid-points of our decades and his are slightly different but not enough to matter for making a comparison.

Before looking at the overall results, let us consider an example of what we are talking about. The Whisky Rebellion of 1794 provides a good case in point. The Federal Government had passed an excise tax on whisky, which the Scots-Irish in western Pennsylvania soon refused to pay. "They needed money; and knowing the Scottish art of whisky making, they set up stills on nearly every farm to produce an easily transported commodity. The excise tax seemed to fall unfairly on this money crop. Moreover, it was inquisitorial. Four counties in the area just south of Pittsburgh were soon being lashed to open resistance by angry leaders . . . When the government tried to arrest men who had defied the revenue officers, violence broke out. Mobs forced a Federal inspector to flee for his life and threatened the little garrison in Pittsburgh" (Nevins and Commager, 1966, p.147). The Federal government finally dispatched 15,000 troops to overawe the malcontents.

This was a form of politically violent protest that stemmed primarily from an economic reason. One would argue, if Southwood's findings are generally true, that in periods of high n Achievement politically violent events of this sort are more likely to occur. It is also an interesting confirmation of the hypothesis that according to our measure, the level of n Achievement in the 1790–99 decade when the Whisky Rebellion occurred, was above average for the whole period under consideration (see Appendix Table 9.8).

Figure 9.5 shows that, on the whole, the fit between the curves for n Achievement level and political violence is surprisingly good. In 11 out of 14 instances, whenever the n Achievement level rises above or falls below the mid-line, the number of politically violent protests also rises above or falls below the mid-line—a result that would seldom occur by chance ($\chi^2 = 4.0$, $p < .05$). This is all the more surprising when one considers that the corrections for the violence measure are necessarily crude, that the time periods do not coincide exactly, and above all, that we had no measure of economic lack of opportunity to match with the changes in n Achievement levels. There are indeed only two periods of major disagreement between

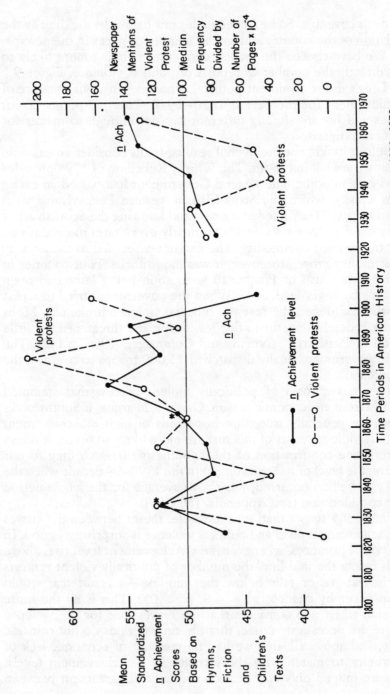

Figure 9.5—Achievement concerns and reports of violent protests United States 1820–1970

the two indexes (which incidentally prevent the correlation between the two indexes from reaching an accepted level of statistical significance).

The first one occurs for the 1900–1910 period when according to our measure the level of violent political protest is very high, and the level of *n* Achievement is very low. In this instance, it appears to be the *n* Achievement measure which is at fault. According to the deCharms and Moeller figures (1962), *n* Achievement level in children's textbooks was at its second highest point in 1910 for the entire period covered in their sample. Unfortunately, as noted earlier, we had available only the shortened sample of material from their study, and it yielded a much lower *n* Achievement score than the full sample did. If the *n* Achievement level for the children's texts is corrected upward in line with the score for the full sample, the discrepancy between the two curves for the 1900–1910 period becomes considerably less.

The other major discrepancy is for the 1950's, when the *n* Achievement level appears to be high and the number of violent protests low. One may speculate that the level of protest was low because this was a post-war period of relative prosperity, when the gap between aspiration and opportunity was not great enough to cause much political violence.

Southwood's hypothesis is thus confirmed on the whole by the American history data: acts of politically violent protest may proceed from a high level of *n* Achievement combined with real obstacles to achieving economic goals. Most violent labor unrest falls in this category. In times of high *n* Achievement, when the economy is expanding rapidly, labor wants its share and will organize violent protests to get it. An anecdote illustrates how the mechanism works. Once some leaders in a Caribbean island community became interested in developing achievement motivation largely as a stimulus to local entrepreneurship and business development. In the course of training various people how to give achievement motivation training, a police officer became so enthusiatic that he decided to train policemen in achievement motivation. A socialized type of power motivation training might have been more appropriate, considering the job the policemen had, but the effect of the achievement motivation training was dramatic: for the first time in history the police force went on strike to get higher wages! Violence that derives from heightened achievement motivation is in a sense more rational and easier to dissipate by allowing people to achieve at least some of their economic goals. Violence derived from the other motivational pattern—high *n* Power and low *n* Affiliation—is much less "rational" and may lead to acts of defiance and bravery that are quite self-destructive.

War, Motive Shifts, and Religious Revivals

The empirical link established between the imperial frame of mind (*n* Power – *n* Affiliation) and subsequent warfare in the history of the United States is interesting but still not completely convincing. We have not yet established clearly how a collective motivational state sets in motion a chain of events eventuating often in warfare. To round out the picture, we need to examine the evidence for the other hypotheses we derived from the study of English history: that a balanced *n* Affiliation and *n* Power are associated with or lead to religious reform (hypothesis 3), that this motivational balance introduces a conflict if *n* Power is fairly strong. In that case *n* Affiliation tends to drop first, producing a strong socialized power drive, reflected often in a zeal for reform (hypothesis 4), which leads to warfare (hypothesis 1), which in turn tends to be followed by a rise in *n* Affiliation (hypothesis 5), and, if this rise produces a balance with *n* Power, starts the cycle all over again.

Figure 9.6 has been prepared to show the occurrence of these predicted sequences several times in American history. The first column on the left demonstrates that the last hypothesis—the rise in *n* Affiliation after wars—is confirmed in an analysis of popular literature in the decade after a war. The need for Affiliation rises to a high level in six out of the eight decades after a war, and in only two of the ten decades following peace. The difference could hardly have arisen by chance (p < .05). The need for Affiliation is especially high in 1780–1790 after the Revolutionary War; it is again high in 1850–1860 after the Mexican War, and reaches an all-time high during, and after the Brothers' War, the American Civil War. It rises a little after the short-lived Spanish-American War and the taking of Panama, and again after World War I and World War II. It is as if doing violence to other people, the experiences of killing others and having friends and relations killed or wounded, arouses almost a reflex response of increased concern for other people.

If the past is any indication of the future, one would have to predict a sharp rise in the need for Affiliation in the 1970's after the violence of the Viet Nam war and the political disturbances of the late 1960's. There was indeed some evidence of such an increased need

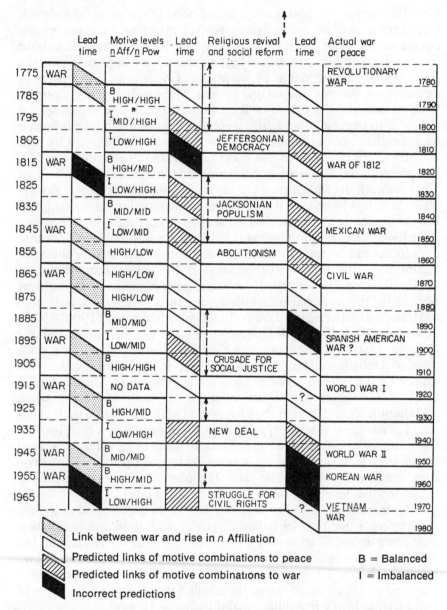

	Lead time	Motive levels n Aff/n Pow	Lead time	Religious revival and social reform	Lead time	Actual war or peace
1775	WAR					REVOLUTIONARY WAR
		B HIGH/HIGH				1780
1785						
		I * MID/HIGH				1790
1795						
		I LOW/HIGH		JEFFERSONIAN DEMOCRACY		1800
1805						
		B HIGH/MID				1810
1815	WAR					WAR OF 1812
		I LOW/HIGH				1820
1825						1830
1835		B MID/MID		JACKSONIAN POPULISM		
		I LOW/MID				1840
1845	WAR					MEXICAN WAR
		HIGH/LOW		ABOLITIONISM		1850
1855						1860
1865	WAR	HIGH/LOW				CIVIL WAR
						1870
1875		HIGH/LOW				
						1880
1885		B MID/MID				1890
1895	WAR	I LOW/MID				SPANISH AMERICAN WAR ?
						1900
1905		B HIGH/HIGH		CRUSADE FOR SOCIAL JUSTICE		1910
1915	WAR	NO DATA			?	WORLD WAR I
						1920
1925		B HIGH/MID				1930
1935		I LOW/HIGH		NEW DEAL		
						1940
1945	WAR	B MID/MID				WORLD WAR II
						1950
1955	WAR	B HIGH/MID				KOREAN WAR
						1960
1965		I LOW/HIGH		STRUGGLE FOR CIVIL RIGHTS	?	VIETNAM WAR
						1970
						1980

Link between war and rise in *n* Affiliation

Predicted links of motive combinations to peace   B = Balanced

Predicted links of motive combinations to war   I = Imbalanced

Incorrect predictions

Figure 9.6—The relation of motivational trends, social reform and war. United States 1780–1970.

for Affiliation in the loving spirit manifested in the great Woodstock jazz festival and in the religious revival affecting so many young people in the early 1970's, particularly the well educated and those from well-to-do backgrounds. Many of them have become devout as Jesus people in the name of traditional Christianity and others as devotees of various Indian gurus like Maharaj-ji, as explained in Chapter 6 in the discussion of Ram Dass. So the stage seems set for the cycle to begin all over again: increased devotion and love followed by a socialized power concern, followed by reform, followed by war.

To check the links in this cycle further, the third column of Fig. 9.6 presents the levels of *n* Affiliation and *n* Power (High, Mid or Low) for each decade. If they are approximately balanced at a moderate to high level—that is, if *n* Power is at least moderately strong, and if *n* Affiliation is not more than 10 standard score units higher or two units lower than *n* Power—that is indicated by a B (balanced) for that decade. As can be seen by looking down the motive levels column of Figure 9.6, this motive combination occurs eight times between 1780–1970, and in six out of seven times it is followed in the next decade by the imperial motivation pattern (I) caused by a drop in *n* Affiliation and a rise in *n* Power. In the eighth instance (1900–1910), no data are available for the following decade. On the other hand, for the nine instances involving other motive combinations, only once does *n* Affiliation drop and *n* Power rise in the next decade. This cannot be due merely to regression toward the mean, since a similar drop in *n* Affiliation and rise in *n* Power does not occur when *n* Affiliation is much higher than *n* Power (1850–1880) and such a shift could occur most easily. Hypothesis 4 is confirmed at a high level of significance (p < .01): when *n* Affiliation balances an *n* Power at least moderately high, *n* Affiliation is more likely to drop and *n* Power rise than would otherwise be the case. The observation we confirmed at the individual level also occurs at the national level.

Unfortunately we have only one-half of an explanation as to how the explosive mixture of balanced power and affiliation motivation may come about. Wars appear to increase the need for Affiliation, but we have no clue at present as to what increases need for Power. All we know is that *n* Power must be at least moderately strong for a balanced *n* Affiliation to create the conflict that results in the imperial mind frame: lower *n* Affiliation and higher *n* Power.

What is the relationship of these motive shifts to religious revivals? Earlier we suggested that religious devotion might be characterized by simultaneously high needs for Power and for Affiliation (the balanced combination). To check this idea (hypothesis 3), we plotted periods of major religious revivals in American history very approximately in Figure 9.6 as dotted vertical lines. It can be observed that some kind of religious revival was going on during six of the eight decades characterized by the balanced motive pattern. The difficulty is to compare this record with decades characterized by other motive patterns. We can scarcely include the imperial pattern decades since they have been shown to follow the balanced pattern so regularly, and there are only three decades that are not characterized by the B or I motive patterns. None of them is associated with a religious revival, but they do not occur often enough to leave one confident that the association of balanced power and affiliation motivations with religion could not have occurred by chance (p is around .10 by Fisher's exact test). Religious revivals may be associated with a balanced motive pattern in the way suggested, but even that conclusion does not help us understand which comes first. There is no evidence in Figure 9.6 to show that either the motive pattern or the religious revival regularly precedes or follows the other. To make the point more clearly it is worth examining the relationship between the two types of events.

The first Great Awakening in American religion started in the 1730's and 1740's under the influence of Methodist preachers and a revised Calvinism whose eloquent spokesman was Jonathan Edwards. The full effect of American Calvinism and Methodism was not generally felt until the end of the 18th century when "general revivals, at frequent intervals, swept across all of New England, except eastern Massachusetts and vast areas of then newly settled areas west of the Appalachians" (Parkes, 1947, p. 87). The major religious event of the 1780's was the spread of the Shaker communities in New England and New York, through the leadership of Ann Lee. Her followers regarded her as the "feminine counterpart of Jesus Christ" and "since the revelation was now complete, men could live without sin, which meant complete chastity and the abolition of private property and of any use of force and coercion." They "established where they lived strictly disciplined monastic lives . . . and became known as Shakers because they were accustomed to dance and shake their bodies during their religious services . . . At times of religious excitement they whirled around like dervishes and fell on the floor in a fit" (Parkes, 1947, p. 80). While Shakerism did not have a wide influence throughout the country, it represented the spiritual enthusiasm, the opening of one's self to divine love and power, which we have argued is characteristic of periods of balanced *n* Power and *n* Affiliation, particularly if both were high. It was symptomatic in an extreme form of a state of mind which we would argue was general throughout the country. In Figure 9.6 we have represented this great religious awakening as occurring in the last quarter of the 18th century, and it is associated roughly with a period of balanced motivation in the 1780's followed by the imperial motive pattern in the 1790's.

The second Great Awakening began some time in the 1820's and lasted at least until 1850. All historians agree it had a profound effect on the social and intellectual life of the American people. Religious revivalism was widespread; many new religions were started, the best known and most influential of which was the Mormon community. Religious schools and colleges were founded. The Methodists alone from 1830 to the Civil War "planted 34 permanent colleges" (Sweet, 1944, p. 149). "Organized benevolence flourished in a hitherto unheard of fashion. Missionary societies, home and foreign, for the conversion of the heathen, came into existence in bewildering numbers" (Sweet, p. 159). There is little doubt that 1820–50 was a period of great religious revival in American history. But it clearly did not begin until after the balanced conjunction of high *n* Power and *n* Affiliation in 1810–1820.

The third religious revival is best associated with the career of the great professional evangelist, Dwight L. Moody, which began after the Civil War and flourished in the last quarter of the nineteenth century. Again it is loosely connected with the shift from a balanced *n* Power and *n* Affiliation (1885) to *n* Power > *n* Affiliation (1895); but if anything it *precedes* the motivational shift rather than follows it as in the Second Great Awakening.

By the 20th century, psychologists had begun measuring religious conviction, at least among college students. Hoge (1969) has collected these studies and attempted to compare attitudes on a common base line from approximately 1906–1968. Figure 9.7 is reproduced from his thesis. Clear from his data is the fact that orthodox religious concern was at a high point in 1900–1910 and again in the mid-1920's when our motivational indexes show that *n* Affiliation and *n* Power were evenly matched and at least moderately high. His curve then shows a sharp drop in religious orthodoxy for the 1930's corresponding in our data to a rise in *n* Power and a drop in *n* Affiliation. And finally, religious concern swings up again in the 1950's, when the two motives are balanced, and down again in the 1960's, when the imperial motive pattern reasserts itself. Religious revivals may be associated with balanced *n* Affiliation and *n* Power, but they do not appear to be moving forces in producing motive changes or in linking them to war or peace.

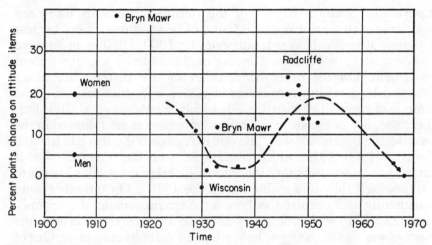

Figure 9.7—Schematic summary diagram of trends in Religious Orthodoxy, United States 1900–1970. From Hoge (1969)

The Imperial Motive Pattern, Reformist Zeal, and War

Figure 9.6 makes clear that the link between the imperial motive pattern and war is reformist zeal. Religious revival in the two instances studied in English history was connected with social reform, as it is in several instances in American history. Usually, in fact, religious revival precedes a concern for social justice, as can be noted from the dotted vertical arrows in Figure 9.6 preceding decades of social concern. The religious revivals, however, do not seem to precede or follow motive shifts in any regular way, and occasionally they seem to follow a wave of social reform, as when the Second Great Awakening occurred after Jacksonian populism. Matters become much simpler if we turn our attention to social reform itself, regardless of its connection with religious revivals.

During periods of social reform, people have been primarily concerned with promoting the welfare of the oppressed—with helping women, blacks, or the poor in their struggle against the "oppressors," the dominant power structure—the trusts, the capitalists, the males, the whites, etc. Periods of major populist reform in the history of the United States, listed in the fifth column in Figure 9.6, occur with amazing regularity in the decade after the shift to an imperial motivational pattern. All six of the reform movements listed are associated with a prior imperial frame of mind, if one allows for less lead time after World War I; only once (in 1800–1810) is an imperial motive pattern *not* followed in the next decade by a major reform movement. On the other hand, other motive patterns are never followed by a reform movement in eleven opportunities, using the same lead times. The difference is highly significant ($p < .01$). Furthermore, five of the six major reform movements are followed in the next decade by a major war. The one exception is the struggle for civil rights in 1960–1970, which overlapped with the Vietnam war. It remains to be seen whether the reformist zeal of the 1960's has yet to express itself fully in a major war in the 1970's. On the other hand wars hardly ever occurred without a reform movement: the Spanish-American War was almost too short to be an exception and the Korean war was in theory at least a United Nations enterprise. Out of the twelve decades when there was no reform, there was peace in nine. Again the differences noted could hardly have arisen by chance ($p < .025$). In other words, reform movements—the passionate concern and action for social justice—are the connecting link between the imperial motive pattern and war established in Figure 9.2. The sequences in Figure 9.6 show a surprising regularity given the extent to which history appears to be determined by external events beyond a nation's control. Let us examine the record in more detail.

The first wave of sentiment on behalf of the Common Man in Figure 9.6 is associated with Thomas Jefferson's years as President (1800–1808). "The year 1800 found the country ripe for a change. Indeed, it proved the year of a great political upheaval. Under Washington and Adams, the Federalists had done a great work in establishing the government and making it strong. . . . But the Federalists . . . had followed policies which did much to give its control and benefits to special classes. Jefferson, a born popular leader, had steadily gathered behind him the great mass of small farmers, mechanics, shopkeepers and other workers. They meant to see that the nation had a people's government, not a government of special interests, and they asserted themselves with tremendous power" (Nevins and Commager, 1966, p. 151). Jefferson "fought for freedom from the British crown, freedom from Church control, freedom from a landed aristocracy, freedom from great inequalities of wealth. He was an egalitarian democrat. He disliked cities, great manufacturing interests, and large banking and trading organizations—they promoted inequality" (*ibid.*, p. 142). His principles and term in office set the tone of strong social reform on behalf of the dispossessed which was to characterize later decades in U.S. history which followed the imperial motive pattern in popular literature (*n* Power > *n* Affiliation). The passion for social reform was later discharged as intense patriotism in the War of 1812.

The second wave of populism began with Andrew Jackson's term of office as President (1828–1836) and continued through the thirties. It too followed a strong imperial frame of mind (1820–1830). Jackson and his crowd of enthusiastic uncultured followers swept the aristocratic Adams and his party out of office in 1828. "Jackson was one of the few Presidents whose heart and soul was completely with the plain people. He sympathized with and believed in them partly because he had always been one of them. He had been born in utter poverty." He had "an intense distrust of Eastern capitalistic organizations . . . it was monstrous that easy living bankers in Philadelphia and New York, should have power to ruin the hard-working people of Tennessee" (Nevins and Commager, 1966, pp. 190–191). He had a "faith in the common man; belief in political equalities; belief in equal economic opportunity; hatred of monopoly, special privilege, and the intricacies of capitalistic finance" (*ibid.*, p. 129). In other words, he stood for and acted on principles of democratic reform, for the people and against the establishment. His views were widely shared. In the words of Nevins and Commager "the thirties were the decade in which manhood suffrage spread throughout most of those states which had hitherto imposed some property restriction . . . Manners were becoming more democratic . . . Life was growing more democratic in many ways. A cheap press was arising . . . Even religion . . . became democratized." The reformers set to work with a passion to fight all authorities or institutions which put impediments in the way of developing the "infinite worthiness of man," in Emerson's words. Once again, reformist zeal was followed by military adventure in the next decade, this time by the Mexican War.

While this was going on in the world of action, motive patterns had shifted, as Figures 9.4 and 9.6 show, back to a balance between strong *n* Power and *n* Affiliation, and the cycle started over again: a heightened imperial motive pattern in the next decade (the 1840's), followed by an even fiercer reformism in the 1850's, which eventually polarized the nation and led to the Civil War in the 1860's. The reform issues on which all energies focused in the 1850's were of course, as noted earlier, freedom for the oppressed Negro slave in the North, and in the South, freedom to live one's own way of life unoppressed by the Northern majority.

Then from 1850–1880 the record shows a period of comparative peace, when *n* Affiliation was very much higher than *n* Power, and a high level of *n* Achievement tended to focus attention on economic matters. But in the 1880's conditions were ripe to set off a new cycle leading to violence: *n* Power and *n* Affiliation came into conjunction, and conflicted; an imperial frame of mind resulted in the 1890's, and once again this led to a tremendous wave of social reform in 1900–1910. Nevins and Commager label the two decades from 1896–1916 the "Age of Reform." "Almost every notable figure in this period, whether in politics, philosophy, scholarship, or literature, derives his fame in part from his connection with the reform movement . . . The heroes of the day were all reformers. Courageously, defiantly, they manned the battlements of democracy and even sallied out to make new conquests. Not since the forties had there been such a ferment in the intellectual world; not since then had reform been so firmly in the saddle" (1966, p. 383). This was the time of the crusade for social justice for the poor, the highpoint of the attempt to rid the country of "demon rum," the establishment of a socialist government which lasted a generation under the La Follettes in Wisconsin. The muckrakers were busy exposing the evils of capitalism in the establishment. This high moral concern, as we have seen, combined with the growing belief that the United States was a world power, made it practically inevitable that we would enter World War II to make the world "safe for democracy."

The cycle of events was the same starting in 1925 and again in 1955. Balanced and conflicting *n* Power and *n* Affiliation in 1925 and 1955 led to an increased imperial concern in the next decades (1930–1940 and 1960–1970); this translated itself more promptly (less lead time) into a passionate reform movement that attempted to do something for the oppressed; and this in turn created a mood which could justify going to war. The only difference is that now the cycle seems foreshortened, since the imperial frame of mind and actions for reform *coincided* in the same decade, whereas earlier there was a longer interval before the reform movements got under way. In 1930–1940 Franklin Roosevelt instituted a far-reaching reform under the New Deal. Like President Jackson, "he had an instinctive faith in the common people," although he himself was a member of the wealthy elite, like Jefferson. He waged war on "powerful reactionary forces" in much the same way as earlier reformers had. In an effort to help the poor who were hard-hit by the depression, he introduced broad-scale programs of relief and spending on public works, and loans for housing. The New Deal introduced legislation to make for permanent reform in banking, water power, farming, labor, social security, and administration of the government. The frame of mind which supported the New Deal concern for social justice also supported our entry into World War II in order to save Europe and the oppressed Jews from the scourge of Nazism.

The style of the Kennedy and Johnson administrations in the 1960's was similar. They too pressed for reforms on behalf of the people, for civil rights, for legislation on behalf of the blacks, for housing and better social security benefits for the poor. They tried to introduce medical care for the aged, and to supply relief to the vast sprawling slums in the cities. The Peace Corps was inaugurated to make American youthful vigor and know-how available to underdeveloped countries everywhere in an effort to lift them out of poverty, disease, and despair.

The striking characteristic about all these instances is their similarity. The themes of American reform movements have always been the same. They aim to fight the establishment and do something for the oppressed—the poor, the blacks, or the women. In six out of six cases, they have been *preceded* by a motive shift which started with *n* Affiliation, and at least moderate *n* Power in balance, and moved on to an imperial frame of mind—an *increased n* Power and decreased *n* Affiliation—apparently a response to the need to do something about one's increased empathy for suffering others.

The paradox of the reform movements is that they have an unintended consequence: they seem to create an action orientation that makes war possible. Before, and more recently during, reformist periods, the need for Power is high, the need for Affiliation is low, and a martial spirit leads to zealous actions to right wrongs on behalf of the oppressed. This atmosphere of righteous action has led to war in too many instances in the history of the United States and England for such consequences to be accidental. The irony, of course, is that the reformers have no intention of starting wars. They are, in fact often pacifists, since pacifism is one other form of protest against traditional right-wing male militarism. Their activities on behalf of reform are usually not closely connected with the wars that follow—the one outstanding exception being the activities on behalf of abolishing slavery which led to the Civil War in the United States. Certainly the New Deal reforms seem superficially unconnected with World War II, except that both actions were taken on behalf of the under dog. Our data suggest that the connection is via the habit of righteous, uncompromising action which the reform movements engender.

Unfortunately this whole line of reasoning only raises questions as to how to interpret the state of the country in the 1970's. In purely statistical terms the Vietnam War is presented in Figure 9.6 as the outcome of the motivation cycle begun in the 1950's; yet even in terms of the speeded-up cycles characteristic of the post-World-War-I period, it seems to have occurred too soon. It can hardly be said to reflect the *outcome* of the zealous reformism of the 1960's, since the reformers were violently opposed to the vietnam War. Thus we must argue either that both the war party and the anti-war party in the 1960's were products of the same reformist spirit—which seems unlikely—or that the Vietnam War is an exception to our general model, reflecting the tag end of the idealism generated in the 1930's which led a whole generation of responsible American statesmen to believe they must intervene to keep the peace and defend the oppressed all over the world. In this case both the Korean War and the Vietnam War represent hangovers of an earlier internationalist reformist spirit, still characteristic of the generation of men who sponsored them. As such they are less exceptions to the model than exceptions generated by our insistence on rigid time sequences.

If the Vietnam War is not the true outcome of the reformist zeal of the 1960's, then we are faced with the awesome probability that it has yet to express itself in some morally justified war in the 1970's. At this writing, it is not difficult to predict the arena in which this war is likely to occur, for the stage is already being set for us to intervene to keep the oppressed Israelis from being wiped out by the Arab nations.

War with the Arab countries can be justified on the score of self-interest, since they can shut off our oil supply; but to run the great risks that such a war would create, the country must be morally prepared to act violently and righteously on behalf of the oppressed— which is precisely what our recent motive cycle and reform movement have prepared us to do.

Are Wars Inevitable?

The picture is alarming. Are we to go on living through cycles of idealism and warfare because of intrinsic motivational connections between these events? Can we do nothing to stop them? One advantage of psychological regularities is that they are not like physical laws in the sense that they "have to" occur. They represent probabilistic statements based on the demonstrated inter-connectedness of psychological events. There is no *necessary* linkage between the events, just a probabilistic one. Note, for example, that in Figure 9.6 the sequences do not automatically recur. There are long periods of comparative quiet; the duration of a given motive pattern is not constant, and it does not *always* produce a given effect. There is room for maneuver.

The first step in getting some control over the sequence of events is to understand the probable linkages. More specifically, we need to understand the possible intrinsic, though paradoxical, linkage between increased devotion, moralistic reform, and later violence. When people repeat the slogan, "Make love not war," they should realize that love for others often sets the process in motion that ends in war. Within the context of Christianity, indeed, some psychologists have long noted that the more devoted Christians are, the more militaristic they are likely to be. Russell (1971), who reviews the numerous empirical studies in support of this finding, observes that "this conclusion is quite paradoxical, since one of the professed aims of the Christian religion has been peace" (1971, p. 26).

Why is it that the more devout a Christian is, the more likely he is to support war and adopt militaristic attitudes? Liberal Christians have regularly tended to accept Gordon Allport's distinction between extrinsic and intrinsic religion, arguing that those who are "really" or intrinsically religious hold attitudes in line with Christian ideals of peaceableness, tolerance for others, and the like. "The extrinsically religious person is he who uses religion to meet his self-serving needs for emotional comfort and salvation. As such, his emphasis will be on the institutionalized or social aspect of religion, not its beliefs" (Russell, 1971, p. 26). Russell points out that the empirical studies do not particularly support this way out of the dilemma, and he goes further. By performing a careful content analysis of the Old Testament and the gospels of the New Testament, he then demonstrates that in these doctrinal sources "love is conditional, so that if one obeys God or accepts Christ, God can forgive past wrongs, but if one continues to defy God or refuses to accept Christ (or even a particular sect's definition of Christ), then one is liable for death and the eternal torment." Orthodox Christian theology is highly intolerant and, in effect, sanctions violence toward any "outgroups" defined as criminal, or heretical, or pagan. "The Fundamentalists and orthodox Christians know their Bible and have attitudes consistent with the Old Testament and the Gospel" (1971, p. 61). Russell argues, in other words, that there is an *intrinsic* connection between increased Christian devotion and violence. So he has come to the same conclusion as we have, based in his case on an analysis of Christian doctrine and in ours on shifts in motivational trends. Increased Christian devotion often leads to warfare in the long run.

As symptomatic of the close association between Christianity and militarism, Russell reminds us of what happened when the Roman emperor Constantine was converted to Christianity. "According to tradition, just before the battle of Milvian Bridge, he saw a vision of a flaming cross with the words 'In Hoc Signo Vinces' ('By this sign you will conquer') written upon it. He fought and won the battle. After converting to Christianity, he continued to make war until he became ruler of the entire Roman empire. Christianity was subsequently accepted as a military religion." In contrast, Russell reports what happened to King Asoka of India who was converted to Buddhism about a thousand years earlier. "As the third in line of military conquerors who created the Mauryan Empire, which covered most of India, he successfully began the conquest of the remaining southern portion of India. At this time, he was converted to Buddhism, which directly taught that the destruction of any living creature was wrong. Then, instead of conquering the rest of India, Asoka gave up conquest, dismantled his army, and devoted his energy to promoting Buddhism—peace, love, and dharma (the moral law)" (Russell, 1971, p. 1).

Is the moral that we should all become Buddhists if we want to avoid destroying one another? Obviously not, if for no other reason than that Buddhism has had no greater success than Christianity in wiping out violence and warfare. The only difference seems to be that Buddhist emperors, after they had completed their conquests, felt guiltier than Christian emperors about having been violent, and spent more of their time and resources trying to make reparations or earn merit by supporting religious institutions. Buddhists are no more exempt than Christians from the motivational regularities that connect increased devotion to violence. Yet there is a clue in the Buddhist prohibition of violence which may help us out of a motivational vicious circle which in the end could destroy mankind. For if we believe that an increase in Christian or any religious devotion leads intrinsically to violence, then to break the cycle we would appear to have to choose between giving up religious devotion and giving up violence.

Here the choice is clear, for we could not give up religious devotion even if we would. In more psychological terms, increases in n Affiliation combined with moderate to high n Power will continue to occur, arising out of natural historical circumstances. Nor would we give up increased devotion, because the increased concern for others that follows from it is an essential ingredient in the civilizing of mankind. So, to prevent Armageddon, we must formally swear off violence as an instrument of collective policy. What the psychological data suggest is that on every church or temple a label should be stuck that reads: "Warning: Christianity (or Judaism, Islam, Buddhism, Hinduism, or Marxism) is dangerous for children and other living things; if you enter here you must renounce violence as an instrument of collective policy." Of course the newer "religions" like Marxism would never consent; they see violence as a necessary means of gaining the good life. It may take a nuclear holocaust to convince them otherwise.

This is exactly the position, as Russell points out, taken by such groups as the Quakers and Anabaptist churches within Christianity, and by similar groups within other major world religions. It is as if, recognizing the dangers of increased religious devotion, they attempted to ward them off in advance by taking the position that they would *never* allow their increased zeal to lead them into collective violence. Such groups typically adopt theological views to support their position. They believe that God is in man, or that the "central part of the human self was identical with God" (Russell, p. 65). Or, as Jesus of Nazareth put it, "I and my father are one." "He who believeth in me, believeth not in me, but in Him who sent me." This belief in the mystical union of man and God makes the concept of a separate God who punishes wrongdoing difficult to accept. "It is contrary to logic and psychological feeling for God to utterly reject and punish Himself, as He would do if He were an essential part of man" (Russell, p. 65). In terms of our model of the evolution of the power drive, such pacifist groups in progressing from Stage I to II to III to IV, do not end by conceiving of themselves as permanently separated from an authority figure (God) or a power outside themselves, but stress continuous unification with Him as they mature. Thus they never consider themselves to have separated from Him as do many people within the Judaic religions, who feel that He can judge them and that they, with His help, can judge and punish others in the name of religion and the moral law. The divinity in all human beings or indeed all living things makes violence against them violence against God and the union with God.

Whatever the justification for their beliefs, they have hit on a formula that holds promise for the future of mankind. They have demonstrated that the only safe Christian (or religious devotee of any kind) is a pacifist.

ACTIVITIES QUESTIONS ASKED FOR CHAPTER 2 STUDY

Code _____

Part I   Background and Personal History Survey

1.   Your name _____   Date _____

2.   Date of birth: Month _____ Day _____ Year _____

3.   Sex: Male _____   Female _____

4.   Height (estimate to nearest half inch) _____

5.   Weight (estimate to nearest pound)   _____

6.   Circle the highest year of school you have completed

      6 7 8 9 10 11 12 | 13 14 15 16 | 17 18 19 20 or more
      elem   high   college or   graduate or pro-
      school   school   special school   fessional school

7.   List all your brothers and sisters according to age and indicate their
    sex. Start with the oldest. Include yourself.

          Age   Sex (M or F)

    1. _____   _____

    2. _____   _____

    3. _____   _____

    4. _____   _____

    5. _____   _____

    6. _____   _____

    7. _____   _____

8.   What nationality did most of your family (grandparents, etc.) come from?
    (Like Irish, Polish, German, etc.) _____

9.   What is your main religious background? Protestant _____ Catholic _____
    Jewish _____ Other _____

10. What did your parents consider the three most important things to teach you?

    1. _____

    2. _____

    3. _____

11. What is (was) your father's occupation? _____

12. Circle the highest year of school he completed

    6 7 8 9 10 11 12 | 13 14 15 16 | 17 18 19 20 or more

    elem   high school   college or   graduate or pro-
    school   special school   fessional school

13. What is (was) your mother's occupation? _____

14. Circle the highest year of school she completed

    6 7 8 9 10 11 12 13 14 15 16 17 18 19 20 or more

    elem   high school   college or   graduate or pro-
    school   special school   fessional school

15. Whom do you resemble most (who are you most like)?

    Mother _____ Father _____

16. In regard to the parent whom you most resemble, try and state briefly how you resemble him or her.

    _____

    _____

    _____

17. Have you or your mother or father had any of the following?
    If yes, indicate who: self, mother, or father.

	Yes	No	Who (self, mother, father)
Epilepsy	___	___	_____
Problem drinking	___	___	_____
Diabetes	___	___	_____
Heart trouble	___	___	_____
Hospitalized in a mental institution	___	___	_____
Hospitalized or treated for alcoholism	___	___	_____

-2-

Were your parents separated or divorced?   Yes _____   No _____
    If yes, how old were you? _____   If you were a child, who did
    you then live with? _____

18. Please list three occupations you have been in, would like to be in,
     or would strongly consider. If you are currently working, list that
     occupation first.   Currently working? Yes _____ No _____

_____

_____

_____

19. Are you married or "living with" someone of the opposite sex? Yes _____
     No _____ . How many years have you been married to or living with this
     person? _____ . Have you ever been divorced? Yes ___ No ___

Part II   Personal habits

Below is a list of habits. Please check the column that describes how much
you are involved in each type of habit. Since some of these are shared, we
are asking you at the outset to answer for both yourself and your spouse.
By "spouse" we mean your husband or wife or person you are living with as
husband or wife. If you are not married or living with someone, just answer
for yourself.

		Have never done	Have done occasion- ally	Have done often	Do regularly
1.	Physical fitness exercises (push-ups, jogging, etc.)	You ‾‾‾	‾‾‾	‾‾‾	‾‾‾
		Spouse ‾‾‾	‾‾‾	‾‾‾	‾‾‾
2.	Yoga or meditation practices	You ‾‾‾	‾‾‾	‾‾‾	‾‾‾
		Spouse ‾‾‾	‾‾‾	‾‾‾	‾‾‾
3.	Prayer	You ‾‾‾	‾‾‾	‾‾‾	‾‾‾
		Spouse ‾‾‾	‾‾‾	‾‾‾	‾‾‾
4.	Dieting	You ‾‾‾	‾‾‾	‾‾‾	‾‾‾
		Spouse ‾‾‾	‾‾‾	‾‾‾	‾‾‾

5. On the average, how often do you or your spouse make bets (with anybody
    about anything) of $1 or more?

You	Your spouse	
‾‾‾	‾‾‾	Twice a week or more often
‾‾‾	‾‾‾	About once a week
‾‾‾	‾‾‾	About once a month
‾‾‾	‾‾‾	About once a year
‾‾‾	‾‾‾	Never

6. Assume a typical situation where you might be drinking <u>beer</u>. How many cans
    would you generally drink? (check below). Now assume a typical situation
    in which your spouse might be drinking <u>beer</u>. How many cans would he or she
    generally drink? (check under "spouse")

<u>You</u>		<u>Spouse</u>
‾‾‾ 9 or more cans		‾‾‾ 9 or more cans
‾‾‾ 6-8 cans		‾‾‾ 6-8 cans
‾‾‾ 3-5 cans		‾‾‾ 3-5 cans
‾‾‾ 1-2 cans		‾‾‾ 1-2 cans
‾‾‾ less than 1 can		‾‾‾ less than 1 can
‾‾‾ don't drink beer		‾‾‾ don't drink beer

-4-

7. How often during the past year have you been in a situation where you were drinking beer? How often during the past year has your spouse been in a situation where he or she was drinking beer?

You	Spouse
_____ 4 or more times a week	_____ 4 or more times a week
_____ 2-3 times a week	_____ 2-3 times a week
_____ 2-4 times a month	_____ 2-4 times a month
_____ 6-12 times a year	_____ 6-12 times a year
_____ 1-5 times a year	_____ 1-5 times a year
_____ never	_____ never

8. Now assume a typical situation where you might be drinking <u>wine</u>. How many wine glasses of wine would you usually drink? (check below). Now assume a typical situation where your spouse might be drinking wine. How many wine glasses of wine would he or she usually drink? (check under "spouse").

You	Spouse
_____ 9 or more glasses	_____ 9 or more glasses
_____ 6-8 glasses	_____ 6-8 glasses
_____ 3-5 glasses	_____ 3-5 glasses
_____ 1-2 glasses	_____ 1-2 glasses
_____ less than one glass	_____ less than one glass
_____ don't drink wine	_____ doesn't drink wine

9. How often during the past year have you been in a situation where you were drinking wine? (check below). How often during the past year has your spouse been in a situation where he or she was drinking wine? (Check under "spouse").

You	Spouse
_____ 4 or more times a week	_____ 4 or more times a week
_____ 2-3 times a week	_____ 2-3 times a week
_____ 2-4 times a month	_____ 2-4 times a month
_____ 6-12 times a year	_____ 6-12 times a year
_____ 1-5 times a year	_____ 1-5 times a year
_____ never	_____ never

10. Assume a typical situation where you might be drinking <u>hard liquor</u>.
    How many drinks would you generally have? (check below). Assume a
    typical situation where your spouse might be drinking hard liquor.
    How many drinks would he or she generally have? (check under "spouse").

    <u>You</u>   <u>Spouse</u>

    _____9 or more drinks   _____9 or more drinks

    _____6-8 drinks   _____6-8 drinks

    _____3-5 drinks   _____3-5 drinks

    _____1-2 drinks   _____1-2 drinks

    _____less than one drink   _____less than one drink

    _____don't drink hard liquor   _____doesn't drink hard liquor

11. How often during the past year have you been in a situation where you
    were drinking hard liquor (check below). How often during the past
    year has your spouse been in a situation where he or she was drinking
    hard liquor? (check under "spouse").

    <u>You</u>   <u>Spouse</u>

    _____4 or more times a week   _____4 or more times a week

    _____2-3 times a week   _____2-3 times a week

    _____2-4 times a month   _____2-4 times a month

    _____6-12 times a year   _____6-12 times a year

    _____1-5 times a year   _____1-5 times a year

    _____never   _____never

12. People drink wine, beer, whiskey, or other liquor for different reasons.
    Here are some statements people have made about why they drink. How
    important would you say each reason is to <u>you</u> for drinking? How important
    would you say each reason is to <u>your spouse</u> for drinking?

                        Circle whichever applies: +2 very important
                                                      +1 fairly important
                                                       0 not at all important

    <u>You</u>   Your Spouse
    +2 +1 0   I drink because it helps me to relax.   +2 +1 0

    +2 +1 0   A drink helps cheer me up when I'm in   +2 +1 0
                 a bad mood.

    +2 +1 0   I drink to be sociable.   +2 +1 0

    +2 +1 0   I drink when I want to forget everything   +2 +1 0

    +2 +1 0   I drink to celebrate special occasions   +2 +1 0

    +2 +1 0   A drink helps me forget my worries.   +2 +1 0

    +2 +1 0   I accept a drink because it is the polite   +2 +1 0
                 thing to do in certain situations.

    +2 +1 0   I drink because I need it when I am tense   +2 +1 0
                 and nervous.

13. Below are some reactions people have to drinking. Please check these as they occur to you and your spouse.

a. How often do you or your spouse awaken the next day not able to remember some of the things you had done while drinking?

You	Spouse
_____never	_____never
_____1-3 times during the year	_____1-3 times during the year
_____4-12 times during the year	_____4-12 times during the year
_____once or twice a month	_____once or twice a month
_____once a week or more	_____once a week or more

b. How often do you intend to have just a few drinks but end up drunk or not entirely in control of what you are doing? How often does this occur to your spouse?

You	Spouse
_____never	_____never
_____1-3 times during the year	_____1-3 times during the year
_____4-12 times during the year	_____4-12 times during the year
_____once or twice a month	_____once or twice a month
_____once a week or more	_____once a week or more

c. Some people worry or feel badly about their drinking, even though they may not be heavy drinkers. How much would you say you worry or feel badly about your drinking? How much would you say your spouse worries or feels badly about his or her drinking?

You	Spouse
_____never	_____never
_____1-3 times during the year	_____1-3 times during the year
_____4-12 times during the year	_____4-12 times during the year
_____once or twice a month	_____once or twice a month
_____once a week or more	_____once a week or more

14. On an average day, how many regular meals do you have? _____
In addition to these meals, how many snacks do you have on an average day? _____.

15. How often do you drink each of the following beverages, <u>in addition to meals?</u> (Please check for each beverage).

	more than once a day (indicate how many times)	once a day	4-5 times a week	1-3 times a week	less often, rarely, never
coffee	____( )	____	____	____	____
tea	____( )	____	____	____	____
soft drinks	____( )	____	____	____	____
milk	____( )	____	____	____	____
juice	____( )	____	____	____	____

16. Do you smoke? Yes _____ No _____ If Yes, what?

_____cigarettes---How many per day? _____

_____cigars-------How many per day? _____

_____pipes--------How many pipefuls per day? _____

17. Before you go to bed, which of the following things do you do? (Check each one that you do).

_____eat

_____take a walk

_____smoke

_____read

_____listen to radio or record player

_____watch TV

_____take a bath

_____take a shower

_____pray or read the Bible

_____empty the pockets of your clothing

_____hang up clothing

_____brush teeth

_____wash up

_____lock the door

_____turn out the lights

_____turn on a night light

_____defecate

_____urinate

_____open a window

_____take a sleeping or other pill

_____drink something

_____other: _____

_____

<u>For those of you who are married or living with someone: a chance to earn $10.</u>

There is another study that you can take part in, which you may find fun and interesting. It would involve both you and your husband or wife (or person you are living with) playing a game together. This game is an adaptation for adults of a child's game, and we are interested in seeing how couples play this game together. It would take about two hours of your time, and can be scheduled at your convenience (morning, afternoon, or evening). We are offering $10 per couple, if you volunteer and are selected to participate.

If you are interested, check here: Yes _____ No _____ Maybe _____

Comments _____

If you are interested, please provide the following information on your spouse or person you are living with:

Name_____

Date of birth: Month _____ Day _____ Year _____

Occupation _____

What is his or her main religious preference? Catholic _____ Protestant _____
Jewish _____ Other _____.

What one nationality did most of his or her family come from? _____

Circle the highest year of school he or she completed

6 7 8 9 10 11 12 | 13 14 15 16 | 17 18 19 20 or more
elem   high school   college or   graduate or
school   special school   professional school

Has this person, or his or her mother or father, had any of the following?
If yes, please indicate who: spouse, mother, father.

	Yes	No	Who (spouse, mother, father)
Epilepsy	_____	_____	_____
Problem drinking	_____	_____	_____
Diabetes	_____	_____	_____
Heart Trouble	_____	_____	_____
Hospitalized in a mental institution	_____	_____	_____
Hospitalized or treated for alcoholism	_____	_____	_____

Were his or her parents separated or divorced? Yes _____ No _____. If yes, how old was she or he? _____. If he or she was a child, who did he or she live with? _____.

PLEASE HAND THIS SECTION IN WHEN YOU FINISH AND YOU WILL BE GIVEN ANOTHER QUESTIONNAIRE.

Part III   Activities, attitudes and feelings

1.   In a typical conversation with friends, do you often find yourself:
      (please check as appropriate as many as apply)

      _____talking less than others

      _____talking more than others

      _____interrupting to say something

      _____talking louder than others

      _____in an argument or heated debate

2.   At a party or social gathering, do you: (please check as appropriate as
      many as apply)

      _____tend to spend most of your time with one person whom you already
              know well

      _____tend to try to meet new people

      _____tend to spend most of your time talking with people of your same sex

      _____tend to spend most of your time talking with people of the opposite sex

3.   Do you find that your work is: (please check one)

      _____often a distraction from things that you would rather be doing

      _____boring and tedious

      _____often a source of enjoyment

4.   Please list as exactly as you can, as many of the clothes that you wore
      the day before yesterday as you can remember.

5.   Regarding members of the opposite sex, do you think it is most enjoyable to:
      (please check one) If you are married, answer the way you would have
      answered before you were married.

      _____have a single stable relationship

      _____have one main relationship, with freedom for others

      _____have several relationships

6.   What organizations do you now belong to? (Include religious or social groups, political groups, etc.) Have you been an officer in any of these organizations?

        Organization   Offices held, if any

       _____   _____

       _____   _____

       _____   _____

       _____   _____

       _____   _____

       _____   _____

7.   Have you ever been involved in a traffic accident as a driver?

      _____ Yes. _____ No.   If yes, how many times? _____

8a. Within the last year, how often have you been in violent physical fights?

      _____ Never. _____ Once or twice. _____ A number of times. _____Frequently.

b.   Within the last year, how often have you been in strong verbal arguments (that did not turn into physical fights)?

      _____ Never. _____ Several times. _____Two to three times a week.

      _____ Almost every day. _____ More than once a day.

9.   Below is a list of various behaviors or actions. For each one, please check the appropriate column.

	have done often	have done once or twice	haven't but would like to do	never considered doing
(a) Yelled at someone in traffic	____	_____	_____	_____
(b) Made hostile remarks to store-keepers, clerks, or the like	____	_____	_____	_____
(c) Walked off during a social occasion, leaving your spouse standing there	____	_____	_____	_____

		have done often	have done once or twice	haven't but would like to do	never considered doing
(d)	Threw things around the room (books, etc.)	___	___	___	___
(e)	Torn up books, course notes, the telephone directory	___	___	___	___
(f)	Screamed or swore at someone because they got on your nerves	___	___	___	___
(g)	Destroyed furniture or glassware	___	___	___	___
(h)	Taken a sign from a public place	___	___	___	___
(i)	Not paid a bill because you were mad at the business firm (telephone, light, dept. stores, etc.)	___	___	___	___
(j)	Deliberately slammed a door hard	___	___	___	___

10.

Please check the answer that applies to you	Nearly all the time	Pretty often	Not very Much	Never
Do you ever have any trouble getting to sleep or staying asleep?	___	___	___	___
Do you have loss of appetite?	___	___	___	___
Do you find it difficult to get up in the morning?	___	___	___	___

Have there ever been times when you couldn't take care of things because you just couldn't get going?	Many times	Some-times	Hardly ever	Never
	___	___	___	___

11. What aspect of religion appeals to you most? Rank order from:
    1 = Appeals most   to   4 = Appeals least

    _____ The way it helps people lead good clean ethical personal lives
    rather than messy or selfish lives

    _____ Its inspirational power, its ability to provide an important
    source of strength to deal with life

    _____ The way it encourages people to go out and change the world
    for the better, fight injustice, help the oppressed

    _____ The way it teaches charity and enables people to help others
    less fortunate than themselves

12. How do you feel about travelling alone in new places?

    _____ Have done it often, enjoy it very much

    _____ Have done it a number of times, sometimes enjoy it

    _____ Have done it a few times, don't enjoy it much

    _____ Have hardly ever done it, or never, because I know I wouldn't
    enjoy it

13. Do you like to try new things to eat that you have never eaten before?

    _____ Have done it often, enjoy it very much

    _____ Have done it a number of times, sometimes enjoy it

    _____ Have done it a few times, don't enjoy it much

    _____ Have hardly ever done it, or never, because I know I wouldn't
    enjoy it

14. Check any of the following experiences that you feel you have
    definitely had.

    _____ A personal religious experience like a feeling of the presence of God

    _____ A strong feeling of being "at one with nature" at a particular moment

    _____ An extra-sensory experience like communication from someone not
    present, dead, etc.

    _____ Being healed, feeling definitely better physically as the result of
    being helped by some spiritual or religious healer

-4-

15. Do you really like to make things (such as special recipes, gadgets, fix up motors, make clothes, etc)? _____Yes _____ No   If Yes, what have you done in this line?

_____

_____

_____

_____

16. Do you play any of the following games? If so, how often?

	Never or once in a great while	Several times a year	Several times a month	Once a week or more
Bridge or other such card games	____	____	____	____
Checkers or chess	____	____	____	____
Bowling	____	____	____	____
Tennis	____	____	____	____
Golf	____	____	____	____

17. Do you collect any objects (shells, stamps, rare books, china, neckties, etc.) now or have you previously? _____Yes _____ No   If Yes, list any kinds of things you collected.

_____

_____

_____

18. Have you loaned anything (like your car, household equipment, clothes) to anyone recently (in the last month)? _____Yes _____No   If Yes, what things?

_____

_____

_____

Do you generally loan things readily? _____Yes   No_____

19.   How many credit cards do you have with you right now? _____

20.   What are your most precious possessions? List as many as are really
      important to you.

      _____   _____

      _____   _____

      _____   _____

      _____   _____

      _____   _____

      _____   _____

21.   Please describe briefly below three incidents that you have found
      personally quite distressing in your life.

      a.   _____

           _____

           _____

           _____

      b.   _____

           _____

           _____

      c.   _____

           _____

           _____

           _____

22. How often do you volunteer to look after kids, either because you like to or don't mind and know it would help someone else? If you have kids of your own, answer in terms of how often you really like looking after them as opposed to have to look after them.

    _____Very often do voluntarily or like to

    _____Many times do voluntarily or like to

    _____Occasionally do voluntarily or like to

    _____Hardly ever do voluntarily or like to

    _____Never do voluntarily or like to

23. Most people have striking or recurrent dreams of some sort. Please try to recall and describe two of your dreams that were unusual or that you have often.

Dream 1 _____

_____

_____

_____

_____

_____

Dream 2 _____

_____

_____

_____

_____

_____

24. How do you like children at different ages?

Like a lot	Some	Not Much	Dis- like			
+3	+2	+1	-1	-2	-3	When they are babies, little and helpless, nice to hold, feed, and make happy
+3	+2	+1	-1	-2	-3	When they are out of the baby stage, able to do things for themselves, look after their own things, learn in school, etc.
+3	+2	+1	-1	-2	-3	When they are teenagers, active, energetic, exploring new skills, emotions, the whole world in front of them to conquer
+3	+2	+1	-1	-2	-3	When they are young adults, just married and learning to be responsible for each other, <u>their</u> kids, etc.

25. If you are having friends in for dinner, what part of it do you enjoy the most? Rank order: 1 = most   to   4 = least

    _____ Thinking about and preparing food for all to enjoy

    _____ Eating a really good meal, especially prepared

    _____ Setting the table or cleaning up afterwards

    _____ The feeling of togetherness that often goes with such a dinner

26. What magazines do you read or look at regularly?

    _____   _____

    _____   _____

    _____   _____

    _____   _____

27. How often do you do the following things? Please check each item either "very often", "occasionally", "rarely", or "never".

a) Go back to the car after you've parked it to make sure you have:	Very often	Occasion-ally	Rarely	Never
1. Turned off the lights	___	___	___	___
2. Turned off the radio	___	___	___	___
3 Locked the doors	___	___	___	___
4. Put the brake on or left it in gear	___	___	___	___
5. Don't drive _____				

b) Go back to the house or
    apartment or room to make   Very   Occasion-
    sure you have: often   ally   Rarely   Never

    1. Turned off the faucets   ____   ____   ____   ____

    2. Locked the doors   ____   ____   ____   ____

    3. Turned off or on
        the lights   ____   ____   ____   ____

    4. Closed or opened the
        windows   ____   ____   ____   ____

28. People have different preferences about where to go for personal help if
     they need it. If you felt that you wanted help, circle how likely you would
     be to go to each of the following. If you are currently consulting any of
     these, check how likely you would be to go again to such a person on another
     occasion.

	Very Unlikely		Maybe		Very Likely	
Minister, priest, rabbi	1 2 3	4 5	6 7	8 9 10		
Consciousness-raising group	1 2 3	4 5	6 7	8 9 10		
Psychiatrist	1 2 3	4 5	6 7	8 9 10		
Parents or relation	1 2 3	4 5	6 7	8 9 10		
A spiritual or holy person (guru, monk, mystic, etc.)	1 2 3	4 5	6 7	8 9 10		
Action therapy (Gestalt, primal scream, bio-energetics, rolfing, dance therapy, etc.)	1 2 3	4 5	6 7	8 9 10		
Friends	1 2 3	4 5	6 7	8 9 10		

29. If someone gave you $10,000, what would you do with it? Please describe
     at least three alternatives.

_____

_____

_____

_____

_____

_____

_____

30. Think for a moment of people in your life who might have been a real
     inspiration to you--people whom you really looked up to. Put their initials
     down as you think of them. They could be related to you or not.

                                            How strong was their influence?
                                            1 = not very strong; 2 = fairly
                                            strong; 3 = very strong, they
     Person's initials   Sex   made a big difference in my life.

     _____   __   _____

     _____   __   _____

     _____   __   _____

     _____   __   _____

     _____   __   _____

31. Below is a list of items. Read each item, and then indicate the extent to
     which you have talked about that item with each person (the column headings)
     --that is, the extent to which you have made yourself known to that person.
     Use the rating scale below to describe the extent that you have talked about
     each item with each person.

     Rating Scale

        0 = Have told the other person nothing about this aspect of me.

        1 = Have talked in general terms about this item. The other person has
            only a general idea about this aspect of me.

        2 = Have talked in full and complete detail about this item to the other
            person. He/she knows me fully in this respect, and could describe
            me accurately.

        X = Have lied or misrepresented myself to the other person, so that he/she
            has a false picture of me.

Item	Father	Mother	Male friend other than husband	Female friend other than wife	Spouse
(a) What I find to be the worst pressures and strains in my work	____	____	____	____	____
(b) The kinds of things that make me especially proud of myself, elated, full of self-esteem or self-respect	____	____	____	____	____

	Father	Mother	Male friend other than husband	Female friend other than wife	Spouse
(c) Whether or not I now have any health problems--e.g., trouble with sleep, digestion, female complaints, heart condition, allergies, piles, etc.	_____	_____	_____	_____	_____
(d) All of my present sources of income--wages, fees, allowance, dividends, etc.	_____	_____	_____	_____	_____
(e) The facts of my present sex life--including knowledge of how I get sexual gratification; any problems that I might have; with whom (if anybody) I have relations	_____	_____	_____	_____	_____
(f) What feelings, if any, that I have trouble expressing or controlling	_____	_____	_____	_____	_____
(g) Whether or not I now make special effort to keep fit, healthy, and attractive (e.g., calisthenics, diet, etc.)	_____	_____	_____	_____	_____

32.　How do you feel about donating parts of your body (like an eye or a kidney) to others after you are dead?

　　_____ I definitely want to, have already made arrangements

　　_____ I definitely want to, and plan to make arrangements

　　_____ I would like to, but feel uneasy about it, and doubt if I will

　　_____ I definitely do not plan to do it

33.　Below are a number of images or metaphors which might be employed by a poet or writer to symbolize the idea of death. Read them over carefully. Then rank them for their capacity to evoke for you an effective image of death. How appropriate do you feel each image is for death? Rank the most effective 1, and the least effective 8, etc. Please rank every metaphor.

a satanic wrestler	_____	a compassionate mother	_____
an infinite ocean	_____	a hangman with bloody hands	_____
silent birds	_____	a crumbling tower	_____
a grinning butcher	_____		

34.   Please indicate the extent to which you agree or disagree with the following
       statements by circling the appropriate number opposite each statment:

	Strongly Disagree	Disagree	Agree	Strongly Agree
	- 2	- 1	+ 1	+ 2

-2 -1 +1 +2   1.   My fantasies are a most important part of my life.

-2 -1 +1 +2   2.   I have several times had a feeling of being one with the
                       external world as a whole which someone described as "an
                       oceanic sensation of eternity."

-2 -1 +1 +2   3.   I find I am able to laugh a little at the mistakes I've
                       made in life.

-2 -1 +1 +2   4.   It is very important for me to understand the underlying
                       motives of other people.

-2 -1 +1 +2   5.   I really enjoy feeling part of an organization like my
                       church or where I work because it makes me feel more
                       useful or more significant.

-2 -1 +1 +2   6.   Knowing the truth is more important to me than acting
                       effectively.

-2 -1 +1 +2   7.   The rich internal world of ideals, or sensitive feelings,
                       reverie, of self-knowledge is man's true home.

-2 -1 +1 +2   8.   Higher authority is really essential for guiding a person
                       in knowing what he should do.

-2 -1 +1 +2   10.   I can't feel right about something I did until I understand
                       why I did it.

-2 -1 +1 +2   11.   I like to associate with people who take life emotionally.

-2 -1 +1 +2   12.   People regard me as a very responsible person. I volunteer
                       for jobs that need doing in an organization and see they
                       are properly done.

-2 -1 +1 +2   13.   I often think about and try to understand my own dreams
                       and fantasies.

-2 -1 +1 +2   14.   Sometimes I think of natural objects as possessing human
                       qualities.

-2 -1 +1 +2   15.   Human problems will be solved by reason rather than by
                       goodwill.

-2 -1 +1 +2   16.   I can really get in a panic about not understanding something
                       profound that I think others understand.

Thank you very much for your time. You have been a great help. If there's any
question you feel you couldn't or didn't answer adequately, please go back and
redo it or mark it with an X so that we can omit your answers.

APPENDIX 1B

PICTURES AND FORMAT USED TO COLLECT STORIES TO ASSESS MOTIVES AND MATURITY FOR CHAPTER 2 STUDY

EXERCISE OF IMAGINATION

Name (Mr/Mrs/Miss)_____Date_____

          Last   First

PLEASE READ THE FOLLOWING INSTRUCTIONS CAREFULLY

An important personal asset is imagination. This test
gives you an opportunity to use your imagination, to show how
you can create ideas and situations by yourself. In other
words, instead of presenting you with answers already made up,
from which you have to pick one, it gives you the chance to
show how you can think things on your own.

On the following pages, you are to make up and write out
a brief, imaginative story for each of the four pictures. You
will have about five minutes for each story. There is one
page for each story (in any case, please do not write more
than about 150 words per story.)

To help you cover all the elements of a story plot in the
time allowed, you will find these questions repeated at the
top of each page:

1. What is happening? Who are the people?
2. What has led up to this situation? That is, what
   has happened in the past?
3. What is being thought: What is wanted? By whom?
4. What will happen? What will be done?

Please remember that the questions are only guides for your
thinking; you need not answer each specifically. That is,
your story should be continuous and not just a set of answers
to these questions.

There are no "right" or "wrong" stories. In fact, any
kind of story is quite all right. You have a chance to show
how quickly you can imagine and write a story on your own.

Try to make your stories interesting and dramatic. Show
that you have an understanding of people and can make up stories
about human situations. Don't just describe the pictures,
but write stories about them.

Now, turn the page, look at the picture briefly, then
turn the page again and write the story suggested to you by
the picture. Don't take more than 5 minutes. Then turn the
page, look at the next picture briefly, write out the story
it suggests, and so on through the booklet.

Total time for the four stories: 20 minutes.

PLEASE PRINT YOUR STORIES

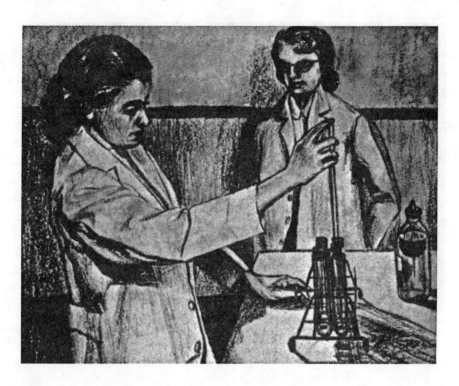

APPENDIX 2

ADDITIONAL TABLES FOR CHAPTER 2

**Appendix Table 2.1—Descriptive characteristics of
samples of men and women tested**

	Men	Women
N	85	115
Age, mean	34.5	36.5
S.D.	8.7	7.9
Marital status, % married	69%	97%
Father's occupation, % blue collar	34%	38%
% mothers who worked	36%	48%
Own education, mean years	15.9	14.6
% only child	18%	15%

**Appendix Table 2.2—Comparison of Maturity Stage and n Power scores for men
and women**

	MEN			WOMEN		
	Stage Score	Modal at Stage*	n Power Score	Stage Score	Modal at Stage*	n Power Score
Stage I mean	.78	16%	3.91	1.17	30%	4.23
SD	.95		3.99	1.12		3.81
Stage II mean	1.11	17%	7.08	1.19	26%	6.46
SD	.85		2.93	1.10		4.48
Stage III mean	.95	19%	9.54	.85	16%	6.38
SD	1.25		3.20	1.10		3.14
Stage IV mean	1.87	48%	6.15	1.64	27%	2.60
SD	1.43		3.61	1.20		2.48
Over all mean			6.06			4.48
SD			3.86			3.85
Number with a mode	69			99		
Number without a mode	16			16		

*Highest score for any of the four stages, if at least two. Ties are decided in favor of the lower stage score.

Appendix Table 2.3–Intercorrelations of Maturity Stage and motive scores (for 85 men above the diagonal, and 115 women below)

	Stage I	Stage II	Stage III	Stage IV	n Power	n Affiliation	Activity Inhibition
Stage I	—	.00	− .22*	.09	− .05	.13	.07
Stage II	.10	—	.28**	− .06	.18	.13	.03
Stage III	− .22*	.03	—	− .08	.49**	− .04	.15
Stage IV	.06	− .12	− .04	—	.19	.16	− .21
n Power	.03	.34*	.44***	− .11	—	− .11	.08
n Affiliation	.22*	.03	− .35***	.02	− .32*	—	.01
Activity Inhibition	.14	.19*	.25**	.00	.26**	− .02	—

*p < .05, **p < .01, ***p < .001

Appendix Table 2.4—Illustrations of how modes of handling aggression may be alternative expressions of n Power

	Individuals	Aggressive acts committed		
		X Haven't but would like to	Y Have Committed	Maximum Score on X or Y
High in n Power				
	A	0	3	3
	B	3	1	3
	C	0	3	3
	D	3	1	3
	E	3	0	3
	F	0 Mean = 1.5	3 Mean = 1.8	3 Mean = 3.00
Low in n Power				
	G	1	1	1
	H	1	1	1
	I	2	1	2
	J	0	2	2
	K	2	1	2
	L	0 Mean = 1.0	1 Mean = 1.2	1 Mean = 1.50
Difference		.5	.6	1.50

APPENDIX 3

ADDITIONAL TABLES FOR CHAPTER 8

Appendix Table 8.1 —Standard scores for motivational variables from stories in children's readers in various countries in 1925

	n Achievement	n Affiliation	n Power	Activity Inhibition
Argentina	.47	.21	.43	− .35
Australia	1.77	− .09	1.24	1.63
Austria	.07	− .30	1.37	− .65
Belgium	− .77	.51	− .59	− .05
Canada	1.58	1.00	.10	− .09
China[a]	− .90	− 2.02	1.53	− 1.17
Chile	− .32	− .94	2.00	− 1.34
Denmark	.66	.67	1.27	2.45
England	.79	1.00	.10	.42
Finland	− .38	− .70	1.53	− .48
France	− .97	.21	1.35	.42
Germany	− .19	− .42	.49	.42
Greece	− 1.56	1.75	− .69	.38
Hungary	.32	− 1.67	.88	.25
Ireland	2.29	.25	.49	.21
Netherlands	− 1.68	.58	− 1.37	− 1.08
New Zealand	− .06	.16	− 1.60	− .22
Norway	− .26	− 1.62	− .23	− 1.13
Spain	− .97	− 1.33	1.06	− 1.30
Sweden	.92	− .40	− .87	− 1.17
Union of S. Africa	− .64	1.02	− .98	1.15
USSR	− .78	− 1.42	1.16	1.41
U.S.	.52	.91	− .39	1.07
Uruguay	− .06	− 1.00	− .07	− .78
Mean raw score				44.17
Standard deviation				23.23

Table 8.2–Standard scores for motivational variables from stories in children's readers around 1950

Algeria	− 1.91	2.04	− .31	− .22
Argentina	1.84	− .09	.40	.27
Australia	.51	− .19	− 1.03	− .80
Austria	− .19	− 1.18	− 1.27	.56
Belgium	− 2.09	.40	.40	− 1.63
Bulgaria	.32	− .19	.00	.36
Canada	.39	.67	.39	− .61
China[a]	.32	− .55	3.27	.12
China-Taiwan[a]	− .25	− 1.91	.57	− 1.19
Chile	− 1.08	1.83	− .23	− .90
Denmark	− 1.27	− .09	.10	.85
England	− .44	1.28	.10	1.48
Finland	− .64	.81	.73	− 1.72
France	.51	− .30	− 1.16	− 1.29
Germany	.19	− .91	.57	1.24
Greece	.39	.58	− .51	.36
Hungary	− .25	− .19	− 1.17	− 1.04
India	.95	− .19	.39	.32
Iraq	− .07	− 1.62	3.39	.12
Iran	− 1.08	− 2.43	.23	− 1.04
Ireland	.39	− .75	− .31	.02
Israel	.44	1.91	− 1.76	1.09
Italy	− .89	1.43	.40	− .51
Japan	− .95	.67	− .20	.90
Lebanon	.95	.51	.39	1.73
Mexico	− .57	.62	1.20	− .51
Netherlands	− .69	.67	− .69	− 1.04
New Zealand	.07	− .84	1.73	− 1.34
Norway	− .39	.25	− 1.60	− .27
Pakistan	.39	− 1.00	.57	1.73
Poland	− 1.52	.21	− 1.17	.56
Portugal	.13	.72	− 1.17	− 1.38
Spain	.44	− 1.51	1.65	− .51
Sweden	− .51	.32	− .23	− .61
Switzerland[b]	− 1.92	− .57	.41	.51
Syria	.13	.21	− .87	− .46
Tunisia	.19	1.32	− .98	− .07
Turkey	2.16	− 1.60	− .88	.75
Union of S. Africa	.44	− .42	.10	− .02
USSR	.13	− .91	.29	2.50
U.S.	.32	.42	.29	1.05
Uruguay	− .19	.51	− .07	.61
Mean raw score				45.49
Standard deviation				20.58

Source: McClelland (1961), _The achieving society_
a. From MClelland (1963a).
b. Based on German and French readers combined in a ratio of 2 to 1.

CODING HISTORICAL
SOURCE MATERIALS
FOR MOTIVATIONAL VARIABLES

THE NECESSITY for coding samples of literary materials written at different times in order to carry out the historical studies in Chapter 9 once again raised all the questions about the validity and reliability of this methodological approach. When I had used it before in *The achieving society* in predicting with some success the rates of economic growth in English history from prior *n* Achievement levels in popular literature, I was very much excited by the results. I wrote a paper published in 1958 and entitled, "The use of measures of human motivation in the study of society," in which I pointed out that coding historical documents for motivational variables provided a method of estimating the strength of various motivational forces at critical periods in history, thus enabling historians to explain better subsequent events. Historians generally have had to rely for such explanations on external events—wars, famines, natural disasters, increasing standards of living, and the like. Yet most historians would agree with Toynbee that it seems impossible to predict just how a people will in fact react to some important external event. There is an unknown factor, "the reaction of the actors to the ordeal when it actually comes. These psychological momenta, which are inherently impossible to weigh and measure, and therefore to estimate scientifically in advance, are the very forces which actually decide the issue when the encounter taskes place" (Toynbee, 1947, p. 68).

I took some delight in pointing out that the method I was proposing could in fact do precisely what Toynbee had said could not be done—measure scientifically and estimate in advance the motivational states that would explain why people reacted in the way they did. Subsequently I sponsored several other such historical studies, summarized in *The achieving society,* to show that the English findings were not just a lucky hit. Then I waited with interest to see what use historians would make of the new technique that seemed to me to promise so much for the historian's craft.

Nearly fifteen years have passed since the publication of *The achieving society.* Historians have not used the technique; nor, by and large, have psychologists. It is hard to know why. Perhaps as humanists historians are allergic to numbers, and do not like to measure things. Perhaps they are allergic to psychology, except in its grand speculative psychoanalytic reaches. Perhaps they simply do not regard psychology as a realm in which one can find hard facts—facts like the existence of a war. They prefer to use psychological *theory* as a kind of mythology to explain whatever other hard facts they dig up. Yet many historians adapted themselves to learning economics when it became fashionable to use economic explanations of historical events. Perhaps I was not persuasive enough, or failed to go into the methodology in enough detail.

My goal here is to try once again, with the findings reported in Chapter 9 as further evidence of the value of the method. I want to explain exactly how one goes about coding historical documents for psychological variables. I shall therefore report in detail the procedure followed by Giliberto (1972) in obtaining his data in English historical trends.

How, then, did he obtain the numbers on which Figures 9.1 and 9.2 are based? How does one code historical documents for motivational variables? The labor involved is not overwhelming and indeed no greater than is involved in reading thousands of pages of historical documents to digest them mentally into some overall impression of what people were thinking about during a particular period. My impression is that social historians do carry out an unsystematic kind of coding in their heads as they read primary source material. What I propose brings some order into the procedure and helps guarantee that the coding is fairer, less influenced by bias or by particularly outstanding or eloquent representatives of specific period in history. Let me summarize what has to be done as a series of "cookbook" steps to be taken in approximately the following order:

(1) Learn something about the codes that you think are relevant. You may of course invent your own codes if you want to prove a particular point—such as, for example, that women appear more frequently as the initiators of action in one period of history than in another. The advantage of using standard codes like those for *n* Achievement, *n* Power and *n* Affiliation is primarily that a great deal is now known about how people motivated by these concerns actually behave. Thus if you know historical levels on these variables, previous evidence from other studies will help you understand what is likely to happen. Manuals exist for learning these coding systems (Atkinson, 1958, and Winter, 1973); you can easily learn to use them yourself, although you may not want to do the coding yourself for fear bias may enter in. You may want to send your materials to be coded by the experienced staff at McBer and Company, 137 Newbury Street, Boston, Mass. of which I am a principal.

(2) Choose for coding written material that is relatively imaginative, that gives the author an opportunity to express his hopes, feelings, dreams, or despairs. The more cut-and-dried and factual the account, the less opportunity there will be for the expression of motivational concerns. Certain types of communications are more likely to be vehicles for expression of one type of motivation rather than another. In Giliberto's study (1972) it was found that street ballads contained practically no sentiments dealing with affiliation— probably because they were primarily political in nature. We would no doubt have reached better estimates of the strength of affiliative sentiments if we had chosen samples of love poetry. The type of literature chosen for coding must be dictated to a considerable extent by the sentiments you are interested in studying.

(3) If you are interested in making comparisons of motivational levels over time, as in the present study, try to select literary forms that have similar significance and similar audiences in the periods compared. There is a danger even in the present study of assuming that plays in Shakespeare's time expressed the sentiments of the same group as in Sheridan's time. The audiences in 1600 and 1800 differed

in important respects. At most we could claim that plays during all of
this time appealed to a more educated segment of the population on
the average than street ballads did. On the other hand, we could not
have continued using street ballads for getting at motivations of the
lower classes in 19th century Britain, and even less today, when they
appear to have survived in only a few places, as in the Calypso songs of
Trinidad.

(4) Make sure the literature was popular in the period it is
supposed to represent. Generally the date of publication must be
within that period, because normally what it communicates reflects the
sentiments of the audience attending to it at that time. Occasionally a
message may become more popular in a later period than when it was
first published, and in that case it should be classified as belonging to
the later period; we try to avoid using such material altogether, as it is
difficult to know just what happened to the message the first time
around. The criterion of popularity at least assures the presence of
something in the material that appeals to a large audience and reflects
their sentiments. A book may be a literary masterpiece as judged by
subsequent generations, but if it is read by nobody at the time it was
published it is useless to include in a study of that historical period.
We are not proposing to get at the motivational level of a class of
people through the motives of *authors* living at the time, but through
the authors' capacity to represent in their work what is of concern to
people in their audience. That is why their works were popular.

(5) Choose material which is representative of the interests of
different audiences or classes of people. If in the analysis of power
motivation we had chosen to look only at plays in England as shown in
Figure 9.1, we would have obtained a misleading picture as to what
was going on in the country at the time. It was only when the trend
line was obtained from the street ballads, representing the concerns of
the lower orders of the population, that we began to understand the
struggles between king and Parliament, and the explanation of their
outcome. Thus you will often want to compare motivational levels
among different classes of the population and perhaps to sum them to
get some overall level of motivation to compare with another time
period.

(6) Choose the selections to be coded *at random*. Whatever you
do, don't read the material first and then decide whether or not to
include it. You will first want to read around in the material to see if it
is sufficiently imaginative or includes thoughts of the type you want to
code, but the final selection of samples to be coded should be done
randomly or completely blindly. Otherwise your own likes or dislikes

or unconscious prejudices will bias the results. Choose authors at random from a list of the most popular, and choose selections at random from their most popular works.

(7) Choose selections from several different authors and texts. Any particular author may himself have a motivational style that is atypical for his age. He may continue to express the sentiments of an earlier period; this you can discover only by sampling from a number of his contemporaries. As a rough rule of thumb, sample from the works of at least ten different authors. Samples of text purporting to represent the concern of any particular group should contain at least 10,000 words or approximately 1100–1200 lines of text. Otherwise the mean scores obtained may be too unstable to give reliable results. The figures provided in Appendix Tables 9.1 and 9.2 illustrate the reason for this rule, and also show how the rules just enumerated were followed in analyzing samples of text used in the study reported in Chapter 9. Note that in every case the unit of measurement is the number of images of such and such a type per hundred lines of text. This gives all scores a common baseline. Often one is tempted to count, say, the number of power images in a particular ballad and divide by the number of lines in the ballad to get the average score for that sample of material. This approach, however, is not satisfactory because the number of images is not always proportional to the number of lines coded. It does not follow that because you find four images in a ten-line segment, you will find forty images in a hundred-line segment. If you use some ten-line segments and some hundred-line segments, you will end with non-comparable numbers.

(8) Appendix Table 9.1 has been prepared to show what the mean n Power scores per hundred lines would look like if they were based on 11 comparable sets of 100 lines each. In the first period shown, the mean based on the odd sets of 100 lines in the sample is 4.24 compared with 4.53 for the even sets in the sample of text. The

Appendix Table 9.1—Mean n Power scores for comparable 100 line sets of drama text

Drama	Historical periods in English history				
	1576–1625	1626–1675	1676–1725	1726–1775	1776–1825
Mean n Power scores/100 lines	4.39	3.58	2.88	3.18	1.59
11 odd sets of 100 lines	4.24	3.76	2.78	2.93*	1.28
11 even sets of 100 lines	4.53	3.39	2.99	3.42*	1.90
σ mean/100 lines	1.2	1.1	.8	1.1	.6

*15 sets of odd lines and 15 sets of even lines

means are very close together and the overall trends are identical for either sample, suggesting that 10,000 word samples (11 sets of 100 lines = 1100 lines × 10 words per line = 11,000 words) are sufficiently large to give fairly stable results. The standard errors of the mean shown at the bottom of the table provide an estimate of how much a mean will vary in successive samples drawn from the same type of material. Means based on samples of 11 sets of 100 lines will usually vary two-thirds of the time not more than 1 point above or below the value given. If the sample size is doubled, as for the mean *n* Power scores for drama shown at the top of Appendix Table 9.1, the means will vary up or down only around .7 of a point. And if it is tripled, as in the mean *n* Power scores for both ballads and drama combined in Appendix Table 9.2, the means will vary most of the time up or down only .5–.6 of a point. These estimates will vary with the size of the mean because generally speaking the variation of means from sample to sample is larger, the larger their actual value. Compare the difference in the standard error of the mean for 4.53 and for 1.90

Appendix Table 9.2–Mean motivation scores per 100 lines of text drawn from different periods in English history

	1501–1575	1576–1625	1626–1675	1676–1725	1726–1775	1776–1825
Drama						
Total authors	5*	13	13	13	14	13
Total lines	500	2200	2200	2200	3000	2200
Mean *n* Affiliation per 100 lines	2.06	4.01	2.16	2.93	1.47	1.55
Mean *n* Power per 100 lines	6.56	4.39	3.58	2.88	3.18	1.59
Ballads						
Total authors	12	17	24	25	23	19
Total lines	1100	1300	1600	1400	1600	800
Mean *n* Power per 100 lines	3.36	3.91	7.55	7.59	4.88	3.25
Totals, *n* Power						
Authors	21**	30	37	38	37	32
Lines	1600	3500	3800	3600	4600	3000
Mean *n* Power per 100 lines	5.00	4.21	5.15	4.72	3.77	2.01
Totals, *n* Ach.***						
Authors	45	42	50	51	49	58
Lines	6048	6048	6048	6048	6048	6048
Mean *n* Ach. per 100 lines	4.79	4.81	3.01	2.99	4.23	6.00

*excludes anonymous plays
**includes anonymous plays
***includes drama, ballads, and accounts of sea voyages

in Appendix Table 9.1. These figures show that there is a diminishing return from increasing sample size beyond 3,000 lines or 25,000 words or so. Even for the *n* Achievement scores which were based on 60,000 lines, the means would vary up or down as much as .4 in two-thirds of the cases.

Thus in the results reported in Chapter 9 the *n* Achievement means are the most representative of all authors and texts and the most stable, the *n* Power means the next most stable and representative, and the *n* Affiliation means the least dependable. The latter are undependable in still another way, because they represent the affiliative interests only of playwrights and playgoers, since we had no sample representative of other groups that could be scored for *n* Affiliation. But in other respects the numbers of authors, lengths of samples, and types of material shown in Appendix Table 9.2 for this study of motivational trends in English history seem adequate.

(9) Make sure that the coding is done blindly, that is, in such a way that the coder either does not know what time period the material represents or does not know what hypotheses are being investigated. Many coding decisions are difficult to make; if a judge has any preconceived ideas as to what should be happening, that knowledge will almost certainly bias the way he decides doubtful issues.

(10) Check the reliability of the coding by having a second coder go over some of the same material to see whether he gets the same results as the first coder. Coders differ in how strictly they code; some tend to be more lenient in applying the coding criteria. Hence it is necessary to correct for this tendency by computing the percentage agreement between two coders. The usual formula is as follows:

$$\frac{2 \times \text{Number of Agreements}}{\text{No. Images, Judge 1} + \text{No. images, Judge 2}}$$

Consider the following numerical example:

		No. Power Images	
100 Line Samples		Judge 1	Judge 2
Sample A		2	1
Sample B		2	2
Sample C		2	2
Sample D		0	0
Sample E		2	1
	Totals	8	6

$$\frac{2 \times 6}{8 + 6} = 85\% \text{ agreement}$$

Note that since this formula does not give credit for agreement on absence of a characteristic, it is on the conservative side. Normally percentage agreement should be at least 80 percent before one can accept the results as reliable.

So much for the cookbook on how to code historical documents to assess the strengths of psychological variables like *n* Achievement, *n* Affiliation and *n* Power. When you finally get the numbers by such a method and plot them as in Figures 9.1 and 9.2, you will need to know something about the correlates of the variables as described in the psychological literature. It is necessary to know a little bit about psychology to interpret psychological data, just as it is to know a little about economics to interpret changes in the terms of trade or income per capita. It is not necessary, however, to be a psychological expert. So far as the motivational levels are concerned, most findings about these three particular variables are summarized in my booklet, *Motivational Trends in Society* (1972). The knowledge involved is by no means as elaborate as the psychoanalytic knowledge required for Freudian interpretations of historical events, and many historians have had no difficulty in mastering the latter. The empirical study of motivational trends, I believe, will lead to historical interpretations sounder in basis than the speculations of psychoanalysis. I hope that the next twenty years will produce a generation of historians as willing to use this approach to the psychological dynamics of history as some recent historians have been to resort to a clinical style of interpreting history.

Tables 9.3–9.8 in this Appendix provide information on the similar investigation of motivational trends in American history also reported in Chapter 9.

Appendix Table 9.3—Children's readers scored for motive levels for Chapter 9
(From deCharms and Moller, 1962)

1800–1809
Stamford, Daniel *The Art of Reading*. Boston: Published for John West by John Russell, 1800.
Cramer, O. *United States Spelling Book*. Pittsburg: Cook and Schoger, 1809.

1820–1829
Pierpont, John *The National Reader*. Boston, Hilliard, Gray, Little and Wilkins, Publishers, 1827.
Leavitt, Joshua *Easy Lessons in Reading. Keene, N. H.: John Prentiss Co., 1823.*

1840–1849
Sanders, Charles W. *School Reader, Boston: C. J. Hendee, 1843.*
Worchester, Samuel *Fourth Reader. Boston: C. J. Hendee, 1843.*

1850–1859
Town, Salem *Third Reader.* Portland, Maine: Sandborn and Carter, 1852.
Tower, Daniel B. *Fourth Reader.* Boston: Sandborn, Carter, Bazin & Co., 1853.

1870–1879
Monroe, Lewis B. *Fourth Reader.* Philadelphis: Cowperthwait and Co., 1872.
Hillaird, Geo. Stillman *The Franklin Fourth Reader.* New York: Tointer Bros., Merrill & Co., 1873.

1880–1899
Swinton, William *Fourth Reader.* New York: Ivison, Blakeman, Taylor & Co., 12883.
Barnes *National Reader 4th,* 1884.

1890–1899
Baldwin *School Reading by Grades (4th).* 1897.
Williams *Book 1.* 1898.

1900–1909
Judson, H. P. and Bender, I. *Graded Literature Readers 4.* Chicago: Charles E. Merrill Co., 1900.
McGuffey's *New Fourth Reader.* New York: American Book Co., 1901.
Jones, L. H. *Fourth Reader.* Boston: Grimm and Co., 1903.

1920–1929
Coleman, Bessie B., Uhl, Willis L., Hosie, James F. *Pathways to Reading 4.*Silver-New York: Burdett& Co., 1926. Plus selections scored in *The Achieving Society.*

1930–1939
Suzzallo, Henry., Freeland, George E., McLaughlin, Katherine L.. Skinner, Ida M., *Fact and Story Readers Book 4.* New York: American Book Co., 1931.
O'Donnell, Mabel, Carey, Alice *If I were Going.* New York: Row Peterson, 1936.
Buckley, Horace Mann et a. *Here and There.* American Book co. New York 1938.

1940–1949
Robinson, Ruth M.   *Toward Freedom.*   New York: Macmillan Co., 1940.
Gates, Arthur., and Ayer, Joan   *Let's Travel On.* New York: Macmillan Co., 1940.

1950–1959
Searles, Ana Hawley   *Fun To Be Alive.* Boston: Allyn and Bacon, 1952.
McKee, Paul, McCowen Annie, Harrison, M. Lucille, Lehr, Elizabeth *High Roads.*
    Boston: Houghton-Mifflin Co., 1952. Plus selections scored in *The Achieving*
    Society.

1960–1972
Fay, Leo and Anderson, Paul S.   *The Young America.* Basic Reading Program Level
    II. Chicago: Lyons & Carnavan, 1972.
Martin, Bill Jr. *Sounds of Mystery. Sounds of Language.* Readers Grade 4. Holt,
    Rinehart and Winston, Inc., 1967.
Evertts, Eldonna L. and Van Roekel, Byron H.   *Trade Winds.* Harper and Row Basic
    Reading Program. New York, Evanston, London: Harper & Row, 1966
Clymer, Theodore; Gates, Doris and McCullough Constance M.   *The Sun That Warms.*
    Boston: Ginn and Company, 1970.

Appendix Table 9.4–Best selling works of fiction (Mott, 1947) scored for motive levels for Chapter 9.

01/01	1782	*M'Fingal*, John Trumbull
01/02	1786	*Clarissa*, Samuel Richardson
02/01	1794	*Autobiography*, Benjamin Franklin
02/02	1797	*The Coquette*, Hannah Foster
03/01	1800	*Life of Washington*, Mason Weems
03/02	1809	*History of New York*, Washington Irving
04/01	1815	*Guy Mannering*, Walter Scott
04/02	1819	*Sketch Book*, Washington Irving
05/01	1820	*Ivanhoe*, Walter Scott
05/02	1826	*Last of the Mohicans*, James Fenimore Cooper
06/02	1832	*Nick of the Woods*, Robert Bird
06/01	1837	*Swiss Family Robinson*, J. Wyss
07/01	1840	*Tales*, Edgar Allan Poe
07/02	1841	*Essays*, Ralph Waldo Emerson
08/01	1851	*Moby Dick*, Herman Melville
08/02	1855	*Ten Nights in a Bar-Room*, T. S. Arthur
09/01	1860	*Malaeska*, Ann Stephens
09/02	1867	*Ragged Dick*, Horatio Alger
10/01	1870	*The Luck of Roaring Camp*, Bret Harte
10/02	1874	*Opening a Chestnut Burr*, E. P. Roe
11/01	1880	*Ben-Hur*, Lew Wallace
11/02	1887	*She*, H. Rider Haggard
11/03	1888	*Looking Backward*, Edward Bellamy
12/01	1895	*Red Badge of Courage*, Stephen Crane
12/02	1898	*Black Rock*, Ralph Connor
13/01	1903	*The Little Shepherd of Kingdom Come*, John Fox
13/02	1903	*The Call of the Wild*, Jack London
13/03	1907	*The Spell of the Yukon*, Robert Service
14/01	1912	*Riders of the Purple Sage*, Zane Grey
14/02	1914	*Tarzan of the Apes*, Edgar Rice Burroughs
15/01	1926	*Topper*, Thorne Smith
15/02	1929	*The Magnificent Obsession*, Lloyd Douglas
16/01	1936	*Gone with the Wind*, Margaret Mitchell
16/02	1938	*Best of Damon Runyan*, D. Runyan
16/03	1939	*Grapes of Wrath*, John Steinbeck
17/01	1940	*Mrs. Miniver*, Jan Struther
17/02	1945	*The Black Rose*, Thomas Costain
17/03	1945	*Forever Amber*, Kathleen Winsor
18/01	1949	*Dinner at Antoine's*, Francis Parkinson Keyes
18/02	1955	*Man in the Gray Flannel Suit*, Sloan Wilson
18/03	1958	*From the Terrace*, John O'Hara
19/01	1960	*Advise & Consent*, Allan Drury
19/02	1967	*The Chosen*, Chaim Potok
19/03	1969	*The Godfather*, Mario Puzo

Appendix Table 9.5–Hymns scored for motive levels for Chapter 9

01/01 1784 Gibbons, Thomas, *Hymns Adapted to Divine Worship*, London

02/01 1791 Wesley, Charles, *Hymns*

03/01 1808 Watts, Isaac, *Psalms of David Imitated in the Language of the New Testament and Applied to Christian State & Worship*. Boston: Manning & Loring

04/01 1810 Dobell, John, *A New Selection of Seven Hundred Evangelical Hymns*. Morristown: P. A. Johnson

04/02 1814 Star Spangled Banner, Francis Scott Key

04/03 1819 from Benson*

05/01 1821 Winchell, James M., *An Arrangement of the Psalms and Spiritual Hymns of Isaac Watts*. Boston, Lincoln & Edmands

06/01 1832 Winchell, James M., *Watts' Psalms Arranged* (another edition of 05/01)

06/02 1832 America (My Country 'tis of Thee)

06/03   from Benson*

07/01 1846 *Christian Hymns for Public and Private Worship; a Collection Compiled by a Committee of the Cheshire Pastoral Association 6th edition*. Boston: W. Crosby

07/03   from Benson*

08/01 1857 Peabody, A. P., *Hymnbook with Additional Services*

08/03   from Benson*

09/01 1865 Cary, Alice, *Ballads, Lyrics and Hymns*. New York: Hurd & Hought

09/02   Battle Hymn of the Republic (by Julia Ward Howe)

09/03   from Benson*

09/04 1867 *One Hundred Songs Devotional, Patriotic, Occasional and Miscellaneous Compiled for Use in Wyman's City University* St. Louis: R. P. Studley & Co.

10/02 1874 *Gospel Songs, a Choice Collection of Hymns and Tunes, New and Old, for Gospel Meetings, Prayer Meetings, Sunday Schools etc.* Cincinnati: J. Church & Co.

10/01 1874 Longfellow, Samuel, and Johnson, Samuel, *Hymns of the Spirit*. Boston: J. R. Osgood & Co.

11/01 1881 *Hymnal of the Methodist Episcopal Church with Tunes*. New York: Phillips & Hunt

12/01 1890 Grosart, Alexander Balloch, *Songs for the Day and Night, or Three Centuries of Original Hymns for Public and Private Praise and Reading*. Edinburgh: Turnbull & Spears

12/02 America the Beautiful

13/01 1904 *Hymns and Prayers for World-Religion* by Martin K. Schermerhorn

14/01 1921 Young, C. E. B., *Hymns of Prayer and Praise with tunes*. London: H. Milford

15/01 1925 Kingsbury, F. G., *Hymns of Praise number two*. Chicago: Hope Publishing Company

15/02 1927 Rodeheaver, H. A., *Praise and Worship Hymns; a Compilation of Hymns and Gospel Songs Adapted to the Present-Day Needs of Church, Sunday Schools and Special Meetings*. Chicago: The Rodeheaver Co.

15/03 1921 Barbour, C. A., *Fellowship Hymns*, New York: The Association Press

16/01 1939 Tiplady, T., *Hymns for the Times*, London: The Epworth Press

16/02 1935 *Pilgrim Hymnal*. National Council of Congregational Churches

17/01 1940 *BMI Hymnal*. Richard Maxwell (ed.), New York: Broadcast Music Inc.

17/02 1942 Tiplady, T., *Hymns for the Pocket*. London, Lambeth Mission

17/03 1943 Bosh, H. G., *Stories of Inspiring Hymns*. Grand Rapids, Michigan: Zondervan Publishing House

17/04 1940 *Protestant Episcopal Hymnal*. New York, The Church Pension Fund

18/01 1952 *Christian Hymns*. Christian Foundation, New York: The North River Press

19/01 1969 *Trial Hymns for Contemporary Worship*. Music Commission of the Diocese of Massachusetts, Boston

19/02 1966 *Hymnal for Juniors*, W. Lawrence Curry (ed.), Philadelphia, Westminster Press

19/03 1966 *Hymnal of Christian Unity*, Bennet, Clifford A. and Hume, Paul (eds.), Toledo: The Gregorian Institute of America

*From Benson, L. F., *Studies of Familiar Hymns*. Philadelphia, Westminster Press, 1902.

Appendix Table 9.6—Need for Power Means and Standard Scores by decade for various types of popular literature, U.S. 1780–1970

| | CHILDREN'S TEXTS | | FICTION | HYMNS | Mean Standard Score |
	Pages Scored	Standard Score	Standard Score	Standard Score	All Sources
1780–89			80.0	43.7	61.9*
1790–99			69.2	58.4	63.8*
1800–09	23	53.4	61.7	58.4	57.8
1810–19			57.1	43.1	50.1*
1820–29	24	57.2	61.7	50.8	56.6
1830–39			41.5	50.2	45.9*
1840–49	12	62.9	37.5	41.9	47.4
1850–59	12	41.5	44.0	36.6	40.7
1860–69			38.5	49.6	44.1*
1870–79	11	50.9	36.0	38.4	41.8
1880–89	12	47.1	46.1	46.0	46.4
1890–99	12	57.2	47.1	39.0	47.8
1900–09	18	66.0	55.6	34.8	52.1
1910–19			49.1		
1920–29	27	37.1	48.6	53.7	46.5
1930–39	18	38.3	61.7	63.7	54.6
1940–49	11	32.1	47.1	60.8	46.7
1950–59	33	49.0	36.5	62.0	49.2
1960–69	24	57.0	61.2	69.0	62.5
Raw score mean		46.54[1]	67.83[2]	44.72[3]	
Standard deviation		15.89	19.84	16.96	

*based on fiction and hymns only

1. Percentage of pages (stories) scored for *n* Power. From deCharms and Moeller (1962), except stories scored by McClelland (1961) added for 1920–29 and 1950–59 decades.
2. Number of page segments (10 lines each) out of 200 for each decade scored for *n* Power. The number for 1780–89 was so extremely high (157) that it was left out of the mean calculation and given an arbitrary standard score of 80.
3. Number of page segments (10 lines each) out of 220 for each decade scored for *n* Power. The value for 1920–29 is based on the average for two samples of 220 page segments each.

Appendix Table 9.7—Need for Affiliation Means and Standard Scores by decade for various types of popular literature, U.S. 1780–1970

	CHILDREN'S TEXTS		FICTION	HYMNS	Mean Standard Score
	Pages Scored	Standard Score	Standard Score	Standard Score	All sources
1780–89			73.2	69.4	71.3*
1790–99			61.0	57.0	59.0*
1800–09	23	53.6	36.4	43.6	44.5
1810–19			61.0	52.9	57.0*
1820–29	24	38.6	43.5	36.4	39.5
1830–39			39.9	48.7	44.3*
1840–49	12	33.4	32.9	45.6	37.3
1850–59	12	60.1	55.7	50.8	55.5
1860–69			69.7	49.8	59.8*
1870–79	11	45.1	43.5	69.4	52.7
1880–89	12	60.1	38.2	47.7	48.9
1890–99	12	43.8	43.5	40.5	42.6
1900–09	18	36.7	54.0	69.4	53.4
1910–19			48.7		
1920–29	27	66.0	45.2	47.8	53.0
1930–39	18	58.8	47.2	39.5	48.4
1940–49	11	51.7	52.2	38.4	47.4
1950–59	33	58.2	54.0	46.7	53.0
1960–69	24	43.8	50.5	46.7	47.0
Raw score mean		42.46[1]	11.74[2]	24.22[3]	
Standard deviation		15.36	5.71	9.69	

*based on fiction and hymns only

1.
2. } as in *n* Power Table
3.

Appendix Table 9.8–Need for Achievement means and standard scores by decade for various types of popular literature, U.S. 1780–1970

	CHILDREN's TEXTS		FICTION	HYMNS	Mean Standard Score
	Pages Scored	Standard Score	Standard Score	Standard Score	All Sources
1780–89			47.2	47.5	47.4*
1790–99			65.8	35.1	50.5*
1800–09	23	33.1	72.8	43.4	49.8
1810–19			42.5	47.5	45.0*
1820–29	24	50.1	35.6	54.5	46.7
1830–39			61.1	43.4	52.3*
1840–49	12	48.7	54.2	40.6	47.8
1850–59	12	39.0	61.1	44.8	48.3
1860–69			56.5	44.8	50.7*
1870–79	11	59.1	49.5	61.4	56.7
1880–89	12	57.6	40.2	58.6	52.1
1890–99	12	70.2	40.2	53.1	54.5
1900–09	18	49.4	49.5	32.3	43.7
1910–19			47.2		
1920–29	27	47.9	51.8	42.0	47.2
1930–39	18	33.1	44.9	68.3	48.8
1940–49	11	53.9	35.6	58.6	49.5
1950–59	33	56.1	40.2	65.5	53.9
1960–69	24	51.7	54.2	58.6	54.8
Raw score mean		39.77[1]	8.21[2]	25.78[3]	
Standard deviation		13.48	4.30	7.22	

*based on fiction and hymns only

1.
2. } as in *n* Power Table.
3.

5

THE RELATION OF POWER
AND AFFILIATION MOTIVATION

IN EACH sample the subjects wrote brief imaginative stories to three or four pictures. The pictures used in the college student samples 1 and 3 included the usual ones designed to elicit power motivation (e.g., two lawyers in an office, a ship's captain, and a man and a woman in a bar) but the three pictures to which the eighth grade students wrote stories were completely different. They had been designed by another investigator to be more appropriate to the age of the children writing the stories. Thus the findings in Appendix Table 9.9 are all the more impressive. In each case those subjects in the top half of the power motive distribution of scores, scored higher in s Power if they were in the bottom half of the *n* Affiliation distribution than if they were in the top half of the *n* Affiliation distribution of scores. This peculiar association of higher s Power with low need for Affiliation could scarcely be due to picture cues eliciting a particular kind of story because the cues differed from sample to sample, particularly in

Appendix Table 9.9—*High n Power expressed as p or s Power When Combined with High or Low n Affiliation*

	A High n Power High n Affiliation	B High n Power Low n Affiliation	Difference B − A	t
Sample 1				
65 college males tested 1969				
N	11[a]	16		
mean p Power	3.27	3.31	+ .04	
SD	1.05	1.10		
mean s Power	1.73	2.69	+ .96	2.00 p < .05
SD	.86	1.53		
Sample 2				
77 8th grade boys & girls tested 1965				
N	20[b]	18		
mean p Power	1.05	1.06	+ .01	
SD	.74	.91		
mean s Power	.55	1.17	+ .62	2.07 p < .05
SD	.67	1.13		
Sample 3				
College summer school males tested 1972				
N	11[c]	20		
mean p Power	1.73	2.70	+ .97	
SD	.86	1.69		
mean s Power	1.09	1.75	+ .66	1.71 p < .05*
SD	.90	1.14		

*predicted direction
a. score of 6 or more on *n* Power, score of 3 or more on *n* Affiliation
b. score of 3 or more on *n* Power, score of 3 or more on *n* Affiliation
c. score of 7 or more on *n* Power, score of 3 or more on *n* Affiliation

sample 2, as compared with the others. Nor does the finding seem to be restricted to a particular sex or social class, since the eighth grade students included both sexes and represented a fairly broad range of socio-economic levels. The hypothesis seems to be amply confirmed. When power motivation is high in individuals, it is expressed more as s Power when the need for Affiliation is low than when it is high.

BIBLIOGRAPHY

Adorno, T. W., Frenkel-Brunswik, E., Levinson, D. J., & Sanford, R. N. *The authoritarian personality.* New York: Harper, 1950.

Almond, G., & Powell, G. *Comparative politics: a developmental approach.* Boston: Little, Brown, 1966.

Anderson, B. R. O'G. The idea of power in Javanese culture. In C. Holt (Ed.) *Culture and politics in Indonesia.* Ithaca, N.Y.: Cornell University Press, 1972.

Argyris, C. *Intervention theory and method.* Reading, Mass.: Addison-Wesley, 1970.

Atkinson, J. W. (Ed.) *Motives in fantasy, action and society.* Princeton, N.J.: Van Nostrand, 1958.

Bach, R. *Jonathan Livingston Seagull.* New York: Macmillan, 1970.

Bacon, M. K., Barry, H. B., & Child, I. L. A cross-cultural study of the correlates of crime. *Journal of Abnormal and Social Psychology,* 1963, 66, 291–300.

Bakan, D. *Sigmund Freud and the Jewish mystical tradition.* Princeton, N.J.: Van Nostrand, 1958.

Bakan, D. *The duality of human existence.* Chicago: Rand McNally, 1966.

413

Baltzell, E. D. *Two Protestant ethics: Puritan and Quaker.* New York: Harper and Row, (In Press).

Barry, H., Bacon, M. K., & Child, I. L. A cross-cultural survey of some sex differences in socialization. *Journal of Abnormal and Social Psychology,* 1957, 55, 327–332.

Bennis, W. G., & Slater, P. E. *The temporary society.* New York: Harper and Row, 1968.

Benson, L. F. *Studies of familiar hymns.* Philadelphia: Philadelphia Westminster Press, 1902.

Boyatzis, R. E. A two-factor theory of affiliation motivation. Unpublished Ph.D. dissertation, Harvard University: Department of Social Relations, 1972.

Boyatzis, R. E. Drinking as a manifestation of power concerns. Paper presented at the Ninth International Congress on Anthropological and Ethnological Sciences. Boston: McBer and Co., 1973.

Bradburn, N. M., & Berlew, D. E. Need for achievement and English economic growth. *Economic Development and Cultural Change,* 1961, 10, 8–20.

Bradford, A. *The volunteer and the bureaucrat: Case studies from India.* Washington, D.C.: Peace Corps, 1968.

Browning, Rufus P. The interaction of personality and political system in decisions to run for office: some data and a simulation technique. *Journal of Social Issues,* 1968, 24, 93–109.

Capote, T. *In cold blood.* New York: Random House, 1965.

Carmichael, L. (Ed.) *Manual of child psychology.* New York: Wiley, 1946

Carstairs, G. M. *The twice born.* London: Hogarth Press, 1957.

Chaudhuri, N. C. *The continent of Circe: An essay on the peoples of India.* Bombay: Jaico Publishing House, 1966.

Chessler, P. *Women & madness.* New York: Avon Books, 1972.

Couch, A. S. Psychological determinants of interpersonal behavior. Unpublished Ph.D. dissertation, Department of Social Relations, Harvard University, 1960.

Dahl, R. A. The concept of power. *Behavioral Science,* 1957, 2, 201–215.

Davis, J. A. & Bradburn, N. O. *Great aspirations: Career plans of America's June 1961 college graduates.* Chicago: National Opinion Research Center, 1961.

deCharms, R. *Personal causation.* New York: Academic Press, 1968.

deCharms, R., & Moeller, G. H. Values expressed in American children's readers: 1800–1950. *Journal of Abnormal and Social Psychology,* 1962, 64, 136–142.

Deutsch, H. *The psychology of women, a psychoanalytic interpretation.* New York: Grune and Stratton, 1944.

Diaz-Guerrero, R. *Estudios de psicologia del Mexicano.* Mexico: Antigua Libreria Roboredo, 1961.

Donley, R. E., & Winter, D. G. Measuring the motives of public officials at a distance: an exploratory study of American Presidents. *Behavioral Science,* 1970, 15, 227–236.

Eisenstadt, S. N. *Charisma, institution building and social transformation: Max Weber and modern sociology.* Chicago: The University of Chicago Press, 1968.

Erikson, E. H. Sex differences in the play configurations of pre-adolescents. *American Journal of Orthopsychiatry,* 1951, 21, 667–692.

Erikson, E. H. *Childhood and society.* (Rev. ed.) New York: W. W. Norton, 1963.

Erikson, E. H. *Gandhi's truth.* New York: W. N. Norton & Co., 1969.

Exline, R. V. Need affiliation and initial communication behavior in problem solving groups characterized by low interpersonal visibility. *Psychological Reports,* 1962, 10, 79–89.

Exline, R. V. Explorations in the process of person perception: visual interaction in relation to competition, sex, and need for affiliation. *Journal of Personality,* 1963, 31, 1–20.

Feierabend, I. K., & Feierabend, R. L. Aggressive behaviors within politics, 1947–1962: a cross-national study. *Journal of Conflict Resolution,* 1966, 10, 249–271.

Fleming, J. Approach and avoidance motivation in interpersonal competition. Unpublished Ph.D. dissertation, Department of Psychology and Social Relations, Harvard University, 1974.

Firestone, J. M. Motives and behavior in large scale political systems: a preliminary analysis. In G. H. Snyder (Ed.) Studies in international conflict. *Buffalo Studies,* 1968, 4, 59–90.

Freeman, J. L. A positive view of population density. *Psychology Today,* 1971, 5, (September), 58–61.

French, E. G., & Lesser, G. S. Some characteristics of the achievement motive in women. *Journal of Abnormal and Social Psychology,* 1964, 68, 119–128.

Gardner, J. W. *The anti-leadership vaccine.* New York: The Carnegie Corporation, Annual Report, 1965.

Gardner, R., Holzman, P., Klein, G., Linton, H., & Spence, D. P. Cognitive controls. *Psychological Issues.* International University Press, 1959, 4.

Gombrich, R. F. *Precept and practice: Traditional Buddhism in the rural highlands of Ceylon.* Oxford: Clarendon Press, 1971

Giliberto, S. M. Motivation and the Methodist revival. Unpublished A.B. thesis, Harvard College, 1972.

Goodenough, E. W. Interest in persons as an aspect of sex differences in the early years. *Genetic Psychology Monographs,* 1957, 55, 287–323.

Greenberger, E. Fantasies of women confronting death. *Journal of Consulting Psychology,* 1965, 29, 252–260.

Gurin, G. *et al., Americans view their mental health.* New York: Basic Books, 1960.

Harrington, C., & Whiting, J. W. M. Socialization process and personality. In F. L. K. Hsu (Ed.), *Psychological Anthropology.* Cambridge, Mass.: Shenkman Publications, 1972.

Harrison, J. *Prolegomena to the study of Greek religion* New York: Meridian Books, 1955. First edition, 1903.

Hendry, L. S. & Kessen, W. Oral behavior of new born infants as a function of age and time since feeding. *Child Development*, 1964, 35, 201–208.

Heider, F. *The psychology of interpersonal relations*. New York: Wiley, 1958.

Hoge, D. R. College students' religion: a study of trends in attitudes and behavior. Unpublished Ph. D. dissertation, Harvard University, Cambridge, Massachusetts, 1969.

The Homeric Hymns, translated by C. Boer from Greek. Chicago: Swallow Press (paperback), 1971.

Horner, M. S. Toward an understanding of achievement-related conflict in women. *Journal of Social Issues,* 1972, 28, 157–175.

Horner, M. S. The measurement and behavioral implications of fear of success in women. In J. W. Atkinson and J. Raynor (Eds.) *Motivation and achievement.* Somerset, N.J.: Wiley (Halstead Press), 1974.

Inkeles, A., & Levinson, D. J., National character: The study of modal personality and sociocultural systems. In *Handbook of social psychology,* Vol. II: *Special fields and applications.* Cambridge, Mass.: Addison Wesley, 1954

Janis, I. L. & Field, P. B. Sex differences and personality factors related to persuadability. In I. L. Janis, *et al. Personality and persuadability.* New Haven: Yale University Press, 1959.

Jourard, S. *The transparent self.* Princeton, N. J.: Van Nostrand, 1963.

Kagan, J. and Moss, H. *Birth to maturity.* New York: Wiley, 1962.

King, S. H. *Five lives at Harvard.* Cambridge, Mass.: Harvard University Press, 1973.

Kluckhohn, F. R., & Strodtbeck, F. L. *Variations in value orientation.* Evanston, Ill.: Row, Peterson, 1961.

Knox, R. *An historical relation of Ceylon.* 1681. Naharajama, Ceylon: Saman Press, 1958.

Kruse, A. Projektive Machtthematik, Verhalten und die Bewertung durch Gruppenmitglieder—eine Erkundungsstudie. Unpublished Diplomarbeit (thesis), Phillips Universität, Marburg, 1971.

Lawrence, D. H. *Mornings in Mexico.* New York: Knopf, 1927.

Leary, T. *High priest.* New York: World Publishing Co., 1967

Lerner, M. J. The desire for justice and reactions to victims. In J. Macaulay and L. Berkowitz (Eds.) *Altruism and helping behavior.* New York: Academic Press, 1970.

LeVine, R. A. Nyansongo: a Gusii community in Kenya. In B. B. Whiting (Ed.), *Six cultures: studies of child rearing.* New York: Wiley, 1963.

Levy, S. G. *A 150 year study of political violence in the United States.* In H. D. Graham, & T. R. Gurr, *Violence in America.* New York: Bantam, 1969.

Lewis, O. *Five families.* New York: Basic Books, 1959.

Lewis, O. *The children of Sanchez.* New York: Random House, 1961.

Litwin, G. H., and Siebrecht, A. Integrators and entrepreneurs: their motivation and effect on management. St. Louis, Mo.: *Hospital Progress,* 1967.

Litwin, G. H., & Stringer, R. A. *Motivation and organizational climate.* Boston, Mass.: Harvard University, Graduate School of Business Administration, Division of Research, 1968.

McClelland, D. C. The calculated risk: an aspect of creative scientific performance. In C. W. Taylor (Ed.), *Research conference on the identification of creative scientific talent.* Salt Lake City: University of Utah Press, 1956, 96–110.

McClelland, D. C. Methods of measuring human motivation, Chapter 1 in *Motives in fantasy, action, and society.* J. W. Atkinson (Ed.). Princeton, N.J.: Van Nostrand, 1958.

McClelland, D. C. *The achieving society.* New York: Irvington Publishers, 1961

McClelland, D. C. Motivational patterns in Southeast Asia with special reference to the Chinese case. *Journal of Social Issues,* 1963, 19, 1, 6–19. (a)

McClelland, D. C. National character and economic growth in Turkey and Iran. In L. W. Pye (Ed.), *Communications and political development.* Princeton, N.J.: Princeton University Press, 1963. (b)

McClelland, D. C. *The roots of consciousness.* Princeton, N.J.: Van Nostrand, 1964.

McClelland, D. C. The two faces of power. *Journal of International Affairs,* 1970, 24, 29–47.

McClelland, D. C. Wanted: a new self-image for women. In R. S. Lifton (Ed.) *The woman in America.* Boston: Houghton Mifflin, 1965.

McClelland, D. C. *Motivational trends in society.* New York: General Learning Press, 1971.

McClelland, D. C. Some themes in the culture of India. In A. R. Desai (Ed.), *Essays on modernization of underdeveloped societies.* Vol. II. Bombay: Thacker and Co., 1971.

McClelland, D. C., Atkinson, J. W., Clark, R. A., & Lowell, E. L. *The achievement motive.* New York: Irvington Publishers, 1953.

McClelland, D. C., Baldwin, A. L., Bronfenbrenner, U., & Strodtbeck, F. L. *Talent and society.* Princeton: Van Nostrand, 1958.

McClelland, D. C., Davis, W. N., Kalin, R., & Wanner, E. *The drinking man.* New York: Free Press, 1972.

McClelland, D. C., Knapp, R. H., Sturr, J., & Wendt, H. W. Obligation to self and society in the United States and Germany. *Journal of Abnormal and Social Psychology,* 1958, 56, 245–255.

McClelland, D. C., Rhinesmith, S., and Kristensen, R. The effects of power training for staffs of community action agencies. *Journal of Applied Behavioral Science,* 1975, 11, 92–115.

McClelland, D. C., & Watt, N. F.   Sex-role alienation in schizophrenia. *Journal of Abnormal Psychology,* 1968, 73, 226–239.

McClelland, D. C., & Winter, D. G. *Motivating economic achievement.* New York: The Free Press, 1969. Paperback edition with an Afterword, 1971.

Malcolm X, *The autobiography of Malcolm X,* New York: Grove Press, 1964. Paperback edition, 1966.

May, Rollo. *Power and innocence.* New York: W. W. Norton, 1972.

May, R. R. Sex differences in fantasy patterns. *Journal of Projective Techniques and Personality Assessment,* 1966, 30, 576–586.

May, R. R. Sexual identity and sex role conceptions in acute schizophrenia. Unpublished Ph.D dissertation, Department of Social Relations, Harvard University, 1968.

McGregor, A. M. *The human side of enterprise.* New York: McGraw Hill, 1960.

Mehta, Prayag. Level of *n* Achievement in high school boys. *Indian Educational Review,* 1967, 2, 36–70.

Minturn, L., & Hitchcock, J. T. The Rajputs of Khalapur, India. In B. B. Whiting (Ed.), *Six cultures,* New York: Wiley, 1963

Mischel, W. *Introduction to personality.* New York: Holt, Rinehart and Winston, 1971.

Mott, F. L. *Golden multitudes: the story of best sellers in the United States.* New York: Macmillan, 1947.

Mowrer, O. H. *The crisis in psychiatry and religion.* Princeton: Van Nostrand, 1961.

Murray, H. A. *Explorations in personality.* New York: Oxford University Press, 1938.

Murray, H. A. American Icarus. In A. Burton & R. E. Harris (Eds.), *Clinical studies of personality.* New York: Harper & Row, 1955.

Mylonas, G. E. *Eleusis and the Eleusinian mysteries.* Princeton, N.J.: Princeton University Press, 1961.

Narain, D. *Hindu character.* Bombay: University of Bombay Press, 1957.

Neihardt, J. C. *Black Elk speaks: being a life story of a holy man of the Oglala Sioux.* New York: Morrow, 1932. Paperback ed. Simon & Schuster, 1972

Nevins, A. & Commager, H. S. *A short history of the United States* (fifth edition). New York: Random House, 1966.

Nyanatiloka. *The Buddha's path to deliverance in its threefold division and seven stages of purity.* Colombo, Ceylon: Bauddha Sahitya Sabha, 1952.

Ogilvie, D. Psychodynamics of fantasized flight: a study of people and folktales. Unpublished Ph.D. dissertation, Harvard University, 1967.

Osgood, C. Semantic differential technique in the comparative study of cultures, *American Anthropologist,* 1964, 66, No. 3, Part 2, 171–200.

Parkes, H. B. *The American experience.* New York: Random House, 1947.

Parsons, T. *Sociological theory and modern society.* New York: The Free Press, 1967.

Paz, O. *The labyrinth of solitude.* (1st ed.) Mexico: Cuadernos Americanos, 1950. Grove Press edition, 1961.

Pérez, T. Saliency of power motivation in machismo Unpublished paper, Harvard University, Department of Psychology and Social Relations, 1974.

Pratt, K. C. The neonate. In L. Carmichael (Ed.), *Manual of child psychology.* New York: Wiley, 1946.

Radhakrishnan, S. *Indian philosophy.* London: G. Allen and Unwin, 1948.

Radhakrishnan, S. *The Hindu view of life.* Bombay: University of Bombay Press, 1957.

Ram Dass (Ed.) *Be here now.* San Cristobal, New Mexico: The Lama Foundation, Box 444, 1971.

Rosenthal, R., & Jacobson, L. *Pygmalion in the classroom: teacher expectation and pupil's intellectual development.* New York: Holt, Rinehart & Winston, 1968.

Ross, H. L. and Glaser, E. M. *A study of successful persons from seriously disadvantaged backgrounds.* Los Angeles: Human Interaction Research Institute, 1970.

Ross, M., Layton, B., Erickson, B., and Schopler, J. Affect, facial regard and reactions to crowding. *Journal of personality and social psychology,* 1973, 28, 69–76.

Rubin, Z., & Peplau, A. Belief in a just world and reactions to another's lot: A study of participants in the national draft lottery. *Journal of Social Issues,* 1973, 29, 73–93.

Russell, E. W. *Christianity and militarism.* Peace Research Reviews. 1971, 4, No. 3, 1–77. Oakville, Ontario, Canada: Canadian Peace Research Institute.

Russett, B. M. and others. *World handbook of political and social indicators.* New Haven: Yale University Press, 1964.

Sarma, D. S. *Hinduism through the ages.* Bombay: Bharatiya Vidya Bhavan, 1961.

Sears, P. S. Doll play aggression in normal young children: influence of sex, age, sibling status, father's absence. *Psychological Monographs: General and Applied,* 1951, 65, No. 6.

Sharaf, M. An approach to the theory and measurement of intraception. Unpublished doctoral dissertation, Harvard University, 1960.

Singer, J. D. & Small, M. *The wages of war, 1816–1965: a statistical handbook.* New York: Wiley, 1972.

Singh, K. *A bride for the Sahib & other stories.* Thompson, Conn.: InterCulture, 1967.

Sinha, J. B. P., Effects of n-Ach/n-Cooperation on group output and interpersonal relations under limited/unlimited resource condition. Unpublished paper, A.N.S. Institute of Social Studies, Patna, India.

Skinner, B. F. *Beyond freedom and dignity.* New York: Knopf, 1971.

Slavin, M. The theme of feminine evil: the image of women in male fantasy and its effect on attitudes and behavior. Unpublished Ph.D. dissertation, Harvard, 1972.

Smith, Bruce. Reflections in a psychedelic mirror: Subjective drug experience, drug use patterns and personality. Unpublished doctoral dissertation, Harvard, 1973.

Solomon, R. H. *Mao's revolution and the Chinese political culture.* Berkeley, Calif.: University of California Press, 1971.

Southwood, K. E. Some sources of political disorder: a cross-national analysis. Unpublished Ph.D. dissertation, University of Michigan, 1969.

Stewart, A. J. Scoring system for stages of psychological development. Harvard University, Department of Psychology and Social Relations, Unpublished paper, 1973.

Stewart, A. J. The nature of woman: Female responses to male definition. Wesleyan University, Middletown, Conn.: Unpublished A.B. Thesis, 1971.

Stewart, A. J. and Winter, D. G. Self-definition and social definition in women. *Journal of Personality*, 1974, 42, 238–259

Stolorow, R. D. The theme of voluntary control, the obsessive-hysteric dimension, and the precipitation of psychological distress. Unpublished Ph.D. dissertation, Department of Social Relations, Harvard University, 1970.

Stone, P. J., Dunphy, D. C., Smith, M. S., & Ogilvie, D. M. with associates. *The general inquirer: a computer approach to content analysis.* Cambridge, Mass.: M.I.T. Press, 1966.

Strodtbeck, F. L. & Mann, R. D. Sex role differentiation in jury deliberations. *Sociometry*, 1956, 19, 3–11.

Strong, E. K., Jr. *Vocational interests of men and women.* Stanford, Calif.: Stanford Univer. Press, 1943.

Sweet, W. W. *Revivalism in America.* New York: Scribner's, 1944. Paperback edition, New York: Abingdon Press.

Szasz, T. *The myth of mental illness: foundations of a theory of personal conduct.* New York: Hoeber-Harper, 1961.

Taylor, W. S. Basic personality in orthodox Hindu culture patterns. *Journal of Abnormal and Social Psychology*, 1948, 43, 3–12.

Terhune, K. W. Motive situation and interpersonal conflict within prisoner's dilemma. *Journal of Personality and Social Psychology*, 1968, 8, (pt. 2), 1–24.

Terman, L. M. & Miles, C. C. *Sex and personality: studies in masculinity and femininity.* New York: McGraw, 1936.

Terman, L. M. & Tyler, L. E. Psychological sex differences. In L. Carmichael (Ed.), *Manual of child psychology.* New York: Wiley, 1946.

Toynbee, A. J. *A study of history.* (Abridgment of Vol. 1–6 by D. C. Somervell.) New York: Oxford Press, 1947.

Trevelyan, G. M., *English social history.* New York: Longmans, Green, 1942.

Tucker, R. C. The theory of charismatic leadership. *Daedalus,* 1968, 97, 731–756.

Tyler, L. *The psychology of human differences.* Chapter 10. New York: Appleton-Century-Crofts, 1956.

Uleman, J. A new TAT measure of the need for power. Unpublished Ph.D. dissertation. Harvard University, 1966.

Veroff, J. Development and validation of a projective measure of power motivation. *Journal of Abnormal and Social Psychology,* 1957, 54, 1–8.

Veroff, J, and Feld, S. *Marriage and work in America: A study of motives and roles.* New York: Van Nostrand Reinhold, 1971.

Walker, E. L., & Heyns, R. W. *An anatomy for conformity.* Englewood Cliffs, N.J.: Prentice-Hall, 1962.

Watt, N. F., Stolorow, R. D., Lubensky, A., and McClelland, D. C. School adjustment and behavior of children hospitalized for schizophrenia as adults. *American Journal of Orthopsychiatry,* 1970, 40, 637–657.

Wearmouth, R. F. *Methodism and the common people of the eighteenth century.* London: The Epworth Press, 1945.

Whiting, B. B. Sex identity conflict and physical violence: a comparative study. *American Anthropologist,* 1965, 67, 123–140.

Whiting, J. W. M., Whiting, B. B., in collaboration with Longabaugh, R. *Children of six cultures: a psycho-cultural analysis.* Cambridge: Harvard University Press, 1974.

Williams, H. D. A survey of predelinquent children in ten middle-western cities. *Journal of Juvenile Research,* 1933, 17, 163–174.

Wilsnack, S. C. *Psychological factors in female drinking.* Unpublished Ph.D. dissertation. Department of Social Relations, Harvard University, 1972.

Winter, D. C. Power motivation in thought and action. Harvard University, Department of Social Relations, Unpublished Ph.D. Dissertation, 1967.

Winter, D. G. *The power motive.* New York: The Free Press, 1973.

Winter, D. G. and Stewart, A. J. Content analysis as a technique for assessing political leaders. In T. Milburn and H. C. Hermann (Eds.) *A psychological examination of political leaders.* New York: Free Press (in press).

Winter, S. K. Being orientation in maternal fantasy: a content analysis of the TAT's of nursing mothers. Unpublished Ph.D. dissertation, Department of Social Relations, Harvard University, 1966.

Witkin, H. A., Lewis, H. B., Hertzman, M., Machover, K., Messner, P. B., and Wapner, S. *Personality through perception.* New York: Harper, 1954.

Zelditch, N. Jr. Role differentiation in the nuclear family. In T. Parsons & R. F. Bales, *Family, socialization, and interaction process.* New York: The Free Press, 1955.

INDEX

423